Matthew

TEACH THE TEXT COMMENTARY SERIES

John H. Walton
Old Testament General Editor

Mark L. Strauss
New Testament General Editor

When complete, the TEACH THE TEXT COMMENTARY SERIES *will include the following volumes*:

Old Testament Volumes

New Testament Volumes

To see which titles are available, visit the series website at www.teachthetextseries.com.

TEACH the TEXT
COMMENTARY SERIES

Matthew

Jeannine K. Brown

Mark L. Strauss and John H. Walton
GENERAL EDITORS

ILLUSTRATING THE TEXT

Kevin and Sherry Harney
ASSOCIATE EDITORS

Adam Barr
CONTRIBUTING WRITER

BakerBooks
a division of Baker Publishing Group
Grand Rapids, Michigan

© 2015 by Jeannine K. Brown
Captions and Illustrating the Text sections © 2015 by Baker Publishing Group

Published by Baker Books
a division of Baker Publishing Group
P.O. Box 6287, Grand Rapids, MI 49516-6287
www.bakerbooks.com

Printed in the United States of America

Library of Congress Cataloging-in-Publication Data
Brown, Jeannine K., 1961–
    Matthew / Jeannine K. Brown
        pages cm. — (Teach the text commentary series)
    Includes bibliographical references and index.
    ISBN 978-0-8010-9218-3 (cloth : alk. paper)
    1. Bible. Matthew—Commentaries. 2. Bible. Matthew—Study and teaching.
    I. Title.
    BS2575.53.B76 2015
    226.2′07—dc23   2014033065

15   16   17   18   19   20   21   7   6   5   4   3   2   1

Contents

Welcome to the Teach the Text Commentary Series

Why another commentary series? That was the question the general editors posed when Baker Books asked us to produce this series. Is there something that we can offer to pastors and teachers that is not currently being offered by other commentary series, or that can be offered in a more helpful way? After carefully researching the needs of pastors who teach the text on a weekly basis, we concluded that yes, more can be done; this commentary is carefully designed to fill an important gap.

The technicality of modern commentaries often overwhelms readers with details that are tangential to the main purpose of the text. Discussions of source and redaction criticism, as well as detailed surveys of secondary literature, seem far removed from preaching and teaching the Word. Rather than wade through technical discussions, pastors often turn to devotional commentaries, which may contain exegetical weaknesses, misuse the Greek and Hebrew languages, and lack hermeneutical sophistication. There is a need for a commentary that utilizes the best of biblical scholarship but also presents the material in a clear, concise, attractive, and user-friendly format.

This commentary is designed for that purpose—to provide a ready reference for the exposition of the biblical text, giving easy access to information that a pastor needs to communicate the text effectively. To that end, the commentary is divided into carefully selected preaching units, each covered in six pages (with carefully regulated word counts both in the passage as a whole and in each subsection). Pastors and teachers engaged in weekly preparation thus know that they will be reading approximately the same amount of material on a week-by-week basis.

Each passage begins with a concise summary of the central message, or "Big Idea," of the passage and a list of its main themes. This is followed by a more detailed interpretation of the text, including the literary context of the passage, historical background material, and interpretive insights. While drawing on the best of biblical scholarship, this material is clear, concise, and to the point. Technical material is kept to a minimum, with endnotes pointing the reader to more detailed discussion and additional resources.

A second major focus of this commentary is on the preaching and teaching process itself. Few commentaries today help the pastor/teacher move from the meaning of the text to its effective communication. Our goal is to bridge this gap. In addition to interpreting the text in the "Understanding the Text" section, each six-page unit contains a "Teaching the Text" section and an "Illustrating the Text" section. The teaching section points to the key theological themes of the passage and ways to communicate these themes to today's audiences. The illustration section provides ideas and examples for retaining the interest of hearers and connecting the message to daily life.

The creative format of this commentary arises from our belief that the Bible is not just a record of God's dealings in the past but is the living Word of God, "alive and active" and "sharper than any double-edged sword" (Heb. 4:12). Our prayer is that this commentary will help to unleash that transforming power for the glory of God.

The General Editors

Introduction to the Teach the Text Commentary Series

This series is designed to provide a ready reference for teaching the biblical text, giving easy access to information that is needed to communicate a passage effectively. To that end, the commentary is carefully divided into units that are faithful to the biblical authors' ideas and of an appropriate length for teaching or preaching.

The following standard sections are offered in each unit.

1. *Big Idea*. For each unit the commentary identifies the primary theme, or "Big Idea," that drives both the passage and the commentary.
2. *Key Themes*. Together with the Big Idea, the commentary addresses in bullet-point fashion the key ideas presented in the passage.
3. *Understanding the Text*. This section focuses on the exegesis of the text and includes several sections.
   a. The Text in Context. Here the author gives a brief explanation of how the unit fits into the flow of the text around it, including reference to the rhetorical strategy of the book and the unit's contribution to the purpose of the book.
   b. Outline/Structure. For some literary genres (e.g., epistles), a brief exegetical outline may be provided to guide the reader through the structure and flow of the passage.
   c. Historical and Cultural Background. This section addresses historical and cultural background information that may illuminate a verse or passage.
   d. Interpretive Insights. This section provides information needed for a clear understanding of the passage. The intention of the author is to be highly selective and concise rather than exhaustive and expansive.
   e. Theological Insights. In this very brief section the commentary identifies a few carefully selected theological insights about the passage.

4. *Teaching the Text*. Under this second main heading the commentary offers guidance for teaching the text. In this section the author lays out the main themes and applications of the passage. These are linked carefully to the Big Idea and are represented in the Key Themes.

5. *Illustrating the Text*. At this point in the commentary the writers partner with a team of pastor/teachers to provide suggestions for relevant and contemporary illustrations from current culture, entertainment, history, the Bible, news, literature, ethics, biography, daily life, medicine, and over forty other categories. They are designed to spark creative thinking for preachers and teachers and to help them design illustrations that bring alive the passage's key themes and message.

Abbreviations

Old Testament

Gen.	Genesis	2 Chron.	2 Chronicles	Dan.	Daniel
Exod.	Exodus	Ezra	Ezra	Hosea	Hosea
Lev.	Leviticus	Neh.	Nehemiah	Joel	Joel
Num.	Numbers	Esther	Esther	Amos	Amos
Deut.	Deuteronomy	Job	Job	Obad.	Obadiah
Josh.	Joshua	Ps(s).	Psalm(s)	Jon.	Jonah
Judg.	Judges	Prov.	Proverbs	Mic.	Micah
Ruth	Ruth	Eccles.	Ecclesiastes	Nah.	Nahum
1 Sam.	1 Samuel	Song	Song of Songs	Hab.	Habakkuk
2 Sam.	2 Samuel	Isa.	Isaiah	Zeph.	Zephaniah
1 Kings	1 Kings	Jer.	Jeremiah	Hag.	Haggai
2 Kings	2 Kings	Lam.	Lamentations	Zech.	Zechariah
1 Chron.	1 Chronicles	Ezek.	Ezekiel	Mal.	Malachi

New Testament

Matt.	Matthew	Eph.	Ephesians	Heb.	Hebrews
Mark	Mark	Phil.	Philippians	James	James
Luke	Luke	Col.	Colossians	1 Pet.	1 Peter
John	John	1 Thess.	1 Thessalonians	2 Pet.	2 Peter
Acts	Acts	2 Thess.	2 Thessalonians	1 John	1 John
Rom.	Romans	1 Tim.	1 Timothy	2 John	2 John
1 Cor.	1 Corinthians	2 Tim.	2 Timothy	3 John	3 John
2 Cor.	2 Corinthians	Titus	Titus	Jude	Jude
Gal.	Galatians	Philem.	Philemon	Rev.	Revelation

General

ca.	circa
cf.	*confer*, compare
chap(s).	chapter(s)
e.g.	*exempli gratia*, for example
esp.	especially
Gk.	Greek
Heb.	Hebrew
v(v).	verse(s)

Ancient Text Types and Versions

LXX	Septuagint or Greek Old Testament

Modern Versions

CEB	Common English Bible
CEV	Contemporary English Version
NASB	New American Standard Version

NETS	New English Translation of the Septuagint
NIV	New International Version
NLT	New Living Translation
NRSV	New Revised Standard Version
RSV	Revised Standard Version

Apocrypha and Septuagint

2 Esd.	2 Esdras
1 Macc.	1 Maccabees
2 Macc.	2 Maccabees
Sir.	Sirach
Tob.	Tobit
Wis.	Wisdom of Solomon

Old Testament Pseudepigrapha

2 Bar.	2 Baruch
1 En.	1 Enoch
Jub.	Jubilees
Pss. Sol.	Psalms of Solomon
T. Iss.	Testament of Issachar

Dead Sea Scrolls

CD	Damascus Document
1QHª	1QHodayotª (Thanksgiving Hymns)
1QS	1QRule of the Community

Mishnah and Talmud

b.	Babylonian Talmud
m.	Mishnah
'Arak.	'Arakin
B. Bat.	Baba Batra
Shabb.	Shabbat
Sanh.	Sanhedrin
Yebam.	Yebamot
Yoma	Yoma (= Kippurim)

Apostolic Fathers

| Did. | Didache |

Greek and Latin Works

Eusebius

| Hist. eccl. | Historia ecclesiastica (Ecclesiastical History) |

Jerome

| Comm. Matt. | Commentariorum in Matthaeum libri IV (Commentary on Matthew) |

Josephus

Ag. Ap.	Against Apion
Ant.	Jewish Antiquities
J.W.	Jewish War

Juvenal

| Sat. | Satirae (Satires) |

Origen

| Cels. | Contra Celsum (Against Celsus) |

Philo

| Decalogue | On the Decalogue |
| Spec. Laws | On the Special Laws |

Seneca

| Ben. | De beneficiis (On Benefits) |

Secondary Sources

BDAG	Bauer, W., W. F. Arndt, F. W. Gingrich, and F. W. Danker. A Greek-English Lexicon of the New Testament and Other Early Christian Literature. 3rd ed. Chicago: University of Chicago Press, 2000.
DJG	Dictionary of Jesus and the Gospels. Edited by Joel B. Green, Nicholas Perrin, and Jeannine K. Brown. Rev. ed. Downers Grove, IL: IVP Academic, 2013.
DNTB	Dictionary of New Testament Background. Edited by Craig A. Evans and Stanley E. Porter. Downers Grove, IL: InterVarsity, 2000.
DTIB	Dictionary for Theological Interpretation of the Bible. Edited by Kevin J. Vanhoozer et al. Grand Rapids: Baker Academic, 2005.

Introduction to Matthew

Matthew has been a favorite Gospel of the church throughout its history. Its place of primacy as the first of the four canonical Gospels corresponds to the frequency of its use by the church for theological reflection across the centuries. A reason for this preference may very well be its concerted attention to Jesus' teachings. For example, the Sermon on the Mount—the first of five great discourses of Jesus in Matthew—contains some of the most familiar phrases attributed to Jesus: "the meek will inherit the earth" (5:5), "turn the other cheek" (5:39), and the Golden Rule (7:12).

Matthew writes in the latter part of the first century to portray Jesus as God's chosen and vindicated Messiah—a Messiah who witnesses to and enacts God's reign in this world through his self-giving ministry and his death on behalf of Israel and for the nations. Matthew's Gospel envisions and shapes its readers toward faith and obedience; they are to be true followers of Jesus and his teachings. Specifically, Matthew desires his readers to be people who value and embody the weightiest matters of the Torah—justice, mercy, and faithfulness—just as Jesus embodied these values in his ministry. In this way, Jesus' followers are drawn into the mission of Jesus to bring restoration to Israel and justice to the nations, empowered by Jesus' ongoing presence with them.

The Reading Approach of This Commentary

There are many ways to read and interpret a Gospel. For example, there is significant precedent from church history for reading one Gospel through the lens of the others, resulting in a harmonized portrait of Jesus from the Gospel accounts. And yet a harmony of the Gospels necessarily loses sight of the individual shaping of Matthew's story, so this commentary avoids harmonizing observations.

For over two hundred years historical-critical inquiry has focused attention on the "world behind the text," by (1) exploring the transmission history of the Jesus traditions before they were written down (tradition and form criticisms), (2) analyzing the literary relationships among Matthew, Mark, and Luke (source criticism), and (3) comparing Matthew with its source material (e.g., Mark) in order to determine its unique emphases (redaction criticism). This commentary shows an awareness of these issues but does not focus its attention on formational and compositional aspects of the "world behind the text."

So what is the approach of this commentary? There are three methodological assumptions guiding its approach. First, Gospels are fundamentally stories about Jesus, so a narrative approach is eminently suitable for understanding them. Specifically, I understand Matthew to be theological history or theological biography, so that analyzing the story line and way the story is told reveals the Gospel's narrative theology.[1] Second, the Gospels are not ahistorical stories; they are "cultural products," having emerged in particular social and cultural contexts.[2] So, although little attention is given to source, form, and redaction analysis in this commentary, focused attention is placed on the first-century setting that illuminates Jesus' story as told by Matthew. Third, the prominence given to theology and teaching in the Teach the Text Commentary Series coheres with my assumption that Matthew as Scripture is meant to shape and form the Christian community. The theological expressions found in the "Teaching the Text" sections are drawn from the passage at hand, based on two values of contextualization (how the biblical text applies to new settings): coherence and purpose.[3] Ideally, these theological and ethical appropriations cohere with the main messages of the text and continue the purposes for which Matthew wrote.

Author

The First Gospel of the New Testament is attributed to the apostle Matthew in early church testimony and by its title, which likely dates from the beginning of the second century. Yet the Gospel itself is anonymous, like the other three Gospels, with no attribution provided in the text itself. The title of the Gospel—*kata Maththaion*—shows up in our earliest manuscripts and probably was added no later than AD 100. The title most likely was added when this Gospel was combined with the other three canonical Gospels for circulation, since

The early church attributed the Gospel of Matthew to the apostle Matthew. This icon of Matthew from a larger piece titled *Christ and Twelve Apostles* was taken from a nineteenth-century Orthodox church in the Antalya region of Turkey.

each title begins with the Greek preposition *kata* ("according to") and so distinguishes one Gospel from another.

The other piece of early evidence comes from Papias, a bishop in Asia Minor, writing sometime in the first third of the second century. A later church writer, Eusebius (died 339), quotes Papias as saying, "Matthew collected [*synetaxato*] the oracles [*ta logia*] in the Hebrew language [*Hebraidi dialektō*], and each translated [*hērmēneusen*] them as best they could" (*Hist. eccl.* 3.39.16). Scholars are divided on whether this saying accurately reflects how and by whom the First Gospel was written, and they also debate the meaning of Papias's words. On the latter, "oracles" (*ta logia*) probably refers to the whole Gospel, at least for Eusebius, given his reference to Mark as an "arrangement of the Lord's oracles [*ta logia*]" just prior to his Matthean discussion.[4] Given that there is no compelling linguistic evidence that the First Gospel is a translation from Hebrew or Aramaic (especially if Matthew used Mark), Papias's reference to *Hebraidi dialektō* might be understood to refer to Hebraic (Semitic) style rather than the Hebrew (or Aramaic) language (with *hērmēneusen* then rendered as "interpreted").[5] It is also possible that Papias is mistaken about the original language of Matthew. Scholars argue both for and against Matthean authorship, and Donald Hagner reflects a middle position: "Matthew the apostle is . . . probably the source of an early form of significant portions of the Gospel, in particular the sayings of Jesus, but perhaps even some of the narrative material."[6]

In the end, determination of authorship is not essential for the interpretation of the First Gospel, since biography as a genre points away from its author toward its subject. The implied author—the author or narrator discernible from the text itself—is a more helpful construct for the interpretation of Matthew than any hypothetical reconstruction of the empirical author. For example, the implied author of the First Gospel is the one who draws extensively on the Old Testament Scriptures through citation and allusion and through ten very particularly shaped "fulfillment quotations" (e.g., 1:22–23). He uses these scriptural references to demonstrate that Jesus is the fulfillment of the Torah and the Prophets (5:17).[7]

Date and Provenance

The range of dates suggested by various scholars for the writing of Matthew spans the latter half of the first century (AD 58–100). More narrowly, most scholars date Matthew after the fall of the Jerusalem temple (AD 70), suggested by 22:7 and 24:15–20. Corroborating evidence includes Matthew's likely use of Mark, which would mean a date after that of Mark, often dated in the late 60s. Matthew probably was written not much later than AD 80, given that the *Didache* and Ignatius appear to show familiarity with Matthew (with both dated late first or early second century).[8]

It is a speculative endeavor to determine the location (provenance) for Matthew's Gospel. Scholars typically derive clues from the Gospel's language and reconstructed social milieu. It is commonly suggested that Antioch in Syria is a likely location, since Antioch had a large Jewish population, would have been a Greek-speaking venue, and had an early Christian presence according to Acts 13:1–3 and Galatians 2:11.[9] Other suggestions of provenance range from Jerusalem to Sepphoris or Tiberias.[10]

Audience

It is commonly suggested that the First Gospel was written for a Jewish audience that has been persuaded that Jesus is God's Messiah. Support for this claim is found in Matthew's use of fulfillment quotations, his emphasis on Jesus as fulfilling the Torah, and the omission of Mark's explanation of Jewish customs (e.g., Matt. 15:2 // Mark 7:3–4). Additionally, recent Matthean scholarship, taking its cue from careful analysis of first-century Judaism of the past thirty years, has suggested that Matthew's Jewish audience continues to have close interaction with their Jewish neighbors who have not been convinced that Jesus is the Messiah. As such, their debates about Jesus are "intramural"; that is, they happen within the parameters of first-century Judaism, of which Matthew's Jewish community is a part. The Jewish author of Matthew uses Jewish sources of authority "to legitimate his particular form of Judaism."[11]

It is also the case that the persistent theme of Gentile inclusion across Matthew may suggest that these Jewish believers in Jesus were just beginning to embark on a Gentile mission (cf. 10:5–6 with 28:19).[12] If so, Matthew's development of this motif would have encouraged that mission as it moved ahead. Finally, while redaction criticism sketched a quite narrow Matthean audience, usually a single community, Richard Bauckham has argued for a broader audience for each of the Gospels.[13] This proposal makes sense of the genre of Gospels as biography (not epistle) and also takes seriously the strong connections and associations among early Christian communities (e.g., Rom. 16:1–2; 1 Cor. 16:1–4).[14]

Occasion and Purpose

The evangelist writes to followers of Jesus in the latter part of the first century, portraying Jesus as God's Messiah, who ushers in God's kingdom through his self-giving ministry and death. Matthew demonstrates that Jesus' messianic claims and mission are vindicated at his resurrection, when God grants him all authority over all the nations. The Gospel of Matthew shapes its reader to respond in ongoing trust and obedience to Jesus, his kingdom message, and his teachings. Matthew's reader is also drawn into the mission that Jesus gives to the apostles, empowered by Jesus' abiding presence, to make disciples of all the nations.

Matthew was likely written to a Jewish audience, probably after the fall of Jerusalem in AD 70. The Gospel was likely transcribed using the common writing implements of this period, such as the bronze pen and inkpot from Roman Britain shown here.

Narrative-Theological Themes

The Kingdom of Heaven/God

The central theological theme that frames Matthew's Gospel is the kingdom of God. And, although the phrase itself is not found in the Old Testament, the kingdom of God is not a new concept in Jewish thought. In Psalms and elsewhere Yahweh, Israel's God, is portrayed as ruler over all and reigning from the heavenly throne. For example, Psalm 99:1 extols Yahweh: "The LORD reigns, let the nations tremble; he sits enthroned between the cherubim, let the earth shake" (also Ps. 97:1). Yet the Old Testament prophets acknowledge that this reign of God is incomplete as they anticipate a future time when Yahweh will fully reign over all creation. Micah, for instance, envisions a day when "the LORD will rule over [the once exiled Israel] in Mount Zion, from that day and forever. . . . The former dominion will be restored to you; kingship will come to Daughter Jerusalem" (Mic. 4:7–8 [see also Isa. 24:21–23; Zech. 14:9]).

Matthew connects this restoration of God's reign and kingdom to Jesus' ministry, life, death, and resurrection. Jesus inaugurates God's kingdom "on earth as it is in heaven" (Matt. 6:10). In fact, the very first words of Jesus' public ministry in Matthew are "Repent, for the kingdom of heaven has come near" (4:17 [cf. 3:2]).[15] Matthew narrates Jesus' ministry to Israel as a preaching and enacting of the kingdom (4:17–9:35; esp. 5:3, 10, 19–20; 7:21; 8:11). Jesus' representative death as the Messiah-King breaks the power of death (27:52) and ushers in the kingdom (e.g., 27:37, 42), and his resurrection demonstrates God's vindication of his kingdom work and role. Across his Gospel Matthew clarifies that the kingdom is an "already and not yet" reality. Because this dual reality of Jesus' kingdom preaching is relatively unanticipated in Jewish expectation, Matthew highlights the still-hidden nature of the kingdom in the present (chap. 13), while pointing ahead to its final consummation at the "end of the age" (28:20 [cf. 25:1, 14, 31]).

An important part of Matthew's vision of the arrival of the kingdom is his focus on Gentile inclusion. In line with Old Testament expectation that Israel's restoration would result in all peoples coming to Jerusalem to honor Yahweh, Israel's God (Isa. 2:2–5; 49:5–7, 22–23), Matthew highlights that Gentiles are receptive to Jesus and his ministry (2:1–12; 8:5–13; 15:21–28), and that the mission initially focused on Israel will expand to all the nations after Jesus' resurrection (15:24; 28:19). Yet Matthew's vision of the church is not one of replacement, in which Gentiles supplant Israel as the people of God. Instead, Jesus promises to build his church beginning with Peter and the other disciples (16:16–20; 18:18–19) and expanding to include those whom they disciple from among all nations (28:19). This mix of Jew and Gentile who follow Jesus is defined as "a people [*ethnos*] who will produce [kingdom] fruit" (21:43).

Matthew's Narrative Christology

Reading Matthew's Christology in and through his narrative is an exploration of how he interweaves his story of Jesus with christological titles and Old Testament references to produce a vision of Jesus as (1) Davidic Messiah, (2) Torah fulfilled and Wisdom embodied, (3) representative Israel, and (4) the embodiment of Yahweh.

Matthew reveals Jesus as the Davidic Messiah, the Torah fulfilled and Wisdom embodied, the representative of Israel, and the embodiment of Yahweh. This mosaic, part of the floor in a villa at Hinton St. Mary, Dorset, England, may be the earliest mosaic picture of Christ (fourth century AD).

Jesus as Davidic Messiah

The primary goal of Matthew's Gospel is to demonstrate that Jesus is the Messiah and to show narratively who he is as Messiah. The title "Messiah" itself (used at 1:1, 16, 18; 2:4; 16:16; 26:63; 27:17, 22) does not immediately clarify what kind of messiah Jesus is, since Jewish messianic views are numerous and varied in the first century (see the sidebar "First-Century Messianic Views" in the unit on 11:2–19). Matthew's attribution of "Son of David" to Jesus affirms him as a royal messiah (e.g., 20:30; 21:9; 22:42; cf. Isa. 11:1; Mic. 5:2; *Pss. Sol.* 17:21), and Matthew's narration of Jesus entering Jerusalem in line with Zechariah's kingly prophecy emphasizes his kingly identity (21:1–9; see also 27:11, 37).[16]

Drawing from the christological category of Davidic Messiah, Matthew shapes a portrait of Jesus as the Messiah-King, who unexpectedly announces that his mission includes his impending death on behalf of his people (16:21; 17:22–23; 20:17–19). Although a first-century would-be messiah could be expected to gather support and head to Jerusalem to claim his throne in the face of Roman occupation, for Jesus to announce his death as "a ransom for many" (20:28) would have confounded royal messianic expectations. Matthew draws on Isaiah's "servant of the LORD" figure to explain how Jesus' suffering and death for Israel and for the nations fits with the Scriptures (with allusions to Isa. 53:11–12 at Matt. 20:28; 26:28; see the sidebar "Jesus as Isaiah's Servant Figure" in the unit on 12:15–21).

Jesus as Torah Fulfilled and Wisdom Embodied

Matthew highlights Jesus as the fulfillment of "the Law [and] the Prophets" (5:17) as well as the teacher who rightly interprets and obeys the Scriptures (5:21–48; 12:1–8). Jesus, not the Pharisees and teachers of the law, interprets the law with its "weightier matters" in view: "justice and mercy and faithfulness" (23:23 ESV [see also 9:13; 12:7]). He also exhorts his followers to obey the Scriptures (5:17–20; 19:17) with these central values in mind. Yet Matthew goes further to imply that Jesus himself is the embodiment of Wisdom and Torah. He does this by aligning the "deeds of the Messiah" (11:2) with wisdom's "deeds"

(11:19) and by portraying Jesus using the language of Wisdom to call his followers to discipleship and rest (see the sidebar "Torah Motifs in Jewish Wisdom Literature" in the unit on 11:20–30).

Jesus as Representative Israel

Another important christological category for Matthew is Jesus as representative Israel. The analogy between Jesus and Israel is introduced clearly at 2:15, where Matthew cites Hosea 11:1. Jesus is God's son in line with Hosea's identification of Israel as God's son; both are brought out of Egypt to the "land of Israel" (Matt. 2:20–21). The comparison continues in Jesus' baptism and temptation (chaps. 3–4). In the latter, Matthew compares and contrasts Jesus with Israel in their respective wilderness temptations (see Deut. 6 and 8, from which verses are cited in Matt. 4:1–11). Unlike Israel, Jesus proves utterly faithful when tempted in the wilderness. Jesus' faithfulness as the Son of God is also highlighted in the Passion Narrative (chaps. 26–27). Through prayer, Jesus remains faithful in spite of his desire to avoid the cross (26:36–46). Matthew draws upon Psalm 22—a psalm about a righteous and faithful Israelite who trusts in God despite unjust suffering—at a number of points during the scene depicting Jesus' crucifixion to portray Jesus as faithful son (see the sidebar "Psalm 22 in Matthew's Crucifixion Scene" in the unit on 27:27–66). Matthew's use of "Son of Man" may also point to Jesus as representative Israel (see comments on 8:20).

Jesus as the Embodiment of Yahweh

Matthew communicates Jesus as the embodiment of Israel's God implicitly for the most part. As Richard Bauckham has argued, Jesus' universal lordship (20:18; also 11:27) signifies his inclusion in the "unique divine identity."[17] Matthew also identifies Jesus as "God with us" (1:23), indicating that in Jesus the divine presence is now manifested with the people of God. In line with this portrayal, Matthew highlights worship of Jesus more than any other Gospel writer (2:2, 8, 11; 8:2; 9:18; 14:33; 15:25; 20:20; 28:9, 17), beginning and concluding the narrative with worship by the magi (2:2) and Jesus' followers (28:9, 17). As Larry Hurtado notes, "It seems undeniable that the intended readers were to take the scenes as paradigmatic anticipations of the reverence for Jesus that they offered in their worship gatherings."[18]

A Vision of Communal Discipleship

Discipleship in Matthew is communal (18:1–35) and defined by trust in and allegiance to Jesus the Messiah. Matthew calls his readers to a robust faith in Jesus and his messianic authority. The twelve disciples, who are portrayed as those of "little faith" (6:30; 8:26; 14:31; 16:8; 17:20), provide a foil to more exemplary discipleship that characterizes various seekers who come to Jesus in faith for healing (e.g., 8:10; 9:2, 22, 29; 15:28). Discipleship in Matthew involves doing the will of God in light of the arrival of the kingdom and as expressed in the teachings of Jesus (7:21–23; 12:50; 19:17; 23:3; 28:19).

For Matthew, discipleship is cross shaped, following the pattern of Jesus' life as service for others (16:24–26; 20:28). A life of service and ministry, especially to those most vulnerable and dispossessed, is characteristic of Jesus himself (e.g., 9:9–13;

19:13–15; 21:14–16). And Jesus commends caring for the vulnerable to his own followers (e.g., "little ones" and "least of these" [10:42; 18:1–20; 25:31–46]). Matthew also defines communal discipleship by the practice of forgiveness based on the extravagant forgiveness of God (6:12–15; 18:23–35). Discipleship that draws from Jesus' own way of living can be summed up as love of God and neighbor (22:36–40) or living out "justice and mercy and faithfulness,"

One of the broad themes in the Gospel of Matthew is that of communal discipleship. This fresco depicting Christ teaching his apostles was painted in the Catacombs of Domitilla, Rome, in the second century AD.

what Matthew calls the "weightier" matters of the law (23:23 ESV). Just as Jesus is portrayed as showing mercy and enacting justice (e.g., 9:13; 12:7, 18–21), so his disciples are called to live out these same values (5:7; 23:23; 25:31–46).

Outline of Matthew

1. Jesus' identity and preparation for ministry (1:1–4:16)
   a. Birth and infancy (1:1–2:23)
   b. Baptism and temptation (3:1–4:16)
2. Jesus' announcement of the kingdom to Israel and resulting responses (4:17–16:20)
   a. Proclamation of the kingdom in word and action (4:17–11:1)
      i. Summary of Jesus' message and ministry (4:17–25)

  ii. Jesus' first discourse: the Sermon on the Mount (5:1–7:29)
  iii. Jesus' enactment of the kingdom (8:1–9:38)
  iv. Jesus' second discourse: the Mission Discourse (10:1–11:1)
 b. Jesus' rejection by Israel's leaders and his withdrawal from conflict to ministry (11:2–16:20)
  i. Rejection of Jesus as the Messiah by Jewish leaders (11:2–12:50)
  ii. Jesus' third discourse: the Parables Discourse (13:1–53)
  iii. Continued conflict and emerging identity (13:54–16:20)
3. Jesus to Jerusalem: kingdom enactment through death and resurrection (16:21–28:20)
 a. Journey to the cross and teaching on discipleship (16:21–20:28)
  i. Jesus predicts the cross and defines discipleship (16:21–17:27)
  ii. Jesus' fourth discourse: the Community Discourse (18:1–35)
  iii. Nearing Jerusalem: illustrations of discipleship (19:1–20:28)
 b. Final proclamation, confrontation, and judgment in Jerusalem (20:29–25:46)
  i. Jesus' royal arrival and controversies with Jerusalem leadership (20:29–22:46)
  ii. Judgment announced on Jewish leadership (23:1–39)
  iii. Jesus' fifth discourse: the Eschatological Discourse (24:1–25:46)
 c. Jesus' execution by Rome and resurrection/vindication by God (26:1–28:20)
  i. Prelude to the cross: betrayal and desertion (26:1–56)
  ii. Jesus on trial (26:57–27:26)
  iii. Jesus' crucifixion, death, and burial (27:27–66)
  iv. Resurrection as vindication and the commissioning of disciples (28:1–20)

Jesus the Messiah from Joseph's Family Line

Big Idea *Matthew, in the opening genealogy, emphasizes Jesus as the Davidic Messiah, whom God has sent to enact Israel's restoration from exile and to include the Gentiles in God's kingdom.*

Understanding the Text

The Text in Context

It may seem surprising to find a genealogy at the opening of Matthew's Gospel, but genealogies were a common means for establishing and substantiating the identity of a person. Matthew's genealogy of Jesus demonstrates that Jesus is Israel's Messiah-King, from David's royal line. Introducing Jesus' identity at the very beginning of the Gospel sets the tone for the next four chapters (1:1–4:16), which focus on elaborating the identity of Jesus as the Davidic Messiah-King who enacts Israel's restoration from exile, as faithful and obedient son, as Gentile hope, and as "God with us." In relation to the rest of Matthew 1, the genealogy poses a conundrum that Matthew will solve in 1:18–25: how Jesus can legitimately appropriate Joseph's lineage even though his biological connection is to Mary (and not Joseph [1:16]). Matthew highlights Joseph's adoption of Jesus through his naming of Jesus (1:21, 25).

Interpretive Insights

1:1 *the genealogy of Jesus.* Ancient genealogies have some recurring features. First, they routinely followed lineage through the male, firstborn family members. Thus, the inclusion of some women (1:3, 5–6) and a few nonfirst sons (e.g., Judah in 1:2; Solomon in 1:6) would have caught the attention of Matthew's original audience. Second, since the form of a genealogy is quite patterned (the repeated "the father of . . ."), additional commentary within the genealogy is a clear way of introducing a theme (e.g., "and his brothers at the time of the exile to Babylon" [1:11]). Finally, it is not unusual for a genealogy to skip some generations; this fits the way ancient genealogies were shaped. Thus, Matthew's formation of Jesus' genealogy into three groups of fourteen is a way of highlighting a thematic or theological point (see below).

the son of David. Given David's role in Israel's history as the prototypical king and the prophetic longing for the return of

Davidic kingship (e.g., Isa. 9:7), this phrase can carry messianic connotations at the time Matthew writes. So his first readers or hearers would have understood "son of David" to point to Jesus as the Messiah, especially given Matthew's explicit affirmations of Jesus as such (e.g., 1:1; cf. *Pss. Sol.* 17:21) (see the sidebar "First-Century Messianic Views" in the unit on 11:2–19).

the son of Abraham. Because Abraham was the patriarch of the Jewish people (Gen. 12:1–3), Matthew's choice to trace Jesus' genealogy back to Abraham indicates an emphasis on the Jewish identity of Jesus (cf. the genealogy in Luke 3:23–38, which reaches back to Adam).

1:1, 17 *Messiah . . . David . . . Abraham; Abraham . . . David . . . Messiah.* Matthew frames Jesus' genealogy with the structural device of chiasm, here an A-B-C-C-B-A pattern. By it, he highlights the Jewishness of Jesus' lineage and especially his Davidic ancestry. (David is prominent in the genealogy in that he is the only ancestor of Jesus to be described with a title, "King" [1:6].) In fact, "son of David" is a favorite identity phrase for Jesus in Matthew (9:27;

Key Themes of Matthew 1:1–17

- Jesus is the Jewish Messiah, from the line of David.
- Jesus, as the Messiah-King, brings restoration of Israel from exile.
- Gentiles are included in God's kingdom, as is intimated from the presence in Jesus' genealogy of four Gentile women.

12:23; 15:22; 20:30, 31; 21:9, 15; 22:42) and is essentially synonymous with "Messiah."

1:2, 11 *and his brothers . . . and his brothers.* The repetition of the phrase "and his brothers" highlights two important moments of the Old Testament story when Israel was away from the land promised to Abraham and his descendants: the time in Egypt ("Judah and his brothers") and the time in Babylon ("Jeconiah and his brothers"). Since Matthew's genealogy emphasizes Jesus as the Messiah (King), who brings God's restoration, these two junctures emphasize the motif of exile that necessitates restoration. Exile and restoration did not only describe particular historical moments in Israel's history; these motifs also carried theological weight to describe Israel's continuing "exile" under foreign oppression (even for those Jews in Judea/Galilee during the Second Temple period), while awaiting God's full restorative work.[1]

Matthew emphasizes the Jewishness of the lineage of Jesus by including the patriarchs Abraham, Isaac, and Jacob in the genealogy list. Cenotaphs (memorials) to these men can be found in the Tomb of the Patriarchs, shown here. This structure was built by Herod the Great in the first century BC on the site of Machpelah, where Abraham purchased a cave in which to bury Sarah, according to Genesis 23.

Comparing Matthew's and Luke's Genealogies

A historical question often posed is how Matthew's genealogy compares to Luke's (Luke 3:23–38), since they are not identical throughout. In fact, the two agree only about a third of the time (from Abraham to David, two names at Matt. 1:12 // Luke 3:27, and Joseph and Jesus). Some have suggested that Matthew draws on Jesus' royal (legal) lineage, while Luke focuses on his biological ancestry.[a] A popular though speculative suggestion is that Luke's genealogy follows Jesus' descent from Mary's family (but see Luke 3:23). While there is no easy answer to this historical question, it is helpful to read each genealogy within its own narrative context to hear the strategy of each evangelist in using a genealogy. Luke includes Jesus' genealogy to tie into his emphasis on Jesus as God's son in the baptism scene (3:21–22, 23–37), while Matthew draws upon the genealogy at the very beginning of his Gospel to evoke Israel's story from Abraham onward and to introduce themes of kingship, exile and restoration, and Gentile inclusion.

[a] See Hagner, *Matthew*, 1:8.

1:3, 5–6 *Tamar . . . Rahab . . . Ruth . . . Uriah's wife.* The women in the genealogy would have caught the attention of Matthew's original audience, since genealogies typically were limited to the male line. What might Matthew be highlighting by including these particular four women? Some have suggested that each woman reflects an Old Testament story that hints of impropriety, thus preparing the reader for the unusual circumstances surrounding Mary's pregnancy (1:16, 18).[2] Jerome (AD 347–420) even suggested that all four women are the sinners of Matthew's genealogy (*Comm. Matt.* 9)! More likely, Matthew is emphasizing Gentile inclusion in Jesus' own ancestry by including these four particular women, since Tamar and Rahab are Canaanite (Gen. 38:1–6; Josh. 2:1), Ruth is Moabite (Ruth 1:4), and Bathsheba, whose national origin is not specified in the Old Testament, is explicitly called "Uriah's wife," emphasizing her connection to her Gentile husband, Uriah the Hittite (2 Sam. 11:3). If so, these women are connected not to Mary in the genealogy (1:16) but rather to a handful of Gentiles who appear in Matthew's narrative to signal God's inclusion of Gentiles in the restored kingdom (e.g., the magi, a Roman centurion, a Canaanite woman, and Pilate's wife).

1:11–12 *the time of the exile.* The exile emphasized at this second hinge of the genealogy is the exile of the southern kingdom of Judah to Babylon in the early sixth century BC. As the book of Kings narrates, the Babylonian king Nebuchadnezzar captured Jerusalem during the reign of King Jehoiachin (called "Jeconiah" in Matt. 1:11–12) and took many captives from among Jerusalem's elite, soldiers, and artisans (2 Kings 24:8–16).

1:16 *Mary was the mother of Jesus.* Matthew makes it clear that Jesus is the offspring of Mary, but he does not tie Jesus biologically to Joseph. In the Greek text a feminine singular relative pronoun (*hēs*) is used to specify that Mary (not Mary and Joseph) "begat" Jesus. This point is important (and will be emphasized again in 1:18) because it raises a genealogical conundrum. Matthew has just traced Jesus' Jewish and Davidic ancestry through Joseph's line, yet he problematizes that connection by indicating that Jesus comes from Mary (and her line) and not Joseph. Matthew will solve this conundrum in Jesus' birth story by accenting Joseph's choice to adopt Jesus as his own son (1:18–25).

1:17 *fourteen generations.* Matthew explains that he has structured Jesus' genealogy in three sets of fourteen generations. Questions arise from this facet of the genealogy. First, since generations may be omitted in an ancient genealogy, it is not problematic if Matthew has done this for some larger purpose. Second, commentators have noted that the final set of fourteen actually contains thirteen generations, unless Jeconiah is counted in the final section (which shortens the middle section by one). As a solution, some have suggested that David be counted twice, given the emphasis on his title as king and his prominence in the genealogy's frame (1:1, 17). Given these numeric difficulties, it is hard to avoid the conclusion that Matthew has chosen three sets of fourteen for a particular thematic purpose, although interpreters have debated its precise meaning. Two primary options are typically raised. First, the importance of the number "seven" to signal completion might indicate that Matthew has arranged his genealogy in multiples of seven (three groups of 2 x 7 = six groups of seven) to signal that Jesus the Messiah ushers in the time of fullness—the seventh period of sevens. Working against this thesis is that Matthew highlights explicitly fourteen rather than seven. A second possibility is that Matthew uses fourteen to stress Jesus' Davidic ancestry, since fourteen is the sum of the numerical equivalents for the Hebrew letters of David's name.

$$\begin{array}{ccccc} \daleth & & \vav & & \daleth \\ 4 & + & 6 & + & 4 \end{array} = \begin{array}{c} D[a]V[i]D \\ = 14 \end{array}$$

The use of such numbering systems, called "gematria," for symbolic or thematic purposes is common in Jewish circles of this time period. Whether or not all early readers of Matthew would have recognized this gematria, it is likely that Matthew uses it to reemphasize David's importance in Jesus' lineage.[3]

Teaching the Text

1. *Jesus is the Davidic king, who will rule God's people.* It is no accident that Matthew draws Jesus' identity from the kingly line of David. David is that prototypical Israelite king, whom the prophets idealize in their depiction of restoration under a kingly descendant from David. For Matthew, Jesus is that rightful king from David's line. Yet it will be Matthew's primary task in the rest of his Gospel to show what kind of king Jesus is and what kind of kingdom Jesus brings. Preaching or teaching Matthew will necessarily mean maintaining a focus on Jesus, placing emphasis where Matthew does.

Matthew follows the kingly line of David in his genealogy from David to the exile. Shown here is one of the domes in the Chora Museum, where Mary, holding Jesus, is surrounded by mosaics of the kings mentioned in Matthew 1:6–11.

2. *Jesus is the Messiah, who brings restoration of Israel from exile.* The pattern of exile and restoration is an important theological motif in both Testaments. According to Matthew's shaping of the genealogy, Jesus is God's agent who brings restoration from Israel's physical and spiritual exile. The time of God's final restoration has actually begun in Jesus the Messiah. Matthew announces this crucial and amazing truth at each hinge of the genealogy:

> Abraham: God chooses a people of promise.
>
> David: God gives them a king of promise.
>
> Exile: They are without their promised king.
>
> Jesus: Kingship and the people are restored.

As we teach or preach this passage, we cannot underscore enough the monumental nature of what God has begun to do in Jesus. All the Old Testament prophetic hopes for restoration converge in this person, Jesus the Messiah.

3. *Matthew accents the inclusive nature of God's kingdom.* The unexpected presence of Gentile mothers in the genealogy (as well as sons other than the firstborn, such as Judah and Solomon) intimates that God's kingdom in Jesus will be one of unexpected inclusion. While some Old Testament prophetic texts indicate that Israel's restoration will be the hope for Gentiles (e.g., Isa. 2:1–5; 51:1–5), Matthew especially emphasizes that God's restorative plan includes Gentiles as well as Jews (cf. 8:11; 12:21). God's restoration also focuses on the marginalized (9:9–13; 21:14–16), since mercy is at the center of God's ways (9:13; 12:7).

The most likely tendency in preaching and teaching Matthew 1 is to skip over the genealogy. Yet Matthew's theology shines through what we might consider to be simply a tedious list. It would be a shame to miss these important theological themes in our preaching or teaching of Matthew. On the other hand, we might be tempted to miss the forest for the trees. Matthew's desire is not that we choose our favorite Old Testament characters who show up in the genealogy and make multiple connections between that character and Jesus (a kind of allegorizing). Instead, we should keep the big picture in view, since Matthew guides us to focus on major junctures of the genealogy. By attending to the broad strokes of the genealogy, we also get a sense of the full sweep of Israel's history portrayed in it. In the genealogy we "enter the narrative world," hearing how Jesus is the fulfillment of Israel's history.[4]

Illustrating the Text

Jesus is the Davidic king, who will rule God's people.

Human Experience: Sharing one's genealogy is not a common way of introducing oneself in our day and age. Yet we routinely ask the question "Where are you from?" to get a sense of who a person is—their identity. The genealogy of Jesus is an answer to this question "Where are you from?" in Matthew's context. And in a similar way, we learn something valuable from hearing about a person's roots and personal location.

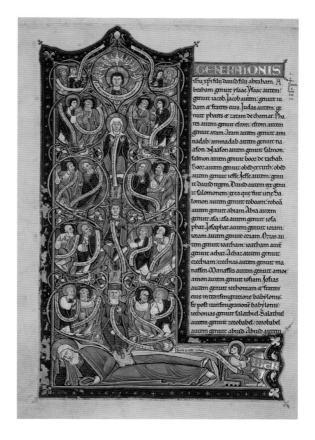

Jesus is the Messiah, who brings restoration of Israel from exile.

Mythology: In the Greek myth of Sisyphus, this famous king was sentenced to a terrible eternity for insulting the gods. In a never-ending cycle of endless toil, Sisyphus would roll a boulder up a hill, only to have it roll back down again. For eternity, he had no hope that the task would be completed. Israel's hope of return from exile had been kindled at various points after the capture of Jerusalem and Judea in the sixth century BC—for example, during the return of exiles under Ezra and Nehemiah and during Israel's brief years of freedom from Greek rule. Yet Rome had invaded and conquered Judea, dashing again their hopes of restoration. Not unlike Sisyphus watching the boulder roll down the hill once more, Israel had to again put their hopes on hold as they struggled under another oppressive regime. Yet Matthew announces that the definitive moment of history, restoration from exile, has arrived in Jesus.

Matthew accents the inclusive nature of God's kingdom.

History: Typically, kings jealously guard their bloodlines, highlighting their noble origins and striving to produce a worthy successor. A good example is King Henry VIII. This king went to great lengths to secure an heir for himself, marrying six wives, two of whom were executed. His mania to divorce his first wife in the hopes of marrying a second was partly responsible for the formation of the Anglican Church. When the pope refused to grant him a divorce, Henry separated the English church from Rome. It is intriguing to note how diverse and messy Jesus' lineage was, and how willingly Matthew highlights this by including non-Jews.

Jesus Adopted by Joseph

Big Idea *Matthew confirms that Jesus belongs to Joseph's genealogy by adoption, showing Jesus to be the Davidic Messiah and the embodiment of God's presence to save.*

Understanding the Text

The Text in Context

Matthew concludes the genealogy from Abraham to Joseph by connecting Jesus' birth to Mary, not to Joseph (1:16). In 1:18–25 Matthew "solves" this conundrum by emphasizing that Joseph names Jesus (1:21, 25), thereby adopting Jesus as his own son. This birth story also moves seamlessly into Matthew 2, where Jesus' birth threatens the ruling "king of the Jews," Herod. Themes introduced in this passage include Jesus as the one who will save his people from their sins (1:21; cf. 26:28), and Jesus as "God with us" (1:23). The latter motif is central to Matthew, given its strategic placement at the beginning and end of the narrative (1:23; 28:20: "I am with you always"; see also 18:20).

Interpretive Insights

1:18 *the birth of Jesus the Messiah.* The word rendered "birth" in 1:18 is the same term used already in 1:1, *genesis* (there translated as "genealogy"). While both translations are quite in line with the different senses of this Greek word,

the connection between the two sections (1:1–17, 18–25) is strengthened in that they both explicate Jesus' "origins." The first half of the chapter gives the genealogical and kingly origins of Jesus, specifically the genealogical line from Abraham through David. The latter half gives the more immediate familial origins, providing the connection between Joseph's genealogy and his adoption of Jesus into his family line.

pledged to be married. Jewish engagements were initiated by a contract of marriage, and a legal action was required to break the engagement. This is what is meant by Joseph's intention to "divorce her" (*apolyō* [1:19]). According to (later) rabbinic traditions, engagements, which usually were arranged when a young woman was about twelve years old, lasted about a year, after which the couple was married, and the wife lived with the husband's family.[1]

1:19 *a righteous man.* Matthew identifies Joseph as "a righteous man" (*dikaios*) and connects this character trait to Joseph's intention to divorce Mary quietly. Matthew might intend to connect Joseph's righteous character to his intention to be merciful to Mary (he meant to divorce her *quietly*, without public disgrace). It is also possible, given Matthew's frequent connection between righteousness and Torah obedience (e.g., 5:20), that he indicates that Joseph felt compelled by the law to divorce Mary. Joseph would have been expected to do just this, according to Jewish, Greek, and Roman law (e.g., *m. Yebam.* 2:8; cf. Deut. 22:23–27 [though it seems that the death penalty was not routinely enacted in the first century]).[2] Both interpretations are consistent with Matthew's emphasis on Torah obedience through merciful action (e.g., 12:7).

1:20 *an angel of the Lord.* Matthew includes angels and/or divine messages, often given in dreams, quite frequently in his early chapters. Joseph is led by angelic instructions and dreams, as are the magi (1:20–21; 2:12, 13, 19–20, 22; 4:11; see also 27:19). By including these plot elements, the author highlights God's protection of Jesus and his family as well as God's guidance through these moments of revelation.

Joseph son of David. Joseph is called a "son of David," just as Jesus is so designated at 1:1 and a number of times across the Gospel. While the descriptor could simply designate one from David's (royal) line, as in Joseph's case, Matthew

applies "son of David" to Jesus with messianic connotations (see comments on 1:1).

from the Holy Spirit. This is the first mention of the Holy Spirit in Matthew's Gospel. Although Matthew tends to prefer speaking of the presence of God with the people of God in terms of Jesus' presence with them (1:23; 18:20; 28:20), references to the Spirit occur often enough (e.g., 3:11, 16; 4:1; 10:20; 12:18, 28, 32; 22:43; 28:19).

1:21, 23, 25 *the name Jesus . . . call him Immanuel . . . the name Jesus.* Each of these three moments in the birth story of Jesus accents the naming of Jesus. Joseph is instructed by an angel in a dream to name Mary's son "Jesus." The final words of the passage indicate that Joseph obeys and does just that. Moreover, Matthew highlights the importance of the meaning of Jesus' name by using that name to form an inclusio (textual bookends) for the passage. In 1:18 he places the noun "Jesus" (*Iēsou*, genitive case) as close to the beginning of the sentence as Greek word order allows, and "Jesus" is also the final word of the passage (1:25).

Joseph "did what the angel of the Lord had commanded him and took Mary home as his wife" (1:24). In modern Nazareth, a house from the early Roman period (first and second centuries AD) has been discovered near the Church of the Annunciation. Archaeological remains from that excavation are shown here.

In terms of the narrative plot, this naming feature of the passage indicates that Jesus is brought into Joseph's Davidic lineage (see comments on 1:25). Matthew also directly shapes his audience's understanding of Jesus' identity by citing Isaiah 7:14 and "naming" Jesus as "Immanuel . . . 'God with us'" (1:23), a theme that begins and ends the whole of Matthew (cf. 28:20).

1:21 *Jesus*. The name "Jesus" derives from the Hebrew name "Joshua" ("Yehoshua"), which means "God is salvation." Matthew both assumes this etymology and emphasizes it for his audience: Jesus is so named "because he will save his people from their sins." Jesus' death for sin as the focal point of his saving work is not made clear at this early stage of Matthew's story, but it will become increasingly clear as the narrative progresses and will find full expression in Jesus' own words in 26:28: "This is my blood of the covenant, which is poured out for many for the forgiveness of sins."

1:22–23 *through the prophet*. Matthew draws on Isaiah 7:14 for his first of ten such fulfillment quotations. Each begins with a similar

Matthew quotes from Isaiah 7:14 to show how Jesus fulfills Old Testament hopes. Isaiah is depicted here in a painting by Duccio di Buoninsegna from the Maesta altarpiece in the Siena Cathedral, Italy (fourteenth century AD).

formula (e.g., "so was fulfilled what was spoken through the prophet" [see 2:15, 17–18, 23; 4:14–16; 8:17; 12:17–21; 13:35; 21:4–5; 27:9–10]). Matthew's use of this formula, along with his many citations and allusions to the Old Testament, demonstrates his interest in Jesus as the one who fulfills the "Law and the Prophets" (5:17–20; 7:12).

Isaiah 7:14 in its context refers to an immediate fulfillment, and specifically the devastation of Judah's enemies Israel and Aram by Assyria before the child soon to be born grows up (Isa. 7:1–17). Matthew seems to draw on a typological reading that sees God's work in Jesus' birth as analogous to (and greater than) God's saving work through the child spoken of by Isaiah (see Isa. 8:1–4; 9:6–7) (see the sidebar "Matthew's Use of the Old Testament"). Matthew uses the Isaiah link to emphasize the importance of the naming of Jesus as well as the conception of Jesus by the Holy Spirit (1:20).[3]

1:25 *And he gave him the name Jesus*. By obeying the angel's directive to name Mary's child (1:20), Joseph becomes Jesus' father via adoption (cf. Isa. 43:1; Luke 1:60–63).[4] The importance of the act of naming for the legal status of a child explains why Matthew accentuates the naming of Jesus, especially since he has raised the problem of Jesus being born from Mary but not from Joseph (1:16, 20).

Theological Insights: The Incarnation

Matthew introduces Jesus as "God with us" (1:22–23), providing the church from its earliest days with a starting point for its doctrine of the incarnation. Various New Testament passages expand on this theological message and enhance Matthew's brief reference. John 1 identifies Jesus with the Word (*logos*), which was with God in the very beginning and was "made flesh" in Jesus (John 1:1, 14, 18), and Colossians 1 joins John 1 in affirming Jesus as the means of creation at the beginning (Col. 1:15–16). Paul in Philippians 2:5–11 "fleshes out" Jesus' incarnation as an emptying (*kenoō* [v. 7], hence the theological term *kenōsis*) of divine prerogative and status.

Teaching the Text

1. *Jesus is the fulfillment of the Scriptures and Israel's story.* Matthew has already indicated through the genealogy in 1:2–17 that Jesus completes Israel's story. With the use of his first fulfillment quotation (1:22–23), he introduces the theme that Jesus is the fulfillment of Israel's Scriptures. This theme of Jesus as the fulfillment of Israel's story and Scriptures is pervasive and can be powerful for preaching and teaching. In doing so, it can be helpful to follow the trail from Matthew back to the Old Testament

Matthew's Use of the Old Testament

Kinds of Usage

- Citations: Often one or more verses of Old Testament text are quoted.
- Allusions: Verbal links (e.g., two to four words) are made between an Old Testament text and Matthew, along with thematic ties.
- Echoes: Some verbal and/or conceptual connections are evident, usually in more than one Matthean passage.

Kinds of Connections between Matthew and the Old Testament Text

- The Old Testament text fits a traditional understanding of prophecy-fulfillment. The Old Testament author envisions an event that is fulfilled in the New Testament context (e.g., Matt. 3:3 // Isa. 40:3: the time of restoration has come).
- The Old Testament text is used by way of analogy to explain an event portrayed by Matthew—that is, "as then . . . so now . . ."—a typological usage (e.g., Matt. 2:15 // Hosea 11:1; and Matt. 15:7–9 // Isa. 29:13: Isaiah's generation compared to Jesus' generation).
- The Old Testament text is used illustratively and/or expressively, often in the form of allusion (e.g., Matt. 10:35–36 // Mic. 7:6). Often in these cases the language and ideas of the Old Testament pervade the imagination of the New Testament writer, who draws from this language for expression.
- The Old Testament text is used to evoke a significant Old Testament salvation-history theme (e.g., Matt. 2:17–18 // Jer. 31:15 with its context). This use may fit another category simultaneously.
- The Old Testament is used to paint the broad strokes of Israel's history (e.g., Matthew's genealogy; and 23:35).

via his frequent citations and allusions. As we connect the story of Jesus with the story of Israel, we would do well to follow Matthew's lead and see the messianic importance of various Old Testament roles and figures. King, prophet, and priest are developed in the Old Testament and other Jewish writings as potential messianic categories, and Matthew draws especially on the first two for his Christology. The evangelist will also make clear an important analogy between Jesus and Israel in these early chapters (e.g., 2:15; 4:1–11). Another significant christological category is the Servant of the Lord from Isaiah's Servant Songs (Isa. 42–53), which Matthew will highlight across his narrative. In preaching and teaching these important connections, we will help our hearers to make the connections that Matthew is making by teaching about these Old Testament categories and figures. Matthew could presume that his audience understood these significant categories for his Christology, but we probably should not presume that our audiences, who are often further removed from Judaism and a rich knowledge of the Old Testament, bring such understandings to their reading of Matthew.

According to Matthew, the birth of Jesus is the coming of Immanuel, "God with us." This nativity scene is from a fourth-century AD sarcophagus.

2. *Jesus is Savior and Immanuel—God with us.* Two key christological affirmations of this passage are that Jesus "will save his people from their sins" (1:21) and that Jesus is "God with us" (1:23). Jesus' saving work is both assumed in his kingdom pronouncement and enactment (e.g., healings) and affirmed at key points in the story. For example, Jesus teaches the disciples that the purpose of his approaching death is "to give his life as a ransom for many" (20:28). The connection between Jesus' death and forgiveness offered is clarified in his words during the Passover meal: his blood "is poured out for many for the forgiveness of sins" (26:28).

Jesus as "God with us" provides a powerful message for Christian communities. While Matthew has been construed by some as focused on "law" more than "gospel," this proves to be a false dichotomy. Matthew does emphasize the importance of obedience (covenant faithfulness) for Jesus' followers (see the sidebar "Matthew's Covenantal Backdrop" in the unit on 3:1–17). Yet he also provides a powerful reminder of the presence of God in Jesus with believers at the beginning and end of his narrative. Jesus is "God with us" (1:23), and Jesus makes an amazing promise in the final verse of the Gospel: "Surely I am with you always, to the very end of the age" (28:20). We can proclaim with confidence that Jesus goes with and empowers his followers as they live out both discipleship and mission (28:19–20). For Jesus has come among us as the one named "Immanuel . . . 'God with us.'"

Illustrating the Text

Jesus is the fulfillment of the Scriptures and Israel's story.

Film: *The Wizard of Oz.* The best-made movies capture a well-written story. One technique of great storytellers is "foreshadowing," whereby later events are portrayed subtly in earlier events. For instance, in *The Wizard of Oz*, the epic battle between Dorothy and the Wicked Witch is foreshadowed by Dorothy's altercation with her heartless neighbor, Miss Gulch. Jesus is the ultimate fulfillment of a story that has been unfolding over centuries, and his coming was foreshadowed in the story of Israel. As we see in Matthew's early chapters, the motifs of Israel's exile and restoration are reenacted in Jesus' story and mission. Jesus brings restoration in definitive ways to Israel's experience of exile.

Jesus is Savior and Immanuel—God with us.

History: Born in the thirteenth century, Saint Elizabeth of Hungary was a German princess, the daughter of King Andrew II of Hungary and Gertrude of Merania, with an impeccable pedigree. Yet after her marriage to Ludwig IV, she established a hospital, where she herself served and cared for the poor in their sickness. Outside the hospital she cared for the poor and downcast, spinning wool and sharing food. For the ways she willingly emptied herself and relinquished her rights, Elizabeth was canonized shortly after her death. Her actions illustrate an incarnational way of life.

Literature: *Aurora Leigh*, **by Elizabeth Barrett Browning.** In this epic poem, Browning wrote the following lines evoking incarnation:

> Earth's crammed with heaven,
> And every common bush afire with
>   God . . .

Poetry: "Ordinary Day," by Jeannine Brown. This 1997 lyric speaks to the meaningfulness of incarnation for ordinary life:

> Ordinary day
> Nothing in the way of unusual
> Doing all the things
> I usually do
>
> Not so very wise
> Not so very spiritual
> Oh so very usual
> Is my life
> But God was not afraid
> To come
> Into this very usual world
>
> Entering our lives
> Taking our humanity
> So very flesh and blood
> The savior's love
>
> Eternal word of God
> From all time existing
> Now to dwell among us
> Eternally
>
> God was not afraid
> To come
> Into this very usual world
>
> Ordinary day
> Nothing in the way of unusual
> Doing all the things
> I usually do
>
> But here in the mundane
> Reminded of reality
> That God is in the usual
> God with me

Jesus as True King of Israel

Big Idea *Matthew contrasts Jesus' identity as the Messiah—the true King who enacts Israel's return from exile—with Rome's client-king, Herod, affirming Jesus' identity through Old Testament testimony, God's protection, and worship of Jesus by the Gentile magi.*

Understanding the Text

The Text in Context

Matthew 2 narrates the political threat that Jesus' birth creates for Herod and the ensuing need for Jesus' family to flee the country. After time in Egypt, they return, settling in Nazareth. Themes of God's protection and direction of Jesus' family through dreams and angelic guidance are prominent, continuing the scene from 1:18–25, where God uses a dream to guide Joseph's decision making. As he has already done at 1:22–23, Matthew uses fulfillment quotations to connect Jesus' story to the Old Testament story of Israel (2:5–6, 15, 17–18, 23). In addition, the theme of Gentile inclusion reappears through the characters of the non-Jewish magi, who seek Jesus and worship him as king.

Interpretive Insights

2:1 *born in Bethlehem.* Bethlehem is located about six miles east of Jerusalem. The reason for Mary and Joseph's presence in Bethlehem is not explained by Matthew, with the likely implication that

Matthew's reader has some knowledge of birth traditions about Jesus (see Luke 2). What Matthew does emphasize through the geography of chapter 2 is the fulfillment of prophecy through Jesus' birth in Bethlehem and the relocation of his family first to Egypt and then to Nazareth in Galilee.

during the time of King Herod. Herod the Great, born around 73 BC, ruled Judea, Samaria, Perea, and Galilee from 37 BC until his death in 4 BC. An Idumean (or Edomite) by birth, he was appointed by Rome in 40 BC to rule Judea because of his alliance with Rome. He gained control of Galilee and then Jerusalem from Antigones, a Hasmonean[1] allied with the Parthians, in 37 BC. He ruled the Jewish people until his death in 4 BC, at which time his reign was divided among three of his sons, Archelaus (over Idumea, Judea, and Samaria [see 2:22]), Philip (over the northeastern sector of his father's territories), and Herod Antipas (over Galilee and Perea) (see the map of first-century Palestine).[2]

Magi from the east. The identity of the magi (Gk. *magoi*) is a matter of debate. Although church history as well as contemporary Christmas scenes and plays depict three opulent wise men of kingly stature, Matthew nowhere indicates the number of magi. Additionally, it is likely that these Gentile star-watchers were servants rather than kings. As Mark Powell indicates, Matthew's reader would have likely identified the magi as royal servants (e.g., Dan. 2:1–12, with *magos* used in the LXX at 2:2, 10).[3] If so, the magi in Matthew 2 would have provided a contrast to King Herod. While kings should be expected to pay homage to the Messiah (see Ps. 72:10–11), Matthew instead portrays royal servants (and Gentiles, at that) doing so.[4] These Gentile worshipers provide a stark contrast to Herod, who claims an intention to worship Jesus but plots his demise instead.

2:2 *king of the Jews.* When the magi ask for information about "the one who has been born king of the Jews," Matthew portrays Herod's response as one of agitation over this potential rival to his throne. The repeated emphasis on Herod as king (2:1, 3, 9) and his power to suppress any rivals (2:16) indicates that Matthew 2 is about political as well as religious authority and claims. For Matthew, Jesus is the Messiah or "king of the Jews." As such, he

Jesus is born in Bethlehem. The area around the modern city of Bethlehem is shown here.

threatens Herod's claim to be king of the Jewish people, the very position granted to him by Roman authority. Herod understands Jesus to be a threat and responds by killing every boy in Bethlehem who might be the one whom the magi came to find (2:16), necessitating that Joseph and Mary take Jesus and flee to Egypt. Even when they return to Israel after Herod dies, they avoid coming under the rule of Herod's son Archelaus by settling in the north, in Galilee.

2:4 *chief priests and teachers of the law.* This first reference to Jewish leaders in Matthew's Gospel couples Israel's temple leaders with its learned men. The chief priests were the key leaders of temple functions and activities; they held both religious and

Key Themes of Matthew 2:1–23

- Jesus the Messiah-King and King Herod are in conflict.
- The Old Testament confirms Jesus' identity as the one who enacts return from exile.
- Gentile inclusion is intimated in the presence of magi.
- God guides and protects Jesus.

political authority centered in Jerusalem and in alliance with and under the authority of Roman occupation. "Teachers of the law" translates *grammateis* (traditionally translated as "scribes") and reflects a group in Judaism that had an interpretive role in the Jewish law (Torah).

2:5–6 *But you, Bethlehem, in the land of Judah.* Micah 5:2 is cited to provide an Old Testament basis for Bethlehem as the birthplace of the Messiah. Although placed on the lips of the chief priests and teachers of the law rather than provided by Matthew as narrator, this quotation functions in similar fashion to the fulfillment quotations that precede and follow it in the birth narrative (1:22–23; 2:15, 17–18, 23). Each citation connects Jesus to the Old Testament story of Israel and to prophetic testimony about God's future work of restoration, which is now coming about in Jesus the Messiah. In the broader context of Micah 5, the Assyrian threat of exile is clearly in view (5:1–6). Micah prophesies that the one who shepherds God's people will bring peace, security, and deliverance from exile.

2:12 *warned in a dream.* Throughout the birth narrative (1:18–2:23) divine protection and guidance are signaled by communication through dreams and angels (1:20; 2:12, 13, 19, 22), as well as in the appearance of the star (2:2). It is striking that Jesus, the true king in contrast to Herod, is not described by active verbs in the birth account. Instead, he is acted upon: Herod tries to kill him, the magi worship him, Joseph takes him to safety, and the prophets testify to him. Accent falls on the theme of divine protection: God watches over the true, yet vulnerable, Messiah-King.

2:15 *Out of Egypt I called my son.* Matthew cites Hosea 11:1, providing the first of numerous analogous connections between Israel and Jesus. In the context of Hosea it is clear that Israel is God's son who is called out of and redeemed from Egypt (Hosea 11:1, 5, 11). Matthew seems to use Hosea intentionally to introduce Jesus as God's son, who will also go down into Egypt and return to the land of Israel (2:20–21 [repeated for emphasis]). By signaling the story of exile and return, this fulfillment quotation provides a second evocation of return from exile in Matthew 2.

2:17–18 *A voice is heard in Ramah . . . Rachel weeping.* Jeremiah 31:15, another fulfillment quotation, is cited in conjunction with Herod's order to kill all boys in Bethlehem under the age of two in order to ensure the removal of Jesus as contender to his throne. Rachel was associated in the Old Testament with the area of Bethlehem and with the town of Ramah (Gen. 35:16–20; 48:7; 1 Sam. 10:2; Jer. 31:15). Ramah was a transport center during the time when Jews were deported to Babylon (ca. 587 BC). In fact, the verses in Jeremiah that follow the one that Matthew cites include the theme of restoration from exile: "There is hope for your descendants. . . . Your children will return to their own land" (Jer. 31:17).

2:22–23 *Archelaus.* Matthew identifies Archelaus as the son of Herod the Great (2:1) and indicates that the former has become ruler of Judea after his father's death (4 BC) (on the division of Herod's kingdom, see comments on 2:1).

District of Galilee . . . a town called Nazareth. Located north of Judea and Samaria, Galilee had a significant Jewish population (see comments on 4:12).

Nazareth was a smaller town in the central area of Galilee, with a population of five hundred or less.[5]

So was fulfilled what was said through the prophets, that he would be called a Nazarene. Though this passage is introduced as a fulfillment quotation, it is likely that Matthew is providing a wordplay to connect Jesus' hometown of Nazareth with his identity as the Messiah. The Hebrew word for "branch" (*netser*) sounds much like "Nazareth" (*Nazōraios*), used in 2:23. The association of David's "branch" in Isaiah 11:1 with messianic hope is well attested in Jewish writings that predate the New Testament (e.g., 1QH[a] 15:19). It would not be far-fetched to expect that certain important Hebrew words had currency in various Jewish circles of the first century, even in ones where the Old Testament was accessed in Greek rather than Hebrew. Matthew's audience could well have caught this wordplay connection between Nazareth and the Messiah.[6] Through this association, "Matthew concludes his telling of the story of Jesus' birth just as he began it (1:1), by emphasizing Jesus as Messiah, Son of David, the hope of Israel's restoration."[7]

Theological Insights: Restoration from Exile

God's promise for Israel's return from exile reverberates across the Old Testament prophets, in and around the texts cited in Matthew 2 and beyond (e.g., Isa. 40; Jer. 31; Ezek. 34; Amos 9:11–15). As Matthew picks up this theme and emphasizes that the arrival of Jesus is precisely return from exile (1:11–12, 17; 2:14–15, 19–21; 3:1–3), so also do other New Testament writers (e.g., Mark 1:1–3; Luke 3:4–6; 9:31 [Jesus'

Map of first-century Palestine

"exodus"]). And yet some New Testament writers also envision the present Christian experience, in the time between the kingdom's arrival and its consummation, as a time of continuing exile. So the letter of 1 Peter refers to its readers as "foreigners and exiles" (2:11; cf. 1:1, 17).

Teaching the Text

1. *Jesus the Messiah brings the restoration of Israel from exile.* The pattern of exile and restoration already established in Matthew 1 continues into chapter 2. This can

be seen most clearly in the quotation of Hosea 11:1 in 2:15, where God's deliverance of Israel from Egypt is the prototype for the promise of God's deliverance of Jesus' family from the evil intentions of Herod by flight to Egypt and return to Israel. Jesus as God's son is protected and delivered. The theme of return to the land, as in the story of Israel, is repeated in 2:20–21 ("the land of Israel") to bring home the point that God is returning his own son, Jesus, from exile as he did for Israel in the time of the exodus. It is significant that the two other specific quotations in Matthew 2 have themes of exile and restoration in their immediate Old Testament contexts (Mic. 5:1–6; Jer. 31:10–17). As we preach and teach this passage, we can offer to our audience the vision of God's promised restoration of this world having its locus in Jesus. From his birth, Jesus is God's son, the Messiah, who ushers in redemption and restoration for God's people.

2. *Gentiles are included in God's redemptive plan.* This theme also spans the first two chapters of Matthew. As the women in Matthew's genealogy signal Gentile inclusion in God's redemptive work, so do the magi in Matthew 2. They represent non-Jewish seekers of God's plan and work who nonetheless are the first worshipers of Jesus in Matthew's Gospel (2:2, 11). Even though Matthew emphasizes Jesus' mission to the people of Israel (e.g., 10:5–6; 15:24), he is also interested in foreshadowing and high-lighting Gentile inclusion in God's messianic people. By the time he writes, the early church has pressed into the implications for Gentiles of God's restoration of Israel in Jesus and is actively engaging the Gentile mission (see 28:19).

3. *Jesus is worthy of worship.* Matthew illuminates Jesus' identity by emphasizing the worship of Jesus by the magi. Matthew, more than the other Gospel writers, portrays various characters worshiping Jesus in his story. In fact, Jesus is portrayed as an object of worship (with the verb *proskyneō* [rendered "knelt" at a number of points]) ten times, more than in the other three Gospels altogether (2:2, 8, 11; 8:2; 9:18; 14:33; 15:25; 20:20; 28:9, 17). These moments of worship include an emphasis at the beginning and the end of the Gospel: the magi worship Jesus at his birth (2:11), and his followers worship him upon his

When the magi find Jesus, they bow down and worship him. The earliest depictions of the "adoration of the magi" are found in the catacombs and on sar-cophagus panels like this one from the fourth century AD from the cemetery of St. Agnes in Rome.

resurrection (28:9, 17). Not only does Matthew clarify his Christology through this emphasis on worship; he also provides a model for Christian practice. The proper response to Jesus the Messiah is worship. And accenting these portraits from Matthew's story can draw our own audiences into deeper worship and praise of Jesus the Messiah.

Illustrating the Text

Jesus the Messiah brings the restoration of Israel from exile.

Human Experience: From a young age, we are wired to make promises and expect promises from others. "I promise" is a vow routinely on the lips of children and adults, and "But you promised!" can be the greatest of constraints on human behavior. Yet in words and actions human beings often let down those to whom they have made promises. We often promise more than we can deliver. According to Matthew, God's promises to Israel are now being fully realized and fulfilled in Jesus the Messiah. As Paul corroborates in 2 Corinthians 1:20, "No matter how many promises God has made, they are 'Yes' in Christ."

Gentiles are included in God's redemptive plan.

Film: *Guess Who's Coming to Dinner.* This 1967 movie challenged audiences to examine their own stereotypes. Breaking boundaries in daring ways for its time, the film depicts a young white woman bringing her black fiancé (played by Katharine Houghton and Sidney Poitier) home for dinner. The plot involves the girl's parents (Katharine Hepburn and Spencer Tracy) struggling to understand what was socially unacceptable in that era and wondering about extending welcome to this young man. For a first-century Jewish audience, the idea of non-Jewish royal servants being the first to worship Israel's Messiah would have provided a similar point of struggle.

Jesus is worthy of worship.

Hymn: **"In the Bleak Midwinter," by Christina Rossetti.** This hymn (1872) highlights the paradox and power of a human child being worthy of human worship. The final stanzas read,

> Angels and archangels may have gathered there,
> Cherubim and seraphim thronged the air;
> But His mother only, in her maiden bliss,
> Worshipped the beloved with a kiss.
>
> What can I give Him, poor as I am?
> If I were a shepherd, I would bring a lamb;
> If I were a Wise Man, I would do my part;
> Yet what I can I give Him: give my heart.

Jesus' Baptism by John

Big Idea *In introducing John the Baptist and narrating Jesus' baptism, Matthew announces the restoration of God's kingdom through Jesus' own covenant faithfulness for all those who will repent.*

Understanding the Text

The Text in Context

Having narrated Jesus' birth, Matthew fast-forwards to the events leading up to Jesus' public ministry, including Jesus' baptism by John (chap. 3). Matthew indicates that John the Baptist's ministry prepares for that of Jesus (3:3; cf. Isa. 40:3) and also resonates with Jesus' ministry, as themes of repentance, warnings of judgment, and Gentile inclusion in the coming kingdom of God resound. Jesus as God's son has already been introduced at 2:15, where Jesus' sonship is compared to that of Israel's ("Out of Egypt I called my son"). Now the motif of Jesus as the faithful Son of God is highlighted at his baptism (3:13–17) and will be contrasted with Israel's unfaithfulness in the temptation narrative that follows (chap. 4).

Interpretive Insights

3:1 *John the Baptist.* The exact background to the purposes of John's baptism is debated, given that Jewish sources do not provide a single, definitive answer for understanding how John's baptism of fellow Jews would have been perceived. Certainly, baptism would have had general associations with various Jewish ceremonial practices of washing for ritual purification (e.g., Num. 19:12; bathing pools for ritual cleansing were commonplace in first-century Israel). The question is whether Jewish ceremonial washings provide the primary lens for interpreting what John was doing, given that John's baptism seems to have been performed upon a person only once. Instead, John may have been mirroring proselyte baptism, the practice of baptizing Gentiles upon conversion to Judaism. The difficulty in definitively supporting this idea is that there are no references to proselyte baptism in pre-AD 70 sources,[1] although Craig Keener notes that proselyte baptism does appear in early Palestinian Jewish texts.[2]

John's baptism also seems to have differed from other Jewish washing practices in its explicit connection to repentance and forgiveness and its focus on eschatological cleansing.[3] The sum of these various rather unusual elements suggests that John's baptism functioned as a call to the people of

Israel to return and embrace a life of covenant loyalty in preparation for the coming reign of God.

3:2 *kingdom of heaven.* With this phrase, Matthew introduces his central concept for communicating God's restoration work. According to Old Testament theology, God is ruler of all and reigns in the heavens (e.g., Pss. 97:1; 99:1). Yet the expectation is clearly expressed, especially in the prophetic books, that a time is coming when God will fully reign over all creation (e.g., Isa. 24:21–23; Mic. 4:1–8). For Matthew, the arrival of God's kingdom—God's reign—is signaled by the arrival of Jesus the Messiah. The preaching of John the Baptist foreshadows the same preaching by Jesus: "Repent, for the kingdom of heaven has come near" (3:2; 4:17) (see "Narrative-Theological Themes" in the introduction).

3:3 *prophet Isaiah . . . "make straight paths for him."* Matthew cites Isaiah 40:3 to illuminate John's mission to prepare Israel for the coming of "the Lord." Isaiah 40 begins a major section that highlights the good news of God's return to Israel and Israel's return from exile (40:1–9). In the Isaiah context "the Lord" refers to

Key Themes of Matthew 3:1–17

- John announces the arrival of the kingdom—God's reign and restoration.
- John's preaching calls for repentance, warns of judgment, and hints at Gentile inclusion.
- Jesus' baptism is a sign of covenant faithfulness and eschatological fulfillment.

Yahweh, Israel's God. It is telling that Matthew applies this text to John's preparation for Jesus and his ministry of restoration. This application implies that Matthew understands Jesus to be enacting and embodying Yahweh's restoration of Israel.[4]

3:4 *camel's hair . . . a leather belt.* This description of John the Baptist echoes the description of Elijah the prophet: "He had a garment of hair and had a leather belt around his waist" (2 Kings 1:8). By connecting John to Elijah, Matthew highlights John's role as forerunner in line with the expectation that Elijah would presage God's return to Israel in the final day (Mal. 4:5).

3:7 *Pharisees and Sadducees.* The Pharisees and Sadducees were two sects within first-century Judaism. The Sadducees were a priestly group of the Jewish aristocracy whose focus was temple service and administration. This means that their role in Matthew is mostly limited to Jerusalem and so to the beginning and ending of the narrative (e.g., here and 22:23, 34). The Pharisees were known for their careful interpretation of the Jewish law. They are Jesus' central opponents in Matthew (e.g., chaps. 12, 15, 23). Narratively, this is because Jesus is portrayed as the right interpreter of the Torah in contrast to them (15:1–20; 23:1–24). It is important to distinguish between this narrative portrayal and the always more complex historical situation. For example, we hear in Acts that some Pharisees became followers of Jesus (Acts 15:5 [note also Nicodemus in John 3:1; 19:39]). Matthew focuses on scribes and Pharisees who challenged Jesus' claims and identity, providing a monolithic group of antagonists for his Gospel. Readers will need to be careful, however, not to assume that this portrayal represents the entire reality about scribes and Pharisees in first-century Judaism.[5]

You brood of vipers! This epithet used by John against Pharisees and Sadducees also occurs in 12:34; 23:33, in both cases leveled by Jesus against the Pharisees. Keener suggests that this image involves more than the negative castigation of these Jewish leaders as snakes. He notes the tradition that the young of vipers killed their mothers during the birth process. Applied to the Pharisees who claim true descent (see 3:9; 23:30–31), the epithet accuses them of being unfaithful to their heritage.[6] These leaders "are excoriated in the prophetic mode as unfaithful members of Israel, but members nonetheless."[7]

3:10 *good fruit.* Matthew introduces a theme that characterizes his Gospel: the importance of doing God's will or, as in the metaphor here, producing good fruit (see 7:16–23; 12:33–37, 48–50; 21:43). In the Old Testament this metaphor is used to connote obedience or covenant loyalty (e.g., Ps. 1; Isa. 37:30–32; Jer. 11:15–20).

3:11 *the Holy Spirit and fire.* John indicates that the baptism that the Messiah brings will occur "with the Holy Spirit and fire." "Fire" appears in context to refer to judgment (3:10, 12), although the point of association between baptism and judgment is not precisely clear. With his reference to the Holy Spirit, Matthew foreshadows the baptism that Jesus' disciples are to administer as they make disciples of all nations (28:19–20). Christian baptism is a baptism "in the name of the Father and of the Son and of the Holy Spirit" (28:19). Although not particularly prominent in Matthew, the Holy Spirit is crucial to Matthew's Christology (see comments on 12:18).[8]

3:15 *to fulfill all righteousness.* When John demurs at Jesus' request for baptism, Jesus provides a reason for his request (unique to Matthew; Mark remains silent on this point): "to fulfill all righteousness [*dikaiosynē*]." This phrase has been vari-

This narrative about John the Baptist is set at the Jordan River. The section of the Jordan River shown here is near Bethabara and is a location traditionally associated with Jesus' baptism.

ously interpreted. It may be that Jesus refers to the necessity of obeying God's will for him. Yet his baptism is not an expression of God's general will expressed in the Torah. More likely, *dikaiosynē* is used in this context to signal God's work of salvation now being inaugurated in Jesus the Messiah.[9] God's faithfulness to the covenant promises to Israel, including final restoration, is beginning to be fulfilled in Jesus' life and ministry. Jesus comes "to fulfill all [God's] righteousness" (cf. 6:33). Of the four Gospel writers, Matthew particularly draws upon language of *dikaiosynē* ("righteousness," "justice") to describe God and God's work as well as Jesus' expectations for his followers.[10]

3:17 *This is my Son, whom I love; with him I am well pleased.* These divine words of commendation at Jesus' baptism evoke at least one Old Testament text. Scholars have argued for three possibilities: Genesis 22 (in which Isaac is referred to as Abraham's beloved son [v. 2]), Psalm 2:7 ("You are my son"), and/or Isaiah 42:1 ("Here is my servant/child"). The most likely candidates are Genesis 22 and Isaiah 42. The latter is especially likely as an intentional Matthean intertext because of a number of alignments that Matthew makes between the words of commendation and the Isaiah passage, which he quotes at length in 12:18–21. There Matthew conforms two verbs ("love" and "well pleased") to the verbs in 3:17 (also 17:5).[11] If Isaiah 42 is the primary backdrop for God's words at 3:17, this is significant for at least two reasons. First, this connection highlights Jesus' role as the Isaianic servant figure (from Isa. 42–53) at the very beginning of his public ministry in Matthew (see the sidebar "Jesus

Matthew's Covenantal Backdrop

Just as we would expect from a (first-century) Jewish writer, Matthew assumes rather than asserts the reality of Yahweh's covenant with Israel. Thus, understanding that covenant is essential for understanding Matthew's Gospel. And the Old Testament story is a story of covenant. Anticipated in the promise of blessing to Abraham and his descendants (Gen. 12:1–3), the divine covenant with Israel is established after Yahweh brings them out of Egypt (Exod. 14–15). At Sinai Yahweh, the God of the whole earth, refers to that salvation and calls Israel into covenant relationship—to living out their identity as God's treasured possession for the purpose of mission to the nations (Exod. 19:3–6):

> Then Moses went up to God, and the LORD called to him from the mountain and said, "This is what you are to say to the descendants of Jacob and what you are to tell the people of Israel: 'You yourselves have seen what I did to Egypt, and how I carried you on eagles' wings and brought you to myself. Now if you obey me fully and keep my covenant, then out of all nations you will be my treasured possession. Although the whole earth is mine, you will be for me a kingdom of priests and a holy nation.'"

Then Yahweh gives Israel the law or the Torah (see Exod. 20–23) to instruct the people how to live in this covenant relationship. Torah is never a means of earning relationship with God; instead, covenant obedience or loyalty is a response to God's salvation and establishment of covenant relationship. The final section of Exodus has to do with the construction of the tabernacle, the place where God chooses to meet with and live among the people of Israel.

Matthew highlights the covenantal identity of those who follow Jesus as Messiah (5:13–16) and frames Torah obedience in terms of (1) God's abiding presence with the people of God in Jesus (1:23; 28:20), and (2) Jesus' own covenant loyalty and faithfulness (e.g., 3:15–17; 4:1–11; 5:17; 26:36–46). And as Jesus is faithful to God and God's ways, Jesus' followers are to be faithful and obedient to Jesus and his teachings (28:20). Matthew, unlike many contemporary expressions of Christianity, has no problem holding together faith (trust) and faithfulness (obedience).

as Isaiah's Servant Figure" in the unit on 12:15–21). Second, Isaiah as backdrop also highlights Jesus as Spirit anointed and his ministry as Spirit empowered, since the second half of Isaiah 42:1 indicates that God's Spirit has been given to the servant (Matt. 12:18b).

Teaching the Text

1. *Jesus is God's faithful son who brings restoration from exile and inaugurates God's kingdom.* Through the narration of Jesus' baptism by John and his use of Isaiah 40, Matthew emphasizes Jesus as the one who begins God's restoration of Israel from exile and who inaugurates God's universal reign over Israel and all nations. The identification of Jesus as God's faithful son has already been introduced in chapters 1–2, especially in the parallel established between Israel as God's son called out of Egypt at the time of the exodus and Jesus now called out of Egypt to bring redemption to God's people (2:15). Jesus as God's faithful son is emphasized at 3:17, where God affirms Jesus as "my Son, whom I love; with him I am well pleased," and where the Isaianic servant as the one who lives out covenant faithfulness and mission is evoked. Teaching this theme can highlight Jesus' faithfulness as the means of redemption as well as the example for believers to follow. While Jesus as redeemer and Jesus as example have often been bifurcated in different branches of Christendom, Matthew would

neither understand nor support such a dichotomy. According to his narration of Jesus' story, Jesus comes to enact God's salvation by his faithful life and death as true representative of Israel. So we need not shy away from preaching both aspects of Matthew's portrayal of Jesus.

2. *The coming kingdom anticipates the final judgment of all humanity and so invites people to repent and return to God's ways.* Matthew's use of Isaiah 40:3 to interpret the ministry of John the Baptist highlights Jesus as the inaugurator of the eschatological time of redemption. John's words about Jesus as the more powerful one who will baptize "with the Holy Spirit and fire" (3:11) also signals that the final day is coming near in Jesus (3:2), especially since the outpouring of God's Spirit was a sign in the Old Testament of the eschatological time of God's restored presence (e.g., Ezek. 39:25–29; Joel 2:28–32). The importance of responding to the final day inaugurated in Jesus' ministry is evident in John's words about repentance, coming wrath, and images of fire (3:7–12). To preach and teach John's message of repentance today (3:2, 8, 11) involves calling people to turn away from sin and its power and return to God in covenant loyalty and trust.[12] An important facet of this motif in both

"And a voice from heaven said, 'This is my Son, whom I love; with him I am well pleased'" (3:17). This nineteenth-century AD icon depicts the baptism of Jesus.

Matthew and Scripture more broadly is the initiating work of God in redemption. It can be relatively easy in preaching repentance to give our congregations the impression that God waits for humans to make the first move. But this would be a misrepresentation of the biblical witness that reveals God as covenant initiator. From calling and giving a promise to Abraham, who was not yet a follower of Yahweh (Gen. 12:1–3; Josh. 24:2), to the frequent refrain that God was initiating a (new) work in Israel (Isa. 43; 44:22; Jer. 24:4–7; Ezek. 36:26–27), the Scriptures portray repentance as a returning to the God who already initiates relationship and restoration. As Søren Kierkegaard expressed God's initiating work,

> When we awake in the morning and turn our thoughts to you—you are the first, you have loved us first. Even if I arise at daybreak and instantly turn my thoughts to you in prayer, you are too quick for me; you have loved me first.[13]

Preachers and teachers cannot emphasize enough the initiating work of God, with all of life to be lived in responsiveness to that work.

Illustrating the Text

Jesus is God's faithful son who brings restoration from exile and inaugurates God's kingdom.

Art: Jesus' baptism has intrigued artists across the centuries. If your context allows, display a set of different paintings portraying Jesus' baptism or use media to display some varied examples of artwork.[14] You might note that various depictions of Jesus' baptism alternately highlight the presence of heavenly figures or of human beings. In doing so, they offer visions of Jesus as representative of God or of humanity in the act of his baptism. Matthew highlights both. Jesus as God's agent and representative inaugurates the kingdom, with his baptism providing that inaugurating moment. And Jesus acts as Israel's representative, proving to be God's true son, as Israel had so often failed to be in the Old Testament story.

The coming kingdom anticipates the final judgment of all humanity and so invites people to repent and return to God's ways.

Quote: *The Adventure*, **by Jerry Sittser.** Sittser offers a compelling picture of Christian discipleship as human responsiveness to God's initiative, which always precedes our response.

> Many of us live as if the Christian life were a matter of feelings about God and duties done for God. We live as religious egotists. We say that we are doing well with God if *we* are disciplined or if *we* are obeying him. We think that we are close to God if *we* feel close to him. We believe that Christianity is true if *we* have been made happy and successful by it or if our religious techniques work. We delude ourselves by thinking, "If only I could conquer this nagging problem, then I would be a true Christian." For many of us, our Christian faith is as good as we are, not as good as God is.
>
> But as long as we make our feelings, our discipline, our consistency, our techniques and our success and happiness the foundation for Christian living, we shall never know true Christianity. It always begins with God, never with us.[15]

Matthew 3:1–17

Jesus Tempted in the Wilderness

Big Idea *Through the temptation narrative woven with Deuteronomy citations, Matthew compares Jesus' faithful sonship to Israel's lack of obedience in their wilderness time and highlights God's protection of Jesus in the wilderness.*

Understanding the Text

The Text in Context

After narrating Jesus' birth and baptism, Matthew concludes his introduction to Jesus' identity (1:1–4:16) with wilderness temptations. The temptation story continues the comparison between Israel and Jesus, emphasizing how Jesus remains utterly loyal to God during his wilderness testing. This motif emerges via Jesus' three citations of Deuteronomy that attend to Israel's lack of loyalty to Yahweh during their wilderness journey (Deut. 6; 8). Matthew displays Jesus as representative Israel who is faithful and true to God's covenant. Later, in the Passion Narrative, Matthew will highlight Jesus' faithfulness at Gethsemane (26:36–46), when Jesus resists the temptation to pursue his own will and remains faithful to God's missional plan for him.

Interpretive Insights

4:1–2 *Jesus was led by the Spirit.* This is the third time in Matthew that the Spirit has had an active role in the early life of Jesus (his conception at 1:20; his baptism at 3:16). This will be the final narration of the Spirit's work before Jesus begins his public ministry, but Matthew returns to the theme of the Holy Spirit as empowering agent at

"Then Jesus was led by the Spirit into the wilderness" (4:1). Matthew likely references the Judean wilderness, a desolate, barren region, as this photograph illustrates.

12:18, where a framing of Jesus' ministry occurs via Isaiah 42:1–4.

tempted by the devil. In this account of Jesus' temptation, his adversary is referenced by multiple descriptors: the devil (4:1, 5, 8, 11); the tempter (*ho peirazōn* [4:3]); Satan (4:10). Matthew locates the temptation of Jesus just prior to his public ministry. Yet Matthew also demonstrates that Jesus is tempted throughout his life to turn away from God's plan for his mission, especially as it relates to his crucifixion. For example, Matthew narrates Peter's opposition to Jesus' first prediction of his death and Jesus' refusal to fall into temptation: "Get behind me, Satan!" (16:23). In 26:36–46 Jesus gains strength from prayer in the face of a fate that he does not desire. And at the climactic moment on the cross Jesus resists any temptation to call upon God to rescue him (27:43). Jesus remains faithful to God and God's purposes from the beginning to the end of Matthew's narrative.

wilderness . . . forty days and forty nights. Matthew signals that he wants readers to compare Jesus' temptation to Israel's testing in the wilderness. In addition to the use of the language of "wilderness," the reference to "forty days and forty nights" evokes Israel's forty years in the desert (Num. 14:33–34). Added to this are the three citations from Deuteronomy 6 and 8, which rehearse Israel's wilderness wanderings.

4:3, 6 *Son of God.* This is the first occasion in Matthew where Jesus is explicitly called "Son of God." Although "Son of God" is easily heard by modern readers as a divine title, its clearest referents within first-century Judaism would be Israel, Israel's king, and, by extension, the Messiah.

Key Themes of Matthew 4:1–11

- Though tempted, Jesus is God's faithful son and Israel's representative.
- Jesus' obedience stands in contrast to Israel's disobedience in the wilderness (via Deuteronomy citations).
- God cares for and protects Jesus.

In the Old Testament Israel is referred to as "son" by Yahweh in Exodus 4:22 and Hosea 11:1 (also *Jub.* 1:25). Since Matthew quotes Hosea 11:1 at 2:15 with reference to Jesus, it is most likely that an Israel/Jesus typology is part of Matthew's use of the term "Son of God." Israel's king is also referred to as God's son in 2 Samuel 7:14 and Psalm 2, with both functioning as early texts in the development of messianic thought (e.g., 2 Esd. 7:28–29). Matthew uses "Son of God" language most frequently with this messianic meaning (e.g., 14:33; 16:16; 26:63). This is demonstrated in the alternation between "Son of God" and "king" in 27:41–44.

4:4, 7, 10 *It is written.* Three times Matthew records that Jesus quotes Deuteronomy to counter the devil's temptations. In each case Jesus finds the answer to the temptation in the story of Israel's own time of wilderness testing recounted in Deuteronomy. In each case Jesus proves to be God's faithful son in spite of temptations, in contrast to Israel's unfaithfulness in testing.

Jesus answers the first temptation (4:3)—to turn stones to bread after forty days of fasting—by citing Deuteronomy 8, which refers to Yahweh's testing of Israel for forty years in the wilderness "to know whether or not [they] would keep his commands" (8:2). Specifically, Jesus cites from Deuteronomy 8:3, which recounts Yahweh's humbling of

Israel by making them reliant on manna to teach them that "one does not live by bread alone, but by every word that comes from the mouth of the LORD" (NRSV). While Israel struggled to learn the lessons of the wilderness, Jesus passes the first test with flying colors by recalling God's words to Israel and the story of Israel's wilderness days.

Jesus answers the second temptation (4:6)—to throw himself down from the top of the temple—by citing Deuteronomy 6:16, a prohibition against testing Yahweh: "Do not put the LORD your God to the test as you did at Massah." The words "at Massah" refer to the particular testing in Exodus 17, in which Israel grumbled and quarreled with Moses over their lack of water. They presumed that God was not with them because of their thirst (Exod. 17:1–7). While Israel most certainly did put their God, Yahweh, to the test, Jesus will not, and so he refuses to do something so presumptuous as to jump off the temple heights.

Jesus answers the third temptation (4:9)—to worship Satan to gain "all the kingdoms of the world" (4:8)—by affirming the most basic command given to Israel: "Worship the LORD your God, and serve him only" (Deut. 6:13 [my translation]) (see also Deut. 6:4–5, the Shema, which calls Israel to love God exclusively). Jesus will not succumb to the temptation to "follow other gods" (Deut. 6:14) as Israel often did in their history as recorded in the Old Testament. Jesus proves to be the true and faithful Son of God, who serves the one true God only and will not bow before any other.

4:3, 6 *If you are the Son of God.* From a narrative perspective, the reader should not trust everything spoken by a character, especially an untrustworthy one (e.g., the devil can be assumed to speak falsely when it serves a purpose) (see the sidebar "Characterization and Narrative Authorization"). Yet the identification of Jesus as God's son has already been authorized by Matthew as true: Jesus is explicitly referred to as "son of David" and "son of Abraham" (1:1) and is implicitly identified as God's son at 2:15. Jesus has also been affirmed as God's son at his baptism, where God says, "This is my Son" (3:17). So the reader will hear the devil's test as containing a truth about Jesus: he is the Son of God. The reader will also be prone to hear this sonship in analogy to Israel (see comments on 2:15), especially in light of the Deuteronomy citations of 4:1–11.

4:6 *He will command his angels.* Jesus is not the only one who cites Scripture in this narrative. The devil is portrayed citing Psalm 91:11–12 to bolster his temptation for Jesus to throw himself from the temple. The psalm promises the one who takes refuge in Yahweh angelic protection against harm. While Jesus surely could rest

According to 4:8, Jesus is taken to a high mountain to be tempted a third time. A location traditionally associated with this Matthean scene is a mountain near Jericho known as Jebel Quarantal.

in the promise of this psalm, Matthew shows that he is not foolish enough to presume God's protection for such a rash and pointless act that would put God to the test (4:7). The lovely irony of the passage is that while Jesus refuses the temptation to seek angelic protection, the passage concludes with the affirmation that "angels came and attended him" (4:11).

4:8–9 *all the kingdoms of the world.* See the sidebar.

Theological Insights: Jesus as Representative Humanity

Matthew portrays Jesus as representative humanity by drawing points of analogy between Jesus and Israel, which was to reflect God's image and embody God's mission to the nations (Matt. 2:15; 3:15–17; 4:1–11). Paul also draws upon Jesus as representative humanity in his argument for the final-day resurrection of believers in 1 Corinthians 15. His logic is that the resurrection of Jesus prefigures and guarantees that of the rest of humanity at "the end" (1 Cor. 15:20–28). His use of Psalm 8 (1 Cor. 15:27) solidifies the argument, since this psalm is about humanity's role in ruling over creation; Jesus now rules as our representative. The author of the Epistle to the Hebrews also draws on this christological category to assure believers of their present freedom from fear of death (2:14–18) and of Jesus' ability to "empathize with [their] weaknesses" (4:14–16).

Teaching the Text

1. *Jesus is faithful to God in spite of temptations.* As noted above, it is shortsighted

Characterization and Narrative Authorization

A basic feature of narrative characterization is the narrator's authorization of various characters. In other words, a narrator of a story will make it clear which characters he or she authorizes and which do not speak from the authorial perspective. Not every word spoken by all characters in a narrative reflects the author's point of view. It can be easy to lose sight of this point when reading the Gospels or other biblical narratives, since a trust in Scripture's reliability might seem to involve treating all its words (even those from characters' mouths) as equally true. But brief reflection on our reading practices indicates that we assess the narrator's authorization rather easily and intuitively. For example, in Matthew, when Peter rebukes Jesus for his prediction of his coming death (16:22), we know that Peter's perspective is flawed and does not represent Matthew's perspective. In this same way, we should be cautious in assuming that the words of the devil in Matthew 4 reflect Matthew's point of view. Matthew does not necessarily authorize the devil's implicit claim to own "all the kingdoms of the world" (4:8–9). Given the Old Testament testimony that all of creation belongs to its creator God, we would do well not to assume that these words are authorized by Matthew as reflective of reality. While God in Jesus sets about reclaiming humanity and all creation, the question of whether the devil can rightly claim to own the world's kingdoms should not be determined by a word from the mouth of an untrustworthy voice in the story.

to imagine Jesus being tempted only at this point in the story line of Matthew. There are several moments in the narrative when Jesus experiences temptation to be unfaithful to God's plan for him (see comments on 4:1). Yet Jesus perseveres, proving to be God's faithful son. While it is common in preaching this text to highlight Jesus as divine (possibly because of his identification as the "Son of God" [4:3, 6]), Matthew emphasizes Jesus as faithful to God's covenant in contrast to Israel's unfaithfulness in the wilderness. This contrast invites the reader to understand Jesus' faithfulness as a part of his role as representative Israel and, by extension, as representative humanity. Preaching that Jesus resists temptation

Matthew portrays the devil tempting Jesus to throw himself from the highest point of the temple. Pictured here is the southeast corner of the Temple Mount complex, which overlooks the Kidron Valley. This is how that location looks today with the more-recent Ottoman-era walls.

because he is divine provides no particular hope for believers struggling with temptation. Yet Matthew does not emphasize Jesus' divinity in this particular text; instead, he highlights Jesus' humanity by means of the comparison with Israel's wilderness temptations. This means that we can preach and teach Jesus' example for his followers as we encounter temptation. As Jesus walked through temptation without succumbing to it, so those who follow him and experience his presence among them (28:20) can have hope for resisting temptation (6:13; cf. 1 Cor. 10:13).

2. *Allegiance to the one true God is the basis for all covenant loyalty.* Each of Jesus' responses from Deuteronomy to the tempter revolves around questions of allegiance. These same questions can provide points of challenge as we teach and preach Jesus' temptations from Matthew. Do we find our sustenance solely in physical bread/food, or do we recognize and affirm the reality that we live by God's word and guidance? Do we test God by our actions that reveal a lack of trust in God's provision, or do we, with Jesus, obey the command to avoid testing the Lord? Do we believe the lie that we can flirt with other allegiances

(gods) while claiming to be faithful to the one true God? For Matthew (and for us), allegiance to God is fundamental to living a life of covenant loyalty. Jesus passes the tests in Matthew 4, preparing the way for his claim to fulfill the Law and the Prophets in the next chapter (5:17). And Jesus provides the example of true Israel and true humanity as one who is able to say no to temptations to trust self or other loyalties and yes to following God wholeheartedly. So we might ask ourselves and the people we teach to examine our allegiances in light of Jesus' own pattern of covenant loyalty.

Illustrating the Text

Jesus is faithful to God in spite of temptations.

History: Mount Everest stands twenty-nine thousand feet above sea level. It is whipped by winds surging up to 120 miles per hour. Since it climbs high into the troposphere, no one presumed that it could be conquered—until, that is, two people climbed and conquered it. On May 29, 1953, Edmund Hillary and Tenzing Norgay did what had seemed impossible. Amazingly, since that time more than three thousand individuals have made the ascent. Hillary and Norgay had blazed the trail, allowing others to imagine that they might succeed and so to walk in their footsteps.

Jesus has paved the way of victory over temptation by living as the one true human being in covenant loyalty to God empowered by the Spirit. He invites us to follow him. The challenge is still great, but the way has been charted by the Messiah, who not only walked that path but also walks with us.

Allegiance to the one true God is the basis for all covenant loyalty.

Quote: *The Screwtape Letters*, by **C. S. Lewis.** In this book Lewis imagines a correspondence between two demons, one a master tempter (Screwtape), the other a novice (Wormwood). In one letter Screwtape teaches Wormwood how to subtly subvert a person's allegiance to God (whom Screwtape calls "the Enemy") through the fallacious idea of human ownership.

The sense of ownership in general is always to be encouraged. The humans are always putting up claims to ownership which sound equally funny in Heaven and in Hell, and we must keep them doing so. . . . It is as if a royal child whom his father has placed, for love's sake, in titular command of some great province, under the real rule of wise counsellors, should come to fancy he really owns the cities, the forest, and the corn, in the same way as he owns the bricks on the nursery floor. . . . We have taught [people] to say "my God" in a sense not really very different from "my boots," meaning "The God on whom I have a claim for my distinguished services and whom I exploit from the pulpit—the God I have done a corner in."

And all the time the joke is that the word "Mine" in its fully possessive sense cannot be uttered by a human being about anything.[1]

Transition to Jesus' Public Ministry

Big Idea *Anticipating Jesus' public Galilean ministry, Matthew affirms Jesus as the bringer of restoration to Israel in line with Isaiah's hopes and intimates the inclusion of Gentiles.*

Understanding the Text

The Text in Context

This passage (4:12–16) transitions between Matthew's introduction of Jesus' identity (1:1–4:11) and Jesus' Galilean ministry to Israel (4:17–16:20). In it, Matthew connects an Isaiah prophecy to Jesus' relocation from Nazareth to Capernaum. Jesus' mission to bring restoration to Israel is implicit in the Isaiah language of "light" dawning upon those in darkness (cf. chaps. 1–2 for restoration themes tied to Jesus' presence). Proclamation and enactment of this restoration will be at the center of Jesus' kingdom ministry in subsequent chapters. In addition, as Matthew has hinted at Gentile inclusion in the opening genealogy (1:3, 5–6) and with the presence of the magi in the birth narrative (2:1), he foreshadows the importance of Jesus' ministry for Gentiles from Isaiah: "Galilee of the Gentiles" (4:15; cf. Isa. 9:1–2). Although Jesus will minister primarily to the people of Israel throughout Matthew's story, the ultimate impact of his work for Gentiles is foreshadowed in his healing for two Gentiles of "great faith" (8:5–13; 15:21–28) and will be fully addressed in the disciples' commission to "make disciples of all nations [*ethnē*]" (28:19).

Interpretive Insights

4:12 *When Jesus heard that John had been put in prison.* Matthew's reader has already witnessed Jesus' baptism by John and heard John's words about "the one who is more powerful than" John who comes after him (3:11). Now, Matthew ties John's imprisonment to the commencement of Jesus' public ministry in Galilee. In chapter 14 Matthew will narrate in a flashback scene the arrest and execution of John by Herod Antipas, tetrarch of Galilee (14:3–12).

he withdrew to Galilee. Galilee in the first century was distinct from Judea in the south in a number of ways. Although Galilee historically had a rather large Gentile population (e.g., during the time of Isaiah), during the time of Jesus it had a large Jewish population, especially in its southernmost region. Jewish communities thrived in the Galilean cities of Sepphoris and Tiberias and especially in the smaller towns and surrounding countryside of southern Galilee. The mixed nature of Galilee, racially and

Key Themes of Matthew 4:12–16

- Jesus' Galilean ministry of restoration is foreshadowed.
- Gentile inclusion is intimated in a quotation from Isaiah.

religiously, would have provided ample reason for Judean Jews to view their Galilean counterparts as distinct from themselves and with some amount of disdain. Matthew illuminates this distinction on a few occasions in his narrative (e.g., 21:10–11; 26:69). As R. T. France highlights,

> Even an impeccably Jewish Galilean in first-century Jerusalem was not among his own people; he was as much a foreigner as an Irishman in London or a Texan in New York. His accent would immediately mark him out as "not one of us," and all the communal prejudice of the supposedly superior culture of the capital city would stand against his claim to be heard even as a prophet, let alone as the "Messiah," a title which, as everyone knew, belonged to Judea.[1]

4:13 *Leaving Nazareth, he went and lived in Capernaum.* Matthew narrates Jesus' relocation from Nazareth (his hometown [see 2:23]) to Capernaum, which will be a primary location for the ministry of Jesus highlighted in subsequent chapters of Matthew (8:5; 11:23).

4:15–16 *Land of Zebulun . . . a light has dawned.* A quotation from Isaiah 9:1–2 serves to connect the location of Jesus' ministry to Israel with words of Isaiah that promise salvation to Israel. Matthew draws on Isaiah 9:1 to connect Capernaum to the quotation; Zebulun and Naphtali are regions corresponding to two of the twelve tribes of Israel. Capernaum is a city located in the region that was originally allotted to the tribe of Naphtali (see the map

of the region of the Sea of Galilee in the first century).

Light, in the context of Isaiah 9, refers to God's salvation and freedom for Israel (9:1–5) through a promised Davidic king (9:6–7). Light dawning, then, points ahead to Jesus' impact upon the people of Israel who experience his teaching and healing ministry (Matt. 5–9). Although light is

Map of the region around the Sea of Galilee in the New Testament period not a prominent theme in Matthew (versus John, for example), Matthew will draw upon the motif to speak of God's people as the light of the world (5:14–16; see also 6:22–23).

Galilee of the Gentiles. Although there is a significant Jewish population in first-century Galilee, Isaiah's description of Galilee as "Galilee of the Gentiles" is not off the mark, given the large Gentile population in its cities and northern region (see 4:12). More importantly, Isaiah's "Galilee of the Gentiles" allows Matthew to highlight once more his theme of Gentile inclusion, already introduced by the women of Jesus' genealogy (1:3, 5, 6) and the magi (2:1). Even though Jesus' ministry will be focused on "the lost sheep of Israel" (15:24; cf. 10:6), Matthew will continue to foreshadow Gentile inclusion by narrating encounters between Jesus and Gentile supplicants (8:5–13; 15:21–28) and will signal the inauguration of the Gentile mission after Jesus' resurrection (28:19).

Teaching the Text

1. *Jesus is the bringer of salvation to Israel.* Matthew draws on Isaiah to frame the ministry of Jesus that he is about to narrate. The ministry of Jesus in Galilee (4:17–16:20) will offer God's eschatological salvation as described in Isaiah to the people of Israel. As he announces and enacts the kingdom, Jesus is the "great light" dawning in the land. While there will be rejection of Jesus' ministry and person, especially by Jewish leadership, many Jews, including the disciples, will respond to this salvation. Matthew holds out hope throughout his narrative that the crowds who hear Jesus will respond by trusting him to be the Messiah (e.g., 9:33; 12:23; 27:64 [see comments there]). It is relatively easy to deal in dichotomies as we preach and teach the Gospels. In real ways, we need to simplify rather than "complexify" Matthew's story for our hearers. Yet we do potential harm by offering a simplified picture of the Jews in Matthew's Gospel that only uses them as a negative foil for right responses to Jesus and his preaching of the kingdom. We will need to make explicit what is implicit yet clear to Matthew's audience: the large majority of those first to believe in Jesus as the Messiah are Jews. In Matthew, these include the twelve disciples and other followers and seekers from the (Jewish) crowds who come to him for healing. And what we see here in the announcement of the scope of Jesus' ministry is that he comes first to preach and enact the kingdom for his own people (see 1:21; 15:24).

2. *God's salvation in Jesus will reach to the Gentiles.* Matthew's Gospel centers on salvation for God's people, the Jews. During his Galilean ministry Jesus will focus almost exclusively on Jewish crowds and seekers. Yet Matthew hints and highlights across his Gospel that Gentiles will be included in the people of God (e.g., 1:3–6; 2:1; 8:11–12; 15:21–28; 21:43). Here in

the headline about Jesus' ministry (4:12–16) Gentile inclusion is intimated ("Galilee of the Gentiles") in the same breath that Matthew speaks of Jesus' forthcoming ministry to Jewish Galileans. After Jesus' resurrection the scope of his ministry through his disciples and followers will be explicitly broadened to "all nations" (28:19).

Given that the church has had millennia to get used to the idea of Gentile inclusion, the power of this theological message might be lost to some extent in our own contexts.

So we might offer the missional vision from the Old Testament of Israel's call to be distinctive and holy, so that they might demonstrate Yahweh's nature and care to the nations. The prophetic picture of the nations streaming into Jerusalem in the final

When Jesus returns to Galilee to begin his preaching ministry, he lives in Capernaum, located on the northwestern shore of the Sea of Galilee. Archaeological evidence from the second and third centuries AD indicates Capernaum was a thriving town supported by fishing, agriculture, and trade. Shown here in the foreground is one of many residences that consisted of several rooms surrounding a small courtyard. Remains of a public building, thought to be the first-century AD synagogue, have been found beneath the white limestone walls of the restored synagogue from the fourth or fifth century AD, which can be seen in the background.

day provides a compelling picture of the task that still invigorates the church today. For Matthew, the kingdom has come near in Jesus, so the time of the universal mission has begun. And our preaching can capitalize on the inclusive nature of Matthew's mission. All people, regardless of ethnicity, nationality, or primary allegiances, are invited to become followers of Jesus.

Illustrating the Text

Jesus is the bringer of salvation to Israel.

Literature: *Tom Sawyer*, by Mark Twain. In Matthew 4:12–16 the salvation that Jesus brings is portrayed in terms of light shining in darkness. In his classic tale *Tom Sawyer*, Twain captures the fear and despair of being lost in the dark. Tom and Becky join a group of adventurers in scouting caves. Soon, they become separated from the group. Unease turns to apprehension. Apprehension morphs into fear. Fear becomes panic. Panic sinks into despair. We read,

> Becky was very weak. She had sunk into a dreary apathy and would not be roused. She said she would wait, now, where she was, and die—it would not be long. She told Tom to go . . . and explore if he chose; but she implored him to come back every little while and speak to her; and she made him promise that when the awful time came, he would stay by her and hold her hand until all was over.[2]

During his ministry in Galilee, Jesus focuses on the people of Israel as the recipients for his message. There were large Jewish communities in Galilee, particularly in the southern and western regions. Shown here is a contemporary aerial view of the area around the southern shore of the Sea of Galilee.

Jesus, the one true light, came into a world that was covered in darkness. To "the people living in darkness . . . a light has dawned" (Matt. 4:16).

God's salvation in Jesus will reach to the Gentiles.

Mission: As foreshadowed in this passage, God's salvation in Jesus, begun in restoration for Israel, will extend to all the nations (28:19). Several websites provide helpful information about the status of missional work to reach all nations and peoples. The Joshua Project, an arm of the U.S. Center for World Mission, defines how much of the world has yet to hear the gospel in their native language. According to the best figures, more than seven thousand people groups remained unreached, a population totaling 2.91 billion people. This resource provides a smartphone app that offers a daily prayer guide. Operation World also provides a prayer guide on its website for Christian mission around the world.

Summary: 1:1–4:16. Matthew's task in the initial chapters of his Gospel is to introduce who Jesus is to his readers and hearers. He begins with the affirmation that Jesus is the Messiah, the longed-for Davidic king ("son of David") and the hope of the Jewish people ("son of Abraham") (1:1–17), who would bring God's eschatological salvation. Moreover, Jesus himself will save Israel from their sins; he is Immanuel, "God with us" (1:18–25). The restoration that Jesus brings is set in the context of return from exile; Jesus is the true king of Israel who enacts God's promise to restore the people of God (2:1–23). Jesus is the Lord announced and prepared for by John the Baptist, and he is God's faithful son, the true representative of Israel (3:1–4:11). Matthew also hints at Gentile inclusion in these first four chapters of his Gospel: Jesus will bring salvation to all peoples through his life, death, and resurrection (1:3–6; 2:1; 4:15–16).

Looking Ahead: 4:17–16:20. Jesus' announcement of the kingdom to Israel and resulting responses:

1. Proclamation of the kingdom in word and action (4:17–11:1)
   a. Summary of Jesus' message and ministry (4:17–25)
   b. Jesus' first discourse: the Sermon on the Mount (5:1–7:29)
   c. Jesus' enactment of the kingdom (8:1–9:38)
   d. Jesus' second discourse: the Mission Discourse (10:1–11:1)
2. Jesus' rejection by Israel's leaders and his withdrawal from conflict to ministry (11:2–16:20)
   a. Rejection of Jesus as the Messiah by Jewish leaders (11:2–12:50)
   b. Jesus' third discourse: the Parables Discourse (13:1–53)
   c. Continued conflict and emerging identity (13:54–16:20)

Jesus Begins His Ministry to Israel

Big Idea *Jesus announces the arrival of God's kingdom by preaching and healing and calls disciples to follow in his mission.*

Understanding the Text

The Text in Context

This passage begins a new section of Matthew's story of Jesus in which Jesus begins to minister to the people of Israel in the area of Galilee (as signaled by the narrative formula at 4:17; 16:21). The inaugural message of Jesus—"Repent, for the kingdom of heaven has come near" (4:17)—is identical to John's earlier preaching (3:2). Jesus' preaching of the kingdom's arrival is coupled with healing and teaching (4:23) and draws large crowds (4:25) as well as particular disciples (4:18–22). With the invitation to four fishermen, Jesus begins his reconstitution of Israel's twelve tribes by calling twelve disciples, or apostles, who are to minister to Israel by preaching and healing in line with Jesus' own ministry (10:1–8; cf. 9:9). Jesus' disciples will be the recipients of his extensive teaching in Matthew (e.g., 5:1–2) and will, after Jesus' resurrection, be expected to pass along his teachings as they make disciples of all nations (28:19–20). Matthew summarizes Jesus' teaching and healing ministry at 4:23 and then repeats this summary almost verbatim at 9:35, indicating that chapters 5–9 are to be understood as a unified segment of his Gospel, composed of Jesus' teachings about the kingdom (chaps. 5–7) and enactment of the kingdom through healings and miracles (chaps. 8–9).

Interpretive Insights

4:17 *From that time on Jesus began to preach.* Here and at 16:21 Matthew repeats a narrative formula that signals a change in the direction of the story: "From that time on Jesus began to . . ." (*apo tote ērxato ho Iēsous* + infinitive). The first use of the formula at 4:17 turns the story line from Jesus' preparation to his ministry of preaching and healing for Israel in Galilee. The second occurrence signals a shift in the story as Jesus heads to Jerusalem and begins predicting for his disciples his coming death (16:21: "From that time on Jesus began to explain to his disciples . . .").

Repent, for the kingdom of heaven has come near. The restoration of God's reign over all the earth was promised in the Old Testament prophets (e.g., Mic. 4:1–8). Matthew's use of "the kingdom of heaven" here reflects his conviction that the restoration of God's reign over all has begun in the ministry of Jesus.

These first words of Jesus in Matthew are identical to those of John the Baptist in 3:2. In both cases Matthew provides the center point of the messages of John and Jesus: the arrival of God's kingdom or reign in this world and the call to respond in repentance—that is, returning to God and God's ways. Matthew's "kingdom of heaven" is essentially identical to "the kingdom of God" as used in Mark (and Luke). Although some have argued for a distinction between Matthew's preferred phrase, "the kingdom of heaven," and his use of "the kingdom of God" (12:28; 19:24; 21:31, 43), there is no substantial difference between these locutions, other than a possible emphasis on the heavenly origin of the kingdom.[1]

That the kingdom "has come near" (ēngiken) introduces at this early juncture the "already and not yet" of God's reign in Matthew. This verb communicates the imminence of the kingdom as Jesus preaches and enacts the kingdom in his own ministry; however, it also allows for the kingdom as a still-future reality, and Matthew will show that the kingdom in its fullness is yet to come (e.g., final judgment will occur at "the end of the age" [13:40]). Matthew will continue to hold the "already and not yet" of the kingdom in productive tension throughout his Gospel.

Jesus calls Simon Peter, Andrew, James, and John to follow him. Immediately these fishermen leave their nets and their boat. Here an artist depicts a dragnet being used along the Sea of Galilee.

Key Themes of Matthew 4:17–25

- Jesus as preacher proclaims the imminent kingdom of God.
- Jesus as healer enacts the arrival of God's kingdom.
- Discipleship means following Jesus and being in mission.

4:19 *Come, follow me.* In 4:18–22 Matthew narrates the call of Jesus' first disciples, Peter and Andrew, James and John. The typical pattern of a Jewish rabbi taking on disciples involved a would-be disciple asking to be accepted by a rabbi as a disciple (see John 1:37–39). It is significant that Jesus is portrayed as the initiator of the discipling relationship here. This difference corresponds to Jesus' heightened authority as compared to other Jewish teachers. Matthew will make this comparison explicit at 7:29: "He taught as one who had authority, and not as their teachers of the law."

4:20–22 *they left their nets . . . they left the boat . . . and followed him.* The first disciples whom Jesus calls are Peter and Andrew, James and John. The calling and authorizing of the twelve disciples waits until 10:1–4, but this initial call narrative introduces the motif of following Jesus in discipleship, which will continue across the

Gospel (9:9; 10:38–39; 16:24; 20:34; 28:19). Important aspects of this discipleship story include the fishermen leaving their livelihood to follow Jesus (4:20, 22; cf. 19:28–29) and the call to mission that accompanies the call to follow: "Come, follow me, and I will send you out to fish for people" (4:19).

4:23 *Jesus went throughout Galilee, teaching . . . proclaiming the good news . . . and healing.* This summary of Jesus' activity of preaching, teaching, and healing is repeated virtually verbatim at 9:35 (where "throughout Galilee" is replaced with "through all the towns and villages"). This repetition forms an inclusio and signals that Matthew wants his hearers and readers to understand chapters 5–9 as a unit. It is significant that Jesus' central activities involve kingdom teaching and preaching and kingdom healing. These will be the very activities that he undertakes in the Sermon on the Mount (chaps. 5–7) and his Galilean ministry (chaps. 8–9).

teaching in their synagogues. The word "synagogue" (*synagōgē*) here may refer to a local gathering of Jews for prayer

According to 4:23–25, Jesus travels throughout Galilee performing miracles of healing and teaching in the synagogues. The restored interior of the fourth- to fifth-century AD synagogue in Capernaum is shown here. Remains of what many believe to be the first-century AD synagogue lie beneath.

and Torah study or the building in which such gatherings took place (see Josephus, *Ag. Ap.* 1.209; 2.175). These local gatherings of Israelites probably began during the period after the exile (late sixth century BC). After the destruction of the temple in AD 70, synagogue buildings became centers of Jewish life and worship.[2]

proclaiming the good news of the kingdom. The connection between the good news (*euangelion*, "gospel") and the kingdom is reminiscent of Isaiah. In Isaiah 52:7 the "good news" of God's promised salvation to Zion is expressed in the message "Your God reigns!" This identification of Isaiah's "gospel" with the future return and reign of God illuminates Matthew's affirmation that Jesus preaches the "gospel" of the kingdom—that is, God's return and

faithfulness and the inauguration of God's kingdom.

Interpretive Insights

5:1–2 *His disciples came to him, and he began to teach them.* Jesus' disciples are the more specific audience of the Sermon on the Mount (chaps. 5–7) on Matthew's story level, even though the crowds are mentioned as present at both the beginning and end of the sermon (5:1; 7:28–29).

5:3 *Blessed are.* These words begin Jesus' announcement of blessing upon the most unlikely audience: those who are destitute, grief-stricken, oppressed, and longing for justice (see below). Two contextual frames help the contemporary reader hear these beatitudes (blessings) along the lines of a first-century audience. First, the broader Greco-Roman world of the first century was highly conscious of status, producing a stratified social system based on various kinds of status (e.g., rich over poor, aristocratic over peasant, male over female, free over slave). Various words and phrases in the beatitudes are best understood from this context and can be described as status language, even though a contemporary reader may not initially hear the language in this way (e.g., "poor in spirit," "meek"). This suggests a reading of the beatitudes as an announcement of status reversals that accompany the arrival of God's kingdom.

Second, in Jewish theology and hope Yahweh was revealed as a God who sides with the poor and lowly (e.g., Isa. 61:1–3). Jewish eschatological hope centered on a day when God would make all things right, so that those who lived to see the time of the Messiah would experience the great

Key Themes of Matthew 5:1–16

- God's kingdom is a reversal of situation.
- God's kingdom upholds countercultural values of mercy, justice, peacemaking, and integrity.
- Jesus' followers in the world have a distinctive, covenantal identity.

Outline for the Sermon on the Mount

5:1–16	**Introduction to the sermon**
5:1–2	Setting
5:3–12	The blessings of the kingdom
5:13–16	The identity and mission of Jesus' disciples
5:17–7:12	**Body of the sermon**
5:17–48	Jesus as fulfillment and authoritative interpreter of the Torah
6:1–18	Practicing covenantal expectations for God alone
6:19–34	Allegiance to the kingdom instead of wealth
7:1–12	Discernment and prayer instead of judgment of others
7:13–29	**Conclusion of the sermon**
7:13–23	Warnings against disobedience
7:24–27	Concluding parable about covenant obedience
7:28–29	Response to Jesus' teaching

blessings of that day. For example, *Psalm of Solomon* 17 announces this blessing: "Happy are those who shall live in those days [of the Messiah], to see the good things of Israel that God shall accomplish in the congregation of the tribes" (17:44 NETS).

for theirs is the kingdom of heaven. The blessings (beatitudes) that Jesus announces in Matthew are carefully structured, with eight stanzas that can be understood as two sets of four blessings. (The final beatitude in 5:11–12 is really an expansion on the eighth and moves outside of the poetic framework of 5:3–10.) It is significant that the first and last blessings (5:3, 10) hold the same affirmation: "for theirs is the kingdom of heaven." This inclusio highlights the "already" of the kingdom. Jesus announces that the reversal of situation and status has already begun. Yet the "not yet" of the kingdom—that is, the fact that final restoration and reversal of fortune is still to come—is signaled by the intervening six blessings: "they will be comforted," "they will inherit the earth," and so on. Each of these is framed in the future tense. In this way, Matthew communicates the "already and not yet" nature of God's reign in Jesus (see comments on 4:17).

the poor in spirit. The first beatitude evokes language from the Old Testament, specifically Psalms and Isaiah. These writings frequently connect those who are most destitute physically with spiritual destitution and despair and also affirm God's particular care for them. For example, Isaiah 61 speaks of the Lord's servant who will proclaim "good news to the poor" and "bind up the brokenhearted" (61:1). The Psalms affirm that the Lord hears "the brokenhearted" and the "crushed in spirit" (Ps. 34:18). In this theological context it is likely that Jesus' words affirm that, quite against normal expectations, the kingdom belongs to those who are poor and despairing.[1]

5:4 *Blessed are those who mourn.* It is likely that Isaiah 61:1–2 sits behind these words. The role of the Isaianic servant is also "to comfort [*pentheō*] all who mourn" (Isa. 61:2 LXX), as in Matthew 5:4. No one

The beatitudes express the blessing that those who are low in status will receive in God's kingdom. The first-century Greco-Roman world was very status conscious, and this is expressed in many funerary reliefs. For example, this funerary monument shows several classes in the Roman social hierarchy. The inscription indicates that the large figures shown in deep relief are a family of freedpersons, both male and female. The smaller figures in shallow relief are the slaves that belong to the family. The visual contrast highlights the difference in social status (Thessaloniki, ca. 50 BC).

would presume that people in the midst of intense grief would be called "blessed." Yet this is the very announcement that Jesus makes. As God's reign becomes reality, those who have mourned will receive God's ultimate comfort.

5:5 *Blessed are the meek.* This blessing clearly echoes Psalm 37:11 (36:11 LXX): "the meek will inherit the land" (LXX: *oi praeis klēronomēsousin gēn*; Matthew: *oi praeis . . . klēronomēsousin tēn gēn*). The word "meek" (*praeis*) can reflect an internal attitude or an external status. The picture from Psalm 37 is one in which the wicked exert their power to oppose and harm the "meek" (e.g., vv. 14, 32–33). So it is likely that the term is used to signal external humiliation and lack of status. As Warren

Carter notes, *praeis* "names the powerless and humiliated who are entreated to trust in God to save them."[2]

5:6 *Blessed are those who hunger and thirst for righteousness.* Given the context of reversal thus far, it is likely that this beatitude also addresses those who are destitute and powerless. The term *dikaiosynē*, which Matthew uses seven times in his Gospel (Mark: 0x; Luke: 1x; John: 2x), can be rendered by any of the following English equivalents depending on context: "righteousness," "justice," or "the act of putting right with/making right." Mark Powell provides a compelling paraphrase: "Blessed are those who are starved for justice."[3]

5:7–10 *Blessed are the merciful . . . pure in heart . . . peacemakers . . . those who are persecuted.* The final four beatitudes in the eight-stanza group confer blessing on those who live in alignment with the values of God's kingdom. There is a reciprocal quality to these values that points back to the first four blessings. Mercy, for example, is shown to those most needing it—those who are destitute (5:3–6). Showing mercy is thematic in Matthew (e.g., 8:3; 9:36; 14:14; 15:32; 23:23; note 9:13; 12:7). The blessing on "the pure in heart" also signals a Matthean motif, especially as it relates to integrity that aligns what is inside with what others see, in contrast to hypocrisy (e.g., 6:1–18; 23). Those who "practice peace" (*eirēnopoioi*) are promised a blessing, along with those who are persecuted because of *dikaiosynē*. How we understand this term in 5:6 impacts its interpretation in 5:10. If "justice" is its connotation in this context, then blessing is granted to those who are persecuted for their commitment

to and solidarity with those experiencing injustice (5:6).

5:11 *falsely.* This word (*pseudomenoi*) is missing from some Greek manuscripts. Although the external evidence (earliest and across a range of manuscripts) favors its inclusion, it is more likely that a scribe added this word to Matthew to explain that blessing occurs only when Christians are *falsely* accused of doing evil.

5:13–16 *salt of the earth . . . light of the world.* The image of salt provides a number of possible metaphorical connections. The covenantal and therefore missional associations of salt are the most likely here, since it is the identity and mission of Jesus' followers that receive attention in 5:13–16. The Old Testament phrases "the salt of the covenant" (Lev. 2:13) and "covenant of salt" (Num. 18:19; 2 Chron. 13:5) suggest this connection, with a likely emphasis on the permanence of the covenant through the metaphor of salt.[4] According to the Scriptures, Israel was called to be "a light for the Gentiles" (Isa. 49:6; 60:1–3; cf. 9:2). Matthew's use of the image of light from the Old Testament is about both identity ("you are the light of the world" [5:14]) and mission ("let your light shine before people [humanity]" [5:15–16]). Salt and light provide two pictures of covenant identity and mission that are now to define the disciples of Jesus.

Teaching the Text

1. *The beatitudes are a pronouncement of blessings and reversals.* It is easy to read Matthew's beatitudes (5:3–12) as essentially a virtue list that describes those

who will participate in God's kingdom. Certainly, there has been a tendency in the history of the church to read the beatitudes in this way. For example, Manlio Simonetti notes that Jerome, in his reading of the beatitudes, saw the kingdom as "the most fitting life for those who are already practicing virtue."[5] Yet, in the reading suggested in this commentary, the beatitudes are blessings first and foremost. They confer blessing on people who are fortunate enough to live in the time of the Messiah. Preaching the beatitudes should follow their contours as blessings of the kingdom now arriving in Jesus. And as God has come in Jesus to make all wrong things right and all upside-down things right side up, reversals are happening. Those most destitute are beginning to receive and will receive blessing. And although these are announcements of eschatological blessing, an ethical invitation flows from them. As we who are followers of Jesus participate in this way of life and the kingdom values of justice, mercy, and faithfulness (23:23), we will also participate in the blessings of the kingdom that Jesus announces.

The beatitudes also provide a clear introduction of the kingdom as "already and not yet." The promise arising from the first and the last beatitudes is clearly cast in the present: "theirs is the kingdom of heaven." So we can preach the kingdom arriving in Jesus. And the rest of the beatitudes are cast in the future tense: "they will be comforted" (etc.). So we should communicate that

there is still a day to come when God will bring the consummation of the kingdom. Balancing both realities is important for the church to live well in the time of the "already and not yet."

2. *Jesus' followers find their identity and mission in covenantal relationship with God*. It is important to notice that 5:13–16 continues the emphasis of the beginning of the Sermon on the Mount on "what is" rather than "what ought to be." Those who follow Jesus, in line with faithful Israel, are declared to be salt and light for the world. These images evoke the covenantal identity of God's faithful people as well as their mission flowing from that identity. This is an important framework to pay attention to in our preaching and teaching. If our preaching and teaching only tell people what they ought to be, and fail to provide them with themes and metaphors for who they are in relationship to the covenanting God, then we do a disservice to God's people. Offering people the pictures that Jesus provides here (and others that help them to understand their new identity) can give them a deeply connected sense of who they are in Christ and why who they are matters for the world that God has created and loves.

Like a lamp giving light from a lampstand, the followers of Jesus are declared to be light to the world as their good deeds bring praise to God. Lampstands from the Roman period have been found that range from two to five feet in height, allowing light from a small oil lamp to shine throughout a room. This lampstand is from first-century AD Italy.

Illustrating the Text

The beatitudes are a pronouncement of blessings and reversals.

Children's Book: *Winnie-the-Pooh,* **by A. A. Milne.** The beatitudes provide an important balance of the "already and not yet" of the kingdom. One might compare the tendency in some parts of the church to overemphasize the "already" with Tigger in Milne's Winnie the Pooh stories: enthusiastic to a fault. We ought not to sketch the present life as a utopian vision that conveniently ignores the presence of suffering and evil. Eeyore, on the other hand, might be analogous to those perspectives that overemphasize the "not yet" of the kingdom: living as if God's reign has not already begun in Jesus. Matthew, along with the other New Testament writers, strikes a careful balance, providing Christians guidance for how to live in light of the kingdom's arrival yet before its final consummation.

Adults as well as children might enjoy seeing images of Tigger and Eeyore in a visual presentation or from a Winnie the Pooh book, with the classic illustrations by E. H. Shepard.[6]

Jesus' followers find their identity and mission in covenantal relationship with God.

Nature: Jesus' own words about salt and light are illustrations of covenantal identity and mission. Thus, it could be helpful to use some salt and a lamp or flashlight to visualize these examples. Keep in mind that many will not immediately connect salt to the idea of covenant and its permanence (see comments on 5:13–16), so you would need to make this connection explicit by drawing on relevant Old Testament texts (e.g., 2 Chron. 13:5). It might be helpful to brainstorm with your audience about the purposes of salt and light, tying some of these to the importance of mission for God's covenant people. It would also help people understand the text to note that when salt and light are "working," they naturally fulfill their purposes (mission)— for example, preserving food and dispelling darkness.

Sermon on the Mount
Jesus Teaches on the Torah

Big Idea *Jesus explains his role as fulfiller and consummate teacher of the Torah (Old Testament law) and expects his disciples to live in covenantal obedience to his expression of the Torah, culminating in the call to love even one's enemies.*

Understanding the Text

The Text in Context

This passage begins the body of the Sermon on the Mount and introduces Matthew's extensive emphasis on the law. In the title sentence (5:17) Jesus claims to fulfill rather than abolish the Law and the Prophets and then calls his kingdom followers to obey the commands of the Torah. Their righteousness should surpass even that of Jewish leaders. In Matthew 5:21–48 Jesus illustrates how this complete covenant loyalty is to be accomplished. Across his Gospel, Matthew will continue to highlight Jesus as fulfillment of the Torah, and even its embodiment (11:2–19; 12:1–13; 15:1–20; 19:1–26; 22:34–40; 23:23). The importance of covenant obedience from his followers, often framed as doing the will of God, is also thematic (7:12, 24–27; 12:50; 19:16–26; 21:28–32; 28:19–20).

Matthew emphasizes Jesus as the fulfillment of the law or Torah. This Torah scroll is from the fifteenth century AD.

Interpretive Insights

5:17 *the Law and the Prophets.* "The Law" (Torah) refers to divine instructions to Israel for living in covenant relationship with Yahweh and with one another. Recent scholarship has clarified the relationships of first-century Judaism to the Torah. Rather than viewing first-century Judaism as consumed by attempts to earn God's favor through Torah obedience, it is more accurate to note that Jews throughout Israel's history understood themselves to be chosen by Yahweh, having experienced redemption from Egypt (Exod. 14) followed by reception of the Torah to guide them in proper allegiance to Yahweh (Exod. 19–24). Obedience to the Torah was not a means of earning their redemption; it was the means of expressing loyalty to the God who had redeemed them.

This basic portrait makes sense of Matthew's positive view of the Torah and Jesus' exhortations to his followers to obey it. The contrast in the six areas of Torah discussed in 5:21–48 is not between the Torah and Jesus' teachings but between one way of understanding the Torah and Jesus' own interpretation of it. Jesus' interpretive lens, which draws on the Old Testament prophetic tradition ("Law and Prophets" here [see also 7:12; 22:40]), views Torah prescriptions through the core values of love, mercy, justice, and loyalty (see 5:43–48; 9:13; 12:7; 22:34–40; 23:23).[1]

I have come . . . to fulfill them. Jesus challenges the notion that he abolishes the Torah, an action that he denounces for his followers in 5:18–19. Instead, he claims to fulfill the Law and the Prophets. Matthew defines this claim first by showing Jesus to be the consummate interpreter of the Torah (5:17–48). Second, Matthew will narrate that Jesus himself honors and obeys the Torah (e.g., 8:4; 12:7; 15:1–20; 19:3–9, 16–19; 22:34–40). Finally, Matthew shapes his Christology to include Jesus as Wisdom, the embodiment of God's will as revealed in the Torah and his own teaching on it (11:2–19, 28–30).

5:19 *whoever practices . . . these commands will be called great in the kingdom of heaven.* The beatitudes have opened the sermon with an emphasis on God's kingdom arriving. With the move to Torah instruction, Matthew's Jesus deftly combines the two primary motifs of the sermon: kingdom and covenant loyalty. As such, the Sermon on the Mount "provides a vision of how discipleship ought to look as God comes to make all things right."[2]

5:20 *unless your righteousness surpasses that of the Pharisees and the teachers of the law.* Here Matthew uses the term *dikaiosynē* ("righteousness") to express all that God requires of Israel, and so all that Jesus requires of his followers as he announces the kingdom. The "righteousness" of Jesus' followers must surpass the righteousness of those most known for their Torah obedience, the Pharisees and teachers of the law. The Pharisees often were admired for their careful adherence to the Torah. They worked to keep in their everyday life the purity laws required for participation at the temple. In this way, their practices were often more strict than practices of other Jewish sects. In Matthew, however, the Pharisees are not portrayed as exemplary in Torah obedience. Instead, Jesus critiques them for disobedience to the Torah (15:3–6; 23:3, 23). So Jesus' disciples are called not to an impossible ethic, but

Matthew's "Antitheses"

In the six commands in 5:21–48 Jesus intensifies a Torah teaching.

Passage	Torah Command/ Prohibition	Jesus' Intensification of It
5:21–26	Prohibition against murder (Exod. 20:13)	Prohibition against even anger
5:27–30	Prohibition against adultery (Exod. 20:14)	Prohibition against even lust
5:31–32	Prohibition against divorce without certificate (Deut. 24:1–4; see Matt. 19:3)	Prohibition against divorce except for sexual immorality
5:33–37	Command to fulfill vows made to God (Deut. 23:21) (prohibition against breaking oaths, if taken)	Command to keep word, with no oath needed (prohibition against oaths)
5:38–42	Implicit: Prohibition against retribution that exceeds initial wrong done (Exod. 21:24)	Prohibition against any retribution at all
5:43–48	Command to love neighbor (Lev. 19:18) (on hating enemy, see comments on 5:43)	Command to love even enemy

rather to a covenant loyalty that revolves around the central values of the Torah.

5:21–48 Matthew 5:21–48 contains six contrasting interpretations of Torah commands (traditionally referred to as "antitheses," though this term is less than helpful). In these six teachings Jesus intensifies a Torah command or prohibition. For example, Jesus does not overturn the prohibition against murder in 5:21–26; instead, he intensifies the intent of the prohibition by proscribing the kind of anger that leads to murder. Jesus' intensified teachings resemble the Jewish interpretive practice of

"making a fence around the Torah" (e.g., *m. 'Abot* 1:1). The idea was to restrict a prohibition further or expand the scope of a command in order to minimize the possibility of transgression (see the sidebar "Matthew's 'Antitheses'").

5:32 *makes her the victim of adultery . . . commits adultery.* In the first phrase the husband "adulterizes" the wife (*poiei autēn moixeuthēnai*), and in the second phrase he commits adultery (*moixatai*).[3] On the exception clause here and in chapter 19, see comments on 19:9.

5:34 *do not swear an oath at all.* Later, Jesus will return to the topic of oaths and clarify that certain practices of taking oaths border on the arbitrary (23:16–22). Philo, a Jewish contemporary, illuminates this tendency when he speaks of the "evil habit of swearing incessantly and thoughtlessly about ordinary matters where there is nothing at all in dispute" (*Decalogue* 92). In 5:33–37 Jesus narrows his teaching from addressing the importance of fulfilling vows made to God to prohibiting oaths entirely. This may seem to contradict the Old Testament, but since making oaths to the Lord was a voluntary practice, Jesus is not contravening Old Testament teaching. Instead, he likely addresses current excesses in oath making by calling his followers to a stricter practice of the Torah.

5:38 *Eye for eye, and tooth for tooth.* This citation of Exodus 21:24 provides what has been termed the "law of retribution" (*lex talionis*). The intent of this Torah command is to limit retribution (no more than an eye for an eye). As Philo writes, "Our law exhorts us to equality when it ordains that the penalties inflicted on offenders should correspond to their actions" (*Spec. Laws* 3.182). Jesus takes this law that provides limits for retribution and limits it further by prohibiting revenge or retaliation, even in like kind.

5:39 *If anyone slaps you on the right cheek, turn to them the other cheek also.* In 5:39–42 three examples are provided to illustrate "do not resist an evil person" (5:39). This passage has been understood to disavow any kind of resistance to evil and violence. Alternately, Walter Wink has suggested that Jesus provides a way of nonviolent resistance for his followers in the face of Roman oppression. For example, a slap on the right cheek implies a slap with an open hand,[4] which would insult a person's honor and typically be done to someone of lower social position. Jesus' exhortation to turn the other (left) cheek would, in effect, challenge the initial act of dishonor.[5]

5:43 *You have heard that it was said, "Love your neighbor and hate your enemy."* While the command to love one's neighbor is clearly from an Old Testament text (Lev. 19:18), its companion, "hate your enemy," is not. Its idea may be extrapolated from certain passages (e.g., Deut. 23:3–6; Ps. 139:21–22). Or it may reflect contemporary sensibilities, such as those found in the Dead Sea Scrolls: "Hate all the Sons of Darkness each according to his guilt" (1QS 1:10; also 1:3–4; 9:16, 21–22).[6] Jesus broadens the command to love one's

neighbor to include love of enemies and prayer for their well-being.

5:48 *Be perfect, therefore, as your heavenly Father is perfect.* This exhortation of Jesus sums up the nature of Jesus' teachings on the Torah from 5:21–48 and clarifies how his followers are to pursue a greater righteousness (5:20). The language of perfection represents the Greek *teleios*, which denotes completion or wholeness. Just as the Torah called Israel to be holy as their God was holy (Lev. 19:2), Jesus calls his followers to complete covenant loyalty.[7]

Theological Insights: Torah in the Time of the Messiah

Matthew emphasizes the goodness and the relevance of the law (Torah) for Jesus' followers, even as he shifts their focus to obeying all of what Jesus himself commands (28:19). This fits well the testimony of the Old Testament itself, which understands the Torah to be God's instructions to Israel after they have experienced God's covenantal promises and redemption from Egypt (Exod. 19, following Exod. 14–15). As the psalmist can say, "The law from your mouth is

As an example of how to respond without retaliation, Jesus says, "If anyone wants to sue you and take your shirt, hand over your coat as well" (5:40). The shirt, or *chiton*, was the garment worn closest to the skin. The coat was a cloak or robe called the *himation*; it is shown draped around the body of this male statue from Herculaneum.

more precious to me than thousands of pieces of silver and gold" (Ps. 119:72). Though Paul has been understood as having no use for the Jewish law, he can be read as holding a place for something like a messianic Torah when he speaks of Jesus as the "culmination of the Torah" (Rom. 10:4) and of believers fulfilling the "Torah of the Messiah" (*nomon tou Christou*) as they carry each other's burdens (Gal. 6:2; see also Rom. 13:8; Gal. 5:14).

In his Sermon on the Mount, Jesus provides his interpretation of the Torah. God gave the law to help Israel understand its covenantal responsibility to God. This section from the sarcophagus of Agape and Crescenziano (AD 330–60) depicts Moses receiving the law.

Teaching the Text

1. *Jesus fulfills the Torah by interpreting it rightly and living it completely, and he calls his followers to live out covenant loyalty in line with the values expressed in the Torah.* Our preaching and teaching of this passage will need to contend with common perceptions (possibly our own) that the law implies legalism and exists only to provide the counterpoint to God's grace and forgiveness. We would do well to remember that the Old Testament affirms the goodness of the law (e.g., Ps. 119:9–16), and that within the law itself a means of forgiveness is provided in the sacrificial system (e.g., Lev. 4). So it is important in our preaching and teaching of Matthew that we do not offer a false dichotomy of law versus grace. This dichotomy is most certainly foreign to Matthew's theology. And Matthew's perspective is a needed corrective for many expressions of Christianity in today's world. Just as the Old Testament affirms the importance of covenant loyalty as a response to God's redemptive work and grace, so Jesus calls his followers to covenant loyalty in light of the arrival of God's kingdom and through the lens of the ultimate values of the Torah. Jesus as its consummate interpreter demonstrates that the center of the Torah is expressed in love of enemy as well as neighbor. And Matthew provides the theological grounding of Jesus (as God) with his people (1:23; 28:20) to indicate the relational (covenantal) basis for obedience to God (for the question of the relationship between contemporary Christians and the Torah, see comments on 28:19–20).

2. *Love of all, even one's enemy, is the ultimate expression of Torah obedience and loyalty.* It is no accident that the six

exhortations of 5:21–48, derived from the Torah but intensified by Jesus, culminate in the command to love both neighbor and enemy. Preaching and teaching this command might seem an easy task, but it is important to help our hearers grapple with the ways this command breaks through long-held and significant barriers. It is all too easy to look for loopholes to this command. For example, did Jesus mean that we ought to put love into action for people who are our military enemies? What about those who have hurt us most deeply? It might be fruitful to reflect upon the ways in which this command actually breaks down barriers between people. As my daughter, then in grade school, once said to me about this verse, "Jesus makes it so enemies aren't enemies anymore." This command really messes with our "us/them" categories. Our preaching and teaching on the passage should do no less.

Illustrating the Text

Jesus fulfills the Torah by interpreting it rightly and living it completely, and he calls his followers to live out covenant loyalty in line with the values expressed in the Torah.

Literature: *Les Misérables*, by Victor Hugo. In Hugo's classic, Jean Valjean steals silver plates from the bishop, Monseigneur Bienvenu (chap. 12). Valjean is stopped by the police, and when they find him in possession of the silver, they bring him to the bishop's residence. Instead of pressing charges, the bishop demonstrates amazing grace to this thief, offering Valjean the silver candlesticks in addition to the silver plates that he stole. The law was in the bishop's favor, yet grace guides the bishop's actions.

At the close of the chapter the bishop explains his actions to Valjean: "Don't forget, don't ever forget, that you promised me to use this silver to make an honest man of yourself. . . . Jean Valjean, my brother, you belong no longer to evil but to good. It is your soul that I am buying for you. I am taking it away from dark thoughts and from the spirit of perdition, and I am giving it to God."[8] The rest of the story beautifully demonstrates how Valjean embodies the grace shown to him by pursuing a life obedient to God in love toward others.

Love of all, even one's enemy, is the ultimate expression of Torah obedience and loyalty.

Testimony: It can be difficult to envision how Jesus' teaching on love of enemies might be lived out in its often messy particulars. We see a powerful example of love of enemy in the work of Dr. C. Timothy Floyd. Floyd, an orthopedic surgeon, tells of his 2003 experience as a member of the U.S. Army's 934th Forward Surgical Team (FST) in Iraq. He writes,

> The FST is located within 10 kilometers of active battle area. We treated wounded at camps near Karbala, Baghdad, Balad, Baqubah, and Tikrit. We often arrived to take wounded at a base just after the Air Force and Army Rangers cleared it, but before other units arrived.
>
> Most of the people we treated were not Coalition forces. We treated Iraqi Army, Republican Guard, Special Republican Guard, foreign terrorists, and unfortunate civilians caught in the crossfire. Military medical doctrine calls for the humane and ethical treatment of all persons wounded in battle—regardless of politics, deeds, or ideology.[9]

Sermon on the Mount

Giving, Prayer, and Fasting

Big Idea *Jesus expects his disciples to practice a covenantal piety that centers on a longing for God's kingdom to arrive and strives to please God, not humans.*

Understanding the Text

The Text in Context

Following on the heels of Matthew's instructions about keeping the law, this passage indicates right ways of enacting religious practices of giving, prayer, and fasting. In each case, believers ought to act "in secret" to receive divine rather than human approval. Their behavior is to contrast with "hypocrites" who care about present, public honor. The problem of hypocrisy will also be addressed by Jesus in chapters 15 and 23. The centerpiece of this passage (and possibly the whole Sermon on the Mount) is the Lord's Prayer (6:9–13). The importance of prayer will also be emphasized in 7:7–11, with the theme of forgiveness (6:12, 14–15) reiterated in the parable of the unforgiving servant in Matthew's fourth discourse (18:23–35).

Interpretive Insights

6:1–18 This passage is clearly divided into three sections on the topics of giving, prayer, and fasting. A pattern is also discernible in each section. (1) There is a parallel prohibition and command: when you do the particular activity, do not do so like the hypocrites, with an accompanying explanation of their way of pursuing the activity to be seen and honored by other people. Instead, Jesus exhorts his followers to do the particular activity "in secret"—that is, for God's eyes only (6:4, 6, 18). This passage does not argue against public giving, prayer, or fasting per se, since Jesus himself prayed publicly (e.g., 14:19), and public prayer was commonplace in synagogues and the temple. Instead, Jesus teaches that one should focus attention on God as audience in these acts of piety (see below). (2) The promise of reward is given for those who practice their righteousness for God's viewing and not for notice and honor before others. The hypocrites "have received their reward in full," but "your Father, who sees what is done in secret, will reward you" (6:2, 4).

6:1 *Be careful not to practice your righteousness in front of others.* Matthew takes a natural turn from narrating Jesus' words on the Torah "righteousness" (*dikaiosynē*) that he expects from his followers (5:20) to the practice (*poeiō*) of *dikaiosynē* in acts of giving to the poor (6:2–4), prayer (6:5–15), and fasting (6:16–18). These three activities are central expressions of Jewish piety and are combined with *dikaiosynē* in the apocryphal book of Tobit: "Prayer with fasting is good, but better than both is almsgiving [*eleēmosynē*, as in Matt. 6:2] with righteousness" (Tob. 12:8 NRSV). In this way, Jesus' message in the Sermon on the Mount continues the theme of covenant obligation and expectation.

6:2 *as the hypocrites do.* Matthew highlights the negative example of "hypocrites" in this passage and elsewhere (e.g., 7:5; 15:7; throughout chap. 23).[1] In this passage these hypocrites pursue righteous actions for wrong motives: they want to receive attention and honor from others instead of from God. This is the essential definition of hypocrisy: motives and actions are not in line with each other. In this way, hypocrisy is the opposite of integrity—a unity of motive and action. Since Jesus' teaching on integrity ("be perfect") has just capped the previous chapter, the exhortations away from hypocrisy toward integrity in 6:1–18 are apropos.

6:4 *Then your Father . . . will reward you.* The promise of reward must be understood in context and, specifically, in relation to the reward that the hypocrites receive. Crucial for understanding

Key Themes of Matthew 6:1–18

- Covenantal expectations include prayer, fasting, and giving to the needy.
- Covenantal practices seek God's commendation rather than human attention and honor.
- Covenantal expectations and practices focus on a longing for the kingdom.

the latter is Jesus' statement that they have (already) received their reward in full; the focus is on when the reward is received, not the particulars of the reward. By giving to the poor, praying, or fasting for the purposes of attention and honor from others, they have received public attention, and that is the only reward that they will ever receive for these deeds. Jesus' followers, on the other hand, are to give, pray, and fast so that they might be seen by God alone. This ensures their future reward. Given this context, it is likely that the reward that they will receive is participation in the kingdom.

Hypocrites will not have a future reward; faithful followers of Jesus will. The kingdom itself seems to be the reward in view.

6:7 *And when you pray, do not keep on babbling like pagans.* In addition to commending the importance of praying with God as one's only audience (6:6), Matthew includes Jesus' commendation of praying with an economy of words (6:7). Unlike the pagans, who "babble" in prayer, Jesus emphasizes that good theology leads to prayer that does not need to pile up words to catch God's attention: "your Father knows what you need " (6:8 [for a similar sentiment, see Eccles. 5:2]).

6:9 *This, then, is how you should pray.* Although 6:1–18 has a fairly precise structural pattern to it (see above on 6:1–18), the middle section on prayer is extended as compared to the sections on giving and fasting. One reason is that Matthew has included the Lord's Prayer as part of this section, as a pattern for Christian prayer (6:9–13).

6:9–10 *hallowed be your name, your kingdom come, your will be done.* After addressing God as "Father," the prayer begins with three petitions in parallelism with one another:

> Hallowed be your name,
> your kingdom come,
> your will be done.

This use of parallelism, common in Jewish poetry, song, and prayer, highlights that this is a prayer for God's kingdom to arrive. All three petitions (with the characteristic *tō* imperatival ending) ask God to come in fullness. We might paraphrase these petitions in this way: "might your name be recognized as holy (by all), might your

kingdom arrive, might your will be done on earth as it already is being done in heaven." The Lord's Prayer is thoroughly kingdom focused and thus focused on God and God's coming reign.

6:11 *daily bread.* The adjective translated "daily" is *epiousios*, a word that occurs nowhere else in extant writings prior to the New Testament (and only here and in Luke 11:3). Although a word's etymology does not always lead to correct conclusions about its meaning, in this case it is the only option for approximating the meaning of *epiousios*. Three options from etymology have been suggested: (1) bread for physical (or spiritual) existence (*epi + ousia*); (2) bread for the present (day) (*epi tēn ousan [hēmeran]*); (3) bread for the coming day, either the literal or the eschatological coming day (from *epeimi*, "to come upon, arrive").[2] Given that the last three petitions are for more immediate concerns prior to the kingdom's arrival, one of the first two options is most likely.

6:13 *deliver us from the evil one.* This prayer in Matthew ends with a request for deliverance from the evil one (Luke's version ends with "And lead us not into temptation" [11:4]). The substantival adjective *ponērou* ("evil one") at the end of this sentence can be either masculine or neuter, since these particular forms are identical in Greek. If it is masculine, then the translation as in the NIV results: "deliver us from the evil one" (the personal use is clear at 13:19). If neuter, it would be rendered as "deliver us from evil" (for a parallel idea, see Sir. 33:1).

The traditional, liturgical use of the Lord's Prayer, in the early days of the Christian church, led to expansions of it in corporate prayer. This continuing usage explains the longer ending of the prayer ("for yours is the kingdom and the power and the glory forever. Amen") that occurs in some Greek manuscripts but is not widespread in the manuscript tradition. It was likely a scribal addition that became fixed over time.

6:14–15 *For if you forgive other people.* Following closely on the fifth petition of the Lord's Prayer asking for God's forgiveness, these verses expand on the notion of forgiveness from God being connected to forgiveness of others. While the "if . . . then" construction could lead to presuming that believers' forgiveness of others is the basis for God's forgiveness of them, a further teaching on forgiveness in chapter 18 clarifies the point. Through the parable of the unforgiving servant Jesus makes it clear that God's astounding and prior forgiveness is the basis for Christian forgiveness of a brother or sister (18:23–35). The requisite for this forgiveness on the human level is essential (18:35, as at 6:14–15) but is grounded in God's initial and ongoing forgiveness.

6:16 *When you fast.* Fasting was a common practice in Judaism (e.g., Neh. 1:4; Esther 4:3; Ps. 35:13–14); it provided "a time of drawing close to God by demonstrating one's commitment."[3] There is evidence that some Jews fasted as a regular practice, twice a week (Luke 18:12; see *Did.* 8:1; according to *Genesis*

Rabbah 76:3, Mondays and Thursdays). In Matthew, John's disciples ask why Jesus' disciples do not fast like the Pharisees do (9:14–15), and Jesus himself has fasted prior to the time of his public ministry (4:2).

Teaching the Text

1. *Jesus calls his followers to practice their covenant loyalty with God as audience rather than to gain honor from others.* Jesus' words ring with great intensity in this passage. His followers are not to do their good deeds so that others will "ooh and aah" and assign them greater honor. Jesus' language is strong: his disciples are not to be hypocrites, pretending to have right motives for their acts of piety while they are really clamoring for human attention. Their integrity is what is at stake. The key to aligning inside and outside, motive and action, is to keep their eyes focused on their true audience: God, their "Father who sees in secret." All acts of covenant loyalty should be done for the sake of God and God alone.

Fasting was a regular Jewish practice. In 6:16–18 Jesus tells his followers that their outward appearance should not indicate whether they have eaten or abstained from a meal. Shown here are several nicely decorated bowls made in Jerusalem in the first century AD and used mostly by the wealthy.

This message is much easier to preach and teach than to live out and model. Especially those whose role in the church often places them in the limelight need these particular words of Jesus to soak into them and shape them. What is the invitation for leaders in not letting their left hand know what their right hand is doing (6:3)? How might this invitation free them from the tyranny of the opinions of others? How might this help them refocus on the only reward that is important: belonging to the kingdom and the King and having the honor that this affords?

2. *Jesus' disciples are given a pattern for prayer that centers on a longing for the coming of God's reign.* In the middle of Jesus' first discourse in Matthew focused on the coming of God's kingdom, it is not surprising that Jesus offers his disciples a prayer that centers on God's reign becoming a reality in this world ("on earth as it is in heaven"). Yet the use of the Lord's Prayer in churches today does not always exhibit or highlight a longing for the kingdom—what Luke Timothy Johnson refers to as the prophetic dimension and thus the countercultural nature of the Lord's Prayer.

The single greatest countercultural act Christians perform is to worship together and proclaim that Jesus is Lord. To cease from the constant round of commerce and consumption, to resist the manipulation of media that insists that working and possessing [define] worth, and to proclaim with the body language of communal gathering that Jesus, not any other power, is Lord is to enact the politics of God's kingdom and to embody the prayer "your kingdom come."[4]

Do we long for God's kingdom to come, especially in a Western, first-world cultural context that seeks first comfort, recreation, and pleasure rather than the kingdom? What might it mean to teach ourselves and our churches to pray with fervor and longing, "Your kingdom come"? As we will see

Jesus instructs his followers to pray that God's kingdom would come. This desire was expressed by early Western Christian artists who depicted Christ on his throne ruling the world. This artistic representation became known as "Christ in Majesty" or "Christ in Glory" and is shown in this reproduction of a painting on parchment by Haregarius (AD 844–51).

later in Matthew, part of the way we might do this is to pursue solidarity with the "least of these" (25:31–46). Longing for mercy and justice for all people propels us to pray for God to come and make all things right.

Illustrating the Text

Jesus calls his followers to practice their covenant loyalty with God as audience rather than to gain honor from others.

Television: Examples of public, extravagant gifts are easy to come by. Take, for instance, the September 13, 2004, episode of *The Oprah Winfrey Show*, in which the host enthusiastically gave away new cars to each audience member. Or one could easily point to several well-known billionaires who have made public displays of their charity. While we should be careful in judging the motives of others, Jesus calls Christians to a different kind of giving: one with no acclaim or notoriety attached to it, one that is done in secret for God alone.

Jesus' disciples are given a pattern for prayer that centers on a longing for the coming of God's reign.

Food: Some flavors are unmistakable, defining entire kinds of food. For instance, tomato, basil, and garlic might make you think of your favorite Italian restaurant. Cilantro, onion, tomato, and jalapeño are essential for a great salsa. And the smell of white rice, ginger, and tuna makes any true sushi lover's mouth water. Our prayer life, Jesus teaches, should be defined by a longing for and focus on the kingdom's arrival. It is the essential ingredient of the church's life of prayer.

Quote: Walter Russell Bowie. Bowie (1882–1969) was the rector of parishes in Virginia and New York, a faculty member at Union Seminary and Virginia Theological Seminary, and author of the hymn "Lord Christ, When First Thou Cam'st to Earth." He penned this prayer:

> O God, go with me as I go out into the confusion of the world. It is often hard to know the right; and even when I know it, still it may be hard to do it. I want to be faithful to the best that I believe in; but the best is high, and the common ways are easy. I need to be reminded of the way I want to go. Help me to keep a clean mind, a generous heart, and a courageous purpose. Let me never willingly bring harm to any [person]; and if in the complexities of things I cannot help, I do bring harm to any, keep me troubled and unsatisfied until I learn to make my good and [theirs] agree. When there seems to be no straight road forward, and I am caught in compromise, teach me to turn where there is least of evil and most promise of a future good. *Let me not only pray, "Thy kingdom come," but do whatever one [person] can to let thy kingdom come through me. Amen.*[5]

Sermon on the Mount
Allegiance and Trust

Big Idea *Jesus calls his disciples to undivided and primary allegiance to God and the kingdom, which will lead to trust in God for their needs.*

Understanding the Text

The Text in Context

This section of the Sermon on the Mount focuses on human allegiances and trusting God for daily needs. The Lord's Prayer in the previous section has already highlighted these themes: allegiance to God and God's kingdom (6:9–10) and requests for daily needs (6:11). Matthew 6:16–24 then deals with issues of allegiance, followed by attention to daily needs such as food and clothing (6:25–34). This passage includes the first reference to "little faith" (6:30), occurring five times in Matthew, each time being Jesus' description of the disciples (8:26; 14:31; 16:8; 17:20). The passage also brings together clearly the two motifs of the entire Sermon on the Mount: God's kingdom and covenant loyalty or righteousness. "Seek first his kingdom and his righteousness, and all these things will be given to you as well" (6:33).

Interpretive Insights

6:19 *Do not store up for yourselves treasures on earth.* This verse provides the headline for Jesus' teaching on allegiances, a theme that flows directly from the first three petitions of the Lord's Prayer. The fervent prayer for God's kingdom to arrive leads naturally into a teaching on what one values in light of God's imminent reign. The exhortation to "store up for yourselves treasures in heaven" (6:20) reflects an allegiance to the "kingdom of heaven," Matthew's favorite expression for God's kingdom (4:17). The motif of treasure communicates specifically how material possessions and wealth can be powerful competition to allegiance to God. In fact, according to Jesus, it is not possible to live in service to both God and money (6:24).

6:21 *For where your treasure is, there your heart will be also.* The reference to a person's treasure and heart being in the same location reflects the understanding of the heart as the seat of allegiance and affection. It is "a term for what is of central importance in a person, what constitutes their true character" (e.g., 15:18–19).[1]

6:22–23 *The eye is the lamp of the body.* This saying is difficult to decipher unless we address ancient views of human physiology and eyesight in particular. The eye is considered a channel for light as it leaves the body (rather than taking in light, as in modern understanding). This leads to the conclusion that the eye illuminates the light (or lack of light) within the body.[2] A healthy eye (*opthalmos haplous*) indicates a body "full of light"; an unhealthy eye (*opthalmos poneros*) attests a body "full of darkness" (6:22–23). And just as light and darkness can have a physical and metaphorical meaning, so these adjectives ("healthy" and "unhealthy") can also carry metaphorical, in this case moral, implications. An unhealthy or evil eye is a sign of stinginess; a healthy eye indicates generosity and sincerity (as noted in the NIV footnotes). These ethical connotations help us to place these verses within the context of the discussion about the relationship between wealth and allegiance to God.

6:25 *do not worry about your life.* Building from the previous passage addressing allegiance and wealth, this section addresses the theme of worry in the face of lack of possessions and sustenance (6:25–34). Such circumstances were commonplace in the Greco-Roman world of the first century, just as they are in many parts of the world today. One model that reflects generally the relative economic levels in the Greco-Roman world suggests that about 3 percent of the population were of elite economic status.[3] Another 17 percent would have been made up of merchants, some freedpersons and

- Allegiance must be given to God and God's kingdom rather than to money or possessions.
- Seeking God's kingdom is the highest priority.
- Trusting God displaces worrying about daily needs.

artisans, scribes and lectors, and military veterans, who would have had a measure of security and greater possibilities of upward mobility. The remaining 80 percent would have lived close to or below subsistence level. As Bruce Longenecker notes of this larger group, "With 55% of the Graeco-Roman world skimming the surface of subsistence and occasionally dropping down below it . . . , and with another 25% living in an extremely fragile suspension above subsistence level . . . , studies of the early Christian movement cannot be immune to the pressing 'realities of poverty' that affected the majority of the imperial world."[4]

6:27 *by worrying add a single hour to your life?* The word here translated "life" (*hēlikia*) may refer either to length of life (i.e., age) or to stature or height. Combined here with *pēchys*, a term of measure ("cubit"), the phrase can refer either to a measured length within a lifespan ("a single hour to your life") or "a single cubit to your height" (as in the NIV footnote). In the latter case, a cubit—the measured length from elbow to end of middle finger, about eighteen inches—would be a significant percentage of a person's height. This would run counter to the logic of the verse. If Jesus is making a point about worry being unable to add (even) a certain measure to a person's height, we would expect the relationship between the additional measure and the full height to be relatively small in percentage (e.g., by worrying could you add even an inch to your height?). So a cubit makes little sense if *pēchys* is referring to height here. Instead, it is more likely that *pēchys* refers to a measure within a lifespan.[5]

6:30 *you of little faith.* This brief characterization of the disciples, the primary audience of the Sermon on the Mount, will be repeated on the lips of Jesus four more times in Matthew (8:26; 14:31; 16:8; 17:20). The twelve disciples are portrayed as having little faith, as distinct from those in Matthew who lack faith (the Jewish leaders and Jesus' hometown) and those who seek healing from Jesus and who show exemplary faith and even great faith (e.g., 8:10; 9:2, 22, 29; 15:28). "Little faith" is defined narratively by worry and fear (6:30; 8:26), wavering doubt (14:31), lack of understanding (16:8), and inability to do what Jesus has empowered his disciples to do (17:14–20; cf. 10:1). In the end, the disciples' little faith is inadequate faith for fulfilling their mission (17:20).

6:32 *pagans run after all these things, and your heavenly Father knows that you need them.* Pagan (*ethnos/ethnikos*; i.e., non-Jewish) views have been referenced already in the sermon as counterpoints to right theology leading to right praxis (5:45–47; 6:7–8). Jesus calls his disciples to live as "children of [their] Father in heaven" (5:45). Like God, they ought to love even enemies. Unlike God and God's children, pagans or Gentiles who do not know or follow God only love and welcome their own people. A right view of God should inform a different way of understanding God and living life. Similarly, pagan people babble in prayer, since they pray to gods who need to be persuaded with many words (6:7). Jesus affirms that the one true God already knows what people need before being asked (6:8). In the passage at hand, worry about daily needs of food and clothing stems from an improper theology that assumes that God is unaware of and unconcerned about people's needs. Jesus counters that "your heavenly Father knows that you need [food and clothing]" (6:32), and that the Father cares deeply about human need and will provide (6:26). In all three cases insufficient understandings of God lead to ways of living that are inadequate.

6:33 *But seek first his kingdom and his righteousness.* In contrast to worry about daily existence, Jesus' followers are to seek God's kingdom and righteousness as their first priority. This is not an insignificant tension. In the first-century world, where provision of food and clothing could

Jesus draws an analogy between his followers and "the flowers of the field" (6:28). If God beautifully clothes the latter (as seen in this landscape from Israel), how much more will he meet the needs of the people who put their trust in God.

be a daily effort and struggle for the poor, Jesus asks believers to trust fully and deeply in God's care so that they might prioritize the kingdom. The coupling here of the language of "kingdom" and "righteousness" highlights the two primary themes of the Sermon on the Mount: God's imminent reign (5:3, 10) and covenant loyalty and faithfulness. The latter theme has been used to describe the covenant loyalty expected of Jesus' followers as they live in light of the coming kingdom (5:20; 6:1). In this case, however, "righteousness" (*dikaiosynē*) clearly refers to God's own righteousness (as some Greek manuscripts indicate by adding "of God" [*tou theou*] to "kingdom"). While it is possible that the reference is to God's moral righteousness, which believers in Jesus should mirror, more likely in view is God's covenant faithfulness to Israel in bringing promised salvation (see comments on 3:15 and also the sidebar "Matthew's Covenantal Backdrop" in that unit). To prioritize God's kingdom and covenant loyalty is to orient oneself fully around God's reign and restoration of all things. As Matthew will make clear, God's reign and restoring work are embodied in Jesus the Messiah, so that responding to God's reign is about responding to Jesus.

Theological Insights: Dangers of Wealth

Matthew emphasizes allegiance to God's kingdom over any valuing of material wealth. Later he will portray wealth as a distraction and a danger to participating in the kingdom (19:16–26). These teachings fit a wider complex of scriptural teachings on care for the poor and avoiding the dangers that wealth can bring. The Torah

made provision for the poor in Israel (e.g., Exod. 23:10–11) and called Israel to generosity: "Be openhanded toward your fellow Israelites who are poor and needy" (Deut. 15:11). Luke develops these themes by announcing blessing on the poor and woe to the rich (6:20, 24). In ways countercultural in the Greco-Roman world and resonant with the Torah, Luke calls his audience to avoid showing favoritism to those with wealth and high status (14:12–14; 19:8) and warns of the dangers of hoarding wealth (12:13–21; 16:19–31). James 2 provides a similar call to avoid favoritism toward the wealthy.

Teaching the Text

1. *Jesus calls his followers to an allegiance to God's kingdom rather than to material possessions, wealth, and worry about the needs of daily existence.* This passage provides a range of applications for believers in Jesus as it relates to wealth and possessions. While all followers of Jesus are called to align their allegiance to God and God's kingdom and to store up treasure accordingly, specific exhortations from this passage will likely land differently with those in our audiences who have much and those who have little. Jesus' warnings about serving money rather than God speak most directly to those in our audience who have the possibility of accumulation of wealth and who can insulate themselves from need and poverty. Alternately, Jesus' call to trust God and Jesus' promises about God's ability and desire to meet needs of daily food and clothing are powerful words for those in our congregations who are poor and struggle to make ends meet. And we should not be afraid to

Jesus warns his disciples, "Do not store up for yourselves treasures on earth," (6:19) because they can be lost due to theft or decay. Six hoards were found during archaeological excavations at Ekron in Israel. Several were discovered under floors. The hoard shown here contains silver, semiprecious stones, and glazed beads and figurines, and serves as an example of valuables that were stored or hidden.

trust in God and the reality of light from within (6:22–23; see also 5:14–16).

2. *Pursuing God's kingdom rather than being consumed by worry about daily needs requires a deep trust in God's goodness and ability to care for those needs.* Matthew highlights the priority of the kingdom in this passage. God has come to make all things right in Jesus, and Christians are to live in light of and in line with kingdom priorities. And according to Jesus, the God who is bringing restoration is a God we can trust with all parts of life and death. This is a powerful message that provides the counterpart for kingdom allegiance. We can exhort our congregations to put God's kingdom first, with all the risks that this entails, because we can assure them that God is fully trustworthy. Kingdom risk without a trustworthy God seems foolhardy. But putting the kingdom as our highest priority in relationship to a God who can be fully trusted is wisdom (7:24–27). Though we are often like the disciples, whom Jesus portrays as having "little faith" here and elsewhere (e.g., 6:30; 8:26), Matthew calls us through the words and deeds of Jesus into a deeper trust of our heavenly Father, who listens, cares, and works in this world for restoration.

preach both messages, even if we risk offending sensibilities on this touchy subject.

And we would be wrong to think that worry about daily life eludes the rich and those with enough to live on. Rather, worry about daily life plagues the rich as well as the poor, even if the worries may not be about putting food on the table or clothing on one's back. Worry can consume the wealthy, who can easily be preoccupied with maintaining wealth and keeping up with the lifestyle of their neighbors. Additionally, concerns and crises in relation to physical and mental health, relationships, and emotional well-being strike rich and poor alike (though not always equally). One powerful application of this passage for those with many possessions and monetary abundance, which characterizes many in the Western world and church, is the freedom from wealth that it offers. Those with much are offered a way out of slavery to wealth by the call to a generous way of life that demonstrates a deep

Illustrating the Text

Jesus calls his followers to an allegiance to God's kingdom rather than to material possessions, wealth, and worry about the needs of daily existence.

Lyrics: Consider the lyrics to Bob Dylan's song "Gotta Serve Somebody." If your context allows, you might play part of the song. In it, Dylan posits that all people will serve someone or something. No one is exempt from this human posture of allegiance and service. Jesus' words make clear the allegiance to material comfort runs against allegiance to the living God: "You cannot serve both God and money."

Pursuing God's kingdom rather than being consumed by worry about daily needs requires a deep trust in God's goodness and ability to care for those needs.

History: In *Sleeping with Bread*, Dennis Linn, Sheila Linn, and Matthew Linn tell this story in their introduction that might help us understand better the angst about daily provision that would have typified the ancient world.

During the bombing raids of World War 2, thousands of children were orphaned and left to starve. The fortunate ones were rescued and placed in refugee camps where they received food and good care. But many of these children who had lost so much could not sleep at night. They feared waking up to find themselves once again homeless and without food. Nothing seemed to reassure them. Finally, someone hit upon the idea of giving each child a piece of bread to hold at bedtime. Holding their bread, these children could finally sleep in peace. All through the night the bread reminded them, "Today I ate and I will eat again tomorrow."[6]

Sermon on the Mount
Praying, Not Judging

Big Idea *Jesus calls his disciples to discernment and loyal actions in their relationships as well as ongoing prayer that trusts in their gracious and good God.*

Understanding the Text

The Text in Context

This passage includes a number of topics that are picked up in other parts of Matthew. The prohibition of judging (7:1) is clarified in chapter 13, where disciples are to avoid judging the eschatological fate of others in the Christian community (13:27–30). Jesus' disciples are also warned against hypocrisy, which has already been exposed at 6:1–18 (see also 15:1–9; 23:13–32). Trusting prayer is a hallmark of Jesus' followers (6:5–15; 21:21–22). The Golden Rule (7:12) brings the body of the Sermon on the Mount (5:17–7:12) full circle, back to the centrality of faithfulness to "the Law and the Prophets" for those who anticipate God's kingdom.

Interpretive Insights

7:1–2 *Do not judge, or you too will be judged.* This teaching of Jesus begins the final section of the Sermon on the Mount prior to its conclusion in 7:13–29. Scholars

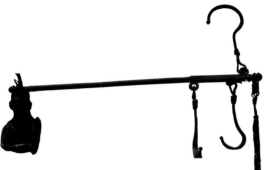

have noted the seemingly disparate topics that are addressed in 7:1–12 yet a few themes emerge. The first in 7:1–6 revolves around judging others. The emphasis is upon avoiding the tendency to judge, although 7:6 introduces the importance of discernment, which is a form of judgment.

An initial question regards the kind of judgment that is prohibited in 7:1. It is likely that the second clause ("you too will be judged") refers to God's final judgment rather

"With the measure you use, it will be measured to you" (7:2). Shown here is a scale from the Roman period.

than judgment by other people. Reference to the final day when God will make right judgments about all people and things is a Matthean motif (e.g., 13:40–43, 47–50; 25:31–33). For this reason, it is likely that Jesus' words "you too will be judged" are a "divine passive" construction indicating that God will judge believers as they judge others.

Another question involves the kind of judgment being rendered to others. The immediate context indicates that an overly critical judgment of a believing brother or sister is an inappropriate kind of judgment, especially when coupled with a lack of awareness about one's own faults (7:3–5). In a wider context, Matthew will also emphasize the inappropriate nature of judging a person's eschatological fate (13:29–30, 36–43). This is God's task alone, and God will make that judgment at the "end of the age" (13:39). Believers are not to usurp God's role as judge.

7:3 *speck . . . plank.* To give an example of the foolishness of judging the faults of others, Jesus uses an image of a believer trying to point out a speck of sawdust in the eye of another believer while at the same time having a wooden plank in their own eye. The latter term refers to a piece of heavy timber often used in construction, overwhelmingly large in comparison to the speck of sawdust. Such powerful hyperbole demonstrates how ridiculous is the presumption of one person's judgment of others (see the sidebar "Imagery and Hyperbole in the Teaching of Jesus").

7:5 *You hypocrite.* As Jesus has warned against acting like "the hypocrites" in 6:1–18, he now speaks to his specific audience as those typified by the same trait. He speaks to any who would presume to judge harshly

---

Key Themes of Matthew 7:1–12

- Disciples must engage in discernment and self-awareness rather than presumptuous judgment of others.
- Prayer offered to the covenant God is effective.
- The Torah is summed up in the Golden Rule.

Imagery and Hyperbole in the Teaching of Jesus

Jesus, much like other Jewish rabbis, used a variety of teaching methods to persuade and compel his audience. His teachings in the Gospels are filled with imagery, both commonplace (e.g., salt and lamps [Matt. 5:13–16]) and striking (e.g., the juxtaposition of speck and plank [Matt. 7:3–5]). In addition to simple images, Jesus told stories (parables) that form more complex images of comparison to illustrate what God's kingdom and God's work are like (e.g., Matt. 20:1–15). Jesus also used hyperbole—exaggeration of images meant to jar sensibilities and prod responses. Jesus has already used hyperbole in 6:1–18, where he calls his followers to give to the needy without concern for public attention or honor. The words "Do not let your left hand know what your right hand is doing" are clearly hyperbolic because the scenario is not a physiological possibility. The point of such hyperbolic speech is to communicate powerfully the necessity of giving with no thought of human praise (even one's own).

---

a fairly insignificant fault while ignoring a major sin or fault of their own. In Jesus' eyes, such persons would be hypocrites, since their motives and actions are out of line with each other. Their presumed motive—to find a reason for judgment of another with little cause—contradicts their own avoidance of self-assessment. They let themselves off the hook for a major fault while calling to account another believer for little or no reason.

7:6 *Do not give dogs what is sacred; do not throw your pearls to pigs.* This teaching provides a point of balance to the strong admonitions against judgment of others. In its general sense, it exhorts Jesus' followers to discernment, that they might avoid giving what is holy to whatever or whoever is unclean. The contrast seems to be taken from purity concerns, though these might be part of the image or metaphor rather than tied to referents of the saying. In its general sense, Craig Keener helpfully compares it to Proverbs 23:9: "Do not speak to fools, for they will scorn your prudent words."[1] In specifics, there is ambiguity about the meaning of the exhortation, since the referents of "what is sacred" and "pearls" and of "dogs" and "pigs" are not specified. (Given that these two clauses are poetically parallel, these two pairs indicate two, not four, referents.)

That which is sacred in Matthew might be connected to the kingdom of God, which has been the centerpiece of Jesus' preaching (4:17). This possible referent fits well with the image of a pearl in a parable in chapter 13, which provides a comparison for the kingdom (13:45–46). Yet Jesus speaks here of "your pearls," making it less likely that he is referring to the kingdom (which belongs to God first and foremost). So another, more likely option is that "pearls" and "what is sacred" refer to wisdom more generally that disciples might offer to others (see Prov. 20:15). The referent of "dogs" and "pigs" is also difficult to discern. While some have suggested that these are references to Gentiles (see 15:21–28), Matthew's commitment to the Gentile mission argues against this connection (28:19). Instead, it might be better to understand "dogs" and "pigs" as standing for those who will not understand the value of wisdom (e.g., "pearls") when it is offered to them. Taking

To encourage his disciples to use discernment, Jesus balances his warnings about judging others by using a figurative phrase, "Do not throw your pearls to pigs" (7:6). Pigs were considered unclean animals, avoided by the Jews, and only the pagans used them for eating and sacrifices. Small votive images, like the pig shown here, have been found in temples to pagan gods (temple of Demeter, Knidos, Turkey, 350–300 BC).

the saying as more general than specific, Warren Carter provides a helpful summary of the teaching of 7:6: "There is no point offering valuable correction when it will be despised and rejected."[2]

7:7–11 In 7:7–11 Jesus invites his disciples to enter boldly into prayer, asking God to grant their petitions for God's "good gifts" (7:11). The three lines that make up 7:7 are formed in Hebraic parallelism, where each line is essentially synonymous with and, in this case, builds upon the previous line.

Ask and it will be given to you;
seek and you will find;
knock and the door will be opened to you.

Jesus then provides an analogy with human parenting to illuminate God's great willingness to answer prayer and "give good gifts to those who ask him" (7:9–11). The argument moves from lesser to greater. If a human parent is more than willing to give what a child asks for, much more so will God as a good Father—the faithful covenant God—willingly give good gifts when asked.

7:9–10 *will give him a stone? . . . will given him a snake?* Although not easily translated into English, these questions begin with the negative particle *mē*, which indicates that the expected answer to these rhetorical questions is no: surely no parent would give a stone to a child asking for bread or give a snake to a child asking for a fish.

7:12 *do to others what you would have them do to you.* This saying of Jesus, known as the Golden Rule, calls Jesus' followers to a way of life that is other-focused. How others would like to be treated becomes the guide for the behavior of a disciple toward them. A similar (converse) saying occurs in rabbinic reflection. The following saying is attributed to Hillel the Elder: "What is hateful to you, do not do to your neighbor. That is the whole Torah; the rest is commentary" (*b. Shabb.* 31a).[3] Jesus also ties this general aphorism to the Torah more broadly: "For this sums up the Law and the Prophets." The teachings of the Torah that Jesus has interpreted and communicated to his disciples in the Sermon on the Mount are summed up in the teaching "Do to others what you would have them do to you." With this reference to the "Law and the Prophets," Matthew has formed an inclusio with Jesus' words in 5:17 at the front of the body of the sermon: "Do not

think that I have come to abolish the Law or the Prophets."

Teaching the Text

1. *Jesus warns his disciples against presumptuous and harsh judgment of others.* Many moments of the Sermon on the Mount have made it into popular parlance (e.g., "This person is the salt of the earth"). Probably no one-liner is as famous as "Judge not lest ye be judged" (in the language of the King James Bible). And this aphorism in its popular usage hits the mark in many ways. If Jesus is calling his followers to be less critical and more gracious, then the perception of Christians as those who are quite judgmental is an indictment that we have not followed this teaching of Jesus with care. We would do well to cultivate church communities that are characterized by a first impulse to extend grace and to forgive (see 18:21–35) rather than to judge. This does not mean, however, that there is no room for discernment in the Christian life and community. Christians should turn a discerning eye inward toward their own faults and sins (7:3–5) as well as practice discernment regarding when to offer correction to others (and when not to [7:6]). Discernment as the pursuit of wisdom and self-reflection is a form of judgment that should characterize Christians.[4]

2. *God will answer prayer; it is part of God's covenant nature and commitment to do so.* As Jesus has done a number of times in the Sermon on the Mount, in 7:7–11 he grounds an exhortation (here to prayer) in right ways of thinking about God. He addresses any tendency to see God as capricious and acting on a whim without

compassion. How could anyone think that the Father in heaven would be a lesser parent than a human parent, who would never give a stone to a child asking for bread? Yet without attentiveness to Scripture, we are prone to such wrong theology. And theology, right or wrong, routinely shows up in our practices of prayer and our interactions with others. In the Sermon on the Mount Jesus illuminates a wrong view about God (and the actions that it produces) as one who shows favoritism (5:45) or as one who is distant and prone to ignore human concerns (6:7, 32). To counter this wrong theology, Jesus affirms a knowledge of Israel's covenant God, who cares, listens, is quick to act, and will answer prayer. Such a message is a crucial one for teaching and preaching in a culture and a world that think and act on wrong views of God on a regular basis. Part of the good news is this: God truly cares about the world and for humanity, made in the image of God. So people can pray with confidence that God acts above and beyond how loving parents act toward their children.

Jesus paints a scenario in which a child asks for a fish. In such a case, a good parent would certainly not give them a snake instead (7:9). Shown here is a modern catch of tilapia, which was also a food source in the first century AD.

Illustrating the Text

Jesus warns his disciples against presumptuous and harsh judgment of others.

Literature: *The Catcher in the Rye*, by J. D. Salinger. This well-known novel provides an intriguing example of judgment of others without a corresponding critical eye on the self. Holden Caulfield, the book's protagonist and first-person narrator, routinely rails against those he encounters for being "phonies."

One of the biggest reasons I left Elkton Hills [a school from which he was expelled] was because I was surrounded by phonies. . . . Haas [the headmaster] would just shake hands with them [ordinary parents] and give them a phony smile and then he'd go talk, for maybe a half an *hour*, with somebody else's parents. I can't stand that stuff. It drives me crazy.[5]

Although Holden prides himself on exposing this lack of authenticity in others, he nonetheless hides behind a persona himself. In spite of regular assertions of his truthfulness to the reader (e.g., "I'm not kidding"; "If you want to know the truth . . ."), he consistently pretends to be what he is not to impress other people. For example, he withholds his real name from people he meets, using pseudonyms such as "Jim Steele." Holden's tirades against phonies are an indictment of his own motives and behavior. In terms that Jesus uses, Holden focuses on the speck in others' eyes and ignores the plank in his own.

God will answer prayer; it is part of God's covenant nature and commitment to do so.

Human Experience: The analogy that Jesus provides in this passage makes for a powerful illustration that we might highlight with our audience. Describe a situation in which parents demonstrate their commitment to their children through thick and thin. If their children ask for something that will keep them fed, warm, or safe, would good parents ever deny them that need if there is the means to provide it? It might be helpful in this regard to recognize two facets of the analogy. First, it presumes good parents. (Although the parent in comparison with God is described as "evil," the analogy works only if the parent wants the best for the child.) We might want to acknowledge that some in our audience may have experienced great harm from a parent; in these cases, the goodness of God may be difficult to understand via this analogy. Second, the analogy presumes that the child is asking for what is needful (not simply something he or she wants). As Jesus has already promised, God will care for the daily needs of God's children who seek the kingdom (6:33).

Sermon on the Mount

Final Warnings and Call to Obey Jesus' Words

Big Idea *Jesus' final words in the Sermon on the Mount warn against those who claim to belong to God but are disobeying God's will. Those who are wise will put Jesus' authoritative words into practice.*

Understanding the Text

The Text in Context

The final section of the Sermon on the Mount focuses on putting into practice Jesus' teachings and provides warnings about those who do not obey God's will. Jesus speaks of bearing fruit being the mark of a disciple (7:15–20; see also 12:33–37; 13:18–23; 21:18–22, 43). Bearing fruit means doing the will of God (7:21) rather than doing evil, a topic to which Jesus will return (12:46–50). The sermon concludes with a parable about the wisdom of putting Jesus' words into practice (7:24–27). The narrative conclusion to the Sermon on the Mount (7:28–29) includes the first of five uses of the formula "When Jesus had finished saying [these things]," which closes each of the five major discourses of Jesus in Matthew (chaps. 5–7, 10, 13, 18, 24–25). The amazement of the crowds at Jesus' teaching authority introduces the theme of authority that will be exemplified in the miracles in chapters 8–9.

Jesus compares false prophets to trees that produce bad fruit. Just as grapevines (like the one shown here) produce grapes but thorn bushes bear no fruit at all, false prophets will be recognized for what they really are by their lack of fruit.

Interpretive Insights

7:13–14 *Enter through the narrow gate.* The saying in 7:13–14 introduces the sermon's conclusion, which centers on doing God's will—a fitting extension of the Golden Rule in 7:12. The call to enter through the narrow gate indicates the difficulty of following the way that Jesus has set forth. Yet it will also be held forth as the wisest of choices (7:24–27). The rhetorical effect of this "two ways" language (narrow gate versus broad road) is to persuade hearers and readers to make the right choice between the two—to follow the way of Jesus.

7:15 *Watch out for false prophets.* This is the first warning against false prophets in Matthew. The warning will resurface in chapter 24, where Jesus speaks of false prophets during the time of the fall of the Jerusalem temple (24:11, 24). Matthew also refers to (good) prophets, who should be treated well by his audience (10:41; 23:34; for Jesus as prophet, see 13:57; 21:11, 46). The false prophets described in 7:15–20 appear in "sheep's clothing"; their outward similarity to true prophets is emphasized. Yet Jesus' followers will be able to recognize false prophets by their evil actions. The repeated phrase "By their fruit you will recognize them" surrounds the picture of good trees naturally bearing good fruit and bad trees naturally producing bad fruit (7:16, 20).

7:21 *Lord, Lord.* Jesus provides another warning at the close of the sermon. This saying is surprising in a few ways. First, although Jesus has just indicated the importance of good deeds for recognizing a true prophet, he reveals here that some who prophesy, cast out demons, and perform miracles in his name may not be true

Who Calls Jesus "Lord" in Matthew?

Matthew has carefully designated various characters by how they refer to Jesus. His disciples and those who come to him in faith refer to him as "Lord" (*kyrios*). Those who are at odds with him call him "Teacher" or "Rabbi," the Aramaic word for teacher.

Characters who call Jesus "Lord"	Characters who call Jesus "Teacher"
The disciples (8:25; 26:22)	A teacher of the law (8:19)
Peter (14:28, 30; 16:22; 17:4; 18:21)	Pharisees (9:11)
Seeker: a leper (8:2)	Pharisees/teachers of the law (12:38)
Seeker: a centurion (8:6, 8)	Collectors of the temple tax (17:24)
A would-be disciple (8:21)	Rich man (19:16)
Seekers: two blind men (9:28)	Pharisees/Herodians (22:16)
Seeker: a Canaanite woman (15:22, 25, 27)	Sadducees (22:24)
Seeker: a man with a sick son (17:15)	A Pharisee (22:36)
Seekers: two blind men (20:31, 33)	Judas, using "rabbi" (26:25, 49)

prophets. It is not "good fruit" of prophetic words or even miraculous deeds that are in mind in 7:16–20; instead, good deeds are best identified with those that have been given priority in the sermon—actions such as seeking reconciliation, faithfulness in marriage, nonretaliation, prayer and love for enemy, giving to the poor, and fasting (e.g., 5:21–46; 6:1–18).

Second, Matthew takes care to show narratively who is a follower of Jesus.

Followers of Jesus and those who come to him in faith call him "Lord" (e.g., 8:2; 26:22) (see the sidebar "Who Calls Jesus 'Lord' in Matthew?"). Given this careful attribution, Jesus likely refers here to those who have been a part of the believing community. They are warned of performing signs but without accompanying good deeds. This fits Matthew's picture of the church in the present as a "mixed community" (see 13:29–30), a characteristic much discussed in Matthean scholarship. As Donald Hagner puts it, "The present age is . . . one in which human society (and thus even the Church) is a mixture of those of the evil one and those of the kingdom."[1]

Finally, it is here in Matthew that "Lord" is first applied to Jesus. In this passage Jesus "presents himself as the one who decides who does and does not enter the kingdom of heaven, and even more remarkably the basis for that entry is people's relationship with *him*, whether or not *he* 'knew them.' "[2]

enter the kingdom of heaven. Jesus speaks of entering the kingdom of heaven, which should not be confused with the more popular, contemporary concept of "going to heaven." The latter is one part of the bigger picture of God's reign over all things in heaven and on earth.[3] Matthew's "kingdom of heaven" speaks to the larger vision of God's restorative work, bringing all things under Jesus' reign (e.g., 1 Cor. 15:20–28).

the will of my Father. This phrase sums up Jesus' expectation for his followers in the Sermon on the Mount (for the same phrase,

According to 7:24–27, obeying the words of Jesus is like building a house on a rock foundation: it provides a firm foundation when adversity comes. In 1927 an earthquake occurred in the Jordan River Valley near the Dead Sea. Houses built on unstable foundations such as clay and soft bedrock, like the one shown here along the Jordan, could not withstand the movement of the earth. Houses built on solid rock remained standing, protecting their inhabitants.

Five Major Discourses	Concluding Formula	Themes
Sermon on the Mount (5:1–7:27)	7:28–29	Covenant expectations in light of the imminent arrival of the kingdom
Mission Discourse (10:1–42)	11:1	Disciples' part in the mission of the kingdom; persecution ahead
Parables Discourse (13:1–52)	13:53	The "already and not yet" of the kingdom; judgment at end of the age
Community Discourse (18:1–35)	19:1	Community life in light of the kingdom; care for the vulnerable and for straying members
Eschatological Discourse (24:1–25:46)	26:1	Prediction of the fall of the temple and the return of Jesus as king and judge at the end of the age

see 12:49–50). The sermon has presumed covenantal categories and relationship (e.g., 5:13–16) as the context for discipleship as doing God's will. As the sermon concludes, Matthew prioritizes praxis. Belief in Jesus as Messiah and as Lord is crucial for those who follow him, but so too is living out the will of God. Actions speak louder than words in this regard (7:21). Matthew will conclude the teachings of Jesus with a parable that indicates a criterion for final judgment that centers on action done for the sake of "the least of these" (25:31–46). For Matthew, responding to God's covenant reaffirmed and renewed in Jesus the Messiah necessarily involves living out covenant faithfulness and obedience.

7:24–27 *puts [these words of mine] into practice . . . does not put them into practice.* Matthew concludes the Sermon on the Mount with a parable, the first parable of Jesus in Matthew. Parables—stories told by Jesus to compare ordinary life to some aspect of God's action or God's kingdom—provide an effective way of placing a choice before Jesus' hearers (and Matthew's readers). Because a parable draws a hearer into a story that usually centers on a compelling choice, a "parable demands total commitment."[4] The parable that concludes

the sermon compels a choice to be either a wise person or a foolish one. The person who hears Jesus' words and "puts them into practice" is like a wise builder who constructs a house on rock rather than on sand. Hearing Jesus' words in the Sermon on the Mount is not enough; obeying them is the wise course that leads to life (7:14).

7:28 *When Jesus had finished saying these things.* This temporal clause is repeated five times by Matthew; each time it marks the conclusion for a teaching discourse of Jesus (11:1; 13:53; 19:1; 26:1). By using this formula, Matthew highlights his arrangement of Jesus' teachings into these five major discourses, with each discourse having a distinct topic and some common features that connect them.

7:29 *he taught as one who had authority.* The notion of Jesus' authority is important in chapters 5–10. In the Sermon on the Mount, Matthew has shown Jesus to be authoritative in his teaching through repeated variations on the refrain "You have heard that it was said . . . but I tell you . . ." (5:21–22, 27–28, 31–32, 33–34, 38–39, 43–44). Jesus' authoritative pronouncements, culminating in his implicit claim to be "Lord" (7:21), provide a contrast to typical Jewish teaching style. Rabbis most often cited past rulings and wisdom of former teachers and traditions to carry on their own teaching.[5] Jesus, however, teaches with an authority that derives from his God-given wisdom and interpretation of the Torah.

Teaching the Text

1. *Doing the will of God—that is, obeying the words of Jesus—is the proper and wise response to Jesus' teaching in the Sermon on the Mount.* In the Sermon on the Mount, Matthew has communicated Jesus' core teachings about how disciples are to live out covenantal faithfulness in light of the arriving kingdom of God. This expectation of obedience may provoke strong reactions, especially from those steeped in dichotomies of law versus grace and faith versus works. Matthew's own setting and messages do not presume these same dichotomies. Instead, covenantal themes are pervasive in the sermon in the identification of Jesus' followers as salt and light (5:13–16), in references to *dikaiosynē* ("righteousness") communicating covenantal loyalty, and in frequent reference to Old Testament theology regarding the covenant-making God to ground the call for believers to trust and act rightly (5:44–47; 6:7–8, 32; 7:9–11). In typical Old Testament fashion, covenantal relationship precedes God's expectation of covenant loyalty and obedience.

So we can be unabashed about preaching and teaching that the response that Jesus calls for is one of obedience or covenant loyalty. This is the narrow gate that disciples are called to enter. Covenant loyalty is the fruit that disciples are called to produce. Covenant loyalty is about doing "the will of my Father who is in heaven" (7:21). Responding to God's covenantal and saving work in and through Jesus is the wisest thing to do; it is like building a house on a rock. And it is also the case that doing God's will is a communal, corporate task for Matthew. The Sermon on the Mount is written first not to individuals, but rather to the community of disciples who have formed around Jesus the Messiah.

2. *Jesus' teachings are authoritative for Christian communities.* Matthew makes it

Entering through the narrow gate means taking the path of obedience to Jesus. John Bunyan picks up this imagery in *The Pilgrim's Progress* when Christian enters the Wicket-Gate as he travels to the Celestial City.

clear that Jesus' words function authoritatively for Christian communities (7:28–29). Jesus affirms the Old Testament Torah in his teachings in the sermon, but Matthew emphasizes at its conclusion that it is the teachings of Jesus (on the Torah's key themes) that are to shape and guide the church. This is communicated most clearly at the end of Matthew, where Jesus refers to the discipleship task of "teaching [other disciples] to obey everything I have commanded you" (28:20). The "everything" encompasses Jesus' teachings across Matthew, including those in the Sermon on the Mount. Jesus' teachings provide the solid foundation for Christian faith and practice. As we have heard in chapters 5–7, Jesus' teachings offer a challenging way of life for the church. It is not an easy way that he calls us to (7:13–14), but it is the way that leads to authentic life. A significant challenge in preaching this message involves not only teaching about Jesus' teachings, but also teaching those whom we lead to obey them. Matthew provides much to help us as we teach what Jesus taught about the arrival of God's kingdom and about living in light of it, but we will not have gone far enough if we only teach Jesus' teachings. We need to press toward helping our churches live out those teachings in their contexts. And this will necessarily involve discipling and modeling by example as well as teaching with words.

Illustrating the Text

Doing the will of God—that is, obeying the words of Jesus—is the proper and wise response to Jesus' teaching in the Sermon on the Mount.

Hymn: "Trust and Obey," by John H. Sammis. This classic hymn nicely brings together what often is kept apart in churches today. All too often we dichotomize "faith" and "works." For Matthew, trusting Jesus as the authoritative speaker of God's truth means putting Jesus' teachings into action—it means to obey them.

> Then in fellowship sweet we will sit at
>   His feet,
> or we'll walk by His side in the way.
> What He says we will do, where He
>   sends we will go;
> never fear, only trust and obey.
>
> Trust and obey, for there's no other way
> to be happy in Jesus, but to trust and
>   obey.

Jesus' teachings are authoritative for Christian communities.

Humor: To illustrate that Jesus' teachings are a solid foundation for living as a Christian (7:24–27), you might give some examples of products that fail to deliver on their promises in advertising. Perform an internet search for strange infomercial products (e.g., *Time* magazine's list of the twenty-five worst infomercials). Taking your setting into consideration, pick some of the silly things that people are willing to purchase to help improve their lives (you might consider showing pictures or video, or even buying and displaying a few of the more outrageous products). Ask a simple question: "Do you think this really works?" Advertising promises many things to make sense of our lives. Jesus' teachings provide a true anchor for living in light of the arrival of God's kingdom.

Jesus, Isaiah's Servant of the Lord, Heals Many

Big Idea *Matthew encourages his readers to trust in Jesus, as he brings the power of God's kingdom to bear upon human sickness and suffering, both to Israel and as a foreshadowing of Gentile inclusion.*

Understanding the Text

The Text in Context

As Matthew's earlier summary of Jesus' teaching (4:23–25) indicates, Jesus' messianic ministry is characterized by preaching (4:17), teaching (5:1–7:29), and healing (8:1–9:38). This section of Matthew introduces Jesus' healing and miraculous ministry in Galilee, accentuating themes of Jesus' authority, the importance of faith for discipleship, and Gentile inclusion in the coming kingdom of God. Jesus' authority and corresponding faith in Jesus will be themes that pervade chapters 8–9. Matthew also cites from Isaiah's Servant Songs (Isa. 42:1–4; 49:1–6; 50:4–9; 52:13–53:12) to connect Jesus' healing ministry to Isaiah's servant figure (Isa. 53:4, quoted in Matt. 8:17). By using Isaiah, Matthew indicates that Jesus is the Isaianic "servant" who willingly and compassionately takes on Israel's suffering as Israel's representative for the purpose of bringing God's kingdom and salvation. Matthew will stress this connection again at 12:18–21 (citing Isa. 42:1–4).

Interpretive Insights

8:1 *When Jesus came down from the mountainside, large crowds followed him.* This transition verse from the Sermon on the Mount to chapters 8–9 parallels 5:1, where we hear that "when Jesus saw the

The first part of Matthew 8 is set in and around Capernaum. This aerial view of the area of Capernaum shows the Sea of Galilee and some of the excavations, which include the fourth- to fifth-century AD synagogue, the octagonal roof covering what some believe to be Peter's house, and walls outlining many insulae and individual dwellings.

crowds, he went up on a mountainside." This repetition forms an inclusio that frames the sermon and highlights Matthew's movement from the words of the Messiah (chaps. 5–7) to the deeds of the Messiah (chaps. 8–9) (see the sidebar "Narrative Outline of Matthew 8–9").

8:2 *A man with leprosy.* The term *lepros* may indicate a number of types of more serious skin diseases, much like the related language in the Hebrew Bible (*tsara'at* [e.g., Lev. 13:2]). Jesus heals this man by touching him (8:3), a gesture not lost on Matthew's audience, which certainly is familiar with the Levitical regulations regarding the impurity contracted by a person who touches someone who is ceremonially impure (e.g., Lev. 5:3). Jesus' command to follow the Mosaic regulations for ceremonial cleansing from such a disease signals his adherence to the Jewish Torah (8:4; cf. Lev. 14:1–32).

8:3 *I am willing . . . Be clean!* With these words, Matthew highlights Jesus' compassion, a theme that will be evident in the various healings of chapters 8–9 and will be mentioned explicitly at 9:13, 36 (see also 14:14; 15:32). And not only is Jesus a compassionate and merciful Messiah, but also he calls his followers to show mercy as a way of living out their covenant fidelity (e.g., 5:7; 9:13; 12:7; 23:23). The request of the leper (8:2) also demonstrates Jesus' authority ("you can make me clean"), another christological theme in chapters 8–9.

8:5 *a centurion came to him.* This healing story focuses on the request from a centurion, presumably a Roman, but certainly a Gentile. There was a Roman military presence in the area of Capernaum, which was near a major trade route and had a customs station. Centurions were commanders of

---

Key Themes of Matthew 8:1–17

- Jesus as healer signals the arrival of God's kingdom in light of Isaianic hopes.
- Disciples are called to have faith in the authority of Jesus over illness.
- Gentiles are included in the coming kingdom.

Narrative Outline of Matthew 8–9

8:1–17	**Three healing accounts: Jesus "takes up infirmities"**
8:1–4	A man cleansed of leprosy
8:5–13	A centurion's servant healed of paralysis
8:14–15	Peter's mother-in-law cured of fever
8:16–17	Exorcisms and healings by Jesus the Isaianic servant
8:18–22	**Discipleship teaching: leaving all to follow Jesus**
8:23–9:8	**Three miracle accounts: Jesus has authority**
8:23–27	A storm calmed
8:28–34	Demons exorcised
9:1–8	A man healed of paralysis and his sins forgiven
9:9–17	**Discipleship teachings: sinners welcomed and fasting explained**
9:18–34	**Three healing accounts: responses of faith, amazement, rejection**
9:18–26	A girl raised from death and a woman healed of bleeding
9:27–31	Two men cured of blindness
9:32–34	A demon exorcised from a man and his muteness cured
9:35–38	**Summary of Jesus' ministry and transition to the Mission Discourse**

---

approximately eighty soldiers. A centurion had a middling role in the hierarchy of the Roman army, being situated below those who commanded cohorts (consisting of six centuries) and those who commanded a legion (consisting of ten cohorts). Matthew highlights this centurion's position as both under and above others in this system (8:9) to make an analogy. The presence of *kai* ("also") at the front of the Greek sentence indicates that the centurion compares his situation in some way with Jesus' authority: "I [also] am a man under authority" (8:9). As Matthew will demonstrate, Jesus receives his authority from God and has authority over the whole created realm (e.g., 8:23–27; 28:18). Somehow, this Gentile centurion understands the nature of Jesus' authority that would allow him to heal from a distance (8:8).

8:6 *my servant.* Here Matthew uses *pais*, which can indicate a "servant/slave" or a "child." Given that centurions were prohibited from legally marrying (although nonlegal marriages were common), it is likely that this *pais* was the centurion's servant and not his son (see the parallel in Luke 7:2, where *doulos* ["slave"] is used).

8:7 *Shall I come and heal him?* Whether this verse is a question or a statement ("I will come and heal him") is debated, as the earliest manuscripts lacked punctuation needed to distinguish between the two. Contextual factors can provide evidence for either rendering, because although the immediate context shows Jesus overcoming boundaries (e.g., touching a leper), the broader context strongly emphasizes the Jewish mission of Jesus (15:24; cf. 10:5–6). Given the lack of punctuation in the earliest manuscripts, we must use grammatical cues to discern the correct reading. In this case, the presence of *ego* ("I") at the front of the sentence provides an implicit contrast as well as an emphasis suggesting that Matthew has framed 8:7 as a question: "Shall *I* come and heal him?"[1] The point of the question would be to express wonder at a Gentile coming to a Jewish healer for help. Jesus expresses similar hesitation toward the one other Gentile seeker included in Matthew, the Canaanite woman, based on his mission to Israel (15:21–28).

8:8 *Lord, I do not deserve to have you come under my roof.* Does this statement illuminate the cultural realities between Jews and Gentiles in the first century, or does it reflect a more general deference on the part of the centurion toward Jesus? Scholars who suggest the former highlight the purity concerns that Jews would have about entering a Gentile's house. Yet these issues should not be exaggerated. Most Jews would be ritually unclean regularly in the course of their lives, since ritual impurity was caused by many common life occurrences (e.g., bodily emissions, births, and deaths), and regaining ritual purity was not a particularly onerous process. Sometimes it only took waiting until sundown for certain impurities to be cleansed. Additionally, Matthew does not highlight purity concerns explicitly in this passage; instead, the missional boundary of Jesus' ministry appears to be the issue in his Gentile interactions (e.g., 15:24).

8:10 *I have not found anyone in Israel with such great faith.* This affirmation of a Gentile's faith is quite startling in the context of Matthew's story, since the focus of Jesus' messianic ministry has been on Israel (4:17; 15:24). It is not coincidental that the two characters in Matthew's story who are described (by Jesus) as having "great faith" are precisely the two clearly identified Gentiles in the story (here and 15:21–28). Prior to his death and resurrection, Jesus is portrayed as staying within the missional parameters set for him (15:24; cf. 10:5–6). After Jesus' resurrection, Matthew affirms the universal scope of the mission: to "all nations," which includes both Jew and Gentile (28:19).

8:11–12 *many will come from the east and the west.* This imagery and language derive from the Old Testament, and specifically from contexts that provide consolation to Israel during the exile. God will bring Israel's exiles back from the east and west (Ps. 107:3; Zech. 8:7). For example, in Isaiah 43:5 we hear Yahweh comforting Israel:

> Do not be afraid, for I am with you;
> I will bring your children from the east
> and gather you from the west.

The astonishing twist in the use of this Old Testament motif in Matthew 8 is that the "many" joining the messianic feast will include Gentiles. The reference to the exclusion of the "subjects of the kingdom" is not meant to be exhaustive; Jews most certainly will be included in the kingdom (e.g., the twelve disciples and the many seekers who put their faith in him [e.g., Matt. 8:1–4; 9:1–8]). The effect of the hyperbole for Matthew's audience, however, is to provide a warning against Jewish presumption of inclusion based simply on heritage (3:9) and to reemphasize the theme of Gentile inclusion in the kingdom.

8:17 *This was to fulfill what was spoken through the prophet Isaiah.* Matthew cites Isaiah to frame Jesus' identity as he does across his narrative.

Matthew	Isaiah
1:23	7:14
3:3	40:3
4:14–16	9:1–2
8:17	53:4
11:5	35:4–6; 61:1 (clear allusions)
12:18–21	42:1–4
13:15	6:9–10
15:9	29:13
21:13	56:7

In 8:17 Matthew draws from Isaiah 53:4, part of Isaiah's Servant Songs (Isa. 42:1–4; 49:1–6; 50:4–9; 52:13–53:12) (see the sidebar "Jesus as Isaiah's Servant Figure" in the unit on 12:15–21). Matthew draws upon the image of God's chosen servant to explain Jesus' healing ministry: "He took our sicknesses and removed our diseases" (8:17 NLT). Although Matthew does connect Jesus' death to the language of Isaiah 53 (e.g., allusions to Isa. 53 at Matt. 20:28; 26:28), this citation makes it clear that Jesus' entire ministry should be understood as connected to Isaiah's servant figure, who acts on behalf of Israel for restoration and wholeness.

Theological Insights: Old Testament Precursors of Gentile Inclusion

Matthew begins and ends his Gospel highlighting the theme of Gentile inclusion. Gentiles are surprising additions to Jesus' genealogy and birth (1:3, 5, 6; 2:1), and the mission to all nations closes out the Gospel (28:18–20). This Matthean theme (also at 4:15; 8:5–13; 15:21–28; 21:43; 24:14) builds on Israel's mission to the nations expressed in the Old Testament. From Abram's call to be a blessing to "all the peoples on earth" (Gen. 12:3) to Israel's mandate to be a "kingdom of priests" (Exod. 19:6), the mission of God through Israel was for the nations. While various historical books give testimony to particular examples of Gentiles included in or ministered to by Israel (e.g., Rahab, Ruth, Naaman, the widow of Zarephath), the prophets often envision a time when the nations will stream into Jerusalem and receive the overflow of Israel's redemption and restoration (e.g., Isa. 2:2–5; 60:1–3; 66:18–21; Mic. 4:1–5; Zech. 14:16–19).

Teaching the Text

1. *As he narrates the healing ministry of Jesus, Matthew indicates the arrival of God's kingdom.* By drawing from Isaiah 53 after narrating three healing miracles (8:1–17), Matthew leads the reader to view Jesus' power and compassion to heal in light of the Isaiah text: "He took up our infirmities and bore our diseases" (8:17). Although Matthew draws on a specific Isaiah text that highlights the Servant of the Lord as healer, Isaiah's broader vision of restoration enacted through this servant figure develops across Matthew's story line, as he layers in Isaiah quotations to explain what Jesus is doing (with likely allusions to Isa. 42:1 at Matt. 3:17; 17:5, and Isa. 53:11–12 at Matt. 20:28; 26:28). In Jesus, the restoration forecasted by Isaiah breaks into this world as Jesus announces the kingdom and performs healings and other miraculous signs. In this way, Matthew shows that Jesus as the Isaianic Servant of the Lord and Messiah-King inaugurates God's reign.

2. *Matthew encourages readers to put their faith in Jesus and his authority over sickness.* In the larger section of 5:1–9:38 Matthew emphasizes Jesus' authority to teach and do miracles. In this specific passage Matthew highlights that Jesus has

As Jesus enters the town of Capernaum, a centurion, a Gentile, asks for his help. Centurions were officers in the Roman military. This funerary monument depicts a centurion who served with the Twentieth Legion (first century AD).

power over illness and disease and encourages his readers to trust that Jesus is both compassionate and powerful to heal (8:2–3, 10–13). Such faith in Jesus' power, however, is not disconnected from Jesus' person as God's agent of restoration and reign. As throughout Matthew, Jesus' words and deeds point to his identity as the Messiah and the bringer of salvation and wholeness. So in our preaching and teaching of this part of Matthew we can help paint a picture of Jesus as the one who brings God's restoration and is both compassionate and powerful.

3. *Gentiles will be included in the coming kingdom of God.* The second healing vignette in this passage again highlights the Matthean motif of Gentile inclusion (already in 1:3, 5–6; 2:1; 4:15). In this text Jesus heals a centurion's servant (8:13) and comments on the inclusion of Gentiles in the coming kingdom (8:11). The fact that contemporary Christian readers are accustomed to and comfortable with the notion of Gentile inclusion in God's people (without conversion to Judaism) should not dull our senses to the surprising nature of Jesus' words and Matthew's point. Although non-Jews would have been welcomed into Israel when they converted to Judaism (via circumcision and Torah obedience), an influx into the church of

Gentiles who remain Gentiles was a surprising development within the early church (see Acts 10; 15).

Two teaching points emerge from this theological emphasis. First, Gentile inclusion is both an expression of God's faithfulness to promises made and a vision of God's wide embrace. Both motifs are eminently suitable for preaching and teaching from Matthew. Second, as the later church will struggle to understand (Acts 10; 15), Gentiles coming into the people of God through Jesus the Messiah should not be required to obey the Torah in all its facets (i.e., convert to Judaism) in order to be equal members in the church with their Jewish brothers and sisters. Matthew gives a prelude to this reality when he narrates the postresurrection Jesus calling his disciples to obey all that *he has commanded* (28:20). Torah obedience is refracted through the lens of Jesus' own Torah teaching. It is his teachings that are now authoritative for the Christian community.

Illustrating the Text

Matthew encourages readers to put their faith in Jesus and his authority over sickness.

Quote: Here is a prayer for healing from the *Book of Common Prayer*: "O God, the source of all health: So fill my heart with faith in your love, that with calm expectancy I may make room for your power to possess me, and gracefully accept your healing; through Jesus Christ our Lord. Amen."[2]

Gentiles will be included in the coming kingdom of God.

Fiction: This "letter" from the perspective of a first-century Jewish believer in Jesus, written by Bethel Seminary graduate Michelle I. Winger, illustrates the complex nature of Gentile inclusion in the early church.

Dearest Mama,

I am half-joyful, half-heartsick and turn to you for help in this time of upheaval and hope. At first I feared this conflict stemmed from my own sinful pride—that I, a Jewish wife and mother, have always kept a clean, kosher home. Now, because our Messiah Jesus has come, I am expected to let little Sarah play and study with Dianna (our pagan neighbor child!) because she too has Jesus—although it seems to be in her own way. It is more than pride . . . it is conscience. We have struggled for centuries to keep the Law, to be pure, to please YHWH, and here this little child simply believes and is accepted into God's Kingdom! Nothing in her is Jewish . . . except her Messiah.

Knowing the resurrected Christ Jesus as my Messiah, having the joy of His Spirit within me has given such peace yet excitement that I can hardly contain it! I hurry to share this Good News with the butcher, the milkman and anyone who will listen—why then, is it almost painful to open my heart and doors, and release my child to the *goyim*? To let her play with their pagan toys and eat their snacks? I am truly happy that the Holy Scriptures have been fulfilled not just for us, but for them as well . . . but here's the rub, that is so much "spiritual talk" while it is on the practical level that I ache. We have been taught not to so much as enter into a Gentile's home, and now it feels that I am breaking vows and a way of life that defined who I was, letting it all go to become who I am in Christ my Messiah. I can hardly bear it.

Can you help me? Your loving daughter

Jesus' Authority to Perform Miracles

Big Idea *Matthew encourages his readers to trust and follow Jesus wholeheartedly, as he shows Jesus' power and authority to be greater than sin, the demonic, and even nature.*

Understanding the Text

The Text in Context

Matthew continues in this passage to emphasize themes of Jesus' authority—here over sin (9:1–8), the demonic (8:28–34), and nature (8:23–27)—and faith as the appropriate discipleship response to Jesus (9:21–22; cf. 8:26). The call to follow Jesus wholeheartedly is issued in 8:18–22, picking up the call stories of the first four disciples (4:18–22) and anticipating that of Matthew, a tax collector, in 9:9. The story of Jesus' calming the storm shares a plot connection with 14:22–33, where Jesus (with Peter momentarily) walks on the sea. Jesus' (messianic) identity and the disciples' little faith are emphasized in both accounts. The story of Jesus' claim to forgive sins (9:2, 8) evokes Matthew's identification of Jesus as the one who "will save his people

from their sins" (1:21) and foreshadows Jesus' death, which will be "for the forgiveness of sins" (26:28).

Interpretive Insights

8:20 *the Son of Man has no place to lay his head.* Jesus here refers to himself as the "Son of Man," a designation familiar from its Old Testament usage. This is the first of thirty occurrences of "Son of Man" in Matthew; in each case Jesus uses the phrase to describe himself (in Matthew as well as in the other three Gospels). Although in many cases it functions primarily as a circumlocution for "I," the echoing of Ezekiel (in which God

The "region of the Gadarenes" (8:28) included the eastern shore of the Sea of Galilee (pictured here).

frequently calls Ezekiel "son of man") may suggest Jesus' solidarity with Israel. At a few key points in Matthew "Son of Man" occurs as part of an allusion to Daniel 7:13–14; these occurrences signal Jesus' vindication and authority (Matt. 10:23; 16:27–28; 24:30–31; 26:64).

8:22 *Follow me.* The message of 8:18–22 concerns discipleship, and specifically the sacrifice (8:18–20) and priority (8:21–22) involved in following Jesus. Jesus has already called four of his disciples to "follow me" (4:18–22). This call comes from Jesus and is not self-initiated, similar to the call of the first four disciples at 4:19 (see comments there). Here Jesus seems to deter one who volunteers to follow by emphasizing the cost involved (a nomadic existence). But the passage also indicates that one who is called must be ready to give uncompromising allegiance to Jesus. Rather than keeping a focus on the particular circumstances of these would-be disciples, the passage highlights the importance of following Jesus as one's highest priority and following him despite the cost (cf. 6:33).

8:26 *You of little faith.* Jesus has already referred to his disciples as those of "little faith," as they are the most explicit audience of the Sermon on the Mount (6:30; see 5:1–2). In the present occurrence their "little faith" (*oligopistos*) is tied to their fear of the storm and waves around the boat. Their fear displaces what should be their trust in Jesus, who has already shown authority over illness (8:1–17). Now Matthew highlights Jesus' authority over creation by calming the storm. The characterization of "little faith" follows the disciples across Matthew (see 14:31; 16:8; 17:20; cf. 28:17).

8:27 *What kind of man is this? Even the winds and the waves obey him?* The disciples' question that concludes the story of Jesus' calming the storm is an important one for Matthew and his readers and hearers. It is the first time in the narrative that the question of Jesus' identity has been raised explicitly since before his public ministry (1:1–4:16). The disciples have heard him teach and have seen him heal the sick. Now when they see his authority extending even over nature, they press to know what kind of man it is who stands before them. This question will guide the narrative in subsequent chapters, as Matthew highlights differing opinions of who Jesus might be (e.g., 11:2–3; 12:23; 14:1–2, 33; 15:22), culminating in Peter's affirmation that Jesus is indeed God's Messiah (16:16).

8:28 *Gadarenes.* Jesus and his disciples have now crossed the lake (the Sea of Galilee) and arrived in the region of the Gadarenes, which is part of the Decapolis (see 4:25).[1] According to Josephus, Gadara was home to Gentiles as well as some Jews (*J.W.* 1.155). A mixed population makes sense of the presence of a herd of pigs (8:30), since Jews considered pigs and their meat unclean (Deut. 14:8). It is not clear, however, whether the two demon-possessed men healed by Jesus are Jew or Gentile. Given that Matthew otherwise clearly delineates Gentile recipients of healing (8:5–13; 15:21–28) and highlights the Jewish scope of Jesus' mission (10:5–6; 15:24), it is more likely that this story also

Matthew 8:18–9:8

Who Has Faith in Matthew?

Matthew highlights the theme of faith through his shaping of different character groups. Although we might expect the twelve disciples to be those who model faith for the reader, Matthew attributes to the disciples "little faith," which is defined by fear, doubt, and lack of trust in Jesus' power (6:30; 8:26; 14:31; 16:8; 17:20). Characters who model faith for the reader include various seekers who come to Jesus for healing (e.g., 8:2; 9:2, 22, 29). "Great faith" is reserved for the two Gentile seekers in Matthew (8:10; 15:28). Finally, it is the Jewish leaders and Jesus' hometown that are characterized as lacking faith in Jesus entirely (e.g., 13:54–58; 12:24; 21:32). Combined with these narrative portraits, Jesus' own teachings on faith emphasize the power of faith in Jesus to accomplish God's work (17:20; 21:21–22).

fits Jesus' ministry to Israel in the regions in and around Galilee (see 4:23–25).

8:29 *before the appointed time.* The *kairos* ("appointed time") indicated here very likely refers to the final day (see the same phrase, *pro kairou*, with this referent at 1 Cor. 4:5), when God was expected to make all things right and Satan and his powers would be destroyed. The only explicit reference to Jesus as "Son of God" in Matthew up to this point has been Satan's taunt during Jesus' temptation ("If you are the Son of God" [4:3]). What the demonic realm seems to know already, Jesus' disciples will come to recognize (14:33; 16:16). For the import of "Son of God" in Matthew, see comments on 4:3, 6.

8:34 *they pleaded with him to leave the region.* Matthew has already begun to narrate a range of responses to Jesus and his kingdom ministry, including great faith (8:10), little faith (8:26), amazement (7:28; 8:27), and hesitance (8:21). Here the people of this town respond to Jesus' display of power over the demonic by begging him to leave. Matthew seems to be indicating

that the restorative power of the kingdom is not welcomed by everyone.

9:2 *When Jesus saw their faith.* Matthew highlights the faith of the friends of the paralyzed man ("their faith"), in concert with others in chapters 8–9 who come trusting that Jesus can heal someone they care for (8:5–6; 9:18). The theme of faith is pervasive in these miracle chapters, both implicitly and explicitly (8:2, 10, 13; 9:2, 18, 22, 28–29; cf. 8:26), as Matthew highlights the importance of trusting in Jesus' authority to heal in line with Isaiah's picture of eschatological restoration (8:17).

Take heart, son; your sins are forgiven. In chapter 8 Jesus has healed the sick, demonstrated power over a storm, and cast out demons. Now Matthew indicates that Jesus has power even to forgive sins. This scene of Jesus forgiving sins is unusual in Matthew: Jesus frequently heals, but only here does he claim to forgive sin. The scene foreshadows the Passover celebration that Jesus shares with his disciples, when he connects the Passover cup to his death (i.e., blood) as a means of "the forgiveness of sins" (26:28).

9:5 *Which is easier: to say, "Your sins are forgiven," or to say, "Get up and walk"?* With this question, Jesus responds to teachers of the law who challenge his claim to forgive a man his sins. It seems clear that it is easier to claim to forgive sins than to claim to heal, since the latter claim is easily and quickly debunked if the man remains unable to walk. But to demonstrate his authority to forgive sins, Jesus heals the man, who then gets up and walks home (9:6–7).

9:8 *they praised God, who had given such authority to man.* While the teachers of the law seem to think that Jesus has crossed a line of authority—they consider

To show that he has the authority to forgive sins, Jesus says to the paralyzed man, "Get up, take your mat and go home" (9:6). This relief from a fourth-century AD sarcophagus shows the healed paralytic carrying his bed.

created world (8:23–27), over evil (8:28–34), and over sin (9:1–8). The cumulative effect of these displays of power is to show that Jesus is the true king of all. His arrival signals the return of the rightful king of all things, whose power will be made explicit in the final moments of the Gospel ("All authority in heaven and earth has been given to me" [28:18]). So the displays of power in chapters 8–9 are displays of kingdom authority. In line with good Jewish theology, God in Jesus is reclaiming what rightfully belongs to God (e.g., Ps. 24:1).

It is fairly common to hear Jesus' miracles, both healings and especially his power over nature, used to prove his divinity. This equation has arisen from modernist debates about Jesus' identity. While Matthew does portray Jesus as the embodiment of Israel's God (see the section "Matthew's Narrative Christology" in the introduction), he does not highlight this portrayal through the miraculous deeds of Jesus. In fact, Matthew makes it clear that these miraculous deeds point to Jesus as the Messiah—that is, the human agent of God's restoring work (e.g., 11:2–5). This is Matthew's burden: to prove that Jesus is God's Messiah. In the Old Testament those who performed miracles by the power of God—both healings and miracles of nature—were not considered divine for doing so (e.g., Elijah in 1 Kings 17; Elisha in 2 Kings 6). So in preaching and teaching on Jesus' miraculous works, we might focus where Matthew does. Jesus' miracles signal that Jesus is God's agent

his offer of forgiveness to be blasphemy (9:3)—the crowd that witnesses the healing attributes the action to God, "who had given such authority to human beings [*anthrōpois*]" (NRSV). If Matthew intends a wordplay here between the "Son of Man" (9:6) and "man" (9:8), as captured in the NIV, then it is precisely Jesus' role as representative humanity that is in view in this passage (see comments on "Son of Man" at 8:20).

Teaching the Text

1. *Jesus, as rightful king of this world, has power over nature and forces that work against God's purposes.* Matthew continues to emphasize Jesus' authority in his Galilean ministry, both in word and deed. Not only does Jesus have authority over illness and disease (8:1–17), but also Matthew demonstrates Jesus' power over the

of restoration—the true Messiah—as God inaugurates the kingdom in this world.

2. *Putting trust in Jesus and following him are right responses to experiencing his authority.* Interspersed in these two chapters focused on Jesus' authority over illness, sin, and evil are discipleship sayings (8:18–22; 9:9–17). The first of these two discipleship moments highlights the cost of following Jesus. It is not enough only to be willing to follow Jesus; potential disciples are called here to count the cost (8:19–20). Since Jesus has no permanent home, his followers must reckon on following him wherever he would lead. Allegiance to Jesus displaces home and even family commitments, something that we see in 8:21–22, where family obligation is shown to be secondary to following Jesus. To first-century ears, this would sound quite countercultural, given the significance of family loyalty and obligation in the ancient world. Jesus in Matthew will speak to this question at a number of points (e.g., 10:37–39; 12:46–50; 19:29). Following Jesus means reorienting oneself in relation to all other commitments. No allegiance is left untouched.

So as we teach this passage, we might ask people to consider their loyalty to Jesus and the kingdom that he is bringing. Have other loyalties displaced this primary one? Do we value comfort and security more than the values of the kingdom? And might our families become places for reflection and practice of kingdom values such as mercy, justice, and faithfulness?

Illustrating the Text

Jesus, as rightful king of this world, has power over nature and forces that work against God's purposes.

Quote: Our modern worldview leads us to assume a God who is distant from creation, with the laws of nature alone explaining natural phenomena. So passages like this one where Jesus demonstrates authority over creation might seem foreign to our way of thinking. G. K. Chesterton, in *Orthodoxy*, suggests an interesting mediating view in this regard.

Because children have abounding vitality, because they are in spirit fierce and free, therefore they want things repeated and unchanged. They always say, "Do it again"; and the grown-up person does it again until he is nearly dead. For grown-up people are not strong enough to exult in monotony. But perhaps God is strong enough to exult in monotony. It is possible that God says every morning, "Do it again" to the sun; and every evening, "Do it again" to the moon. It may not be automatic necessity that makes all daisies alike; it may be that God makes every daisy separately, but has never got tired of making them. It may be that He has the eternal appetite of infancy; for we have sinned and grown old, and our Father is younger than we.[2]

Putting trust in Jesus and following him are right responses to experiencing his authority.

Poetry: "A Tent for a Home," by Jeannine Brown. This lyric about allegiance and security is drawn from Matthew 8:18–22:

> The fox has its hole and the bird its nest,
> But the Son has no place to lay his head,
> So they followed the Lord and they gave up their homes,
> And they journeyed as strangers.
>
> My roots go too deep, I care far too much,
> For all of the things of this world.
> So I'll follow my Lord and I'll give up my home,
> And I'll find my home in you.

"He is no fool who gives what he cannot keep to gain that which he cannot lose." This reflection was written by Jim Elliot in his journal (the page is shown here). Elliot's death at the hands of those with whom he sought to share the gospel in the jungles of Ecuador is a modern example of one who was willing to pay the ultimate cost for following Jesus.

Jesus Eats with Sinners and Heals the Sick

Big Idea *Matthew encourages his readers to trust and follow Jesus, whose healing power and mercy toward sinners signal the arrival of God's kingdom.*

Understanding the Text

The Text in Context

The final section of chapters 8–9 continues to accent themes of Jesus' authority to heal—with three healing accounts in this section—and faith as the appropriate response (9:22, 29). The call narrative of the tax collector Matthew includes a paradigmatic meal scene in which Jesus eats with "tax collectors and sinners" (9:9–13; see also 11:19; 21:31; 22:8–10). Jesus cites Hosea 6:6 in response to complaints from Pharisees that he eats with such people (9:13; also 12:7). For Matthew, Jesus rightly interprets God's law through the lens of mercy, justice, and faithfulness (23:23; also 5:7). So Jesus' pattern of eating with "sinners" demonstrates his merciful kingdom ministry. This section introduces the conflict between the Jewish leaders and Jesus and his ministry (9:34), which will intensify in coming chapters (especially chaps. 12 and 21–27).

Interpretive Insights

9:11 *Why does your teacher eat with tax collectors and sinners?* In Matthew, tax collectors are paired with sinners or prostitutes to represent those on the outer edges of Jewish society (11:19; 21:31–32). The category of sinners identifies those Jews with a reputation for routinely transgressing the Torah and its regulations. Tax collectors, because of their frequent interaction with the Roman establishment, were viewed as Jews colluding with those occupying their own land. Jesus' critics, the Pharisees, lodge the accusation that Jesus eats with such sinners and tax collectors. Banquets and other occasions for eating were significant social situations in the ancient world. Association by eating was a signal of relationship and close identification with another person.

9:13 *I desire mercy, not sacrifice.* Jesus draws from Hosea 6:6 in his response to Pharisees who question him (likewise at 12:7). In Hosea's setting, Israel's covenant unfaithfulness was condemned in spite of their seemingly appropriate worship practices (e.g., participating in sacrifices [Hosea 5:7; 6:6]). In Hosea, "I desire mercy, not sacrifice" prioritizes faithful living in relation to God and neighbor over participating in cultic (worship) practices while living disloyally. Yet neither Hosea nor Matthew drives a wedge between worship practices and other covenantal expectations. The statement in Hosea is a statement of priority, and Matthew uses the text for the same purpose of prioritization. Mercy, along with justice, faithfulness, and love, is at the center of the Torah; these four are the lens through which the rest of the Torah is understood and practiced (Matt. 12:7; 23:23; also 5:43–48; 22:34–40). Applied to the accusation that Jesus eats with "tax collectors and sinners," the Hosea citation indicates that mercy toward those who need God's restoration takes priority over purity required for Jewish worship. Purity parameters were important to Pharisees, whose more stringent purity practices mirrored those of priests at the temple (see 15:1–2), and made association at meals with some groups of people, including tax collectors, problematic.

9:14 *How is it that . . . your disciples do not fast?* See comments on 6:16.

9:17 *new wine into old wineskins.* Two sayings of Jesus (about a new patch on old cloth, and new wine in old wineskins) emphasize that Jesus' disciples do not fast because of the arrival of something new: God's kingdom. In this new time it is inappropriate to act as if the kingdom has not arrived. Yet Jesus indicates, through another analogy, that his disciples will

Key Themes of Matthew 9:9–34

- Jesus as the authoritative healer signals the arrival of God's kingdom.
- Jesus' demonstration of mercy toward sinners signals the arrival of God's kingdom.
- Placing faith in Jesus and following him are the appropriate responses to his authority.

indeed fast when he (the bridegroom) is taken from them (9:15).

9:18 *My daughter has just died.* Matthew has narrated a number of healings in chapters 8–9 (8:1–17; 9:1–8), but this is his first and singular example of resuscitation (see 11:5). Stories of raising the dead also appear in the Old Testament (1 Kings 17:17–24; 2 Kings 4:32–37), and these may form a narrative backdrop to the Gospel accounts (also Luke 7:11–17; John 11).

9:20 *woman who had been subject to bleeding for twelve years.* The account of the healing of this woman occurs in intercalation with the raising of a girl, with Matthew drawing on one of Mark's famous "sandwich" story pairs (using an ABA pattern; see Mark 5:21–43). So the two intertwining stories should be read as mutually interpretive. In both stories Jesus' compassion and authority are emphasized, along with exemplary faith (9:18, 22). Although it is possible, depending on the source of her bleeding, that the women was ritually unclean (see Lev. 15:25), it is not clear that she would

"[People] pour new wine into new wineskins" (9:17). This replica is on display at a restored third-century AD home at Qatzrin on the Golan Heights.

Matthew 9:9–34

have caused impurity to those with whom she came in contact.[1] In any event, Matthew does not highlight purity concerns in this passage; instead, he accents faith in Jesus' authority to heal.

touched the edge of his cloak. The word "edge" represents the Greek word *kraspedon*, which here refers to the tassel (Heb. *tsitsit*), which a Jewish man wore on the corners of his outer garment in accordance with the Torah (Num. 15:38; see BDAG 564).

9:22 *your faith has healed you.* Faith in Jesus' authority is exemplified by the woman and the girl's father (with faith also highlighted at 8:2, 10; 9:2). These seekers show exemplary faith, in contrast to the disciples, who only show "little faith" (8:26). Through these examples and counterexamples, Matthew's audience is encouraged to trust in Jesus' compassion and authority to heal.

9:23 *Jesus . . . saw the noisy crowd and the people playing pipes.* Matthew here reflects Jewish mourning practices, in which professional mourners were hired to weep and grieve along with the family and friends of the deceased (see Jer. 9:17–18; Amos 5:16). The playing of musical pipes often accompanied such mourning activity (Josephus, *J.W.* 3.437).

9:27 *Have mercy on us, Son of David!* The theme of compassion is reiterated (5:7–10; 9:13), once again coupled with Jesus' power to heal (9:28). The attribution of "Son of David" to Jesus by these two blind men affirms what Matthew's readers have been told from the start (1:1). Jesus as "Son of David" is a messianic affirmation (see the section "Matthew's Narrative Christology" in the introduction). Here and elsewhere in Matthew seekers coming to Jesus for healing seem to recognize his messianic status (15:22; 20:30–31). When Jesus arrives in Jerusalem, the crowds will hail him as "Son of David" (21:9, 15).

9:30–31 *Jesus warned them . . . But they . . . spread the news.* The two men ignore Jesus' warning to keep news of their healing to themselves. While Matthew picks up this motif of the "messianic secret" from Mark (e.g., Mark 1:44; 3:12; 5:43; 7:36), its use makes sense in historical context. Jesus' activity of healing begins to catch the attention of Jewish leaders (9:34) and will,

The "noisy crowd and people playing pipes" (9:23) are the professional mourners who were summoned as part of the funeral ritual. The flute players shown here are part of a larger relief of a funeral procession from the first century AD.

according to Matthew, lead to a plot to kill him (12:14). Under Roman occupation, activity by an occupied people that was perceived as potentially seditious caused alarm, both for the occupiers and for local leaders who had to give account to Rome. The large groups of people following Jesus, the spreading news of his proclamation of the kingdom of God (not that of Caesar), and the accompanying healings could have raised such concern. Jesus is portrayed as attempting to limit the impact of his growing infamy (see also 8:4; 12:16; 16:20).

9:33 *Nothing like this has ever been seen in Israel.* In response to Jesus healing needy people, the Jewish crowd is amazed. Their exclamation highlights that Jesus' ministry has been focused on the people of Israel (as noted at 4:15), although a few Gentiles of great faith appear in Matthew's telling of Jesus' ministry (8:5–13; 15:21–28). The exclamation also indicates that the crowds are open to Jesus and his work. Across Matthew, the Jewish crowds exhibit various positive responses to Jesus (e.g., 9:8; 15:31), as they recognize, in part, who Jesus is (e.g., 12:23; 21:9, 11). This should raise questions about characterizing the crowds in Matthew in a uniformly negative manner (see comments on 27:25).

9:34 *by the prince of demons . . . he drives out demons.* The Pharisees claim that Jesus' power to cast out demons derives from the demonic realm, a claim Jesus will refute (12:22–37). Matthew has provided a number of possible responses to Jesus' healing power in chapters 8–9: (1) the negative example of the Pharisees (9:34); (2) the more positive example of the

crowds (9:33); (3) the responses of faith exemplified by various seekers (8:2, 10; 9:2, 18, 22, 29).

Theological Insights: Mercy Triumphs

Matthew draws on Hosea 6:6, prioritizing mercy over sacrifice (Matt. 12:7), to highlight the centrality of mercy in God's kingdom. Already, the Torah affirms God as merciful, gracious, compassionate (e.g., Exod. 33:18–19; 34:5–7; Deut. 4:31), and the prophets assert God's mercy as the basis of their prayer for Israel's restoration (e.g., Isa. 63:7–19; Mic. 7:18–20). The songs of both Mary and Zechariah in Luke's Gospel thematize God's mercy (Luke 1:50, 54, 72, 78). And Paul exhorts his Roman audience to live a life of service because they have experienced God's mercy (Rom. 12:1), with Titus 3:4–5 affirming that salvation comes because of God's mercy. And as God is, so should God's people be. The call to be merciful resounds from Old Testament to New (Hosea 6:6; Mic. 6:8; Matt. 23:23; Luke 6:36; Jude 1:22). James, in his call

---

What's "New" in Matthew?

Matthew 9:14–17 is one of only a few places where the evangelist uses "new" (*kainos* or *neos*) language. As much as contemporary Christians are comfortable speaking about "new covenant," "new Israel," and so on, Matthew seems just as uncomfortable using the adjective. His other few uses are telling. In 13:52 teachers of the law who have become Jesus' disciples are adept at handling "new treasures as well as old" (13:52). Jesus at the Passover meal with his disciples indicates that he will not drink the Passover wine with them until he drinks it "new with you in my Father's kingdom" (26:29). Here, as in 9:16–17, the new thing is the kingdom, which is still future in its fullness. Finally, Jesus is placed in a new tomb (27:60). Such limited use of "new" language indicates Matthew's strong sense of continuity between God's promises to Israel and the actualization of these promises in Jesus the Messiah.

---

for believers to show mercy, frames it well: "Mercy triumphs over judgment" (James 2:13).

Teaching the Text

1. *Jesus' table fellowship with those on the margins flows from the centrality of mercy in God's kingdom.* In this passage we hear of Jesus' choice to associate closely (by eating at table) with tax collectors and sinners. These morally suspect individuals would have been avoided by more scrupulous Jews such as the Pharisees, especially in the close association represented by table fellowship. Matthew indicates that the priorities of Jesus rank mercy above concerns over associations that may result in ritual impurity. By citing Hosea 6:6, Matthew is not degrading Jewish purity regulations any more than Hosea is. For Hosea, it is clear that proper sacrifice and worship are important, but they mean nothing without merciful and just action toward one's neighbors (see Hosea 6:7–9). Matthew clearly upholds the Torah (5:17); Jesus is never portrayed as breaking the commandments, even when he is accused of doing so (e.g., 12:1–8). In fact, in this same passage Jesus is portrayed, almost incidentally, as paying attention to what many Christian readers would consider a less important command: the wearing of tassels on his cloak (9:20; cf. Num. 15:38). But Matthew also clearly shows that Jesus prioritizes the "more important matters of the law—justice, mercy and faithfulness" (23:23). Jesus inaugurates and casts a vision for a kingdom in which mercy is a central value. Rather than avoiding "sinners" and associating only with the "righteous," Jesus, guided by the mandate for mercy, lives among and announces God's salvation to sinners (1:21). This is a powerful message to preach in our churches. But it likely will have little impact unless coupled with a corporate way of life that embraces those considered to be outsiders. If Jesus was known as "a friend of tax collectors and sinners" (11:19), should not the church be typecast the same way?

2. *Jesus as healer and miracle worker comes from God and is worthy of our trust.* These are not new themes; instead, they continue the motifs begun already in chapter 8: Jesus' authority and the importance of faith in response to it. But as Matthew tells story after story about Jesus' ability and willingness to heal and do other miracles, the reader is led to the conclusion that Jesus

> In this passage Jesus associates with tax collectors and sinners. This relief from a second-century AD mausoleum shows a tax collection scene (Treviri, Rheinisches Landesmuseum).

is truly from God (in contrast to the Pharisees' deduction that he casts out demons by the prince of demons [9:34]). His identity as the Messiah, which emerges along the story line (e.g., Son of David [9:27]), is confirmed by his compassionate use of power. By wedding Jesus' compassion and authority (across chaps. 8–9, but explicitly at 9:35–36), Matthew provides a compelling picture of one in whom we can place all our trust.

Teaching on the message of faith is best done not by talking about faith in isolation but by focusing on the object of faith, Jesus. One of the best ways to engender faith for those we teach (and ourselves) is to provide a sustained and compelling portrait of Jesus as worthy of our faith. Fortunately, this is precisely what Matthew (and the other Gospels) provides. As much as possible, we might follow the contours of his story of Jesus. In 8:1–9:34 the vision of Jesus healing and performing miracles with power and compassion is one that can encourage people to trust him more fully.

Illustrating the Text

Jesus' table fellowship with those on the margins flows from the centrality of mercy in God's kingdom.

Quote: Mark Batterson explains why National Community Church decided to build a coffeehouse rather than a church building in Washington, D.C.

> [Jesus] hung out at wells. Wells weren't just places to draw water. Wells were natural gathering places in ancient culture. Coffeehouses are postmodern wells. . . . Too many churches expect unchurched people to come to them, but the church is called to go to the unchurched people. The church is called to compete for the kingdom in the middle of the marketplace.[2]

History: Oskar Schindler is an example of what it means to use power in compassionate ways—extending mercy to the powerless. Schindler spent his entire fortune to save the lives of some twelve hundred Jewish workers from Nazi death camps like Auschwitz. The final scene from Steven Spielberg's film *Schindler's List* movingly portrays Schindler's compassion and his regret at not working to save more Jews from death.

Jesus as healer and miracle worker comes from God and is worthy of our trust.

Literature: *The Lion, the Witch and the Wardrobe*, by C. S. Lewis. Jesus' ministry of healing, power, and compassion already enacts the redemptive purposes of the kingdom, even before his representative and salvific death. Lewis's classic tale depicts Aslan the lion healing citizens of Narnia who have been trapped by the power of the White Witch. Aslan, Susan, and Lucy visit the witch's castle, where her victims wait, trapped as statues of stone. Aslan breathes on the prisoners, and these giants, talking animals, and fauns are set free, healed from the witch's curse. Then this troupe of creatures follows Aslan to the great battle that awaits them. Even before he vanquishes the White Witch, Aslan proves to be the true king of Narnia.

Mission Discourse

The Twelve to Follow Jesus' Lead

Big Idea *In the second major Matthean discourse Jesus calls the Twelve to lead in mission to Israel, following his model as an authentic shepherd of God's people despite persecution.*

Understanding the Text

The Text in Context

The brief narrative transition between chapters 8–9 (9:35–38) and Jesus' second teaching section in chapter 10 highlight Jesus' Galilean ministry to a people who are without true shepherds (leaders) and Jesus' call to pray for "harvest workers." These themes of shepherding and mission dominate chapter 10 (especially its first half [e.g., 10:6]), often referred to as the Mission Discourse. The authority that Jesus bequeaths to his twelve disciples is for the empowerment of their mission, which is to parallel his own (10:1, 5–8). While their mission at this early stage is limited to Israel, a mission to "all nations" opens up after his resurrection (28:19). The themes of standing firm without worry in the face of persecution and opposition concludes the first half of the Mission Discourse (10:19, 22; see also 24:13).

Interpretive Insights

9:35 *Jesus went through all the towns . . . healing every disease and sickness.* This verse repeats almost verbatim the introductory summary at 4:23, indicating that Matthew is bookending chapters 5–9 to show it as a discrete section. These chapters have highlighted Jesus as teacher (chaps. 5–7) and enactor of the kingdom (chaps. 8–9). His kingdom actions focus on healing the sick, since seven of the ten miracles in 8:1–9:34 are healings.

9:36 *sheep without a shepherd.* In the brief summary in 9:35–38 Matthew introduces the topic that will characterize chapter 10: Jesus' call to his disciples to be "workers [in the] harvest field" (9:38), looking after the sheep of Israel. The motif of sheep is introduced in 9:36 and recurs in 10:6, 16: "lost sheep of Israel" and "like sheep among wolves."

10:1 *Jesus called his twelve disciples.* The people of Israel came from twelve tribes from the lineage of Jacob and continued to be identified by tribe throughout their history (e.g., Phil. 3:5). Thus, choosing twelve disciples would have been a symbolic act communicating that Jesus was restoring and reconstituting Israel around himself and his ministry.

gave them authority to drive out impure spirits and to heal every disease and sickness. The pattern of and power for the ministry enacted by Jesus in 4:23–9:34 is given to the twelve disciples here. Specifically, Jesus empowers his disciples to heal and cast out demons. The disciples, however, will not live up to what they have been given as the narrative progresses. A key example occurs at 17:14–20, where the disciples are unable to cast out a demon and heal a young boy. Jesus will attribute their inability to their "little faith" (17:20).

10:2–4 *These are the names of the twelve apostles.* Jesus' twelve disciples are called "apostles" only here in Matthew. While the term *apostolos* can be used generally to refer to someone who is sent (a "messenger"), in much of the New Testament it has a more technical sense and refers to "a group of leaders within the early church who fulfilled a role vested with some authority."[1] Matthew uses *apostoloi* to refer to the Twelve in such a technical sense. The twelve disciples are named, with some being identified by two names (e.g., "Judas Iscariot"). This was a common practice that provided a way of specifying a particular person who had a popular name. Two disciples are described by an activity: "Matthew the tax collector" and "Simon the Zealot [*Kananaios*]" (*Kananaios* reflects the Aramaic for "zealot"; cf. NRSV: "Simon the Cananaean"). The latter category indicated someone who was committed to freedom for Israel from its Roman oppressors. Several zealot movements occurred at various times during this period of

Key Themes of Matthew 9:35–10:23

- The disciples' mission is modeled upon Jesus' mission.
- The shepherding of God's people must be authentic.
- Disciples are to be bold in their witness despite persecution.

Roman occupation (see, e.g., Josephus, *Ant.* 17:273–77; Acts 21:38).

10:5–6 *Do not go among the Gentiles . . . Go rather to the lost sheep of Israel.* Matthew has indicated narratively that Jesus' ministry has been focused on Israel (4:12–16). Now he explicitly indicates the

Jesus equips his disciples with the power to heal and authority to cast out demons. He then sends them to the "lost sheep of Israel" (10:6; also 15:24), a scene perhaps captured on this ivory plaque called *The Mission of the Apostles* (tenth century AD, Constantinople).

scope of the disciples' ministry to be limited to Israel. Gentiles (*ethnē*) and Samaritans are not the focus of their itinerant mission. This resonates with Jesus' words at 15:24, where he says that he "was sent only to the lost sheep of Israel." In Matthew, the universal scope of God's mission in Jesus will emerge only after his resurrection. In the closing words of the Gospel, "Go and make disciples of all nations [*ethnē*]" is the clear directive for Jesus' followers (28:19).

The disciples are instructed not to take extra sandals and to shake the dust off their feet when leaving homes or towns that do not welcome them or the message of the kingdom. Shown here are the remains of leather sandals found in the Cave of the Letters in the Judean Desert (second century AD).

10:7 *proclaim this message: "The kingdom of heaven has come near."* The twelve disciples are given the same kingdom-centered message to proclaim that has characterized the preaching of both John the Baptist and Jesus (3:2; 4:17). The call that follows to "heal the sick, raise the dead, cleanse those who have leprosy, drive out demons" (10:8) reflects precisely what Jesus has been doing in chapters 8–9, with its various healing stories (including a leper [8:1–4]), exorcisms (8:28–34; 9:32–34), and a resuscitation (9:18–26). The disciples' call to kingdom ministry derives from the kingdom ministry of Jesus himself. Scholars have noted that the one activity characteristic of Jesus' Galilean ministry that is not reflected in chapter 10 is teaching. In addition to preaching about or proclaiming the kingdom (4:17), Jesus has been teaching

about the kingdom (4:23; 5:2; 9:35) and will continue to do so throughout the narrative (e.g., chaps. 13, 18, 24–25). The disciples, although called to proclaim the kingdom here (10:7), are not called to teach until the final commissioning scene of Matthew (29:18–20), where they will be called to teach the nations "to obey everything" that Jesus has commanded them. For Matthew, it is not until Jesus, as consummate teacher, has finished teaching his disciples that they are ready to teach others.

10:11 *Whatever town or village you enter, search there for some worthy person.* The import of 10:9–15 is to guide the Twelve in their mission to rely upon the hospitality of people within the various towns they visit. This explains the prohibition against bringing money and extra supplies (10:9–10). The reception in these towns of the disciples and their kingdom message determines whether they "let [their] peace rest" on a home or whether they "shake the dust off [their] feet" (10:13–14).

10:14 *shake the dust off your feet.* This phrase reflects the action of Jews shaking the dust from foreign soil off their feet when returning to their own land.[2] It functions here as a sign of judgment (cf. 10:15).

10:15 *Sodom and Gomorrah.* The story of the destruction of Sodom and Gomorrah because of their great wickedness (Gen.

18:16–19:29) provides the backdrop to this reference within Jesus' discourse. These ancient cities that epitomize wickedness in the Old Testament (e.g., Deut. 32:32; Jer. 23:14) are compared favorably to any towns that reject the kingdom mission of the Twelve as they travel across the land.

10:17 *handed over to the local councils and be flogged in the synagogues.* After speaking about their reception by the towns they will visit (10:9–15), Jesus alerts the Twelve to the reception they will receive from leaders and authorities. He begins by warning them that they will come before various Jewish ruling groups, signaled by *synedria* ("local councils" [see 5:22]) and *synagōgai* ("synagogues").

10:18 *brought before governors and kings as witnesses to them and to the Gentiles.* The twelve disciples will be brought before Gentile authorities as well as Jewish ones; Matthew specifies governors and kings and then mentions the Gentiles more broadly.

10:20 *the Spirit of your Father.* This phrase is unique in Matthew and in Scripture generally. It echoes ideas from John 15:26, where the Spirit is said to be sent by the Father and to testify about Jesus. In Matthew the Spirit's role in the life of the believer is promised at 3:11 (Jesus "will baptize you with the Holy Spirit") and invoked in the trinitarian formula in 28:19.

10:23 *you will not finish going through the towns of Israel before the Son of Man comes.* These words of Jesus are often read as a reference to his second advent. Yet in the New Testament, *parousia* (not used here) is the term commonly used to refer to his second advent. In Matthew *parousia* occurs at 24:3, 27, 37, 39, with

these instances clearly referencing Jesus' reappearing in the final day (see comments on 24:3). Here at 10:23 and elsewhere in Matthew the evangelist uses *erchomai* (a common Greek word for "come") along with other phrases from Daniel 7:13–14 to evoke the picture of "one like a son of man, coming [LXX: *erchomai*] on the clouds of heaven" (cf. Matt. 10:23; 16:28; 24:30; esp. 26:64). Alluding to the Daniel passage allows Matthew to picture Jesus as enthroned in God's heavenly presence and therefore vindicated by God. It becomes clear that, for Matthew, Jesus' vindication is tied both to his resurrection and to his prophetic announcement of the temple's destruction (see comments on 24:30). If this allusion and its meaning are correct, then in 10:23 Matthew's Jesus indicates that the mission to Israel will still be happening at the time of the temple's destruction.

Teaching the Text

1. *Disciples of Jesus follow in his footsteps for their mission and ministry.* While it is important to keep in mind that not all the instructions that Jesus provides for the twelve apostles are applicable to Matthew's audience, including contemporary readers (e.g., mission to Israel only, no extra clothing [see comments on 10:32]), it seems clear that Matthew wants followers of Jesus to understand that their ministry is to be patterned in particular ways on Jesus' own mission. First, the picture of Jesus as a shepherd to Israel (2:6; 9:36) connects with his call to the Twelve to go to the "lost sheep of Israel" (10:6). The shepherd picture is one of care, protection, and rescue. This is how Matthew has been portraying Jesus

in chapters 8–9, and this is how disciples of Jesus should think of their own leadership roles. Second, the centerpiece of Jesus' ministry is also the center for the preaching of the Twelve: "The kingdom of heaven has come near" (10:7; likewise 4:17). While a post-Easter message will rightly include and emphasize Jesus as rightful king and his life, death, and resurrection as the inauguration of God's reign in this world, it is important that the Christian message continue to be centered on the kingdom. God in Christ has come to reclaim and put back in right order all that belongs to God. The Christian message is not, as some have criticized, just pie in the sky—a message about how we can escape from this world and go to heaven. The gospel of Jesus Christ is written on a much bigger canvas than this. The Christian message is about God's work in this world, drawn from God's covenant with Israel, established inexorably in the coming of Jesus the Messiah and culminating at the final day when heaven and earth will be renewed and all who have trusted in and followed Jesus will experience resurrection from the dead.

2. *Followers of Jesus can live with boldness in spite of opposition because "the Spirit of [their]*

Jesus was often portrayed as a shepherd in early Christian art. This statuette is from the fourth century AD.

Father" will be with them. Jesus speaks to the twelve apostles about the inevitability of opposition and persecution in their kingdom mission and will continue to do so throughout chapter 10 (see 10:24–25, 34–36). Especially as the chapter progresses, it becomes clear that Matthew understands Jesus' words to apply to a wider audience than the Twelve. When opposition comes because of the message of the kingdom, all of Jesus' followers are assured that they will not be alone. God's Spirit will be with them, providing words for them in their defense. Later in the chapter Jesus provides a word of comfort for disciples: they need not fear those who oppose them, since God cares for them deeply and personally (10:29–31).

Illustrating the Text

Disciples of Jesus follow in his footsteps for their mission and ministry.

Human Metaphors: Various leadership books draw attention to Jesus as a leader using various metaphors of CEO, life coach, mentor, entrepreneur, and even the corporate turn-around expert. Yet we would do well to highlight Matthew's (and other evangelists') identification of Jesus as shepherd, who cares for and leads his sheep. To explore this image more thoroughly, you might draw upon Ezekiel 34 or John 10.

Quote: In his book *In the Name of Jesus*, Henri Nouwen comments on Christian leadership:

> [Future leaders] will think of themselves as enablers, facilitators, role models, father or mother figures, big brothers or big sisters, and so on, and thus join the countless men and women who make a living by trying to help their fellow human beings to cope with the stresses and strains of everyday living. . . . But that has little to do with Christian leadership because the Christian leader thinks, speaks, and acts in the name of Jesus, who came to free humanity from the power of death and open the way to eternal life. . . . The task of future Christian leaders is not to make a little contribution to the solution of the pains and tribulations of their time, but to identify and announce the ways in which Jesus is leading God's people out of slavery, through the desert to a new land of freedom.[3]

Followers of Jesus can live with boldness in spite of opposition because "the Spirit of [their] Father" will be with them.

Quote: In her memoir *The Hiding Place*, Corrie ten Boom tells of her sister's final days when they were prisoners together in Ravensbrück in northern Germany during World War II. Betsie, who had cared for other women in Jesus' name throughout their imprisonment (for harboring Jews in their home), was still preoccupied with mission even as her body was wasting away. As she was being brought to the hospital with barely any life left in her, she whispered to Corrie, "[We] must tell people what we have learned here. We must tell them that there is no pit so deep that He is not deeper still. They will listen to us, Corrie, because we have been here."[4]

Mission Discourse
Call to Allegiance to Jesus

Big Idea *Jesus calls his disciples to be loyal to God above all, to the God who protects and cares.*

Understanding the Text

The Text in Context

In the second half of the Mission Discourse, Jesus instructs the disciples how to respond to the persecution that will attend their mission. Matthew also records Jesus speaking to the crucial issue of loyalty among his followers. His paradoxical teachings about finding life by losing it (10:38–39) will resurface later (16:24–26). The theme of caring for "little ones" (10:42) will also prove thematic in Matthew in later discourses (18:6, 10; cf. 25:40, 45). The narrative conclusion to the Mission Discourse (11:1) echoes the virtually identical conclusions of the other four major sections of Jesus' teaching in Matthew (7:28–29; 13:53; 19:1; 26:1) and

leads into a narrative section (chaps. 11–12) focusing on the reception of Jesus and his message in Galilee among the Jewish leaders and people.

Interpretive Insights

10:24 *servant above his master.* A number of Jesus' proverbial sayings occur in this discourse (e.g., 10:34), including this one about slaves and masters. Jesus uses a commonplace picture, given the ubiquitous nature of slavery in the ancient world. For example,

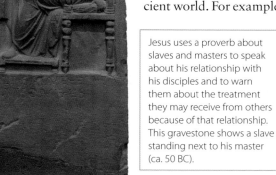

Jesus uses a proverb about slaves and masters to speak about his relationship with his disciples and to warn them about the treatment they may receive from others because of that relationship. This gravestone shows a slave standing next to his master (ca. 50 BC).

about a third of the inhabitants of Italy were slaves in the time of the Roman emperor Augustus.[1] The point of the saying is that since Jesus himself is being reviled, so too will his disciples be mistreated. Such is the pattern of slaves and masters, students and teachers.

10:26 *do not be afraid.* Three times in this part of the discourse Jesus exhorts his disciples to be unafraid (10:26, 28, 31). Given the betrayal, persecution, and mistreatment that Jesus has been predicting, this admonition is necessary. Disciples can be unafraid because God will make known every hidden thing. They can be confident to speak their message boldly and in the open (10:26–27). They can be unafraid because those who persecute them can kill only the body, not the soul (10:28). They can be unafraid because they are supremely valued by God their Father (10:29–31).

10:28 *be afraid of the One who can destroy.* Instead of fearing those standing against Jesus and against their own mission, disciples should have an appropriate fear or reverence for God, who has ultimate power over their future. This one with ultimate authority is also the one who cares for them to such an extent that even the hairs on their heads are numbered (10:30).

10:29 *Father's care.* The theme of God's attentiveness and care is reminiscent of the Sermon on the Mount, where God is portrayed as a loving Father who avoids favoritism (5:45–46), anticipates what people need before they even ask (6:8, 32), and is the perfect parent who gives good gifts to all those who ask (7:9–11). Jesus' disciples can trust that their God, the God of Israel, cares deeply for them.

Key Themes of Matthew 10:24–11:1

- Disciples are to fear only God, not others.
- Disciples are of great value to God.
- Allegiance to God supersedes all other (even family) loyalties.

10:32 *Whoever acknowledges me.* From this point on in the Mission Discourse the audience address changes from second-person (the "you" presumably aimed at the Twelve) to third-person generics: "whoever" (10:32, 38, 39, 41) and "anyone" (10:37, 40, 42). The effect of this change is a broadening of the scope of the discourse's audience to include more explicitly Matthew's readers. Reviewing the entire Mission Discourse, Jesus' quite specific instructions in 10:5–15 (e.g., do not go to the Gentiles; take no bag for the journey) keep the Twelve more keenly in mind as the recipients of these words. However, even the second-person pronouns (which are plurals throughout) begin to draw the reader into Jesus' teachings, especially as the chapter proceeds without narrative interruption (e.g., 10:19–20). As Jesus' teachings become more broadly applicable and begin including the third-person generic references, readers are encouraged to hear Jesus' words as intended more directly for themselves.[2]

10:35 *a man against his father . . . his own household.* Micah 7:6 is used here to illustrate and specify Jesus' proverbial saying "I did not come to bring peace, but a sword" (10:34). In terms of their genre, proverbs are generalities that prove true in most situations. Interestingly, Matthew will use another proverb about swords later in his Gospel. Jesus will reprimand one of his followers for

"Anyone who loves their father or mother more than me is not worthy of me" (10:37). This was a radical idea given the importance of family ties during this time. Shown here is a funerary monument depicting a Roman family from the first century BC.

focuses on allegiance to Jesus. Disciples are to count Jesus and the kingdom as their highest priority, even ahead of family and their own life. These sentiments were quite countercultural in Jewish society, where family obligations and loyalties were foremost in importance.

> On the story level focused on Jesus teaching the twelve, the metaphor of a cross would pose a vision of discipleship as a path to death, since carrying one's cross was what Rome forced criminals to do on the way to execution. Matthew is also foreshadowing for his readers Jesus' own death by crucifixion. While it is possible to romanticize the cross today, the analogy of cross to discipleship would have been stark and sobering for Jesus' hearers.[3]

using a sword to defend him during his arrest: "For all who draw the sword will die by the sword" (26:52). Understanding the proverbial (i.e., general) nature of these two sayings helps to avoid accusing Jesus (and Matthew) of incoherence; it also helps to clarify the meaning of these statements. In this case, Jesus specifies what this proverb means by reference to Micah: family discord will be a normal part of some accepting and some rejecting Jesus, who is messenger and enactor of the kingdom. Micah 7 rehearses the prophet's dismay with the covenantal disloyalty all around him. The oracle (7:1–7) ends with his affirmation to trust and hope in God alone (7:7). In analogous fashion, Jesus speaks of family loyalties that will undergo great strain when some family members acknowledge Jesus and others do not (see also 10:21–22).

10:38 *take up their cross and follow me.* This section of the discourse (10:32–39)

Matthew 16:24–26 will repeat and elaborate on the ideas of following Jesus, carrying one's cross, and losing one's life.

10:40 *Anyone who welcomes you welcomes me.* The idea of welcome for the mission of the disciples has already been introduced in 10:9–15. Here Jesus intensifies his point by identifying with his disciples to such an extent that to welcome them is to welcome both Jesus and Yahweh, who has sent him (see a similar saying in regard to children at 18:5). The three groups mentioned—prophet, righteous person, little one (10:41–42)—seem to refer to the twelve apostles and others like them who participate in Jesus' mission. God will reward anyone who welcomes and receives these missionaries and their message.

10:42 *little ones.* The final group from the saying about extending welcome is "little ones" (*mikroi*). In one sense, this group does not seem to fit well with the prophets and righteous ones of this saying. Unlike the first two groups, "little ones" does not signal a group naturally esteemed in the believing community, as prophets and the righteous are. In fact, "little ones" seems to refer to those with little status and value. This reading is clarified in Matthew's subsequent narrative. In chapter 18 the *mikroi* are those of lower status and those most vulnerable who are to be cared for by the church (18:6–14). The word *elachistos*, the superlative form of *mikros*, is used in the parable of the sheep and the goats to identify those with whom Jesus closely aligns himself: "the least of these" (25:40, 45).[4]

11:1 *After Jesus had finished instructing his twelve disciples.* The formulaic "After Jesus had finished [+ verb]" occurs at the conclusion of each of the five major discourses in Matthew and signals a transition to the narrative that follows (7:28; 11:1; 13:53; 19:1; 26:1; see comments on 7:28). The transition from chapter 10 to 11:2–16:20 involves a refocusing on Jesus' Galilean ministry (as in 4:17–9:35), with clearer indications of the rejection that accompanies his kingdom preaching and work (foreshadowed in 10:24–25). Although the disciples have been given instructions for their mission to Israel, Matthew does not narrate their actually going out in mission (cf. Mark 6:12–13; Luke 9:6). Instead, he returns his attention to Jesus' ministry and its reception. Some have suggested that to include the mission of the Twelve in the story at this point, and specifically their return, might imply that the mission to Israel expressed in 10:23 had been accomplished.[5] Instead, Matthew highlights the universal mission of the disciples in the closing scene of his Gospel. At 28:19 he makes it

clear that the disciples are now to go out in mission to all nations (including Israel). In addition, by delaying the narration of the Twelve going out, Matthew may want to draw his readers more clearly into the commissioning at 28:18–20.[6]

Theological Insights: A Singular Allegiance

A significant refrain across Scripture is the call to a singular allegiance. In the Torah Yahweh commands Israel, "You shall have no other gods before me" (Exod. 20:3 [cf. Exod. 19:5]). And Isaiah declares Yahweh as the only God, who deserves complete allegiance (e.g., Isa. 45:18–25). Matthew affirms here that same necessary allegiance and places Jesus at the center of human response to God and God's work (10:32–39). We hear similar refrains throughout the New Testament. For example, Paul writes to Roman citizens in the Roman colony of Philippi to reorient their perspective toward a kingdom "citizenship" (*politeuma* [Phil. 3:20; in 1:27 the verb *politeuesthe*, "conduct yourselves," is related to this word for "citizenship"]). And in Revelation, where the stakes for human loyalty are particularly pronounced, we hear a warning that some have "forsaken the love you had at first" (2:4).

Teaching the Text

1. *In the face of opposition, Jesus gives the counterintuitive exhortation "Do not be afraid."* A natural response to opposition and persecution is to fear those who have power to oppose and harm. Jesus encourages a different response in 10:26–31. His three exhortations to not be afraid draw

from a right theological understanding. Disciples need not fear others who might harm them, since God will disclose all things in the end, including any injustice enacted toward Jesus' followers (10:26). They need not fear, for it is God, not others, who holds the power over ultimate destiny (10:28). And they need not fear, because God cares deeply and personally for each disciple, so much so that "even the very hairs of your head are all numbered" (10:29–30). As we have seen at other points in Matthew, deep theological currents run under and through Jesus' teaching. A right view of God is rooted in a covenantal, relational vision of Israel's God (see comments on 6:32).

2. *Jesus' followers are called to acknowledge and love Jesus as their first priority.* Jesus calls his disciples to a new set of allegiances. In a cultural context that emphasizes honoring and sacrificing for one's family, Jesus speaks difficult words. He speaks of the division that may come to families if some family members follow Jesus and some do not (10:34–35). This kind of division in families occurs in our own contexts today. If family loyalty requires denying or turning away from Jesus as Lord, Christians must be ready to love Jesus more than family by remaining true to him and to his ways.

After humanity's fall (Gen. 3), idolatry—at root an issue of competing allegiance—becomes the bane of human existence. Just as Israel was called to untainted loyalty to Yahweh, Jesus calls his followers to be fully loyal to him (10:37). Following Jesus involves a path of service and devotion to him, even to the point of losing one's life (10:38–39). While not all disciples of Jesus will be pressed to that extreme,

it is instructive to note that, according to church tradition, quite a number of the twelve apostles (the specific story audience of chap. 10) died as martyrs because of their allegiance to Jesus.

3. *Welcoming Jesus' followers who go out in mission is like welcoming Jesus himself.* This idea will be reiterated later in Matthew, especially in relation to those most on the margins of the believing community, whether because of their lack of status or their meager resources (18:5; 25:40, 45). The category of "little ones" begins that idea here, since this is a status term (see comments on 18:6). Caring for those disciples least likely to be valued will bring great reward from God. In our teaching on this passage and on this theme in Matthew, we would do well to consider who in our own faith communities has little status and so potentially little value from a human perspective. According to Jesus in

"Whoever loses their life for my sake will find it" (10:39). Many early Christians were martyred for giving witness to Jesus. This column capital from the Crusader period depicts the beheading of James, the brother of John.

Matthew, we are to value and provide care for precisely these "little ones."

Illustrating the Text

In the face of opposition, Jesus gives the counterintuitive exhortation "Do not be afraid."

Mission: Elisabeth Elliot, in *Through the Gates of Splendor*, chronicles the story of five missionaries, including her husband, Jim, who were martyred in their attempt to bring the gospel to the Huaorani tribe in eastern Ecuador. Before leaving on their mission, the five missionaries (Pete Fleming, Ed McCully, Nate Saint, Roger Youderian, and Jim Elliot) sang the hymn "We Rest on Thee." The lyric of this great hymn, by Edith Cherry, exhibits the courage that we can have when we fear the Lord alone. The first stanza reads,

> We rest on Thee, our Shield and our Defender!
> We go not forth alone against the foe;
> Strong in Thy strength, safe in Thy keeping tender,
> We rest on Thee, and in Thy Name we go.
> Strong in Thy strength, safe in Thy keeping tender,
> We rest on Thee, and in Thy Name we go.

Hymn: "His Eye Is on the Sparrow," by Civilla D. Martin. The author of this hymn shared the story behind her famous chorus. One spring, while she and her husband were on holiday, they met another couple, Mr. and Mrs. Doolittle. This godly couple had experienced their share of hardship.

Mrs. Doolittle had been confined to her bed for nearly twenty years. Mr. Doolittle was in a wheelchair. Through it all, however, they had maintained an abiding joy. When asked their secret, Mrs. Doolittle shared, "His eye is on the sparrow, and I know he watches me." The promise of God's care and presence can sustain us through the most difficult trials.[7]

Jesus' followers are called to acknowledge and love Jesus as their first priority.

Church History: Early church writings contain various accounts of how the early apostles died. Some of the accounts evidence embellishment, but some of them carry marks of historical witness. All of them underline the point that these apostles considered acknowledging Jesus as more important than their own lives.[8]

Apostle	Reported Fate
James the brother of John	Killed by sword (see Acts 12)
Peter	Sentenced to death by crucifixion. Requested to be hung upside down, feeling unworthy to face death in the same manner as his Master
Andrew	Crucified
Thomas	Killed by spear
Matthew	Killed by sword
James the Lesser	Thrown down from the temple
Simon the Zealot	Crucified
Judas Thaddeus	Beaten to death
Matthias (replaced Judas)	Stoned and beheaded
John	Not martyred but reportedly scarred by boiling oil
Paul	Beheaded

Jesus as Isaianic Messiah and Wisdom Embodied

Big Idea *Matthew demonstrates Jesus to be the Messiah, who signals the kingdom's arrival by his acts of healing and preaching of good news and confounds human expectations by embodying the wisdom of God.*

Understanding the Text

The Text in Context

This passage begins a two-chapter account of various responses to who Jesus is and to his kingdom message among the Jewish people of Galilee. Beginning with John the Baptist's wonderings about Jesus, the reader hears of various responses, from the very negative responses of Jewish leaders in Galilee (12:1–45) to the positive responses of those who do "the will of [Jesus'] Father" and so are considered Jesus' family (12:46–50). The proper response to Jesus is outlined at the end of chapter 11, where

Jesus calls his fellow Jews to come to him as they would to the Torah and to Wisdom itself (11:28–30). The motif of rejection by "this generation" (11:16) will recur in subsequent chapters (12:39–45; 16:4; 17:17; 23:36). Centrally, Matthew highlights Jesus as the Messiah, who comes to enact Isaiah's restoration message (11:3–5; cf. 8:17; 12:18–21; 20:28).

Interpretive Insights

11:2 *When John . . . heard about the deeds of the Messiah.* John the Baptist reappears in the story as an inquirer about Jesus' identity. His question of whether Jesus is the "one who is to come" is prompted by what he has heard Jesus is doing. The phrase "the deeds of the Messiah" forms an inclusio

The imprisonment of John the Baptist mentioned in Matthew 11:2 would have occurred at the fortress palace of Herod Antipas at Machaerus. The archaeological remains of Machaerus are located on this mountaintop to the east of the Dead Sea.

with "[wisdom's] deeds" (*erga*) in 11:19 and suggests a wisdom Christology. Jesus has already been identified as the consummate teacher and fulfillment of the Torah (chaps. 5–7, esp. 5:17–48). Matthew now extends his Christology to identify Jesus as the embodiment of Wisdom (see comments on 11:28–30).

11:3 *Are you the one who is to come?* The characterization of John the Baptist in chapter 3 leads the reader to believe that he speaks in line with Jesus' (and Matthew's) values (see 3:1–17). Yet in this passage John wonders (through his disciples) whether Jesus is the Messiah, suggesting that Jesus is not acting in ways fully consonant with messianic expectations. Jesus' healings have been in the foreground in Matthew's narration of his Galilean ministry, and Jesus will draw from Isaiah to indicate that his healing work signals his messianic identity (11:5). Yet healings and miracles were not necessarily associated with Jewish messianic expectations, especially in terms of Davidic messianic views (see the sidebar "First-Century Messianic Views"). And the location of his itinerant healing ministry in the backwater region of Galilee also defied expectations. So John's question provides an opportunity to clarify what kind of Messiah Jesus is. In fact, Jesus' identity will be central in chapters 11–16 (e.g., 14:1–2, 33; 16:13–16).

11:5 *The blind receive sight . . . and the good news is proclaimed to the poor.* Jesus responds to the question about his identity by allusion to Isaiah 35:4–6; 61:1. Both Isaiah passages picture a day of restoration for Israel, and Isaiah 61 draws on the image of the Servant of the Lord empowered by the Spirit of the Lord (from Isa. 42:1).

Key Themes of Matthew 11:2–19

- Jesus is the expected Messiah in unexpected form.
- Jesus as the Messiah enacts Isaiah's message of healing and preaching good news.
- Jesus is the embodiment of Wisdom who experiences rejection.

First-Century Messianic Views

Within first-century Judaism there was no single view of the Messiah. In addition to conceptions of the Messiah as a royal figure, there are Jewish writings that sketch a picture of a priestly Messiah (e.g., Qumran's "Messiah of Aaron" mentioned in 1QS 9:11; CD 12:23). And the Jewish writing *1 Enoch* pictures a heavenly, exalted figure based on Daniel's vision of "one like a son of man" who takes on messianic features (e.g., 1 En. 48:1–5; cf. Dan. 7:13–14). One prominent strain of messianic expectation, drawn from Israel's prophetic writings, was a Davidic king who would reign on Israel's throne and bring about Israel's restoration (e.g., Isa. 11:1–9; Jer. 23:5–6; Mic. 5:1–9; see also Zech. 9:9–13). Within this configuration, the Messiah would confront and defeat Israel's enemies. So messianic expectations in the first century could have easily included the confronting and overthrowing of Israel's Roman occupiers. As the writer of *Psalm of Solomon* 17 prays (ca. 70 to 45 BC),

> See, O Lord, and raise up for them their king,
> the son of Dauid,
> at the time which you chose, O God, to rule over Israel
> your servant.
> And gird him with strength to shatter in pieces
> unrighteous rulers,
> to purify Ierousalem from nations that trample her
> down in destruction,
> in wisdom of righteousness, to drive out sinners from
> the inheritance,
> to smash the arrogance of the sinner like a potter's
> vessel,
> to shatter all their substance with an iron rod,
> to destroy the lawless nations by the word of his
> mouth. (17:21–24 NETS)

The message communicated via Isaiah at Matthew 11:4–5 is that Jesus' ministry of healing and preaching the good news of the kingdom fulfills Isaiah's vision of restoration. In this way, Jesus is God's agent of restoration to Israel. He has come as Israel's Messiah to heal and restore.

11:6 *stumble.* Given the unexpected nature of Jesus' messianic activity—he heals rather than overthrows—Jesus pronounces a blessing on "anyone who does not stumble on account of me." The term "stumble" translates *skandalizō*, a word used at key points by Matthew to indicate a negative response to Jesus and his ministry. Jesus' hometown takes offense (*skandalizō*) at him because they consider him a known quantity (13:57), and the Pharisees are offended by his teaching (15:12).

11:9 *Yes, I tell you, and more than a prophet.* Across Matthew, John the Baptist has been portrayed as a prophet. He eats and dresses like Elijah, the prototypical Israelite prophet (3:4; cf. 2 Kings 1:8). Here John is called "more than a prophet"; he is the one to prepare the way for God's return to Israel (3:3; cf. Mal. 3:1). John's preeminent role is clarified in 11:11: he comes at the crucial juncture of salvation history. In his preparatory role, John signals the imminent arrival of God's kingdom but does not participate in it: "Whoever is least in the kingdom of heaven is greater than [John]." He is the last of the prophets pointing forward to the time of restoration (11:13–14).

11:12 *the kingdom . . . has been subjected to violence, and violent people have been raiding it.* Although *biazetai* can be either a middle ("forcefully advancing") or passive ("subjected to violence") verb, most take it here in the passive. A related interpretive issue is whether *biazetai* should be rendered positively or negatively. If the former, then the two parts of 11:12 involve a contrast:

Jesus speaks to the crowd about John the Baptist, telling them that "he is the Elijah who was to come" (11:14). This mosaic from the Hagia Sophia in Istanbul depicts John the Baptist. The words on the mosaic can be translated to read, "Saint John, the forerunner."

"From the days of John the Baptist until now the kingdom of heaven presses forcefully, [yet] those who are violent grab at it."[1] Most take the latter tack (e.g., NIV), understanding the two lines of the verse as essentially synonymous. In either option the specific referent of "violent people" is ambiguous. Given John's demise soon to be narrated (14:1–12), Herod Antipas may be a type of the violent ones raiding the kingdom. The conflict generated by the kingdom (10:21–22) was an expected one in Jewish thought. The time of the Messiah would be preceded by "messianic woes" or tribulation for the faithful (e.g., 1QH[a] 11:7–11).

11:14 *he is the Elijah who was to come.* John the Baptist is explicitly identified with

Elijah, as he implicitly is in 3:4. This identification, based on expectations arising from Malachi 4:5–6, will be highlighted and explained at 17:10–13 (for discussion of eschatological expectations associated with Elijah, see comments on 17:10).

11:15 *Whoever has ears, let them hear.* This refrain recurs at 13:9, 43 and evokes Isaiah, where the Israelites of that time are characterized as having ears but not hearing (Isa. 6:10; 30:9; 42:19–20; 43:8; 65:12). Matthew borrows this Isaianic hearing motif in 11:2–16:20 to explain the frequent rejection of Jesus' message by many in Israel (epitomized by the Jewish leaders). He also uses this motif to highlight that the eschatological time of reversals of spiritual deafness and blindness has arrived, just as Isaiah announced (e.g., 13:11–17; cf. Isa. 29:18; 32:3–4).[2]

11:16 *To what can I compare this generation?* The term "generation" is first used here in Matthew (see also 12:39, 41, 42, 45; 16:4; 17:17; 23:36; 24:34) and refers to those who have heard and experienced Jesus' ministry and yet rejected it. This rejection and ensuing judgment are epitomized by the Jewish leaders who claim that Jesus' authority comes from the demonic (see 12:24, 38–45). The specific complaint regarding "this generation" is their fickleness and obstinacy: they accept neither John nor Jesus, even though they lodge contradictory claims about them (11:16–19).

11:19 *Here is a glutton and a drunkard, a friend of tax collectors and sinners.* Matthew has indicated that Jesus has no difficulty eating with "tax collectors and sinners," and that he is questioned by Pharisees for doing so (9:9–13). Here, in the mouths of his critics, this accusation of

Jesus' pattern of befriending tax collectors and sinners is potent. Not only does Jesus associate with those on the (moral) margins of Jewish society; he is characterized by these friendships. The accusation of being a glutton and drunkard could arise from the portrayal of Jesus' disciples (and him?) as those who do not practice the Jewish discipline of fasting (see 9:14).

But wisdom is proved right by her deeds. The deeds of Wisdom correspond to "the deeds of the Messiah" (see comments on 11:2).

Teaching the Text

1. *Jesus comes as a Messiah who enacts Isaiah's message of healing and the good news of God's reign.* It is common to hear from pulpits that Jesus was a completely unexpected kind of Messiah. However, if Jesus had defied *all* expectations for the Messiah, he would have been completely unintelligible. It is important then to discern in what ways Jesus defied expectations. This passage gives us some clues. When asked by John's disciples if he is the Messiah ("the one who is to come"), Jesus responds with a list of activities from Isaiah that would typify the time of Israel's restoration, including various kinds of healing (11:4–5). These activities, however, usually were not tied to messianic expectations. Instead, conceptions of a Davidic Messiah focused more on conquest of Israel's enemies and the ensuing restoration of Israel as a free people. Most certainly, in the first century this would involve conquest of Rome. Although Jesus will be executed by Rome, his own mission as described by Matthew is not centered on military

Matthew 11:2–19

or political victory. Yet it is not the case that Jews were expecting a political kingdom but Jesus instead brought a spiritual one—another common way of speaking of Jewish expectation and Jesus. Jewish expectation was always a thoroughgoing combination of "political" and "spiritual" goals and beliefs. And Jesus enacts a kingdom that is tangible, embodied, and politically significant. What we do see in Matthew is that, by drawing on Isaiah, Jesus is shown to be a Messiah who inaugurates a kingdom of mercy and justice on behalf of those most downcast (the blind, lame, poor [11:5]). So we might avoid preaching the kingdom that comes through Jesus as just a "spiritual" reality. Instead, we might focus people's attention on the ways that Jesus brings holistic restoration to people and to the created world.

2. *Even though Jesus' actions show him to be the Messiah and Wisdom embodied, faith is needed to recognize who he is.* Jesus indicts "this generation" for the first time here, a complaint also issued in the Old Testament toward Israel (e.g., Deut. 32:5, 20; Jer. 7:29). Jesus' complaint against his generation does not involve all Israel (since his disciples and many others show faith across the narrative), but it does signal that Jesus' identity is not transparent to the majority of those who have experienced his ministry. Matthew indicates that Jesus' deeds should be sufficient to vindicate him (the christological connection to "wisdom is proved right by her deeds" [11:2, 19]). Yet the evangelist also implies that there is an opacity to Jesus' identity, enough so that it is easy for people to stumble over him (11:6). The hiddenness of the kingdom emerges as a prominent theme in 11:2–16:20. This might also prove a helpful theme in preaching and teaching about Jesus. Although there is good reason to trust in Jesus as the Messiah, this is not readily apparent to all who are introduced to him. Rather than assuming that we can convince people of Jesus' identity by proofs alone, we may do better to acknowledge, with Matthew, that it takes faith to recognize Jesus as the Messiah.

In Matthew 11, Jesus points to his healing and preaching ministry when he is asked if he is the Messiah. James Tissot artistically captures these healing activities in his painting *In the Villages the Sick Were Brought unto Him* (illustration for *The Life of Christ*, ca.1886–94).

Illustrating the Text

Jesus comes as a Messiah who enacts Isaiah's message of healing and the good news of God's reign.

Mythology: In Homer's *Odyssey* we read of the adventures of Odysseus returning home from the Trojan War. After incredible trials and amazing feats of cunning and strength, Odysseus arrives in his home country only to hear that his wife is being courted by a gaggle of unscrupulous suitors. Operating under the assumption that Odysseus is dead, these men are hoping for her hand in marriage and a cut of his estate. When he finally comes into his household again intent on winning back his wife, Odysseus is dressed as a beggar. No one recognizes him. No one besides his aged dog realizes that he is, in fact, the master of the house. Jesus' healing ministry was an unexpected aspect of his role as the Messiah, making it difficult for some (even John the Baptist) to recognize him as such.

Applying the Text: We might encourage people to consider how they can experience healing in their own lives and their communities. One of the first steps is to identify where healing is needed. For some, the answer will be obvious; for others, it will take discernment. The following questions might be helpful:

- Is there a place of physical need in my life?
- Is there a memory and/or experience that seems to hurt any time I revisit it?

- Is there an area of discord or fracture in a community that I belong to?

Jesus has come to bring restoration. And although living in the "already and not yet" means that we will not experience full restoration from every sickness and struggle, we can and should encourage people to pray together for God's restoration.

Even though Jesus' actions show him to be the Messiah and Wisdom embodied, faith is needed to recognize who he is.

Scripture: In Proverbs 8–9 we see Wisdom personified, crying out and offering guidance to all. Yet fools and scoffers often turn away. They are confident in their own power to navigate life. But it is those who trust in and respond to Wisdom's offer who find life. These verses provide a helpful backdrop for understanding how Jesus is Wisdom personified in his offer of truth and experience of rejection. Wisdom's words are expressed in this way:

> Now then, my children, listen to me;
>   blessed are those who keep my ways.
> Listen to my instruction and be wise;
>   do not disregard it.
> Blessed are those who listen to me,
>   watching daily at my doors,
>   waiting at my doorway.
> For those who find me find life
>   and receive favor from the LORD.
> But those who fail to find me harm
>   themselves;
>   all who hate me love death. (Prov. 8:32–36)

Jesus as God's Wisdom Is a Hidden Reality

Big Idea *Rejection of Jesus as God's wisdom both deserves judgment and fits a divine pattern in which truth is hidden from the wise and revealed to unexpected ones.*

Understanding the Text

The Text in Context

In this passage Matthew's Jesus critiques various Galilean towns for failing to respond to his message of repentance (see 4:17). As in 11:2–5, the miracles that he has done are directly linked to this message and his identity (11:21–24), so their rejection of his miracles is an implicit rejection of his message and self. In contrast to the judgment that they will experience (11:22, 24; cf. 12:39–42), Jesus praises God for those "little children" who have responded rightly to Jesus' message (11:25–27). Matthew here begins the motif of hiddenness and revelation, which will recur later (chap. 13; cf. 16:17). The passage concludes with an invitation by Jesus to come to him, much like Wisdom's call to hear and obey in Proverbs and other Jewish wisdom literature, thus emphasizing Jesus as the fulfillment and even embodiment of the Torah (see 5:17–20).

Interpretive Insights

11:20 *Jesus began to denounce the towns in which most of his miracles had been performed.* After introducing the fact of opposition to Jesus' ministry in the first half of chapter 11 (11:6, 12, 16–19), Matthew turns to Jesus' predictions of judgment on those cities that have experienced his powerful enacting of the kingdom. Matthew has been highlighting these miraculous deeds

Although the residents of Bethsaida have seen Jesus perform miracles in their city, they do not respond in repentance (11:21). This aerial view shows the excavations of Bethsaida Julius near the Sea of Galilee, one of three possible locations for the village of Bethsaida referenced in Matthew.

in chapters 8–9 and has referred to these healings and other miracles as the "deeds of the Messiah" (11:2).

they did not repent. Repentance has been tied to the reception of the kingdom in the preaching of both John the Baptist and Jesus (3:2; 4:17). This theme of repentance is one that draws from Israel's prophets, who called God's people to repent and return to their God in covenant loyalty (e.g., Isa. 59:20; Jer. 18:8; Ezek. 14:6; 18:30–31; Hosea 14:1–3). In Matthew a lack of repentance is evidenced by the Jewish leaders, who have rejected John's call to repentance (3:2, 7–8; also 21:32) and will soon be characterized as lacking repentance in their demand for "a sign" from Jesus (12:38–41).

11:21 *Chorazin . . . Bethsaida.* Chorazin and Bethsaida are just to the north of the Sea of Galilee and are identified here as towns that have experienced the kingdom ministry of Jesus. Although Matthew mentions these towns nowhere else, Bethsaida is attested as a location of Jesus' ministry elsewhere in the Gospels (e.g., Mark 8:22; Luke 9:10).

Tyre and Sidon. As Chorazin and Bethsaida have been paired here, so too are Tyre and Sidon, cities that had oracles of judgment spoken against them in the Old Testament Prophets (e.g., Jer. 25:17–22; Ezek. 28:21–22; Joel 3:4–5; Zech. 9:1–3). With great irony, their fate is favorably compared to the cities that have seen Jesus' miracles but have not repented.

11:23 *Capernaum.* Jesus made Capernaum, on the northern side of the Sea of Galilee, his hometown (4:13), and it is the setting for many of the healings and miracles of chapters 8–9 (see 8:5; 9:1). Since Capernaum is Jesus' home base, it

Key Themes of Matthew 11:20–30

- Warnings of judgment are issued to those who have rejected Jesus.
- Jesus' identity is revealed to unexpected ones (little children).
- Jesus is Wisdom (Torah) personified, whose teaching is easy to bear.

is particularly incriminating that the town as a whole fails to receive Jesus' message and repent in preparation for the coming reign of God.

No, you will go down to Hades. Allusions to Isaiah 14 are evoked in Jesus' incriminations against Capernaum. The language of being "lifted to the heavens" and "going down to Hades" comes from Isaiah 14:13, 15, and is set in the context of a taunt against the king of Babylon. Babylon was Israel's archnemesis in the sixth century BC, and in Isaiah 14 Yahweh speaks of a time when Israel will mock Babylon for its arrogance (14:4–23). Although the rulers of Babylonian think they are indestructible ("I will ascend to heaven" [14:13 NETS]), Babylon will be humiliated and destroyed ("you will descend into Hades" [14:15 NETS]; cf. 14:22). "Hades" in the Septuagint (*hadēs*) renders the Hebrew (*she'ol*), which refers to the "realm of the dead" (NIV). Jesus' message to those in Capernaum who have rejected the message of the kingdom and resisted his ministry is an analogous warning: their presumptuous arrogance will actually result in their destruction.

Sodom. As the prototypical city receiving judgment in the Old Testament (see Gen. 18:16–19:29), Sodom is used in a comparison with Capernaum: "It will be more bearable for Sodom on the day of judgment

Torah Motifs in Jewish Wisdom Literature

In Sirach, a Jewish wisdom book, the author writes from the vantage point of Wisdom, much like what we see in Proverbs 8. In Sirach 24:19 Wisdom calls out, "Come to me, you who desire me, and eat your fill of my produce." This resonates with Matthew 11:28, where Jesus calls out to those who will listen, "Come to me." The author of Sirach also writes of grappling with Wisdom (*sōphia*) and directing his soul toward Wisdom (51:19–20). Then he describes the fruits of Wisdom with much the same language that Matthew uses in 11:28–30.

Sirach 51:26–27

Put your neck under the yoke [*zygos*],
   and let your souls [*psychē*] receive instruction;
   it is to be found [*heuriskō*] close by.
See with your eyes that I have labored [*kopiaō*] little
   and found myself much rest [*anapausis*].

Matthew 11:28–30

Come to me, all you who are weary and burdened [*kopiaō*], and I will give you rest [*anapauō*]. Take my yoke [*zygos*] upon you and learn from me, for I am gentle and humble in heart, and you will find [*heuriskō*] rest [*anapausis*] for your souls [*psychē*]. For my yoke [*zygos*] is easy and my burden is light.

than for [Capernaum]" (11:24). Both sayings (about Chorazin/Bethsaida and about Capernaum) function as warnings against rejecting Jesus and the kingdom, and they function as encouragements to repent and respond in allegiance to Jesus, who demonstrates his authority by performing these miracles.

11:24 *day of judgment.* Jewish expectations included a final day of reckoning. At that time God would both vindicate the righteous—his covenantal people—and bring judgment on the wicked. The prophets most frequently refer to this eschatological time as the "day of the LORD" (e.g., Isa. 13:9; Ezek. 30:3; Joel 2:31; Amos 5:18; Obad. 1:15; Zeph. 1:14; Mal. 4:5; also used in 1 Thess. 5:1–2; 2 Pet. 3:10).

Matthew here and in the surrounding context (10:15; 12:36) uses "day of judgment" to refer to that same final judgment (see also 2 Pet. 2:9; 3:7; 1 John 4:17).

11:25 *hidden these things from the wise and learned, and revealed them to little children.* In Jesus' prayer to the Father (11:25–27) the twin motifs of revelation and hiddenness come to the fore. Matthew will highlight these themes across this section of his Gospel (11:1–16:20) and will particularly focus on them in the Parables Discourse (13:1–53). Given the hiddenness of the kingdom (its "not yet" quality), revelation and corresponding faith are needed in order to receive the word of the kingdom. Jesus' prayer also signals the reversals of the kingdom: those who respond favorably to the kingdom message and messenger are unlikely recipients (as already at 5:3–10). Those of low status and who lack understanding—here exemplified by "little children"—will receive revelation about the kingdom (see comments on 18:2). Those expected to respond with understanding—"the wise and learned"—will experience the kingdom as hidden from them.

11:28–29 *Come to me, all you who are weary . . . you will find rest.* Jesus' invitation to come to him for rest echoes motifs from Jewish wisdom literature, in which Wisdom (or the Torah) is personified as calling to all those who will listen and obey (e.g., Prov. 8; Sir. 6; 51; Wis. 6) (see the sidebar "Torah Motifs in Jewish Wisdom Literature"). Thus, in this context, Matthew portrays Jesus as the embodiment of Wisdom. This christological portrait is confirmed by the other references to and emphases on wisdom in chapter 11: (1) the

Jesus says that his "yoke is easy" (11:30). One type of yoke that could be envisioned here is a wooden frame that fit around a person's neck and shoulders with the weight of things to be carried suspended equally from each side. This Roman mosaic depicts a man carrying baskets with a yoke.

inclusio formed by 11:2 and 11:19, which identifies Jesus' actions with the actions of Wisdom; (2) the inversion of expected wisdom at 11:25.

11:30 *my yoke is easy and my burden is light.* "Yoke" (*zygos*) is a word frequently associated with the Jewish law, the Torah (e.g., Jer. 5:5; Sir. 6:30; 51:26; *2 Bar.* 41:3; Acts 15:10). As a yoke would assist an animal or person in their work, the Torah was understood in Judaism to be God's instruction, providing guidance for Israel's communal life. It is significant for Matthew's view of Jesus and the law that, while Jesus can speak of his yoke as a "light load" (*phortion elaphron* [11:30]), the Jewish leaders are characterized as placing "heavy loads" (*phortia barea* [23:4]) on the Jewish people's shoulders in their interpretation and use of the Torah. For Matthew, it is not the Torah that is burdensome, but instead particular ways of interpreting it and drawing from it for living.

Theological Insights: Jesus as God's Wisdom

As we have seen in this passage, Proverbs 8 (along with some Second Temple Jewish texts) prefigures the connection that Matthew makes between Wisdom and Jesus. Other New Testament writers take up this connection and develop it. John's Gospel begins by identifying Jesus with the "Word" (*logos* [1:1, 14]), which in Jewish writings was fairly interchangeable with Wisdom (e.g., Wis. 9:1–2).[1] John indicates that the Word was present and active at the creation of the world (compare with Wisdom in Prov. 8:22–31). A similar christological picture is present in Colossians 1:15–16. By this implicit comparison, "Paul has shifted the focus from God's creation through . . . Wisdom to God's creation through Christ."[2] Finally, Paul makes explicit the connection between Jesus the Messiah and Wisdom when he writes of "Christ the power of God and the wisdom of God" (1 Cor. 1:24 [cf. 1:30]).

Teaching the Text

1. *Jesus warns the people who have heard his message and seen his signs but have not responded in repentance.* In concert with the Old Testament prophets, Jesus announces that God's judgment will come upon those towns that have rejected his message of the kingdom. In fact, even the most evil cities of the ancient world

are compared favorably with the fate of Capernaum, Chorazin, and Bethsaida, the towns that have been the recipients of Jesus' ministry. Some have wondered if part of the reason John the Baptist does not fully recognize Jesus as doing what the Messiah would do (11:2–3) is that John envisions the Messiah as the bringer of judgment upon those unrepentant in Israel, as he himself has preached (3:7–12). In the present passage we see Jesus announcing that God will respond to people's lack of repentance "on the day of judgment" (11:22, 24), but we do not see him enacting that judgment in the present. For Matthew, judgment waits until that final day (see 13:24–30; 16:27). Jesus does warn of the coming judgment based on how people have responded to his kingdom message and actions, but his work in the present focuses on giving rest to those who are weary and burdened (11:28–30).

2. *The reversals of the kingdom extend to the revelation of God's reign.* According to Jesus in 11:25–27, those most expected to understand who he is and the signs of the arrival of the kingdom will experience the kingdom as hidden and opaque. The unexpectedness of the kingdom is due, in part, to the unlikely nature of the recipients of the kingdom. Those who are characterized as lacking understanding and status—little children—are those who receive revelation of the kingdom. This fits the theme of kingdom reversals elsewhere in Matthew (e.g., 18:1–5; 21:14–16; see also 9:9–13). What about this theme for preaching and teaching Matthew? It is a good reminder for us that no one sits outside the scope of God's restoration activity. In fact, those whom we might be most likely to write off as unresponsive to and unable to understand Jesus and his kingdom message may be precisely those to whom God is revealing Jesus.

3. *As Wisdom personified, Jesus offers rest for all those who will follow his ways.* In contrast to those who teach the law in ways that are onerous and who fail to show people how to live faithfully by it, Jesus teaches and lives out the Torah in a way that provides rest for his followers. Since he is the very embodiment of Wisdom, his yoke is easy and light. His covenant loyalty provides the model for our own. Even more than this, because he is Wisdom, joining ourselves to Jesus and his way of living means that he teaches us the way: "Learn

Jesus warns the people of Chorazin of future judgment because they do not repent in spite of the miracles they have witnessed (11:21). This aerial view shows the third- and fourth-century AD reconstructed remains at ancient Chorazin. Earlier structures have yet to be found.

from me, for I am gentle and humble in heart, and you will find rest for your souls" (11:29).

Illustrating the Text

Jesus warns the people who have heard his message and seen his signs but have not responded in repentance.

Literature: *A Christmas Carol*, by Charles Dickens. In Dickens's famous story, Ebenezer Scrooge is warned about his miserly way of life by three visiting ghosts: the Ghost of Christmas Past, the Ghost of Christmas Present, and the Ghost of Christmas Yet to Come. Scrooge has spent his whole life pursuing and hoarding money rather than caring for others, and these ghosts come to warn him of the dire future that awaits him for living this way. Yet the warnings are intended to change Scrooge—to stop him in his tracks and cause him to change his course. What the ghosts envision for Scrooge may not come to pass, if only he will embrace a life of generosity. Jesus' warnings of future judgment for rejecting him are meant to function as a similar kind of deterrent for Matthew's audience. Matthew highlights these warnings (11:20–24) alongside Jesus' offer of wisdom and rest (11:25–30) in order to provide his readers with a choice. Which path will they take? Will they respond in faith to Jesus or reject him as Messiah? Only one path leads to life and rest.

It might be useful to share Dickens's preface to *A Christmas Carol*. It illustrates the impact that the warnings to Scrooge were meant to have on Dickens's audience: "I have endeavoured in this Ghostly little book, to raise the Ghost of an Idea, which shall not put my readers out of humour with themselves, with each other, with the season, or with me. May it haunt their houses pleasantly."[3]

As Wisdom personified, Jesus offers rest for all those who will follow his ways.

Film: *The Mission*. In this 1986 movie, Rodrigo Mendoza (played by Robert De Niro) is a mercenary slaver who makes his living off of kidnapping the natives from the Guaraní community and selling them to plantations. Mendoza murders his brother in a fit of passion and is then overcome by depression after the murder. A Jesuit priest, Father Gabriel (played by Jeremy Irons), who is ministering to the Guaraní, challenges Mendoza to take on a penance for his actions by carrying a large net full of heavy armor and weapons up a steep cliff along a waterfall in the South American jungle. Mendoza struggles with the weight of this penance in the rugged terrain. In a powerful scene, others seek to assist him, trying to remove the burden from him, but in the end the only ones who can offer him release are those he has sinned against. They alone can remove his burden. Once atop the cliff, he encounters a group of the very same people from among whom he had made slaves, and they cut loose the heavy net and push it into the river. His repentance and their forgiveness lead to true transformation and rest.

Matthew 11:20–30

Sabbath Controversies with the Pharisees

Big Idea *Matthew portrays Jesus (versus the Jewish leaders) as the true interpreter of the Torah, who understands its center to be mercy and who keeps the Sabbath while also being Lord over it.*

Understanding the Text

The Text in Context

This passage, which focuses on Jesus as rightly interpreting the Torah, follows directly Matthew's comparison of Jesus to Wisdom, whose instruction (yoke) is "easy" (11:28–30; cf. 11:19). Here Matthew begins to narrate the heightened conflict between the Galilean Jewish leaders, specifically the Pharisees, and Jesus. This conflict will be the focus of chapter 12. Jesus' earlier altercations with Galilean Pharisees resulted from his eating with tax collectors and sinners (9:9–13) and his healing activity (9:34). In chapter 12 the conflict arises from his interpretation of Sabbath regulations (12:1–14) as well as the origins of his healing power (12:22–29). In subsequent chapters Matthew will introduce oral traditions concerning the law as another point of conflict between the Pharisees and Jesus (15:1–20). In these various debates Matthew emphasizes that Jesus rightly interprets the Torah through the lens of mercy (9:13; 12:7), a theme that Matthew connects closely with Jesus' works of healing (e.g., 9:34–38; 12:15–21).

Interpretive Insights

12:2 *When the Pharisees saw this.* The Pharisees as opponents of Jesus have already made their appearance in the narrative before this point (3:7–10; 5:20; 9:9–17, 32–34). Here in chapter 12 the Pharisees contest a point of Torah interpretation with Jesus, namely, whether Jesus' disciples are breaking the Torah by gleaning and eating grain from a field on the Sabbath (12:1–2). Given that the Pharisees had a reputation among the Jewish people for their careful and scrupulous adherence to the Torah, it is not surprising that they are Jesus' primary opponents in Matthew. The evangelist frequently compares Jesus' interpretation and adherence to the law with that of the Pharisees to show Jesus as the consummate Torah interpreter (12:1–14; 15:1–20; 19:1–12; 22:34–40).

Your disciples are doing what is unlawful on the Sabbath. Matthew follows Mark in clustering the Sabbath controversies here (see Mark 2:23–3:6). In this first account (12:1–8) it is Jesus' disciples who are accused of breaking the Sabbath. Adherence to the Sabbath was a pillar of Judaism. It was one of the commandments given to Israel as God established the covenant with them (Exod. 20:8–11), and it defined Judaism within its first-century Roman context. The Roman writer Juvenal describes the Jews as those "who have had a father who reveres the Sabbath, worship nothing but the clouds, and the divinity of the heavens, and see no difference between eating swine's flesh . . . and that of [humans]" (*Sat.* 14, 96–99). In fact, in the time of Jewish persecution during the reign of Antiochus IV (175–164 BC), Jews were killed for keeping the Sabbath against royal edict (1 Macc. 1:41–64). So the debate that we hear in this Matthean passage is fundamental to Jewish identity and values.

12:3 *Haven't you read what David did . . . ?* Jesus' answer to the Pharisees' accusation that his disciples are breaking the Torah involves a scriptural precedent from 1 Samuel 21:1–6. In that text David's men are given bread to eat from the bread consecrated for the priests. David justifies this action because his men are on a holy mission. The implication of this textual reference is to exonerate Jesus' disciples based on the nature of their mission: they serve the mission of Jesus, who will prove to be not only the son of David but also David's Lord (22:41–46). So the disciples are innocent of the charge of transgressing the law (12:5–6).

Key Themes of Matthew 12:1–14

- Jewish leaders reject Jesus.
- Jesus is both keeper and Lord of the Sabbath.
- Mercy takes priority over sacrifice for interpreting Torah.

12:5 *Or haven't you read in the Law . . . ?* If there is a specific Scripture text in mind here, it may be Numbers 28:9–10, which instructs Israel's priests to make sacrificial offerings on every Sabbath day. As in 12:3–4, the argument here is that Jesus' disciples are innocent of breaking the Sabbath, based on their special role in God's present work. As the priests were allowed special exemption to serve in the temple, so also the disciples, who are involved in service to "something greater than the temple."

12:6 *something greater than the temple is here.* This part of Jesus' argument indicates that Jesus' disciples are free from blame because what they are a part of is greater than the mission that David's men

When the Pharisees criticize the actions of the disciples on the Sabbath, Jesus points to the example of David taking and eating the consecrated bread from the tabernacle. This model of the table for the bread of the presence holding the consecrated bread is part of the tabernacle replica at Timna, Israel.

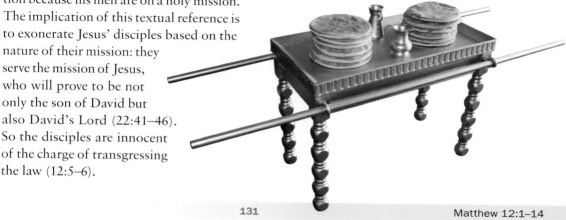

and Israel's priests were serving. "Something" renders the Greek word *meizon*, a neuter adjective that here indicates the comparison is between the temple and a nonpersonal entity. This means that Jesus is not part of the comparison being expressed here, although some have read it this way (e.g., NIV 1984; NLT).[1] In the context of Jesus' comparison between the situation of David (and the Old Testament priests) and the current situation of Jesus and his disciples (and in the wider context of 11:11–12; 12:25–28), the most likely referent for the "something greater" is the kingdom.

12:7 *I desire mercy, not sacrifice.* Matthew draws upon Hosea 6:6 for the second time in his Gospel (see 9:13), reflecting Jesus' prioritization of mercy and compassion in line with Hosea's prophetic message. Applied to the Pharisees' accusation against the disciples of Jesus, the Hosea citation indicates that compassion toward the disciples in their hunger and need for sustenance as they go about kingdom ministry is more important than the Pharisees' way of interpreting and applying Sabbath regulations. Matthew vindicates Jesus' interpretation and practice of the Sabbath (12:3–6); neither Jesus nor his disciples break the Sabbath (12:7).

you would not have condemned the innocent. With these words of Jesus, Matthew clearly exonerates the disciples of the charge that the Pharisees make against them. Matthew uses here the same term, "innocent" (*anaitios*), that he uses of the priests in their temple service in 12:5 (the only occurrences of this word in the New Testament).

12:8 *For the Son of Man is Lord of the Sabbath.* This final maxim of Jesus

fits well in his Jewish context. A Hebrew commentary on the book of Exodus offers the following: "The Sabbath is given to you; you are not given to the Sabbath" (*Mekilta* on Exod. 31:14). This similar teaching (whether known by Matthew or not) suggests that we interpret Jesus' statement with a view to his role as representative Israel and humanity (see comments on "Son of Man" at 8:20). If this is the case, Jesus as humanity par excellence illumines the truth that the Sabbath was always intended as a gift for Israel's benefit. The Sabbath command is given for people, not vice versa. In line with 12:6, however, other commentators have read this maxim as highlighting the unique authority that Jesus as Son of Man has over all things, including the Sabbath.

12:10 *Is it lawful to heal on the Sabbath?* This question by the Pharisees is their second challenge to Jesus regarding the Sabbath. Matthew explicitly narrates their motives: "looking for a reason to bring charges against Jesus" (12:10).

12:11–12 *If any of you has a sheep . . . ? How much more valuable is a person than a sheep!* Jesus makes an argument from lesser to greater in his response to the Pharisees. This a fortiori argument is a common form of Jewish argumentation. A similar one is used in the Talmud to teach that the Sabbath may be broken when a human life is in danger (*b. Yoma* 85a–b). Yet Jesus' argument is based on the value of a human being above an animal's life. An animal that falls into a pit, he argues, would engender the owner's compassion and so would move the owner to rescue it. Jesus seems to draw on general practice here rather than any particular scriptural text or example. The theme of compassion or mercy is highlighted in Jesus' argument, as at 12:7. On doing good as the centerpiece of the law, see 7:12.

12:13 *it was completely restored.* This account of a Sabbath healing anticipates the summary of Jesus' healing activity that comes in 12:15. As such, it signals a return to Matthew's focus on Jesus' healing ministry (begun in 8:1–9:34), which will be in the spotlight in 12:15–26, as well as in chapters 15, 17, and 21.

12:14 *the Pharisees went out and plotted how they might kill Jesus.* The reader has already heard of the Pharisees' antagonism toward Jesus: they attribute his healing power to the demonic (9:34). Here, however, Matthew makes explicit that they begin to plot Jesus' death. This intensification of the conflict between Jesus and

Jewish leaders will eventually lead to Jesus' death (see 16:21; 26:1–4; 27:20).

Teaching the Text

1. *God's mercy is the lens through which we ought to understand our covenant obligations.* In teaching on the topic of Jesus and the Sabbath, it is common enough to portray Jesus as one who breaks Sabbath rules for greater purposes (to see this tendency, search the internet for "Jesus Sabbath breaker"). The resulting portrayal fits well with our cultural affinity for mavericks and nonconformists. In fact, sometimes our portrait of Jesus resembles a figure from our imaginings of the Wild West more than a first-century Jewish man. Part of this tendency arises from our ambivalence about the Jewish law, particularly the parts that focused on the Jewish temple, purity concerns, and Sabbath regulations. Yet

> "If any of you has a sheep and it falls into a pit on the Sabbath, will you not take hold of it and lift it out?" (12:11).

When the Pharisees ask Jesus if it is lawful to heal on the Sabbath, Jesus responds by showing the importance of mercy and healing a man with a shriveled hand. This scene is depicted on a fourteenth-century AD mosaic in the Chora Monastery, now a museum, in Istanbul.

Matthew has no problem accenting Jesus' adherence to the Torah and his claims that he and his followers are innocent of the charge of breaking the Jewish law. For Matthew, Jesus differs from certain Jewish teachers in his care for the central theme of mercy (9:13; 12:7). This theme itself is inherent in the Torah and is emphasized by the Hebrew prophets as they expound on the Torah (Hosea 6:6). So instead of making the Jewish law the foil in order to preach about the greatness of Jesus (i.e., law = bad; Jesus = good), we might follow Matthew's lead. We might help people understand how Jesus, as a good Jew, kept the Torah. And we might help them understand how, as the Jewish Messiah, he was the consummate teacher and embodiment of the Torah, even though he will call his followers to obedience to *his* commands after his resurrection (28:20 [see comments there]). In the end, Jesus rightly places mercy at the center of his teaching on God's law. And so it might just be that the Christian way of nonconformity is best defined by our compassion.

2. *The time of the kingdom has begun; something (and someone) new has arrived.* With the statement that "something greater than the temple is here," Matthew's Jesus points to the arrival of God's reign over all of life. The mission of Jesus and his disciples has precedence over what came before, not because what came before was deficient but because the kingdom is the climax of the covenant. When the kingdom comes in its fullness, it will bring about the culmination of God's restoration of Israel and the nations for all those who follow the ways of Jesus. And as Matthew will make very clear by the end of his narrative, Jesus is the king who inaugurates God's reign, and Jesus is Lord of the Sabbath and of everything "in heaven and on earth" (28:18).

Illustrating the Text

God's mercy is the lens through which we ought to understand our covenant obligations.

Human Experience: When you take an eye exam, the optometrist has you look through various sets of lenses to determine your prescription. Bit by bit, the doctor zeroes in on the proper numbers. "Which looks clearer, A or B?" Some more adjustments. "Now which looks clearer, A or B?" More adjustments are made until, finally, the doctor leans back, jots a few notes, and lets you know what degree of correction your eyes require. According to Jesus, the proper lens for clearly understanding God's requirements is the lens of mercy. In this way, mercy toward others should guide our attitudes, behaviors, and dispositions.

Scripture: Prior to Jesus' emphasis on mercy, the Old Testament highlights the priority of mercy. In Psalms the writers cry out for God to show mercy again and again, on the assumption that God is a God of mercy. Indeed, God's "great mercy" is emphasized in, for example, Psalms 25 and 69. Sharing some examples could help people understand the continuity between Old and New Testaments on this issue.

> Remember, LORD, your great mercy and love,
> > for they are from of old.
> Do not remember the sins of my youth
> > and my rebellious ways;
> according to your love remember me,
> > for you, LORD, are good. (Ps. 25:6–7)

> Answer me, LORD, out of the goodness of your love;
> > in your great mercy turn to me. (Ps. 69:16)

The time of the kingdom has begun; something (and someone) new has arrived.

Quote: In her book *The Misunderstood Jew*, Amy-Jill Levine notes how often we make Judaism a "fall guy" in the Gospels. Warning against this tendency, she writes that Christians often attempt to make Jesus relevant "by projecting a negative stereotype of Judaism or by erasing Judaism entirely. The proclamation of the church can, and should, stand on its own; it does not require an artificial foil, an anti-Jewish basis, or an overstated distinction."[2] The newness of the kingdom does not require us to malign what is old, especially since Matthew does not lead us in this direction.

Human Experience: You might draw upon the ways we anticipate and celebrate major events in life: a new job, a wedding, the birth of a baby, a retirement, or an exciting vacation. This anticipation and celebration give just a glimpse of the way many first-century Jews would have anticipated the kingdom's arrival.

Jesus as the Isaianic Servant of the Lord

Big Idea *Matthew shows Jesus' withdrawal from his antagonists and his admonition to secrecy to be signs of his identity as the Isaianic Servant of the Lord, who will proclaim justice to all the nations.*

Understanding the Text

The Text in Context

Following the Sabbath debates between the Pharisees and Jesus, Matthew narrates that Jesus withdraws from controversy and turns to the crowd, which needs and receives his compassionate healing activity (12:15). This first of three withdrawals from controversy (also 14:13; 15:21) is followed by a warning against publicly reporting Jesus' healings (cf. 8:4; 9:30). Matthew then provides direct commentary on the compassionate healings and subsequent call to secrecy by inserting a quotation from Isaiah 42, the longest citation in Matthew's Gospel (Isa. 42:1–4; Matt. 12:18–21). Matthew has already

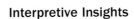
Matthew connects the phrase from Isaiah 42, "I will put my Spirit on him," with the descent of the Holy Spirit on Jesus after his baptism (3:16–17). This scene is depicted on this ivory panel from the fifth century AD.

drawn upon Isaiah's Servant Songs to identify Jesus and his ministry in line with Isaiah's servant figure (8:17). He further emphasizes Jesus as God's chosen servant here and will do so again via allusions to Isaiah 53 in 20:28; 26:28.

Interpretive Insights

12:15 *Jesus withdrew from that place.* Matthew narrates Jesus withdrawing from controversy three times in 11:2–16:20, each time using the verb *anachōreō* (12:15; 14:13; 15:21). In each case the previous passage recounts a point of controversy: in two cases between Jesus and the Pharisees (12:1–14; 15:1–20), and in one case between Herod and John. In all three instances Jesus withdraws from these points of controversy to focus his attention on healing (12:15; 14:14; 15:22, 30). This narrative motif connects nicely to the part of the quotation from Isaiah 42 that speaks of Yahweh's servant not quarreling or crying out (12:19a).

A large crowd followed him, and he healed all who were ill. This summary of Jesus' healing ministry resembles the other summaries that Matthew provides for Jesus' Galilean ministry. The initial twin summaries (4:23–25; 9:35) frame Jesus' teaching and enacting of the kingdom (chaps. 5–9). The three summaries interspersed in 11:2–16:20 remind the reader that Jesus announces the arrival of the kingdom not only in his words but also by the healings that he performs (12:15; 14:34–36; 15:29–31). These healings signal Isaianic restoration (11:5; 12:18–21).

12:16 *He warned them not to tell others about him.* Matthew's use of this "messianic secret" motif (8:4; 9:30; 16:20) makes sense within the context of Roman occupation and Jewish messianism (see comments on 9:30–31). The subsequent Isaiah quotation speaks of how "no one will hear his voice in the streets" (12:19) and links the portrait of the servant figure with Jesus' warning to remain quiet about his healings.

12:17 *what was spoken through the prophet Isaiah.* The ensuing scriptural citation is the longest one in Matthew and provides a number of narrative and thematic connections for his purposes. First and foremost, Jesus is identified with the servant of Yahweh who brings restoration to Israel and to the nations. Narratively, Isaiah's identification of the Spirit upon the servant figure corresponds to Matthew's

baptism scene, where the Spirit comes upon Jesus as he begins his public ministry (3:13–17). In fact, the baptism scene includes evocations of Isaiah 42:1. A connection to the immediate narrative context of Matthew is the reference to the messianic-secret motif. Thematically, three additional themes are expressed in the Isaiah quotation that Matthew utilizes: justice (12:18, 20), mercy (12:20), and Gentile inclusion in restoration (12:21).

12:18 *Here is my servant.* Matthew has already implicitly affirmed Jesus as Isaiah's servant figure (3:17; 8:17). At 12:18–21, close to the midpoint of Jesus' Galilean ministry, Matthew makes it clear that Jesus is the Spirit-anointed servant of Yahweh who enacts a ministry of justice and mercy for Israel and on behalf of the nations (see the sidebar "Jesus as Isaiah's Servant Figure").

the one I love, in whom I delight. These two verbal descriptors of the Isaianic servant (*ho agapētos* and *eudokēsen*) have already been used of Jesus at his baptism: "This is my Son, whom I love [*ho agapētos*]; with him I am well pleased [*eudokēsen*]" (3:17). Matthew has aligned 3:17 and 12:18 to strengthen the allusion to Isaiah 42 in the baptism scene (the two verbs differ from those in Isa. 42:1 LXX). For Matthew, Jesus is portrayed as the Isaianic servant from his baptism onward.

Jesus as Isaiah's Servant Figure

Isaiah is crucial to Matthew's Christology. The evangelist repeatedly cites and alludes to the Servant Songs of Isaiah (Isa. 42:1–4; 49:1–6; 50:4–9; 52:13–53:12). Citations occur at 8:17 (Isa. 53:4) and 12:18–21 (Isa. 42:1–4). Both clearly set Jesus' ministry in the context of the mission of Isaiah's servant figure. Allusions to the Servant Songs occur at 3:17 and 17:5 (Isa. 42:1), and 20:28 and 26:28 (Isa. 53:11–12). Other likely allusions to Isaiah 53 occur especially in Matthew's Passion Narrative (Isa. 53:5, 7, 9 in Matt. 26:63, 67; 27:12, 14, 57).

What is the nature of this connection between Isaiah's servant figure and Jesus? First, it is important to note that in Isaiah this figure, although personified individually (e.g., 49:5–6), is also identified with the nation of Israel (41:8; 44:1, 21; 45:4; 49:3). The identity and mission of Israel were to be enacted by Israel or by this servant figure on behalf of Israel. This means that Matthew's use of these Isaiah texts heightens the comparison that he already has introduced between Jesus and Israel (e.g., 2:15). Second, Matthew uses Isaiah to explain Jesus' ministry and mission. He interprets Jesus' ministry in terms of the servant's mission to bring mercy and justice to Israel and the nations (see Isa. 42:1–4; Matt. 12:18–21). And he interprets Jesus' death in light of the servant's role in dealing with evil, sin, and suffering for Israel and for the nations (Isa. 53).

I will put my Spirit on him. Matthew applies these words from Isaiah to Jesus, confirming the narrative portrayal of the Holy Spirit coming upon Jesus at his baptism (3:16–17). Early on in Matthew the Holy Spirit has an active role in the life of Jesus. Jesus is conceived through the Holy Spirit (1:18, 20). Jesus is anointed by the Spirit at his baptism (3:16), and the Spirit leads him into the wilderness where he is tempted (4:1). Yet when Jesus begins his public ministry, the Spirit seems virtually absent. But Matthew makes it quite clear in 12:18 that the Spirit has been upon Jesus throughout his ministry: "Here is my servant . . . I will put my Spirit on him, and he will proclaim justice to the nations."

12:19 *no one will hear his voice.* Although this line of the Isaiah quotation may

be most closely linked to the messianic-secret motif in 12:16, it also contributes to a motif of hearing woven though Matthew 11:2–16:20.[1] By making the verb "hear" active rather than passive (as in the Hebrew text and the LXX), Matthew has heightened an emphasis on hearing as a human response to Jesus. In the case of the quotation and its context in Matthew, the emphasis falls on those who lack the ability or inclination to hear in a positive sense the message of Jesus.[2] In the immediate context, the Pharisees reject Jesus' teaching and ministry and plot his demise (12:14, 24).

12:20 *A bruised reed he will not break, and a smoldering wick he will not snuff out.* These two images from Isaiah are compelling visions of compassion. The Lord's servant, now identified as Jesus by Matthew, will not even break off a reed bruised at its bending point, though this seems a natural enough thing to do. And while it is commonplace to snuff out a wick that no longer has a flame but only a bit of smoke remaining, the Lord's servant will not even do this. This fits Matthew's vision of Jesus as merciful Messiah (see 8:3; 9:36; 14:14; 15:32).

till he has brought justice through to victory. For a second time the Isaiah 42 citation accents the theme of justice in the mission of the Servant of the Lord (cf. 12:18: "he will proclaim justice to the nations"). For Matthew, this theme is a natural one to apply to Jesus' ministry and mission on behalf of the poor and downcast. As Richard Beaton notes, "Matthew's Jesus, in a non-confrontational manner, offers justice to the poor, sick and lame and to the harassed crowds."[3] In addition to this

use of Isaiah 42 to frame Jesus' ministry of justice, elsewhere Jesus speaks of the centrality of justice for interpreting and obeying the Torah, where justice is one of three most important values (23:23). Also, if *dikaiosynē* in the beatitudes is best rendered "justice" (see 5:6), then God's coming reign as typified by the arrival of justice headlines the Sermon on the Mount.

12:21 *In his name the nations will put their hope.* Although Matthew focuses Jesus' ministry on Israel (10:5–6; 15:24), he also consistently points ahead to the promise of Gentile inclusion (e.g., 1:3–6; 4:15; 8:10–11; 28:19). Isaiah 42:1–4 provides him another opportunity to do so, with its references to "the nations" (*ethnē* [12:18, 21]). Jesus, in his role as the Isaianic servant who acts on Israel's behalf, will "proclaim justice to the nations" so that "in his name the nations will put their hope."

Theological Insights: Mission for Justice

Matthew has already signaled the connection between the kingdom and restoration of justice (5:6, 10 [see comments there]). In chapter 23 he alludes to Micah 6:8 to emphasize the "weightier matters of the Torah," which include justice (23:23). The Torah held Israel accountable for practicing justice (e.g., Exod. 23:1–9; Deut. 16:18–20), and the Old Testament prophets emphasized Israel's obligations to enact

Matthew identifies Jesus, who in 12:15 heals all the sick who come to him, as the servant figure described by Isaiah who enacts mercy and justice. This mosaic from the Chora Monastery (now a museum) in Istanbul, shows a group of people who have come to Jesus for healing (fourteenth century AD).

justice in line with the Torah (e.g., Ezek. 22; Hosea 12:6; Amos 5; Hab. 1:4; Zech. 7:8–10). Luke highlights this prophetic call to enact justice for the most needy of society (Luke 1:52–53; 3:12–14; 11:42; 18:1–8; 20:45–47). Jesus as the ultimate restorer of justice is the focus in Matthew 12:18–21 (as the Isaianic servant bringing justice to the nations), in Revelation 19:11, and in Hebrews 1:8: "About the Son he says, 'Your throne, O God, will last for ever and ever; a scepter of justice will be the scepter of your kingdom.'"

Teaching the Text

1. *Jesus is the servant of Yahweh who announces and enacts God's restoration for Israel and for the nations.* By citing Isaiah 42:1–4 in 12:18–21, Matthew frames the ministry of Jesus to Israel in light of Isaiah's servant figure, who acts for and on behalf of Israel. In Isaiah Yahweh's servant is commissioned to gather Israel back from exile (49:5) but also to fulfill Israel's God-given mission to bring God's salvation to the nations (49:6). By drawing from Isaianic servant texts at key moments, Matthew frames and interprets

Jesus' ministry both for Israel and for the nations. As we have already noted, Jesus' ministry in Galilee has been and continues to be focused on Israel—preaching and enacting the kingdom and gathering Jewish followers. The one story so far that highlights a Gentile interacting with Jesus is the exception that proves the rule. Jesus marvels at the centurion's great faith and heals on his behalf (8:5–13; for another such story, see 15:21–28). Yet in the final scene of Matthew, Jesus' mission to the nations will be announced and begun through his disciples: "Go and make disciples of all nations" (28:19). For Matthew, understanding Jesus and his mission means understanding Isaiah's vision of restoration that is enacted through the figure of the Servant of the Lord. So we would do well to help people understand Jesus and his mission by giving them some of this backstory from Isaiah, as well as from other Old Testament writings. When teaching this passage, we should point out the close connection between the restoration of Israel and the mission to the Gentiles. Jesus calls Israel back to God so that they can proclaim God's name among the nations.

2. *Jesus, as the servant of Yahweh, enacts the dual kingdom values of mercy and justice.* It is easy enough to consider mercy and justice as two values on differing poles of a spectrum, or, worse yet, as somehow contradictory. Clearly Matthew has no problem joining these together to describe Jesus' kingdom ministry, both in 12:15–21 and elsewhere (23:23; 25:31–46). The ease with which he joins together mercy and justice fits well the scriptural witness to God as one who is just and merciful, as in Exodus 34:6–7: "The LORD, the LORD, the compassionate and gracious God, slow to anger, abounding in love and faithfulness, maintaining love to thousands, and forgiving wickedness, rebellion and sin. Yet he does not leave the guilty unpunished." A just God does not ignore injustice (e.g., Ps. 140:12); a merciful God waits patiently for people to respond in right ways. In our preaching and teaching we may tend to lean into one or the other of these primary values of mercy and justice. This passage reminds us to bring mercy and justice—as qualities that characterize God and should characterize Christians—into balance.

Jesus' ministry in Galilee has focused on preaching the kingdom and healing the sick. This view from Mount Arbel shows the Sea of Galilee and some of the area of Galilee.

Matthew 12:15–21

Illustrating the Text

Jesus is the servant of Yahweh who announces and enacts God's restoration for Israel and for the nations.

News: Neal Peckens and Jason Hiser were just hoping for a little time away, a hike in the mountains. The Virginia natives had traveled to Glacier National Park for a trek into the backcountry. They wound up lost in the wilderness. Unexpected snow obscured their trail. A hard wind blew their topographical map away. Soon, all they could do was hunker down in their tent and hope for a rescue. When rescue finally came, the men were fifteen pounds lighter and ready for home.[4] Like the wandering sheep in Jesus' parable (Matt. 18:12–14), Israel had strayed from God, and they had been sent into exile for their idolatry, scattered among the nations (see 2 Kings 24). Jesus came to lead the mission to bring them, and all people, back to God.

Nature: The human heart is an incredible pump. This muscular organ, just the size of the fist, beats nearly 100,000 times per day, propelling 2,000 gallons of blood through the body; some 60,000 miles of blood vessels depend on the heart to bring oxygen to organs and tissues (if your context allows, consider using pictures or video of the heart in action). For just a moment, consider what would happen if the heart stopped giving out what it took in. What if the heart ceased this pattern of receiving-giving-receiving-giving? God's people have been blessed so that they might be a blessing (Gen. 12:1–3). We are given life so that we might extend it to others.

Jesus, as the servant of Yahweh, enacts the dual kingdom values of mercy and justice.

History: When apartheid finally came to an end in South Africa in the early 1990s, leaders sought a way forward that would include both justice and mercy with the goal of national healing. They formed the Truth and Reconciliation Commission, which provided a venue for victims to share their stories and perpetrators to confess their crimes, so that forgiveness might be extended and authentic reconciliation might take place. Under the leadership of people such as Archbishop Desmond Tutu, this commission was a critical part of helping South Africa move into a new era and begin writing a redemptive chapter in the life of that nation.

Pharisees Reject the Divine Origin of Jesus' Power

Big Idea *Although Jesus is accused of healing by Satan's power, Matthew shows him to be enacting the kingdom by God's Spirit and so warns of judgment upon those who fail to accept Jesus' identity and respond in obedience.*

Understanding the Text

The Text in Context

The controversy between Jesus and Galilean Pharisees intensifies in this passage. The Jewish leaders again accuse Jesus of casting out demons by the prince of demons (12:24; cf. 9:34). Jesus addresses their accusation with a set of analogies, claiming in the process to be the one who, led by the Spirit, is bringing God's kingdom (12:28; cf. 4:17; 10:7). Jesus' references to the Holy Spirit in Matthew cluster here (12:18, 28, 31, 32), indicating that Matthew ties the Spirit's work to the inauguration of God's kingdom in the

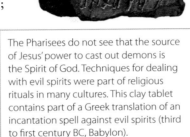

The Pharisees do not see that the source of Jesus' power to cast out demons is the Spirit of God. Techniques for dealing with evil spirits were part of religious rituals in many cultures. This clay tablet contains part of a Greek translation of an incantation spell against evil spirits (third to first century BC, Babylon).

person of Jesus (connection also in 1:18, 20; 3:11, 16; 4:1; 28:19). Themes of judgment for unbelief and the importance of good deeds also are reiterated in chapter 12 (earlier at 3:7–12; 7:15–20).

Interpretive Insights

12:23 *Could this be the Son of David?* Jesus' healing of a man who is blind and mute evokes this response from the people looking on. Although the use of *mēti* with a question can imply that a negative answer is expected ("He's not the Son of David, is he?"), this particle is also used in the sense of "perhaps" to signal that those asking the question are unsure of its answer (BDAG 649). The latter fits better with the astonishment that Matthew attributes to the crowds (rather than unbelief, which better characterizes the Pharisees in 12:24 and following). Matthew's penchant for "Son of David" is seen here in this crowd's response. It is used to express their wondering about his messianic identity.

12:24 *It is only by Beelzebul, the prince of demons.* Beelzebul is defined as "the prince of demons," the same way the name is defined in a contemporary Jewish text, the *Testament of Solomon* (6:1). As such, it likely functions as one of the names for the devil or Satan in the first century.[1] Matthew has alluded to this kind of accusation by Jesus' adversaries already in 10:25: "If the head of the house has been called Beelzebul . . ." The accusation that Jesus' power derived from the demonic seems to have been fairly widespread (e.g., John 10:20). For example, the Talmud records that Jesus was executed because he practiced sorcery and led Israel into apostasy (*b. Sanh.* 43a). Jesus counters this claim with reference to the kingdom. His logic goes like this: If Satan is involved in driving out Satan (demons), then Satan's kingdom will, in essence, self-destruct. So Jesus must be driving out demons by the power of God as a sign of the kingdom of God (12:25–28).

12:28 *Spirit of God.* As Matthew has affirmed the role of the Spirit of God in empowering Jesus' ministry (12:18), Jesus here affirms that it is by the Spirit of God that he has driven out the demon. Matthew emphasizes the Spirit-anointed nature of Jesus' ministry at Jesus' baptism (3:16; see comments on 12:18).

the kingdom of God has come upon you. In 4:17 Jesus announced that the kingdom had come near, and he has preached about

Key Themes of Matthew 12:22–50

- Jesus is the Spirit-led enactor of God's kingdom.
- Jewish leaders accuse Jesus of being in league with Satan.
- Jesus warns of judgment upon those who refuse to recognize him as God's servant.
- Jesus' family of disciples is characterized by doing God's will.

the kingdom and enacted the vision of healing and restoration portrayed in Isaiah. But Jesus makes an even clearer and more direct claim about his role in the kingdom. In his healing of a demon-possessed man, Jesus makes a direct claim that his actions are bringing God's kingdom to this world. The "you" in "upon you" (*eph hymas*) is plural, so the point is not that the kingdom has come upon specific people (here, the Pharisees would be unlikely persons for Jesus' reference), but rather that the kingdom has come to people—that is, this world.

12:31 *blasphemy against the Spirit will not be forgiven.* There have been many interpretations in the history of the church of what the "blasphemy against the Spirit" entails. The literary context suggests that the Pharisees' response to Jesus should guide our understanding of this phrase. The Pharisees have attributed Jesus' act of casting out a demon to Satan; they have denied that Jesus works miracles by the power of God's Spirit. This seems to be the best frame for understanding the "blasphemy against the Spirit." To attribute the work of God's Spirit to the enemy of God is a blasphemous act, and it fundamentally shapes the trajectory of the Pharisees' other responses to what God is doing in Jesus' ministry. In this sense, it sets the course for their ongoing rejection of Jesus' ministry and mission.

12:36 *everyone will have to give account . . . for every empty word they have spoken.* Matthew routinely emphasizes the importance of faithful actions, as he does in 12:33 with the imagery of good fruit (cf. 3:7–10; 7:16–23; 21:43). Here Matthew makes it clear that faithful actions include the words that people speak.

12:38 *Teacher, we want to see a sign from you.* Pharisees and teachers of the law refer to Jesus as "teacher" here and elsewhere in Matthew (9:11; 22:16, 36). Matthew places "Lord" on the lips of characters who respond positively to Jesus, while "teacher" is used for those who are antagonistic to him (see the

sidebar "Who Calls Jesus 'Lord' in Matthew?" in the unit on 7:13–29). Pharisees ask Jesus for a "sign," seemingly to prove the authenticity of his identity and action, here and in 16:1 (accompanied by teachers of the law in 12:38 and Sadducees in 16:4). In both passages Jesus refuses to give a sign and instead offers a riddle: "the sign of the prophet Jonah" (12:39; 16:4).

12:39 *A wicked and adulterous generation asks for a sign!* The motif of the obstinacy of the present generation occurs across the narration of Jesus' ministry (11:16 [see comments there]; 16:4; 17:17; 23:36; 24:34). The phrase "a wicked and adulterous generation" echoes Deuteronomy 32 in its reference to the Israelites of the wilderness generation (32:5, 20; see comments on 17:17). Matthew seems to highlight the similarities between that generation in the wilderness, which frequently turned away from Yahweh in spite of God's miraculous works, and the generation that is experiencing the miraculous kingdom ministry of Jesus but does not, as a whole, respond in faith and loyalty.

Here in 12:22–50 it is the Pharisees who epitomize this rejection of the work of God by attributing Jesus' power to heal to the demonic.

the sign of the prophet Jonah. Jesus rebuffs the Pharisees' request for a sign. His provision of "the sign of . . . Jonah" functions more like a riddle than a sign, especially since there is no indication that the Pharisees

When the Pharisees and teachers of the law ask for a sign, Jesus instead speaks a riddle about Jonah. This sarcophagus fragment from the fourth to fifth century AD depicts Jonah being swallowed by the great fish.

understand it (they ask for a sign again at 16:1). Jonah's time in the belly of a fish provides an analogy for the Son of Man's "three days and three nights in the heart of the earth" (12:40). Matthew's first hearers almost certainly would have recognized this reference to Jesus' time between crucifixion and resurrection from the Gospel traditions, which would have been commonplace in early Christian communities. On the story level, however, Jesus' words are obscure and function as a riddle that confounds his opponents.

12:41 *now something greater than Jonah is here*. As at 12:6 ("something greater than the temple is here"), the "something "greater" is likely the kingdom, especially given the close proximity to Jesus' discussion about the kingdom in the previous verses.

12:45 *That is how it will be with this wicked generation*. The analogy in 12:43–45 compares "this wicked generation" (see 12:39) to a scenario in which a person is freed from an impure spirit only to have that spirit return with seven other spirits even more wicked ("seven" being a number of fullness). The point of the analogy is to reaffirm the ideas already communicated in 12:39–42 (also 11:20–24). Just as the kingdom being inaugurated is even greater than previous expressions of God's work in this world, so the judgment on those who reject this climactic work of God in Jesus will be greater.

12:46 *his mother and brothers stood outside*. Matthew 12:46–50 is the narrative unit that leads into Matthew's third major discourse of Jesus' teaching (13:1–53). As with the other discourses (e.g., 5:1–7:29; 10:1–11:1), Matthew carefully arranges material leading up to and surrounding these teaching units. In this case, stories involving members of Jesus' family form an inclusio around the Parables Discourse (12:46; 13:55–56). Matthew uses these references to Jesus' family to highlight issues of loyalty.

12:47 *Someone told him*. This verse, although missing in some Greek manuscripts, seems necessary, since otherwise Jesus answers (*apokrinomai* [12:48]) not a person's question (12:47) but his family's arrival (12:46). It is likely that 12:47 was omitted due to a scribal eye skip, since the same word (*lalēsai*) concludes both verse 46 and verse 47, which could easily account for this omission.

12:50 *whoever does the will of my Father in heaven is my brother and sister and mother*. Matthew has already emphasized the motif of doing "the will of my Father in heaven" (the exact phrase occurs in 7:21; see also 6:10; 21:31; 26:42). Here the phrase identifies those whom Jesus considers to be his true family members. In a social context in which (physical) family ties are paramount, these words are potent and surprising. The closest of loyalties, even family connections, are reordered based on covenantal loyalty to God (see also 10:34–39).

Teaching the Text

1. *Jesus brings God's kingdom to this world by the power of the Holy Spirit*. This passage clearly shows Jesus to be God's agent in bringing God's reign to bear in this world. A clash of cosmic powers is front and center in this passage. Although the Pharisees have accused Jesus of casting out a demon because he himself takes his power

from the demonic realm, Matthew has been communicating across his Gospel that Jesus derives his power from God (3:16–17; 8:8–9; 9:6–8; 12:18). In this passage Jesus' words make the source of his power clear: "It is by the Spirit of God that I drive out demons" (12:28). And in line with Jewish expectation, the pouring out of God's Spirit signals the turn of the ages and the arrival of the kingdom of God (see Joel 2:28–32). Sometimes our preaching of Jesus focuses on the internal change that Jesus can bring to individuals, and this is a valid and important message to communicate. However, this passage highlights for us the cosmic change that Jesus' presence in this world has begun. As John Timmer puts it, "Jesus' coming into the world was not a visit; it was an invasion."[2] The power of Jesus in bringing God's kingdom to this earth is a crucial message to proclaim—to both believers and seekers—and should be a regular theme of preaching and teaching. Following this perspective, we can speak about an invitation to join what Jesus is already doing in this world. Into a context that easily speaks of Jesus living within us, we can invite people to consider how they might participate with Jesus in his kingdom work. Fundamentally, following Jesus is about joining in Jesus' ministry, not Jesus joining in ours.

2. *Matthew calls people to recognize Jesus as authorized by God and to respond to his kingdom work with repentance and covenant loyalty.* Proper response to Jesus and his kingdom message includes repentance—returning to God and God's ways

The healing miracle narrated in 12:22–23 is illustrated in this painting by James Tissot called *The Blind and Mute Man Possessed by Devils*, part of his series *The Life of Our Lord Jesus Christ*.

(12:41).[3] It also involves covenant loyalty, characterized by producing fruit in word (12:34–37) and deed (12:33). The disciple's life will be characterized by doing the will of God (12:50). Yet Jesus also makes clear that forgiveness is available to all (12:31). Nonetheless, 12:31 has also been misunderstood and misused by many, given its provocative words "blasphemy against the Spirit will not be forgiven." Speculation about what falls under this category of an unforgivable sin has harmed many sensitive souls who might convince themselves that they have somehow committed this unforgivable sin. We should be very careful when teaching this text to locate Jesus' words in the context of the passage: it is stubborn unbelief in Jesus as God's agent that is the sin of these particular Pharisees. And their lack of belief here is part of their persistent resistance to Jesus' ministry (e.g., 9:34; 12:1–14; 22:15). So we can help those who read this text and wrongly think of themselves as being outside God's grace and forgiveness. We help them by interpreting the text rightly and assuring them that God in Christ does forgive their sin whenever they come in repentance (6:12).

Illustrating the Text

Jesus brings God's kingdom to this world by the power of the Holy Spirit.

History: If John Timmer is right to liken Jesus' coming to an invasion to reclaim the world for God (see above), the following event might provide a captivating illustration. On October 30, 1938, CBS radio aired a broadcast that has become legend in the annals of pop-culture history. On Halloween night, as listeners were enjoying the music of Ramón Raquello and his orchestra, a "news" bulletin suddenly interrupted programming. A grave voice announced the invasion of Earth by Mars. Many people did not realize they were listening to a dramatic adaptation of H. G. Wells's *The War of the Worlds*, produced by up-and-coming actor and director Orson Welles. They listened in horror, believing that the earth really was under attack. According to reports, one police station received more than two thousand phone calls in a fifteen-minute span. This fictive "coming" can turn our thoughts toward the significance of Jesus' coming from God to do his kingdom work and remind us to respond rightly, with repentance and covenant loyalty.

Politics: As the role was defined in the early nineteenth century (at the Congress of Vienna in 1815), an ambassador was an authorized representative of the head of state of the sending country. As such, ambassadors had full authority to represent their government in the host country to which they were assigned. This framing of the role of ambassador provides a partial analogy for God's authorizing of Jesus to fulfill the mission of God.

Popular Culture: Internet and social media make it easier than ever for words to be both ubiquitous—people can say whatever they want, whenever they want, to a wide audience—and potentially harmful. Even words spoken in private can be recorded and posted for others to see, often to the embarrassment of the speaker. And in our digital age we are increasingly realizing how much of what we do and say may be accessed long after the event. Now, more than ever, it matters that our actions and our words reflect our covenant faithfulness.

Parables Discourse

Importance of Response to the Kingdom Message

Big Idea *Though the kingdom has a hidden quality so that some do not see or understand it, Jesus teaches his disciples the importance of receiving the kingdom message and bearing fruit.*

Understanding the Text

The Text in Context

The third major Matthean discourse, the Parables Discourse (chap. 13), explores through teachings and parables the varied responses that have been narrated in chapters 11–12. Matthew's two previous discourses have introduced the kingdom —its covenantal nature (chaps. 5–7) and its mission (chap. 10). The Parables Discourse elaborates on the nature of God's kingdom and reveals it as an "already and not yet" reality. In the chapter's first parable (parable of the soils) and its explanation a variety of responses to the message of the kingdom are delineated. Rejection of the kingdom message is explained by a similar rejection in Isaiah's time (13:14–15; see Isa. 6:9–10). Acceptance of the kingdom message is expressed in terms of hearing (i.e., receiving) and bearing fruit—motifs already introduced earlier in Matthew (hearing: 11:4–5, 15; 12:19b; bearing fruit: 3:8; 7:15–20; 12:33–37).

In the parable recorded in Matthew 13:3–9, a farmer goes out to sow seeds. He uses the broadcasting technique, where handfuls of seed are tossed over the prepared soil. This photograph shows a Palestinian farmer sowing seeds using this method. Although meant for the ground that was already cultivated or would be turned under with a plow, the seeds could settle anywhere.

Interpretive Insights

13:1 *Jesus went out of the house.* According to 12:46, Jesus has been teaching inside a house. Now in 13:1–2 Matthew narrates that Jesus comes out of the house to teach the crowds. Later in the Parables Discourse Matthew will indicate that Jesus leaves the crowd and goes back into the house, where he will explain his parables to the disciples (13:36). These changes of location contribute to the motifs of hiddenness and revelation in the Parables Discourse. Revelation comes to Jesus' true family, who do the will of God (12:50) and who follow Jesus in discipleship (13:10–12). The kingdom, because of its unexpected nature, remains opaque to those whose hearts are calloused and who have closed their eyes (13:15).

13:2 *Such large crowds gathered around him.* The primary, initial audience of the Parables Discourse is the crowds. Of the five major discourses of Jesus in Matthew, four are focused on the disciples (see 5:1–2; 10:1; 18:1; 24:1–2). While the Sermon on the Mount does include the crowds (7:28–29), the Parables Discourse is the discourse focused on the crowds most specifically. Yet the narrative audience shifts in 13:36, where Jesus focuses on the disciples by entering "the house."

13:3 *Then he told them many things in parables.* Parables will be used frequently by Jesus with the disciples and in his confrontations with his opponents (chapters 18–25), but chapter 13 contains the greatest concentration of parables in Matthew. Jesus uses eight parables and interprets three of them in the span of the Parables Discourse (see the sidebar "Structure of the Parables Discourse"). The use of

Key Themes of Matthew 13:1–23

- To truly hear the kingdom message means to receive it and bear fruit.
- In the present time the kingdom is hidden.
- Hidden truths are expressed through parables.

Structure of the Parables Discourse

This third major discourse in Matthew is carefully structured. An inside/outside motif follows the narrative frame of the chapter: Jesus speaks to the crowds (outside the house) in 13:1–35 and to his disciples (inside the house) in 13:36–52. Four pairs of parables also provide a structural pattern for the chapter. Each pair highlights some aspect of the nature of God's kingdom.

Outside:

13:1–9	Parable of the soils	A
13:10–17	Reason for parables: Isaiah quotation	Reason
13:18–23	Interpretation of the soils	
13:24–30	Parable of the wheat and weeds	B
13:31–32	Parable of the mustard seed	C
13:33	Parable of the yeast	C
13:34–35	Reason for parables: Psalms quotation	Reason

Inside:

13:36–43	Interpretation of wheat and weeds	
13:44	Parable of the treasure	D
13:45–46	Parable of the pearl	D
13:47–50	Parable of the fish and net (+ interpretation)	B
13:51–52	Parable of the house owner	A
13:53	Conclusion to Parables Discourse	

parables for teaching about the kingdom is tied to its hidden nature (13:13, 44).

A farmer went out to sow his seed. The first parable pictures a farmer sowing seed to gain a harvest. Three of the four soils receiving seed produce no lasting plants and so no harvest. Only the good soil (13:8) produces a harvest. The emphasis of this parable of the soils lands not on the farmer but on the four soils. As Jesus will explain in the parable's interpretation in 13:18–23, the seed refers to the message of the kingdom, and the soils represent four different responses to it.

13:8 *other seed fell on good soil, where it produced a crop.* The picture in the parable is of a bumper crop that comes from seed falling on good soil (i.e., the message of the kingdom falling on ready and responsive ears). This picture corresponds to the Matthean motif of fruit bearing (e.g., 12:33).

13:9 *Whoever has ears, let them hear.* Matthew highlights this refrain of Jesus three times (11:15; 13:9, 43). In each case Jesus gives an invitation to hear in such a way as to receive his teaching about the kingdom. This invitation evokes Isaiah's hearing motif, which communicates Israel's obstinacy against hearing Isaiah's message, Yahweh's promise of a future time of hearing, and the corresponding invitation to Israel to hear and understand. In Matthew 13 this invitation mitigates the idea that revelation is fully withheld from the crowds (e.g., 13:11–15). All who hear Jesus' parables are invited to hear and understand.[1]

13:10 *Why do you speak to the people in parables?* The disciples' question and Jesus' answer (13:10–15) delineate the disciples and the crowds as two distinct audiences for kingdom revelation in this chapter. The theme of revelation has already been introduced at 11:25–27, where Jesus has indicated the unexpectedness of the recipients of kingdom revelation (11:25).

13:11 *knowledge of the secrets of the kingdom of heaven.* Although this phrase can be read in gnostic fashion to indicate that God arbitrarily reveals fully to one group and withholds fully from another, the context of chapter 13 provides the actual contours of revelation and hiddenness. The crowds hear of the kingdom, though in parabolic form (13:34). The disciples are privy to Jesus' additional interpretation of the parables (13:18–23, 36–43, 49–50), yet they will continue to be characterized by frequent misunderstanding (e.g., 15:15–16; 16:5–12). And in Matthew thus far Jesus' teaching and preaching has been available to all (e.g., 4:17; 5:1–7:29). So "the knowledge of the secrets of the kingdom" must be understood in light of these narrative realities. The difference between just hearing and hearing followed by receiving is somehow tied to the very nature of the kingdom, which is both hidden and revealed (see "Teaching the Text" below).

13:14–15 *In them is fulfilled the prophecy of Isaiah.* Isaiah 6:9–10 is used to explain why the crowds do not respond in faith to Jesus' message and ministry en masse. Isaiah is called to preach to a people who will be essentially unresponsive to his message (Isa. 6:8–13). In analogous fashion, Jesus' ministry meets much unresponsiveness in Israel (e.g., 11:20–24), especially as represented by the opposition from Jewish leaders (12:1–45). Yet the Isaiah text also evokes the wider context of Isaiah, especially through the motifs of hearing and seeing in the latter that Matthew draws on in 11:2–16:20.[2] This means that although "this people's heart has become calloused" and "they have closed their eyes" (13:15), the possibility for reversal exists. In Isaiah God promises to bring about such reversals of response (32:3–4), and Israel is invited to hear and see in spite of their current obduracy (e.g., 42:18). So in Matthew Jesus invites the crowds to hear and respond (13:9), and some from the crowd will continue to respond to Jesus in faith (e.g., 15:31; 20:29–34).

13:16–17 *But blessed are your eyes because they see and your ears because they hear.* This beatitude (*makarios*, as in 5:3–11) announces blessing on those present for the arrival of the kingdom. Here it is the disciples specifically who are beneficiaries of God's work in Jesus, which they have been seeing and hearing. The crowds have not been privy to the same kind of revelation as the disciples; they hear about the kingdom only in parables (see 13:11). But Matthew also compares the disciples to those in Israel's past in order to emphasize the temporal nature of the blessing on the disciples. Prophets and righteous people in Israel's history longed for this moment but did not see it (13:17). Jesus' disciples are blessed to be alive at this point in history, when God is bringing the kingdom in the ministry and work of Jesus.

13:19 *When anyone hears the message about the kingdom and does not understand it.* Here Jesus provides the first of three parable interpretations (also 13:37–43, 49–50). The seed of the parable is identified as the message of the kingdom. The emphasis then falls on four ways of responding to the good news about God's reign. For one person, "the evil one . . . snatches away" the message (13:19). Another person "receives it with joy," but, lacking deep roots when trouble comes, "they quickly fall away" (13:20–21). For yet another person, the gospel is made unfruitful by "the worries of this life and the deceitfulness of wealth" (13:22 [cf. 6:19–21]). In each case fruitlessness demonstrates that the gospel could not take root and remain.

13:23 *someone who hears the word and understands it . . . produces a crop.* The climax of the parable of the soils is the reception of the gospel by the "good soil." This soil represents the person who hears and understands the message of the kingdom and therefore produces a bumper crop. A harvest of thirty, sixty, or one hundred times the original seed sown indicates an amazing yield. What begins as small and seemingly insignificant will surpass expectations, a motif woven throughout the Parables Discourse.

Teaching the Text

Jesus teaches that the kingdom has an element of hiddenness in the present time that takes eyes of faith to see. Jesus'

In Jesus' parable of the soils, some seed falls "along the path" (13:19). Shown here is a path at the edge of some fields in Galilee near Capernaum.

words about "the secrets of the kingdom of heaven" could be taken to support a kind of gnosticism, in which some people have an inside track on divine knowledge. Certainly, in some strands of the early church gnosticism became one way of interpreting such sayings of Jesus. And it is all too easy for Christians to claim special knowledge and act superior to others who have not yet responded to Jesus in faith. Yet God's revelation is a gift, and God often "gifts" it to those whom we least expect to receive it (9:9–13; 11:25–27). So we ought to be careful not to presume to know who will and will not be responsive to the message of the kingdom. As the parable of the soils indicates, the message goes out to all.

In addition, there is an ebb and flow to the giving of revelation, as Matthew tells it. Chapter 13 sits midpoint in the story line of Jesus' Galilean ministry and explains the rejection and antagonism that Jesus has already been experiencing from the Jewish leaders and from some others in Israel (12:1–45; 11:20–24). So Jesus' words in chapter 13 must be heard in this wider narrative context. Jesus speaks these words in 13:12: "Whoever has will be given more, and they will have an abundance. Whoever does not have, even what they have will be taken from them." In context, this provides a picture of revelation given and received, which begets more revelation (and so on). Conversely, when revelation is given and not received, God's revelation will eventually be taken away—like a plant that cannot find what it needs in inhospitable soil (13:5–7). So human response and divine revelation

In the parable, some of the farmer's seed falls among thorns, perhaps like those pictured here on a hillside near Capernaum. Just as thorns crowd out other, more valuable, plants, Jesus explains that worries and wealth prevent the gospel from bearing fruit.

are not mutually exclusive in Matthew. As God's revelation in the preaching of Jesus finds soil in which to take root, more is revealed, which then provides opportunity for greater faith and trust. When Jesus' message of the kingdom does not find fertile soil to take root, this revelation of God through Jesus cannot find a place to remain and grow.

This passage also warns about the ways in which wealth and worry can inhibit the gospel finding a place to grow in our lives. God does not snatch the gospel away from people, but wealth and worry about daily life can do this damage. As Jesus has indicated in the Sermon on the Mount, serving God rather than money allows the believer to trust fully in God's provision for daily life and needs (6:24–34).

Illustrating the Text

Jesus teaches that the kingdom has an element of hiddenness in the present time that takes eyes of faith to see.

Quote: Anthony Thiselton suggests that the parables of Jesus themselves have an element of hiddenness for an important reason. He suggests that for Jesus,

the purpose of using parables rather than "direct" discourse may well be *to prevent premature understanding unaccompanied by inner change*. For a hearer to imagine that he or she has "seen" the point of a packaged truth in terms of a take-it-or-leave-it attitude is disastrous. Postponement of understanding until the heart is ready may be part of the shared hermeneutical strategy here. To "know" in a way that fails to *engage* because it is too soon is more likely to invite judgement than appropriation. Those who are ready, however, receive the "more" that additional direct communication may provide. Indirect communication is a necessary strategy when illusion blocks the way.[3]

Education: Coaches and teachers offer students the chance to experience a stronger performance or deeper knowledge. Perhaps you could tell your audience about a great coach or teacher who has been a part of your ongoing growth in a particular area. Yet in the end, a coach, no matter how great, cannot run the race for the sprinter; and a piano teacher cannot truly help the student who does not practice. The student must take responsibility by responsive engagement with the teacher or coach and by putting into practice what he or she has learned so far. And with faithful response comes the possibility of richer experience in the process of growth and maturity.

Scripture: It is a common human fault to claim special knowledge for oneself and one's own group. "We have the corner on the truth" is a very tempting claim to make. This is not simply a contemporary phenomenon; we see this kind of spiritual pride in the Corinthian church, as evidenced in 1 Corinthians. From boasting about their connections to the best leaders ("I follow Paul . . . I follow Apollos . . . I follow Cephas" [1:12; cf. 4:6–7]), to their presumptuous claims to heavenly tongues, prophetic utterances, and all mysteries and knowledge (13:1–3), some of the Corinthian believers were under the erroneous impression that they, in contrast to others, had an inside knowledge of the divine. Paul addresses these gnostic-like assumptions by identifying those who hold them as "puffed up" (*physioō* [4:6, 18; 5:2]). And the antidote to being puffed up (presuming special knowledge) is love (13:2). As Paul writes in 8:1b–3, "Knowledge puffs up while love builds up. Those who think they have knowledge do not yet know as they ought to know. But whoever loves truly knows."[4]

Parables Discourse

The "Already and Not Yet" of the Kingdom

Big Idea *Though the kingdom and people's responses to it have a hidden quality in the present time, everything will be made clear in the end—both people's responses and the great value of the kingdom.*

Understanding the Text

The Text in Context

The parables in this section of the Parables Discourse build upon the varied responses to the kingdom introduced in 13:1–23 by indicating the hidden nature of the kingdom in the present. What will be clear in the end is partially hidden in the present, so that it takes eyes of faith to see it. Thus, the kingdom is like weeds and wheat growing together in a field, a mustard seed, and yeast hidden in a lump of dough. Its impact and its true followers will be clear only at the final judgment. Yet the kingdom is also of far greater worth than a great treasure or an exquisite pearl. The theme of God's final judgment continues to be prominent in the chapter (13:40–43, 49–50; cf. 3:7–12; 7:15–20), along with a motif of insiders and outsiders (13:36). The latter motif actually surrounds the discourse with

bookending accounts of Jesus' family and hometown (12:46–50; 13:54–58).

Interpretive Insights

13:24 *The kingdom of heaven is like.* This phrase introduces six of the eight parables in chapter 13 (13:31, 33, 44, 45, 47) and also occurs at 18:23; 20:1; 22:2. The first and final parables in chapter 13 focus on responses to the kingdom rather than providing comparisons to the kingdom itself, as the six others do. What these six parables communicate about the kingdom is its hiddenness and seeming insignificance in the present, its future consummation at "the end of the age," and its supreme value.

13:30 *Let both grow together until the harvest.* As Jesus' interpretation of this parable will indicate (13:37–43), the wheat and the weeds signify the righteous and wicked, respectively. Here the parable indicates that until the harvest (end of the age [13:39]), the wheat and weeds will necessarily grow alongside each other. There is no way to pull out the weeds and at the same time avoid "uproot[ing] the wheat." The implications of this picture include the truth that God will be the one to judge human responses at the time of final judgment. People are not to do this kind of judging. The idea of deferring judgment to God and to that final day has already been introduced in 7:1–2 ("Do not judge") and will be emphasized in Jesus' final parable (25:31–46).

13:31 *The kingdom of heaven is like a mustard seed.* Another comparison to the kingdom that Jesus offers comes from the mustard plant. Although the mustard seed is very small (cf. 17:20), it produces the largest of plants. In the same way, the kingdom is so small that it seems insignificant. But in the future the presence of the kingdom will become obvious. Although growth is mentioned in the analogy of the mustard seed, this does not seem to be the focus of the analogy. Rather, contrast between the smallness and largeness of the beginning and end points is where the emphasis lies.

13:33 *The kingdom of heaven is like yeast that a woman took and mixed into . . . flour.* This parable is paired with that of the mustard seed (13:31–32). The analogy indicates that the kingdom, though now small and seemingly insignificant, will have an influence beyond expectations. In the end, the kingdom will be clearly and fully revealed. Matthew introduces the motif of hiddenness in this parable by using the verb *enkryptō* (NIV: "mixed"; RSV: "hid"), which

Key Themes of Matthew 13:24–53

- At the present time, the kingdom is hidden and seemingly insignificant.
- Judgment of the righteous and the wicked is deferred until the end of the age.
- The kingdom is of immeasurably great value.

indicates something becoming concealed by being mixed in with something else. This motif is explicit at 13:35, 44.

13:34–35 *Jesus spoke all these things to the crowd in parables . . . So was fulfilled.* The Old Testament citation in 13:35 comes from Psalm 78:2. In the psalm's context the "hidden things" now uttered are not truths heretofore unknown; they are "things we have heard and known, things our ancestors have told us" (Ps. 78:3). The problem of the psalm is that previous generations were "stubborn and rebellious" and unfaithful to God (78:8). Because of their unfaithfulness, they "forgot what [God] had done" for them (78:11). In Matthew the use of this psalm highlights that Jesus teaches in

Jesus compares the kingdom of heaven to a mustard seed that will become a large plant in which birds can perch. The plant referred to is probably the flowering black mustard plant (*Brassica nigra*), shown here.

parables in line with the prophets of the past, and that, as has always been the case, it takes eyes of faith to see and interpret rightly the works of God. Without faith, there is a hidden quality to God's revelation (see 13:12–13).

13:36 *Then he left the crowd and went into the house.* This verse acts as a hinge in the Parables Discourse. According to 13:2, Jesus has been teaching the crowds; now he turns to teach his disciples and interpret the parables for them (13:37–43, 49–50).

13:37 *Son of Man.* What is left unidentified in the interpretation of the parable of the soils (13:18–23) is made explicit here: the Son of Man (Jesus himself [see comments on 8:20]) is the one who sows the seed—that is, the one who preaches the message of the kingdom.

13:39 *The harvest is the end of the age.* The phrase "end of the age" is a favorite of Matthew; it occurs three times in this chapter (13:39, 40, 49) and also in 24:3; 28:20. Matthew uses the phrase to signal the final day, in which God will judge all matters and people (13:40–43).

13:44 *The kingdom of heaven is like treasure hidden in a field.* This parable, along with the following one about the pearl, teaches that the kingdom is of great value. This might seem too obvious a point to make, yet the hiddenness of the kingdom in the present has been thematic in chapter 13 (13:35; see comments on 13:33) and is emphasized here: it is "hidden" treasure. Although the kingdom is at present seemingly insignificant, these two parables make it clear that the kingdom is of much greater worth than everything a person has (13:46).

13:47 *Once again, the kingdom of heaven is like a net.* This parable forms a

Jesus explains to his disciples that the kingdom of heaven is like a net full of fish where the good fish, symbolizing the righteous, will be separated from the bad fish, the wicked. Shown here is a modern fishing net full of fish from the Sea of Galilee.

pair with that of the weeds and the wheat to highlight that God will be the one to judge right and wrong—the righteous and the wicked—and will do so at the end of the age.

13:51 *"Have you understood all these things?" Jesus asked. "Yes," they replied.* Jesus' question and the disciples' answer often are taken at face value to prove that the disciples in Matthew essentially understand what Jesus teaches them. However, narrative methodology pushes us to ask whose point of view is represented in any particular moment of direct speech (see the sidebar "Characterization and Narrative Authorization" in the unit on 4:1–11). The key issue is whether Matthew communicates that the disciples actually do understand, not whether they claim to do so. The fact that Jesus questions their level of understanding in 15:16 and 16:9 cautions against attributing understanding to the disciples as a general character trait. Although they are privy to Jesus' interpretation of parables in chapter 13, the disciples continue to struggle to understand what Jesus teaches about the kingdom and about their role in its mission.[1]

13:52 *every teacher of the law who has become a disciple of the kingdom of heaven.* In Matthew the usual use of *grammateus* ("teacher of the law," traditionally rendered "scribe") is in the plural, often coupled with "the Pharisees" (e.g., 5:20; 12:38; 23:2) or "the chief priests" (e.g., 16:21; 20:18). Here, as in the other singular usage (8:19), a (potential) disciple of Jesus is envisioned. Some have wondered if this positive use of *grammateus* indicates that Matthew comes from and writes to a scribal community of believers in Jesus. What is significant in 13:52 is the combination of *grammateus* and "a disciple of the kingdom of heaven." In chapter 13 Jesus has taught about the nature of the kingdom as an "already and not yet" reality by drawing from the Scriptures (Isaiah, Psalms). Expounding the Scriptures is precisely the role of the *grammateus* (see 7:29).

like the owner of a house who brings out of his storeroom new treasures as well as old. This final brief parable compares a learned disciple of the kingdom to a householder with a storeroom who brings out new and old treasures from storage. So a disciple of the kingdom knows enough to draw upon both old and new to understand the nature of the kingdom and to follow accordingly. In context, the parable seems to point to the use of what has been known about God's coming reign and what is new about the kingdom in Jesus' proclamation. The new may correspond to the surprising hiddenness of the kingdom, which was not a part of Jewish expectation about the arrival of God's reign in this world but which

has been emphasized in chapter 13. The old may correspond to the teachings of the Scriptures that Jesus draws upon to teach about the kingdom (Isa. 6; Ps. 78).

This final parable forms an inclusio with the first one in chapter 13, the parable of the soils, to illustrate the proper response to Jesus' message about the kingdom: understanding and receiving the kingdom and so producing fruit.

13:53 *When Jesus had finished these parables.* This concluding formula ("When Jesus had finished . . .") occurs after each of the five Matthean discourses (7:28; 11:1; 19:1; 26:1).

Theological Insights: The Kingdom's "Already and Not Yet"

Matthew has already introduced the "already and not yet" realities of the kingdom in the beatitudes (5:3–10): "the kingdom *is* theirs . . . they *will be* comforted." In chapter 13 Matthew highlights the hiddenness of the kingdom—its still-future dimensions. This dual reality of the kingdom cuts across the New Testament writings. Paul, for example, can speak in the same letter about the already and the not yet. In 1 Corinthians 10:11 he speaks of the Corinthians as those "on whom the culmination of the ages has come." Yet five chapters later Paul affirms that "the end," and so believers' resurrection, is still to come (1 Cor. 15:24). In Galatians Paul combines both dimensions in a single thought: Jesus "rescue[s] us from the present evil age" (Gal. 1:4). And, like Matthew, Paul identifies a hiddenness to kingdom reality in the present: "Your life is now hidden with Christ in God" (Col. 3:3).

Teaching the Text

1. *Although the kingdom has a hiddenness to it in the present, all will be made clear at the end of the age, and God then will judge everything and everyone.* The paradox of the kingdom—its reality as both "already and not yet"—is highlighted in the Parables Discourse. At present there is a hiddenness to the kingdom, as expressed in the parables of the weeds and wheat, mustard seed, and yeast. People's responses to the kingdom are not always clear to human judgment in the present, hence the call to leave the weeds and wheat growing together in the present time (13:30). Yet Matthew makes it clear in the parables of the weeds and wheat and of the net that a day will come when all will be clear. The implication is that Christians should leave judgment of people to God, since God will judge rightly at the end of the age (cf. 7:1). This is an important message for preaching and teaching, since it is all too easy to assume that we know who people are and where they stand in relation to faith. Matthew cautions against our rushing to judgment, since responses to the kingdom as a hidden reality are themselves fully discernible only to God.

2. *Although the kingdom is seemingly insignificant in the present (hidden from sight), it is of the greatest value and is worth all that a person has.* Given Matthew's emphasis in chapter 13 on the hiddenness of the kingdom, it might be easy to assume that the kingdom is relatively insignificant. Matthew counters this assumption by indicating that the kingdom will be of the utmost greatness and influence at its future consummation (parables of the mustard seed and of the yeast). Its apparent insignificance at present should not be mistaken for a lack of worth. Indeed, it is worth more than everything a person might possess (parables of the hidden treasure and of the pearl). It is worth one's full commitment and loyalty. And given that the kingdom's full significance and influence are still in the future, faith is required to believe that God will bring its consummation. The hiddenness of the kingdom means that Christians always walk by faith in this life. This is an important message for the church in an age that longs for certainty and requires proofs for every claim. Scripture in general and Matthew in particular make it clear that we are not offered certainty in this life. We are called to put our faith and trust in the God who is making all things right. We can have the deepest conviction of the reality of the kingdom—a conviction grounded in trust in Jesus the Messiah, who is the firstfruits and promise of what is still to come.

Jesus compares the kingdom of heaven to a valuable pearl. Shown here are a variety of pearls on an oyster shell.

Illustrating the Text

Although the kingdom has a hiddenness to it in the present, all will be made clear at the end of the age, and God then will judge everything and everyone.

Metaphor: In chemistry, use of a litmus test allows someone to check a substance's acidity or alkalinity. Litmus is a mixture of dyes that changes color upon coming into contact with acidity (to red) or alkalinity (to blue). This test has become a metaphor for occasions when judgments are made based on a singular criterion. Christians have often used various litmus tests—religious, social, and political—as a means of determining true faith. For Matthew, however, it is God, not humans, who will determine the presence of authentic faith. And God will wait until the final day to do so.

Although the kingdom is seemingly insignificant in the present (hidden from sight), it is of the greatest value and is worth all that a person has.

Television: In the PBS series *Antiques Roadshow*, experts appraise garage-sale purchases, family heirlooms, and recently found articles to determine their value. Often, individuals discover that they have "hidden" treasures, items worth a great deal more than their appearance suggests. In one episode, a man with a passion for collecting Chinese rhinoceros-horn cups discovers that the set that he spent about $5,000 to acquire—a large amount of money to him—is worth at least $1 million. The appraiser notes how, simply by

pursuing something he loves, the man has gained a fortune.[2]

Quotations: If the kingdom is in a real sense hidden in the present, then there continues to be a sense of mystery or ambiguity to our walking by faith and not by sight. Luke Johnson speaks of this ambiguity of "learning Jesus," by which he means living in relationship to "the mystery of a living person in the present."[3] For Johnson, learning Jesus

> involves a considerable amount of ambiguity. . . . Ambiguity is the element of tentativeness, of risk, of gamble, in committing to a path of understanding and action that is definite but also open-ended. If the church is committed to learning Jesus as a living person, then it is also committed to ambiguity as an inevitable—and positive!—dimension of its existence.[4]

As Barbara Brown Taylor writes, "If it is true that God exceeds all our efforts to contain God, then is it too big a stretch to declare that *dumbfoundedness* is what all Christians have most in common? Or that coming together to confess all that we do not know is at least as sacred an activity as declaring what we think we do know?"[5]

Herod and Hometown Misunderstand Jesus' Identity

Big Idea *Although Jesus' miraculous powers are acknowledged, this leads not to universal faith but rather to unbelief (in his hometown) and confusion over his identity (by Herod).*

Understanding the Text

The Text in Context

Matthew concludes the third discourse of Jesus' teaching with the transition formula (13:53) that he also uses at 7:28–29; 11:1; 19:1; 26:1. In two pericopes (13:54–58; 14:1–12), Matthew narrates two kinds of rejection of Jesus and his kingdom message: the unbelief of Jesus' hometown (13:58) and Herod's confusion about Jesus' identity (14:1–2). This section continues the focus on Jesus' identity tied to his healing power introduced at 11:2–5 (see 11:20; 12:15, 22; 13:54; 14:2). The passage also follows up the plotline about John's imprisonment (4:12; 11:2; 14:3–12). The motif of "stumbling" ("taking offense") over Jesus is also important in this section of Matthew (13:57; see also 11:6; 15:12; 26:31–33).

Interpretive Insights

13:54 *Coming to his hometown.* Matthew has indicated earlier that Jesus' family comes from the town of Nazareth (2:23).

Where did this man get this wisdom and these miraculous powers? Although people in Jesus' hometown question the origin of his wisdom and miracles, Matthew has already portrayed Jesus as Wisdom and has clearly indicated that his power comes from God (11:2–12:45). Like the Pharisees (9:34; 12:22–24), the people of Jesus' hometown question the source of his power to do the miracles (*dynameis*) that they have witnessed. The language of *dynameis* connects back to chapter 11 and misperceptions about Jesus' identity and forward to Herod's misconceptions about Jesus (see 11:20–24; 13:54; 14:2).

13:55 *mother's name Mary . . . brothers . . . sisters.* Mention of Jesus' family parallels 12:46–50, where Jesus' mother and brothers come looking for him. In this way, these sections (12:46–50; 13:54–58) provide an inclusio for the Parables Discourse.

13:57 *And they took offense at him.* Matthew draws upon the motif of "stumbling" (*skandalizō*, commonly rendered as "take offense") here to indicate the negative response of Jesus' hometown to his ministry (see also 11:6 [see comments there]; 15:12; 26:31).

A prophet is not without honor except in his own town. This proverbial saying of Jesus indicts the lack of faith of the people in his hometown, since they cannot see beyond his family context to imagine him in the exalted role implied by his miraculous actions.

13:58 *because of their lack of faith.* Jesus' hometown is one of two character groups (the other being the Jewish leaders [12:1–45]) that are portrayed as being "without faith" (*apistia*) in Jesus and his authority. Whereas the disciples are characterized by "little faith" (*oligopistia, oligopistos* [e.g., 14:31]), a number of seekers from the Jewish crowds are commended by Jesus for their faith (*pistis* [e.g., 9:2, 22, 29]).

14:1 *Herod the tetrarch.* This Herod is a son of Herod the Great (2:1) and was put in charge over one-fourth of the territory that his father ruled (*tetraarchēs* derives

Key Themes of Matthew 13:54–14:12

- Jesus' powerful deeds are recognized.
- In Jesus' hometown there is "stumbling" and lack of faith.
- Herod is confused about Jesus' identity.

in part from the Greek word for "four"). Specifically, this Herod—Herod Antipas—ruled over Galilee and Perea from 4 BC to AD 39. His brother Archelaus ruled over Judea, Samaria, and Idumea (see 2:22; see commentary on 2:1) until he was deposed by Caesar in AD 6 and replaced by Roman governors. Pontius Pilate was one such governor.

This scene in 14:3–12 provides a flashback within the narrative. The passage begins with Herod Antipas, ruler of Galilee,

Jesus returns to his hometown of Nazareth, a small agricultural village in the mountains of Lower Galilee. This view of modern Nazareth from Mount Tabor shows how it nestles within a bowl formation in the Nazareth Range.

responding to reports about Jesus with concerns that John the Baptist has been resurrected (14:1–2). Matthew then proceeds to tell the story of John's execution by Herod (14:3–12), which occurred sometime earlier, as is made clear in 14:2, where Herod expresses his belief that John has risen from the dead.

14:2 *This is John the Baptist; he has risen from the dead!* Herod's notion that Jesus is somehow John raised from the dead will find a counterpart in various people's opinions about Jesus in 16:14. Some scholars attribute such a belief to the prophetic tradition of resurrection, especially as a signal of the end of the age,[1] while others attribute Herod's association of Jesus with John resurrected to populist superstition.[2]

This passage continues Matthew's emphasis on Jesus' identity in 11:2–16:20. At 11:2–5 John the Baptist wonders if Jesus is the Messiah. At 12:1–44 the Pharisees attribute Jesus' healing power to the demonic, thereby implying that his identity is quite different from the one that he is implicitly claiming. Here Herod wrongly construes Jesus to be John raised from the dead. At 14:33 and 16:13–20 the disciples rightly recognize Jesus' messianic identity.

miraculous powers. Matthew uses *dynameis* ("miracles"; NIV: "miraculous powers") to describe Jesus' messianic deeds (see 11:2–5). In chapter 11 Jesus' miracles performed across Galilee were not met with corresponding repentance (11:20–24). These christological miracles have just been questioned by those in Jesus' hometown (13:54), resulting in fewer miracles being performed there (13:58). Now Herod attributes Jesus' miracles to John brought back from the dead. Across chapters 11–16 Jesus' actions are misconstrued and do not necessarily prove to those who observe them that he is the Messiah.

14:3–4 *Now Herod had arrested John.* Matthew has already indicated that John was imprisoned at 4:12 in order to signal the beginning of Jesus' public ministry. In 11:2 John sends a question to Jesus about his miracles that John has heard about while in prison.

because of Herodias, his brother Philip's wife . . . It is not lawful. According to Josephus, Herodias was first married to Herod, son of Mariamme II (*Ant.* 18.136), who was possibly named "Herod Philip." Josephus agrees with Matthew that she divorced her first husband and then married Herod Antipas, an act that "flout[ed] the ways of our fathers" (*Ant.* 18.136 [see 17.341]). The specific Old Testament regulation is found in Leviticus 20:21: "If a man marries his brother's wife, it is an act of impurity; he has dishonored his brother" (see also Lev. 18:16).

14:5 *but he was afraid of the people.* Herod's fear of the people mirrors the language of the chief priests and elders in 21:23–27, who are also afraid of the people (*ochlos*) because they consider John to be a prophet (21:26).[3] Matthew characterizes the Jewish and Roman leaders differently than he does the Jewish people (*ochlos*). So it is not helpful to collapse Matthew's distinction between Jesus' antagonists, comprised of Jewish and Roman leaders, and the Jewish crowds. The crowds remain open to Jesus' ministry and so continue to be those who respond to Jesus' message (see comments on 27:64).

they considered John a prophet. Matthew indicates that the Jewish people consider John to be a prophet (here and 21:26). In both cases their assessment causes key leaders to fear taking action against John (or speaking against him [21:26]).

14:10 *and had John beheaded in the prison.* See the sidebar "Josephus on John the Baptist's Death."

14:12 *John's disciples came and took his body . . . told Jesus.* John's disciples,

mentioned here and at 9:14 and 11:2, bring news of John's death to Jesus, which returns the story line from this flashback about John's death to Jesus and his Galilean ministry.

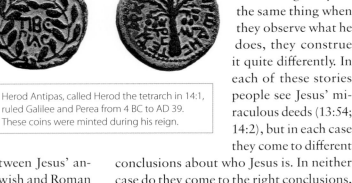

Herod Antipas, called Herod the tetrarch in 14:1, ruled Galilee and Perea from 4 BC to AD 39. These coins were minted during his reign.

Teaching the Text

1. *Jesus' miraculous power signals his messianic identity but does not guarantee acceptance and reception.* The accounts of how people respond to Jesus and his kingdom actions (see 11:2–5) make it clear that although they see the same thing when they observe what he does, they construe it quite differently. In each of these stories people see Jesus' miraculous deeds (13:54; 14:2), but in each case they come to different conclusions about who Jesus is. In neither case do they come to the right conclusions, according to Matthew. The people of Jesus' hometown stumble over him (take offense at him) because, despite his miracles, they cannot be free of seeing him in the categories of his youth and his family of origin. They cannot quite shift their frame of reference to see and recognize Jesus as the Messiah—not Jesus the carpenter's son. Herod, on the other hand, seems to give Jesus' miracles more weight, but he comes to the wrong conclusion that Jesus is somehow John the Baptist, the prophet, come back from the dead to haunt him.

In a modernist context, Christians often think that Jesus' miracles provide fail-safe

Matthew 13:54–14:12

proof of his identity. Yet the people in this narrative, who were quite ready to grant the existence of Jesus' miraculous power, did not come to the right conclusion, that Jesus is Israel's Messiah. This is a good reminder that people will not come to recognize who Jesus is through proofs and even through demonstrations of power. There is something beyond the realm of indisputable demonstration about Jesus and his identity. As we have seen already in Matthew, it takes faith and trust to look at what Jesus is doing and come to the conviction that he is acting by God's power and on God's behalf to bring the kingdom to this world. In our preaching centered on Jesus and his words and works, we would do well to remember to call people to trust in a reality that, though eminently reasonable, calls for something beyond reason.

2. *Some people stumble over Jesus and his kingdom actions.* In line with the previous teaching point is the text's message that some people will stumble over Jesus. People of Jesus' hometown are portrayed as taking offense at him, because they cannot see him in categories that are new or different from what their past experience provides. In

the end, they stumble over the uniqueness of Jesus. We are invited to preach Jesus as the Messiah, the unique one who acts with God's own authority. We ourselves should not put stumbling blocks in the ways of others (see 18:6–7), but neither should we try to make Jesus more palatable by downplaying his uniqueness. In this regard, it is all too easy to create Jesus in our own image. We can see something of this in the array of views about Jesus popular today inside and outside of the church: Jesus as simply a teacher of good deeds, Jesus as the epitome of Western masculinity, or Jesus as poster boy for any and every political perspective. Yet to preach Jesus from Matthew's point of view is to highlight Jesus' true identity as the Messiah and inaugurator of the kingdom, even if this challenges people's comfortable assumptions about him.

Illustrating the Text

Jesus' miraculous power signals his messianic identity but does not guarantee acceptance and reception.

Literature: *The Last Battle*, by C. S. Lewis. In this children's novel, Lewis weaves the theme of testing through his portrayals of the characters. Who will prove faithful? Who can be trusted? Some characters stay true to the end, even to death. Others betray. One group simply refuses to place its faith in anyone or anything, deciding that all reality is deceptive. The dwarves, who make this decision, enter "the next world," a beautiful paradise. But because of their resolute skepticism, they are unable to experience the delights that surround them. Instead, they are convinced that they are bound by the four walls of a dirty stable. When delicious fruit is presented, they smell only straw. When wine is offered, they reject what they are sure is water from a dirty trough. They lack the crucial lens of faith to see what is truly real.

Some people stumble over Jesus and his kingdom actions.

Quotes: It is all too easy to make Jesus more palatable to ourselves and others. More often than not, we do this by making Jesus in our own image. Albert Schweitzer critiqued this tendency over a century ago: "The mistake was to suppose that Jesus could come to mean more to our time by entering into it as a man *like ourselves*. That is not possible . . . because such a Jesus never existed."[4]

Scot McKnight, a New Testament professor, notes this same tendency.

On the opening day of my class on Jesus of Nazareth, I give a standardized psychological test divided into two parts. The results are nothing short of astounding.

The first part is about Jesus. It asks students to imagine Jesus' personality, with questions such as, "Does he prefer to go his own way rather than act by the rules?" and "Is he a worrier?" The second part asks the same questions of the students, but instead of "Is he a worrier?" it asks, "Are *you* a worrier?" The test is not about right or wrong answers, nor is it designed to help students understand Jesus. Instead, if given to enough people, the test will reveal that we all think Jesus is like us. Introverts think Jesus is introverted, for example, and, on the basis of the same questions, extroverts think Jesus is extroverted.

Spiritual formation experts would love to hear that students in my Jesus class are becoming like Jesus, but the test actually reveals the reverse: Students are fashioning Jesus to be more like themselves. If the test were given to a random sample of adults, the results would be measurably similar. To one degree or another, we all conform Jesus to our own image.[5]

Matthew 13:54–14:12

Jesus' Compassion and Authority to Do the Miraculous

Big Idea *Matthew shows Jesus to be worthy of trust as the Son of God, as he acts in compassion and authority to heal the sick, feed hungry crowds, and even walk on the sea.*

Understanding the Text

The Text in Context

Matthew narrates Jesus healing the sick, feeding the five thousand, and walking on the water to demonstrate Jesus' authority over sickness and even the natural elements. Through these miracles Matthew reaffirms Jesus' identity as the Messiah ("Son of God" [14:33]). The evangelist has already emphasized Jesus' authority and compassion through healings and miracles in chapters 8–9. In chapters 11–16 he makes more explicit Jesus' messianic identity demonstrated through these actions (see 11:2–5). The feeding of a large crowd (five thousand men along with women and children) is the first of two such feedings (the second is in 15:29–39). These feedings echo the Old Testament stories of Moses as he provides food for the Israelites in their wilderness journeys. These feedings also provide an opportunity for Jesus' disciples to put their faith and service into practice (see 14:16), although they fall short of Jesus' expectations for them, exhibiting "little faith" instead (14:17–18, 31; cf. 6:30; 8:26; 16:8; 17:20).

Interpretive Insights

14:13 *When Jesus heard what had happened, he withdrew.* This is the second instance of Jesus withdrawing after controversy in 11:2–16:20 (see 12:15; 15:21). In this case he withdraws after hearing of John's death at the hand of Herod. Given that Herod closely associates John with Jesus (14:1–2), it is not improbable that Herod's violence against John could spill over into violence against Jesus. So Jesus withdraws from controversy and possible harm to focus on his healing ministry (as at 12:15; 15:21).

14:14 *he had compassion on them and healed their sick.* Matthew provides several summaries of Jesus' healing activity in this section (12:15–16; 14:14, 35–36; 15:29–31). In this particular summary Matthew makes explicit the theme of Jesus as compassionate Messiah (also 12:7; 14:14; 15:32), although this motif is implicit in many of the healing stories.

14:16 *You give them something to eat.* Jesus seems to expect his disciples to provide for the crowds in some miraculous way. This coheres with the Mission Discourse, in which Jesus grants authority to the Twelve to do the miraculous (10:1) by following the pattern of Jesus' own ministry (10:7–8). Yet the disciples will fall short of Jesus' expectations for them in this regard (see 15:33; 17:14–20). As Donald Verseput notes, in 14:17 the disciples focus "upon their limited means and [fail] to reckon with the magnitude of Jesus' awesome power . . . an obvious expression of 'little faith.'"[1]

14:17 *five loaves of bread.* This reference to bread (*artos*) begins a bread motif that ties together the two feeding miracles (14:13–21; 15:32–39) and connects to Jesus' warning to the disciples about the "yeast of the Pharisees and Sadducees" (16:6), which recapitulates the lessons of the two feeding miracles (16:8–10; see also 15:26).

14:19 *he gave thanks and broke the loaves. Then he gave them to the disciples.* The specific language that Matthew uses here foreshadows his narration of the Passover celebration that Jesus shares with his disciples the night before his death (26:26–29). The common language between the passages includes four verbs and two nouns: taking the bread, giving thanks (*eulogeō*), breaking it, and giving it to the disciples. A similar composite of terms is also used in the feeding of the four thousand (15:36). By tying together the two feeding miracles with the Passover celebration, Matthew signals that these miracles should be understood as echoing Israel's experience in the wilderness (see comments on 14:20). Jesus is portrayed as the one who inaugurates the new exodus in line with Isaiah's related theme.

When Jesus multiplies the loaves and fishes, all eat and are satisfied. The disciples gather the remains, filling twelve baskets. This fourteenth-century AD mosaic emphasizes the twelve baskets of leftovers.

14:20 *They . . . were satisfied, and the disciples picked up twelve basketfuls of broken pieces.* This feeding miracle evokes Yahweh's miraculous provision of manna for Israel in the wilderness (see Exod. 16; Deut. 8:1–5). Not only is the connection offered by the implicit comparison between Yahweh's provision for Israel and Jesus' provision for the same; the verbal links between Jesus' actions at 14:19 and the Passover celebration of 26:26–29 also highlight connections with Exodus. Additionally, the mention of "twelve basketfuls" of leftovers from the miracle evokes the provision for Israel's twelve tribes. While the number "twelve" would not in itself be enough to evoke the Old Testament story, its combination with the other features in 14:13–21 supports the Exodus allusions.

14:23 *he went . . . by himself to pray.* Although Jesus' praying is not thematic as in Luke (who often mentions Jesus' prayer life), Matthew does show him praying here and at 19:13–15, where he blesses and prays for children. In Gethsemane Jesus is shown in concerted prayer as he anticipates his coming death (26:36, 39, 42, 44).

14:25 *Jesus went out to them, walking on the lake.* As at 8:23–27, where Jesus calms a storm at sea, Matthew portrays him as one with authority over the natural world.

14:26 *they were terrified . . . and cried out in fear.* The fear experienced by the disciples is understandable, given the appearance of Jesus on the water. This story functions in similar ways to theophanies in the Old Testament, in which the Lord or an angel of the Lord appears to a person. In these instances fear is an expected response, and comfort in the form of an exhortation not to fear is commonplace. For example, when Daniel experiences a vision of a supernatural being, he trembles in fear but is comforted with the words "Do not be afraid" (Dan. 10:4–12 [see also Gen. 15:1; 26:24; Judg. 6:23; Luke 1:13, 30]). Jesus' words to his disciples in 14:27 are similar.

14:29 *Then Peter got down out of the boat.* Peter is the most prominent of the disciples in Matthew's Gospel. He often functions as their spokesperson (e.g., 15:15; 16:16; 17:24–27; 18:21; 19:27). At other points in the narrative he is portrayed in somewhat distinctive terms. For example, here and elsewhere he appears as rash or impulsive (16:22; 17:24–25; 26:33).

The boat used by Jesus' disciples to travel across the lake may have been similar to the first-century AD vessel whose remains are shown here. It was found in 1986, buried in the mud of the drought-exposed shoreline on the northwest side of the Sea of Galilee.

14:31 *You of little faith . . . why did you doubt?* Jesus refers to Peter as one with "little faith," the same description that Jesus uses for the twelve disciples across the narrative (6:30; 8:26; 16:8; 17:20). At other points "little faith" is defined by the presence of worry (6:30), fear (8:26), and lack of understanding (16:8); in this passage it is further explicated by Peter's "doubt" (*distazō*, also rendered as "waver"). This word is used in the New Testament only in Matthew and only two times (14:31; 28:17). In both cases it describes a wavering of faith in the disciples. Little faith is a faith that does not hold firm in the midst of adversity or confusing circumstances.

14:33 *those who were in the boat worshiped him, saying, "Truly you are the Son of God."* This is the first time in the story line that the disciples respond to Jesus in worship. It parallels the final scene of the Gospel, where the eleven disciples respond to the resurrected Jesus with both worship and doubt (*distazō* [28:17; as at 14:31]). The confessional statement "You are the Son of God" by the disciples here is a fitting answer to their rhetorical question at 8:27: "What kind of man is this?" It also parallels Peter's confession at the end of this section of Matthew: "You are the Messiah, the Son of the living God" (16:16). In first-century Judaism "son of God" language could be used for the Messiah (e.g., 2 Esd. 7:28–29), and this seems to be the way Matthew uses it (16:16 as appositional; 26:63; see comments on 4:3, 6).

14:34 *Gennesaret.* Gennesaret is a region on the northwest shore of the Sea of Galilee. The last location specified in Matthew was Nazareth, Jesus' hometown (13:54–58). The setting for the feeding miracle that has just occurred is an unspecified "solitary place" (14:13) set apart from a number of towns and villages (traditionally, it is associated with Tabgha and/or Bethsaida [cf. Mark 6:45; Luke 9:10]). In 14:22 Jesus then sends the disciples in a boat across the Sea of Galilee. They land at Gennesaret, on the other side from where they started out.

14:35 *when the men.* The Greek *andres* typically refers to a group of men, as in 14:21 (as opposed to *anthrōpos*, which is typically generic); but *andres* may also indicate a group of people, as the quite general nature of the activity of the subsequent verbs would seem to suggest ("they [the people vs. the men] brought all their sick to him" and "they begged him" [cf. NRSV; CEB; CEV]).

14:36 *begged him to let the sick just touch the edge of his cloak.* Jesus' power and compassion are implicitly communicated in this description of people coming to him for healing. The power of Jesus that comes through simply touching the edge of his cloak is reminiscent of an earlier incident in which a woman with chronic bleeding touches the edge of Jesus' cloak (9:20) and is healed. Reference to the "edge" of Jesus' cloak renders the Greek *kraspedon*, which refers to the tassels worn by Jewish men on the corners of their robes (see comments on 9:20).

Teaching the Text

1. *By fostering connections with the Exodus narratives, Matthew emphasizes Jesus' authority and compassion toward Israel in line with a similar portrait of Yahweh from Exodus.* At a defining moment in the story of Israel from the Old Testament,

God establishes a covenant with them after redeeming them from Egypt. In the giving of the covenant stipulations, Yahweh is revealed as a God who is gracious as well as powerful to redeem Israel: "The LORD, the LORD, the compassionate and gracious God, slow to anger, abounding in love and faithfulness" (Exod. 34:6). This picture of this God of all authority who compassionately brings Israel out of Egypt by signs and wonders and then feeds them in the wilderness provides a fitting backdrop for Matthew's portrayal of Jesus. As Jesus has acted with compassion and authority to heal and save (chaps. 8–9; 11:2–5), now he acts with compassion and authority to feed and provide. Preaching a God who has all authority but no compassion would offer a terrifying divine portrait, and preaching a God who has great compassion but no power to save would offer an anemic one. The beautiful good news, as Matthew tells it, is that Jesus, like Yahweh, is compassionate and powerful to save. This is the good news that we are invited to preach and teach.

2. *Matthew 14:22–33 focuses primarily on Christology, not on discipleship.* It is easy to focus our attention in preaching and teaching on the figure of Peter. His impulsive actions in jumping out of the boat are captivating and fit nicely with our cultural propensities to glorify risky behavior. Matthew, however, provides no indications that Peter's behavior is particularly commendable. Peter is neither criticized nor praised for attempting to

All four Gospels record Jesus demonstrating his authority over the forces of nature on the Sea of Galilee. In Matthew 14:33 the response of the disciples is to worship Jesus as the Son of God. This sarcophagus fragment from the fourth century AD shows the Gospel writers John, Luke, and Mark in a ship that Christ is steering through storm-tossed waters.

do what Jesus does. Instead, the focus of his role in the story is on his faith, which is compromised by his fear of the elements. He succumbs to fear; his faith wavers. In the end, he is portrayed as one with "little faith," in line with the disciples generally in Matthew. The right action of the disciples is clearly their worship and confession of Jesus as "Son of God" (Messiah) at the end of the story (14:33), which points to Matthew's christological focus of the story. When preaching or teaching this passage, we might well emphasize Jesus as one with authority over even the forces of nature. As such, he is worthy of our faith and worship.

Illustrating the Text

By fostering connections with the Exodus narratives, Matthew emphasizes Jesus' authority and compassion toward Israel in line with a similar portrait of Yahweh from Exodus.

Film: *The Ten Commandments.* Cecil B. DeMille's 1956 classic movie offers a famous scene in which Moses stands at the water's edge just as God parts the sea, making a way of escape for the Israelites from Egypt's army. This scene captures the imagination and emphasizes God's authority over creation—an authority that Jesus demonstrates in this passage.

Matthew 14:22–33 focuses primarily on Christology, not on discipleship.

Quote: The focus of this passage is primarily on Jesus' identity and authority and not so much on Peter's trust or lack of it. By focusing on Jesus, Matthew commends trust in Jesus' authority to his reader. In *The Reason for God*, Timothy Keller notes,

> The faith that changes the life and connects to God is best conveyed by the word "trust." Imagine you are on a high cliff and you lose your footing and begin to fall. Just beside you as you fall is a branch sticking out of the very edge of the cliff. It is your only hope and it is more than strong enough to support your weight. How can it save you? If your mind is filled with intellectual certainty that the branch can support you, but you don't actually reach out and grab it, you are lost. If your mind is instead filled with doubts and uncertainty that the branch can hold you, but you reach out and grab it anyway, you will be saved. Why? It is not the strength of your faith but the object of your faith that actually saves you. Strong faith in a weak branch is fatally inferior to weak faith in a strong branch.[2]

Education: "Show and tell" is a favorite part of most children's experience in elementary school. They hunt through the house for something unique to bring to show their classmates. To simply describe one of these personal treasures with words without bringing it to class would defeat the purpose of show and tell. In analogous fashion, Matthew shows what Jesus does in order to lead his readers to respond in worship. To simply say that Jesus has power over God's creation and so is worthy of our worship falls short of showing this power through scenes such as the one in 14:22–33. Just as the disciples are led to worship when they experience Jesus' authority ("Truly you are the Son of God"), so Matthew draws his readers into worshiping Jesus by showing his power over wind and wave.

Jesus, Not Jewish Leaders, Interprets the Torah Rightly

Big Idea *Jesus and his followers are shown to be true adherents of the Torah, contrasting with the Jewish leaders who disobey the law and so are defiled even as they follow their traditions.*

Understanding the Text

The Text in Context

In this passage Matthew narrates another conflict between Jesus and the Pharisees and teachers of the law (15:1). This controversy, like the earlier one (12:1–14), focuses on Torah observance, particularly teaching traditions on the Torah. Matthew affirms Jesus as the one who rightly interprets and obeys the law, while the Pharisees are portrayed as those who disregard the law in their efforts to obey their own tradition (15:3). Jesus as the one who rightly interprets the Torah is thematic in Matthew (e.g., 5:17–20; 9:13; 12:7). Later in the Gospel Jesus will give a thoroughgoing critique of the Pharisees and teachers of the law for circumventing obedience to the law in their very efforts to keep oral tradition (23:13–36). This passage also emphasizes

The Pharisees ask Jesus why his disciples do not follow the purity practices before eating food. Stone mugs like this one found at Masada may have been used to pour water for ritual hand washing (first century AD).

the important of hearing and understanding (15:10), with the disciples functioning as a less than ideal example of such understanding (15:15–16; cf. 16:9).

Interpretive Insights

15:1 *Then some Pharisees and teachers of the law came to Jesus from Jerusalem.* Matthew frequently groups together Pharisees and teachers of the law as Jesus' opponents about the Torah (12:38; 23:2–29; cf. 5:20). While there have been Pharisees and teachers from the environs of Galilee who have opposed Jesus (e.g., 12:2, 14, 24, 38), Matthew indicates that some have come from Jerusalem to question Jesus about Torah observance. This implies that news of this Galilean prophet and teacher has reached the center of Judaism.

15:2 *Why do your disciples break the tradition of the elders?*

The term "tradition" (*paradosis*) refers to oral regulations and laws that developed around the written Torah; such tradition was intended to help those keeping it to avoid transgressing the Torah (see comments on 5:21–48). Attributing their tradition to "the elders," as the Pharisees do here, grants it a greater sense of authority (for teachings attributed to "the elders," see Josephus, *Ant*. 10.51). Pharisees affirmed the authority and value of oral tradition, while other groups did not (e.g., Sadducees). In this way, the Pharisees held themselves to a stricter legal code than did others.

They don't wash their hands before they eat! The particular criticism lodged against Jesus' disciples (not Jesus himself) is that they do not perform ceremonial hand washing before they eat. This is not a universal regulation of the Torah; instead, it was a requirement for priests serving in the temple (see Exod. 30:17–21). Given that the Pharisees sought to keep more routinely various commandments that were required of the priests performing temple service, they show a concern for hand washing before meals (as a cultic, not a sanitary, measure). Although we lack first-century evidence for such an expectation for all Jews, the influence of the Pharisees with the general Jewish populace might account for such an expectation, as we see reflected here in Matthew.

15:3 *And why do you break the command of God for the sake of your tradition?* The crux of Jesus' countercomplaint against the Pharisees and teachers is that they care more about the traditions meant to help keep the Torah than about the Torah

itself (see 23:16–22). The basic charge is leveled again at 15:6.

15:4 *Honor your father and mother.* Jesus draws on the fifth commandment (Exod. 20:12) and a related prohibition against cursing one's parents (Exod. 21:17) to illustrate the irony of elevating a human tradition meant to keep one from disobeying the Torah above the very commandments themselves.

15:5 *devoted to God.* This phrase renders the Greek *dōron*, which is used to translate the Hebrew term *qorban* (e.g., Lev. 2:1). The Hebrew word refers to something no longer used for ordinary purposes but consecrated to God (BDAG 559; cf. Mark 7:11, where the Greek equivalent *korban* is defined by *dōron*). In the first-century setting, *dōron* refers to a vow made to dedicate some part of one's property to God, specifically to the temple treasury.[1] In Matthew, the example that Jesus gives is of property devoted to God that might have been used to support one's parents. Such a vow, which is not itself a Torah requirement, actually causes one to transgress the commandment to honor parents (Exod. 20:12).

15:7 *You hypocrites!* The reference to the Pharisees as hypocrites also occurs in the woes in 23:13–29 and the conflict at 22:15–22 (v. 18). For Matthew, a hypocrite is one whose inner life and outer life are incongruent (see 6:2, 5, 16; 23:25). This lack of integrity is captured well in the words of Isaiah at Matthew 15:8: "These people

Matthew 15:1–20

Jewish Purity Considerations and Regulations

It is fairly common in Christian interpretations of first-century Judaism to misread Jewish sensibilities about ritual purity. A more nuanced portrait emerges from recent scholarly studies.

1. In the Old Testament material no clear distinction is made between what we might categorize as moral laws and purity laws. For example, the call to love one's neighbor (Lev. 19:18) sits in the middle of the holiness code that focuses on purity concerns. This carries over into the practices of Judaism, where the purification or sin offering "was offered both for certain moral offenses and for the pollutions incurred without any moral failure."[a]

2. Adherence to the Torah provided the basis for Jewish distinctiveness from Gentiles around them. This was true for the various food regulations, by which Jews were "confronted daily at the dinner table" with God's call for a distinctive holiness.[b]

3. Being ritually unclean was not considered moral failure. "Uncleanness is not a disease, and it implies no moral censure; it is a ritual state in which both men and women likely found themselves most of the time."[c] So "being an observant Jew . . . did not mean avoiding all uncleanness but rather knowing when he or she had incurred pollution so as to attend to its purification at once."[d]

4. Some Jews, such as the Pharisees and Essenes, were concerned with purification not only from primary pollution but also from secondary pollution, which involved coming into contact with something touched by a person or a thing in an unclean state. This additional commitment would involve, for example, avoiding a meal with someone who was ritually unclean.

[a] deSilva, *Honor, Purity*, 268.
[b] Milgrom, *Leviticus 1–16*, 730.
[c] Levine, "Discharging Responsibility," 387.
[d] deSilva, *Honor, Purity*, 275n62.

honor me with their lips, but their hearts are far from me."

15:9 *their teachings are merely human rules.* Jesus cites Isaiah 29:13, which indicts Israel of the past for their hypocritical behavior. In analogous fashion, Jesus applies the text to the Pharisees' hypocrisy. The second half of the citation fits well with the present situation, since Jesus' concern is that the Pharisees have elevated human rules (traditions about hand washing) above the teachings of God.

15:10 *Listen and understand.* As in the Parables Discourse (chap. 13), Jesus invites the crowds and his followers to hear and understand ("Whoever has ears, let them hear" [11:15; 13:9, 43]).[2]

15:11 *What goes into someone's mouth does not defile them.* Jesus tells a parable to illustrate his point. His parable addresses purity issues (see the sidebar "Jewish Purity Considerations and Regulations"), which are central to the Pharisees' question in 15:2.

15:12 *the Pharisees were offended.* The term used here for "offended" is *skandalizō*, which can refer to taking offense or falling away. Matthew uses both senses in the course of his story, the former to describe Jesus' hometown and the Pharisees (13:57; 15:12) and the latter to describe Jesus' disciples (26:31; see also 13:21).

15:13 *Every plant that my heavenly Father has not planted will be pulled up.* This saying is reminiscent of the parable of the wheat and weeds (13:24–30) as well as the theme of revelation introduced at 11:25–27.

15:14 *they are blind guides.* This is a significant indictment of those meant to lead the people of Israel, as the Pharisees and teachers of the law were supposed to do (see 23:2–3). The influence of these teachers in leading the people astray is emphasized in the picture of the blind leading the blind (similarly in 23:16–26). These leaders are blind because they misinterpret and misapply the laws of God.

15:16 *Are you still so dull?* Jesus' exasperation with the slowness of the disciples to understand corresponds to his care in interpreting parables for them (13:18–23, 36–43, 49–50). This exasperation leads the reader to wonder at the disciples' claim to understand the parables (13:51). The disciples continue to need Jesus' explanations, and they misunderstand his repeated teachings. The terse parable in 15:11 is explained in 15:17–20 as teaching that evil thoughts produce evil words and actions. These are the things that come "out of the mouth."

15:20 *eating with unwashed hands does not defile.* The parable in 15:11 includes the aphorism "What goes into someone's mouth does not defile them." According to Jesus' interpretation at 15:17–20, this aphorism addresses the Pharisees' complaint about his disciples and not food laws themselves (cf. Mark 7:19). Matthew's Jesus is addressing the problem of adding external regulations in order to protect oneself against defilement that comes from eating, while ignoring defilement that comes from the interior person, where evil and good are produced (see 12:35).

Teaching the Text

1. *For Matthew, Jesus interprets the Torah rightly; it is the Pharisees and teachers of the law who are misguided in their understanding and practice of the Torah.* It is sometimes tempting to pit Jesus against the law, so that the law is the enemy and Jesus the champion of freedom from such strictures. This is especially true of many Christian readings of Jewish purity laws, which are deemed tedious and onerous. This certainly would be a misreading of Matthew. In this passage we have seen that

Jesus' problem with some of the Jewish leaders is that they substitute their traditions on the Torah for the commands themselves. What should be central has become, at best, peripheral and, at worst, ignored. Purity regulations are not the problem per se in this passage. Given that the Pharisees do not accuse Jesus directly of being lax in this regard (they address concerns about his disciples only), we should not assume that Matthew is giving a negative portrait of purity laws. So in our preaching and teaching we should be careful to help people understand what purity regulations were about and why Jews attempted to be faithful in following them. Our preaching should focus on what Matthew emphasizes: the importance of keeping God's commands and not allowing our own traditions to become more important than or even replace these commands.

It is necessary, however, in our postresurrection context to recognize that Gentile inclusion among the covenant people has shifted expectations about the Old Testament food laws and their applicability. In an unexpected turn, it was revealed to the early church that Gentiles coming into the faith did not have to convert to Judaism in order to be full participants in the messianic community (see Acts 10:1–11:18; 15:1–35). Thus, Gentile believers were not required to be circumcised or to follow Jewish food laws from the Torah. Although this part of the formation of the Christian faith falls outside of Matthew's story line, it is appropriate to bring this truth to bear when teaching about this passage.[3] But it would be important to do so without disparaging Jewish food laws in the process.

2. *Jesus teaches about how evil thoughts*

and actions defile a person. Jesus points to the source of evil thoughts and actions—the human heart—to illustrate the nature of defilement. Through Jesus' teaching, Matthew cautions his reader to look inward to address where actions and thoughts come from. As we have heard in 12:33, "Make a tree good and its fruit will be good." By addressing the inward life, a person's actions and words will come into alignment with God's will.

Illustrating the Text

For Matthew, Jesus interprets the Torah rightly; it is the Pharisees and teachers of the law who are misguided in their understanding and practice of the Torah.

Applying the Text: As you think about re-contextualizing this passage, the following questions might provide analogous points of reflection for contemporary congregations. In this process it would be helpful to realize that discerning the lines between tradition and Scripture is often more difficult than we imagine (as the Pharisees illustrate in this passage), since traditions are often closely tied to Scripture as extensions of our understanding of Scripture.

- Where do your own denominational or cultural traditions add to or detract from biblical commands?
- What are some traditions in your local church context that would be difficult to change without significant fracturing of your church? These might provide examples of ways in which our own traditions have overshadowed Scripture.

Cultural Experience: What was it like to live in a culture that explicitly fostered an awareness of ritual purity and impurity? David deSilva provides a helpful analogy from our own cultural context, which, though not technically a purity culture, cares about defilement boundaries.

Watching how people handle their food is an especially fruitful way to discover their purity codes and the places where defilement threatens to creep into their lives. Food spread out over the kitchen counter (while one is preparing dinner, for example) is clean and in its proper place. Food might even be able to enter the living room if it is properly contained. If the food, however, were spread out over the staircase, we would see it as "unclean" and polluting—we would cleanse the stairs and probably dispose of the food as "defiled" as well. Eating out poses many threats to a person's purity, hence the proliferation of hand sanitizers, the care taken not to eat what falls onto the bare table or the floor, and the inspection of the silverware for particles of food left from the last meal.[4]

Jesus teaches about how evil thoughts and actions defile a person.

Quote: Parker Palmer, in *A Hidden Wholeness*, commends integrity to his reader—the unifying of internal and external worlds—and speaks of the problem of a divided life.

In a culture like ours—which devalues or dismisses the reality and power of the inner life—ethics too often becomes an external code of conduct, an objective set of rules we are told to follow, a moral exoskeleton we put on hoping to prop ourselves up. The problem with exoskeletons is simple: we can slip them off as easily as we can don them.[5]

Jesus' Compassion and Authority to Feed and Heal

Big Idea *Matthew demonstrates Jesus' compassion and authority in a miraculous feeding and in healing that extends even to a Gentile, indicating that trust is the right response to Jesus.*

Understanding the Text

The Text in Context

For a third time in Matthew, Jesus withdraws from controversy (15:21; see also 12:15; 14:13) to minister with healing to the crowds (15:22, 30–31). Given that Matthew focuses almost exclusively on Jesus' ministry to Israel (10:5–6), it is significant that the story of the healing of a Canaanite woman's daughter is included (15:21–28; note 15:24). This is only the second encounter between Jesus and a Gentile supplicant; the first is the centurion in 8:5–13. In both cases Jesus responds to the "great faith" that these Gentiles exhibit (8:10; 15:28). The feeding of the four thousand follows just one chapter after the feeding of the five thousand (14:13–21) and reiterates Jesus' compassion and authority as well as motifs of a new exodus (15:32, 36–37).

Jesus travels from Galilee to the vicinity of Tyre and Sidon and then heads back toward the Sea of Galilee.

Interpretive Insights

15:21 *Leaving that place, Jesus withdrew to the region of Tyre and Sidon.* This is the last of three times that Matthew narrates Jesus' withdrawing (*anachōreō*) from controversy to focus on compassionate healing (12:15; 14:13; 15:21). Tyre and Sidon are on the coast of the Mediterranean

immediately northwest of Galilee. It is unclear whether Jesus enters these predominantly Gentile cities or remains in their general vicinity, which, as with much of this part of Galilee, was predominantly Jewish in makeup.[1]

15:22 *A Canaanite woman.* The use of "Canaanite" (cf. "born in Syrian Phoenicia" in Mark 7:26) evokes the story of Israel and Canaan and particularly the enmity between the two in Israel's early history.[2] This heightens the power of the theme of Gentile inclusion that emerges from 15:21–28.

Lord, Son of David, have mercy on me! Interestingly, this Gentile woman appears to know enough about Jesus to call him "Son of David," a favorite Matthean term to signal Jesus' messianic identity (1:1–17).

My daughter is demon-possessed. Jesus' ministry of exorcism is introduced in the summary in 4:24 (also 8:16) and illustrated in 8:28–34; 9:32–33; 12:22; 17:14–20.

15:23 *Jesus did not answer a word.* In spite of the woman's plea and her apparent recognition of his messianic identity, Matthew narrates that Jesus gives no response to her.[3] Commentators and other readers are prone to rescue Jesus at this point by attributing altruistic intentions (e.g., he is testing the woman to draw out her faith). Yet unless we provide motives for the characters, the story reads as if Jesus expresses hesitation in granting healing to a Gentile (15:24, 26), as in 8:5–7 (see comments there). The problem with importing such motives is that the text gives no particular clues for doing so. This fits the practices of ancient characterization, which tended to avoid providing the thoughts and motives of its characters.

15:24 *I was sent only to the lost sheep of Israel.* The scope of Jesus' ministry has been indicated from the start as focusing on Israel: "Jesus went throughout Galilee, teaching in their synagogues" (4:23). Jesus has indicated to his disciples that they are to confine their ministry (which is an extension of his) to "the lost sheep of Israel" and avoid going "among the Gentiles" or entering "any town of the Samaritans" (10:5–6). Here Jesus makes it clear that the people of Israel are the God-given focus of his Galilean ministry. After the resurrection Matthew will narrate a dramatic shift to include "all nations" (28:19). The latter emerges from (1) the isolated instances of Gentile ministry by Jesus (here and in 8:5–13); and (2) the theme of Gentile inclusion across Matthew that points ahead to this postresurrection expansion (e.g., 1:3–6; 2:1–2; 4:15–16; 12:18–21; 21:43; 24:14).

One interesting feature of this part of the dialogue is that Jesus makes this statement not directly to the woman but rather in response to the disciples' request that Jesus send her away from them. This may indicate that Jesus is unwilling to send the woman away, while also affirming that her request sits outside the scope of his God-given mission at present. As such, his comment invites further conversation.

15:26 *It is not right to take the children's bread and toss it to the dogs.* In their second exchange Jesus responds to the Canaanite woman's "Lord, help me!" with a picture of the Jews as the children eating at a table and Gentiles as the dogs waiting to catch a dropped morsel. He makes the point that it would not be right to throw the bread intended for the children to the dogs. It is difficult to attribute these words to Jesus if we view him as one who agrees to every request for healing that comes to him. It seems significant that both occasions in Matthew where Jesus initially demurs to heal involve a Gentile seeker (here and 8:5–13).

Yet in this particular story Jesus hesitates not just once (as at 8:7), but first through silence (15:23), then for reasons related to his mission (15:24), and now with what seems to be a derogatory statement: Jesus portrays the woman in his analogy as one of the dogs. Jews did use the term *kyōn* ("dog"), a ceremonially unclean animal, as an invective for Gentiles (e.g., ironically in Phil. 3:2). Here the diminutive form, *kynarion*, is used, possibly to indicate a smaller, domestic dog (though it can also be used without diminutive force [BDAG 575]). While reading *kynarion* as indicating the family pet offers a softer reading of Jesus' words here, it does not remove their sting fully. Yet the woman does not take the words as a sign of defeat; instead, she pushes back one more time.

15:27 *Yes it is, Lord.* The woman's response to Jesus' qualifier that his ministry is limited to Israel can be read two ways. The "yes" (*nai*) might indicate agreement with Jesus' statement about bread to the dogs, in which case her next words qualify her agreement ("yet even the dogs eat the crumbs"). The NIV's rendering interprets the *nai* as a contradiction of Jesus' words "It is not right to . . . toss it to the dogs."

The women disagrees, "Yes, it is [right]." This interpretation fits well the use of *gar* ("for, because"), quite seldom contrastive, which follows the "yes." Her reasoning follows: "Even the dogs eat the crumbs that fall from their master's table." In her ingenuity, she is like the centurion who works around Jesus' initial hesitation ("Shall I come and heal him?" [8:7]) by recognizing that Jesus is able to heal even without accompanying him home (8:8–9).

15:28 *Woman, you have great faith!* The passage concludes with Jesus' exclamation of this woman's great faith and his healing of her daughter. The only other occurrence of "great faith" in Matthew describes the one other Gentile supplicant coming to Jesus for healing, the centurion in 8:10, again tying these two stories together thematically as well as in a number of their narrative details.

15:29 *went along the Sea of Galilee.* Matthew omits reference to the Decapolis (cf. Mark 7:31), thereby showing Jesus to be in Jewish territory (along the northwest side of the Sea of Galilee) for the following feeding miracle.

15:30 *Great crowds came to him . . . and he healed them.* Matthew provides another summary of Jesus' healing activity (see 4:23–25; 9:35; 12:15; 14:34–36).

15:31 *The people were amazed . . . And they praised the God of Israel.* While some have taken the inclusion of the phrase "God of Israel" to signal that these crowds are made up of Gentiles, the phrase is used across the Old Testament in the mouth of Israelites (e.g., Deborah in Judges 5:3; Jonathan in 1 Kings 1:48; the psalmist in Ps. 41:13; see also Luke 1:68).[4] Matthew mutes any indication in his Markan source that

Matthew 15:29–39 records that Jesus miraculously feeds a hungry crowd for a second time. This tenth-century AD ivory plaque from the Magdeburg Cathedral, Germany, illustrates the multiplication of the loaves and fish.

(as some scribes seem to have assumed by substituting "Magdala[n]" for "Magadan"), then it is located on the western side of the Sea of Galilee, southwest of Capernaum. Unlike Mark's related accounts, Matthew's narrative portrays Jesus' ministry focused in Galilee and on the people of Israel (see 15:21).

the feeding of the four thousand focuses on Gentiles (e.g., Mark 7:31; 8:10).

15:32 *I have compassion for these people.* The Matthean theme of Jesus as compassionate Messiah is again reiterated (see 8:3; 9:36; 14:14; 20:34).

15:33 *Where could we get enough bread in this remote place?* The disciples continue to evidence "little faith," since they have just recently witnessed Jesus feeding over five thousand people (14:21). Getting enough bread is not a problem! "The deliberate parallels between this episode and the first feeding account render the disciples' continued lack of insight into the mighty power of Jesus all the more incomprehensible."[5]

15:36 *when he had given thanks, he broke them and gave them to the disciples.* For the linguistic parallels between this verse, the first feeding miracle, and Jesus' Passover celebration with his disciples, see comments on 14:19. Matthew makes these parallels in order to highlight the theme of new exodus.

15:39 *went to the vicinity of Magadan.* If Magadan is to be identified with Magdala

Theological Insights: Gentile Inclusion—New Testament Trajectories

Matthew portrays Jesus as ministering to Gentiles only twice in his Gospel (here and 8:5–13). Yet Matthew highlights the theme of Gentile inclusion at the beginning and end of his Gospel, with the inclusion of Gentiles in Jesus' genealogy and at his birth (1:3, 5, 6; 2:1) and when Jesus commissions his followers to disciple all nations (28:18–20). This Gentile mission becomes a central issue in other New Testament writings. In Acts the Holy Spirit falls upon Gentiles prior to their conversion to Judaism, signaling the inclusion of Gentiles in the messianic community on full terms with Jewish believers (10:1–11:18; 15:1–35). In Galatians Paul argues vigorously that Gentile believers must not be compelled to be circumcised and obey the Torah in order to be full members of the messianic community; they are already fully included through Jesus and by the Spirit (2:14–3:29; cf. Rom. 3:21–26).

Teaching the Text

Matthew portrays Jesus following his God-given mission to announce the kingdom's arrival to Israel and moving outside these missional parameters only when observing great faith. This passage often provokes in its readers a need to explain away various details of the story that seem to cast Jesus in a bad light. Interpreters often state quite categorically that Jesus is testing the Canaanite woman (or his disciples) and intends all along to heal her daughter, although there are no textual clues that point in this direction. Sometimes readers focus on the distinction between *kyōn* and *kynarion* ("dog" and its diminutive form) to indicate that Jesus compares Gentiles to the family pet versus a wild dog. Yet even if this diminutive is meant to soften the comparison, the comparison still seems less than complimentary.

If it is the case that Matthew here offers a portrait of Jesus being hesitant to cross the missional boundary from Jew to Gentile, how do we preach this Jesus, especially when the tendency in much preaching is to emphasize Jesus as a maverick who transgresses social and cultural boundaries without a thought? This passage reminds us that the priority of Israel's restoration was a fundamental expectation arising from the Old Testament itself. God's return to and restoration of exiled Israel from among the nations would then set in motion a redemptive harvest of the nations (e.g., Isa. 2:2–5; 60:1–3; 66:18–21; Mic. 4:1–5). It was Israel's privilege and responsibility as God's chosen people to be a light to the nations. Matthew highlights this temporal priority of Jesus' messianic ministry in 10:5–6; 15:24 (see also 8:5–7; this priority is evident in Acts as well). So we can draw from the Old Testament to frame Jesus' own ministry, in which mission to Israel matters and remains the focus of his ministry until after the resurrection. He truly is the one who will "save his people from their sins" (1:21). The powerful inclusivity of salvation available to all nations (28:18–20) is accented when we acknowledge, with Matthew, that it comes as a result of Jesus' death and resurrection. And the corresponding truth is that we who follow Jesus have the privilege and responsibility to be a light to the nations today.

In the end, we do not need to domesticate Jesus in these particular moments where he does not quite fit our stereotypes or to make him more palatable to our audiences. In this story Jesus does provide healing for a Gentile in spite of missional

Jesus commends the Canaanite woman's great faith after she answers his objection to healing her daughter by saying, "Even the dogs eat the crumbs that fall from their master's table" (15:27). Shown here is a Greek funerary relief in which a dog investigates the floor underneath a table in this banquet or symposium scene (fourth century BC).

constraints. And he does so because he sees an amazing display of faith from this Canaanite woman. And that is the message of the passage. Trust in this Jewish Jesus. Trust in him and bring your needs to the one who is Israel's Messiah, and you will not be disappointed.

Illustrating the Text

Matthew portrays Jesus following his God-given mission to announce the kingdom's arrival to Israel and moving outside these missional parameters only when observing great faith.

Literature: *The Lion, the Witch and the Wardrobe,* by C. S. Lewis. In our attempts to domesticate Jesus we risk losing the power of his distinctive identity as a Jew and the priority of his mission to restore Israel. In C. S. Lewis's famous book, the rightful ruler of Narnia, Aslan (a lion), is described in terms that seem relevant to attempts to domesticate Jesus. Lucy, a child who has recently arrived in Narnia, asks Mr. and Mrs. Beaver about Aslan.

"Is he—quite safe? I shall feel rather nervous about meeting a lion."

"That you will, dearie, and no mistake," said Mrs. Beaver; "if there's anyone who can appear before Aslan without their knees knocking, they're either braver than me or else just silly."

"Then he isn't safe?" asked Lucy.

"Safe?" said Mr. Beaver; "don't you hear what Mrs. Beaver tells you? Who said anything about safe? 'Course he isn't safe. But he's good. He's the King, I tell you."[6]

Matthew 15:21–39

The Disciples Confess Jesus as the Messiah

Big Idea *While Matthew warns his readers against the unbelief and wrong teachings of the Jewish leaders, he provides the right response to Jesus in the disciples' confession of Jesus as the Messiah, which comes via revelation from God.*

Understanding the Text

The Text in Context

This passage provides a climactic summary of a number of key story elements that Matthew has introduced thus far. First, the request from the Jewish leaders for Jesus to provide a sign (16:1–4; see 12:38) culminates the various controversies that Matthew has narrated between the Jewish leaders and Jesus (e.g., 9:34; 12:22–24; 15:11–20). Second, the confusion of the disciples over bread (16:5–12) highlights the continued struggle of the Twelve to understand and trust in Jesus and his authority (16:8). Most importantly, Jesus' identity as the Messiah is confessed in explicit terms for the first time by a person in Matthew's story (16:16), providing the climactic moment of Jesus' Galilean ministry (4:17–16:20). Matthew highlights themes of revelation (16:17; see 11:25; 13:35) and the promise of authority for Peter and the Twelve (16:18–20; see 18:18; 28:18–20). Yet the placement of this confession immediately before Jesus' first passion prediction (16:21) and Peter's subsequent rebuke (16:22) indicates that Peter and the other disciples do not understand the kind of Messiah Jesus has come to be. In 16:21–28:20 Matthew will make clear the nature and destiny of Jesus as Israel's Messiah.

Interpretive Insights

16:1 *tested him by asking him to show them a sign from heaven.* Similar to 12:38, the Pharisees (now with the Sadducees) ask Jesus for a sign to prove his authority. In this instance Matthew makes it clear that the request is actually a test (for a series of tests of Jesus' authority, see 22:15–40).

16:2–3 *When evening comes . . . signs of the times.* Some early Greek manuscripts do not include these verses, beginning with "When evening comes." It is likely that this description of weather, which fits the region of Palestine, was omitted by scribes copying the text in other areas of the Mediterranean world, where the particulars of a red sky and what it signaled made less sense.

In other words, 16:2–3 are quite possibly original to Matthew, since their omission is explained by their regional particularity.

16:4 *A wicked and adulterous generation looks for a sign.* Jesus has already used this phrase to describe the Pharisees (12:39) in their request for a sign, evoking Deuteronomy 32:5, 20. For Jesus' riddle about the "sign of Jonah," see comments on 12:39.

16:5 *forgot to take bread.* Matthew has woven a bread motif through chapters 14–16, culminating with this passage, which recalls the twin feeding miracles that Jesus has performed (14:17; 15:33) and leads into Jesus' riddle about the yeast of the Jewish leaders.

16:6 *Be on your guard against the yeast of the Pharisees and Sadducees.* This warning from Jesus comes in the form of a riddle, which the disciples misunderstand to be about the bread that they had forgotten to bring along with them.

16:8–9 *You of little faith . . . Do you still not understand?* Matthew portrays the disciples as those of "little faith," always with this description on the lips of Jesus. Little faith has been variously defined contextually as worry (6:30), fear (8:26), and doubt or wavering (14:31). In all cases it is an inadequate faith in Jesus' power to rescue and provide (see also 17:20). Here little faith is tied to the disciples' lack of understanding. Although some have argued that Matthew's concept of faith is quite distinct from understanding, this passage indicates a closer tie between them.[1]

Don't you remember . . . ? Jesus references the two recent feeding miracles (14:13–21; 15:32–39) in order to demonstrate the obvious point that if he and the disciples were low on bread, he could easily solve that dilemma. The irony is palpable.

Key Themes of Matthew 16:1–20

- The unbelief of the Jewish leaders has the potential to influence disciples and others.
- Jesus' disciples are characterized by misunderstanding and little faith.
- The disciples' confession of Jesus as the Messiah comes through divine revelation.

16:12 *Then they understood.* Jesus has just reiterated his warning about "the yeast of the Pharisees and Sadducees" (16:11). Matthew indicates that the disciples now understand the nature of the riddle to be about the teaching of the Pharisees and Sadducees. This specific understanding, however, does not allow us to attribute the trait of understanding to the disciples, since they will continue to misunderstand Jesus' teachings (e.g., 16:22; 19:10, 13).

the teaching of the Pharisees and Sadducees. By comparing the teaching of these leaders to yeast, Jesus implies that the disciples should be on guard against the pervasiveness and influence of their teachings. This warning fits the contours of Matthew's narrative, in that the Jewish leadership rejects Jesus and his message (12:1–14, 22–45; 21:45–46; 26:3–5) and many of the Jewish people are influenced by their leaders in destructive ways (21:33–46; 23:1–4, 13; 27:20; cf. 9:36).

16:13 *the region of Caesarea Philippi.* This area is located about twenty-five miles north of the Sea of Galilee. The importance of highlighting the location likely stems from its close identification with the disciples' confession of Jesus as the Messiah in the Gospel tradition (see Mark 8:27).

16:14 *John the Baptist.* Matthew has already narrated the view of Herod Antipas that Jesus is John the Baptist raised from the dead (14:1–12); here others think the same.

Elijah. This identification fits the portrait of Yahweh sending "the prophet Elijah to [Israel] before that great and dreadful day of the LORD comes" (Mal. 4:5). Jesus' activity, possibly his warnings of coming judgment (e.g., 11:20–24; 13:40–43, 49–50), has caused some to identify him with this preparatory figure. For fuller discussion, see comments on 17:12.

Jeremiah or one of the prophets. Matthew indicates elsewhere that the Jewish people consider Jesus to be a prophet (21:11, 46). While Matthew portrays Jesus within the stream of prophetic tradition (13:57; 23:29–39),[2] he also wants his readers to understand that Jesus is more than a prophet. Jesus should be recognized as the Messiah in all the ways that this is defined within the narrative.

16:16 *You are the Messiah, the Son of the living God.* Peter, as spokesperson for the Twelve (note the plural "disciples" and plural Greek verb for "tell" in 16:20), confesses the true identity of Jesus. He is Messiah, which is then further explained by the title "Son of the living God" (similar to 14:33). "Son of God" is a messianic title in first-century Judaism (2 Esd. 7:28–29; see comments on 4:3, 6). This confession provides a climactic moment in the narrative, since this is the first such explicit confession of Jesus as the Messiah by any person in the story.

16:17 *this was . . . revealed to you . . . by my Father in heaven.* In this section of Matthew (11:2–16:20) the theme of revelation has been prominent (11:25–27; 13:11–12, 34–35; 16:17). The theme of revelation is paired with the theme of faith—a faith that

is able to perceive and respond to the hidden nature of the kingdom in Jesus' ministry and preaching.

16:18 *you are Peter, and on this rock I will build my church.* Matthew highlights a wordplay as Jesus gives Simon the name "Peter" (*petros*) and references "this rock" (*petra*). Much attention has focused on whether Jesus promises to build his church upon Peter himself (a Roman Catholic view) or upon Peter's confession (the typical Protestant perspective). If the confession is in view, it is still the case that there is a certain authority given to Peter in the subsequent words of Jesus (16:19). Alternately, if Peter is "the rock" upon which Jesus' church will be built, the same authority given to him in 16:19 is broadened at 18:18–19 to include at least the Twelve, and, more likely, the entire church. In all the Gospels, reference to the "church" (*ekklēsia*) occurs only here and in 18:17 (see comments there).

the gates of Hades will not overcome it. The picture that Jesus draws is of the church having the strength to withstand the power of death. For Hades as the realm of the dead, see comments on 11:23.

16:19 *keys of the kingdom of heaven.* The "keys of the kingdom" are likely defined by the subsequent reference to the authority to bind and to loose that Jesus promises to give to Peter. These promises of authority should be understood in light of their expansion to the Twelve (and likely the whole church) at 18:18–19 as well as Jesus' own claim to all authority in 28:18 (see comments on 28:19–20).

whatever you bind . . . whatever you loose. Mark Powell helpfully locates the language of binding and loosing in Jewish discussions of Torah application (see 16:19;

18:18; cf. 23:4). To bind a particular law is to judge it binding for a specific situation. To loose a law involves determining that it is not applicable in a specific context (as Jesus does in 12:1–12).[3] So Matthew seems to be indicating that Jesus promises future authority to his followers to interpret and apply the Torah (and, by extension, his own teachings) for particular situations.

16:20 *Then he ordered his disciples not to tell anyone that he was the Messiah.* This warning fits Matthew's motif of the messianic secret in 8:4; 9:30; 12:16; 16:20 (see comments on 9:30–31). Given that when Jesus does publicly display his messianic identity (21:1–11), he is crucified soon afterward, concern to keep his identity under wraps is understandable in historical context.

Teaching the Text

1. *To confess Jesus to be the Messiah, the Son of the living God, is to demonstrate a right understanding of who Jesus is.* This confession by the disciples at the climactic point of Jesus' Galilean ministry points to its centrality. As Matthew has communicated from the opening of his Gospel, Jesus is the Messiah (1:1). And, although there are many ways that Matthew develops his Christology (e.g., Jesus as representative Israel, Jesus as Wisdom), confessing Jesus as the Messiah is paramount for Matthew.

It is interesting, though not surprising, that in the modern period the church has often accented the confession of Jesus as divine as the most important confession to make. And Matthew does portray Jesus as the embodiment of Yahweh, Israel's God (see the section "Matthew's Narrative Christology" in the introduction). Yet the

Jesus says he will give Peter the keys of the kingdom of heaven. Artists often picture this literally by depicting Peter holding keys, as in this fourteenth-century AD carving from Tuscany.

people in Matthew's audience in their context needed to hear the affirmation that Jesus was God's true Messiah; and Matthew calls them, through this passage and others, to reaffirm this confession themselves. What would it mean for us to preach and teach Jesus as the Messiah in fresh ways in our own contexts? First, such teaching would necessarily require us to explain what "Messiah" means, and that would be a good thing. It would require us to provide the Jewish backdrop for Jesus more so than we have been accustomed to doing, since "Messiah" means something only in the story of God's work in and for Israel. Second, focusing our hearers on the truth that Jesus is the Messiah should follow the same trajectory that Paul followed when he preached Messiah Jesus ("Christ Jesus") to non-Jewish audiences. Paul translates this category for his audience by emphasizing Jesus as "Lord" over all, a title that had great significance in his own context, as "Caesar is Lord" was a common affirmation in the first-century world. Jesus as Lord—God's agent who has all authority—remains an understandable and powerful affirmation in our context, where powers, people, and institutions can provide counterclaims to Jesus' authority. By faith, we say "Jesus is Lord," and that *he* has all power (see 1 Cor. 15:24–28), in the

Matthew 16:1–20

face of a world where perceived evidence to the contrary abounds.

2. *Although Peter and the rest of the Twelve confess Jesus' true identity, they do not provide an exemplary portrait of discipleship.* We might be tempted to preach how the disciples are exemplary in their confession of Jesus as the Messiah. We are justified in doing so only if we also provide the alternate portrait of the disciples as a foil for discipleship, as they are in 16:5–12. The disciples continue to misunderstand much of what Jesus teaches, and they will misunderstand the nature of his mission as the Messiah (16:21–23). So preaching discipleship in Matthew does not mean idealizing the disciples, since Matthew sketches a picture of disciples by using them as both exemplars and foils and by drawing on other exemplars of faith and discipleship in the story.[4]

More generally, there is a tendency to idealize various biblical characters and then preach them as moral examples. This is certainly the case in teaching the Bible to children, where we tend to minimize the faults of biblical figures, especially those we have difficulty explaining to children (e.g., sexual sins of Judah, of David, etc.). Yet by idealizing and moralizing these characters, we not only do a disservice to the authors' intentions; we also run the risk of downplaying the theological themes of these narratives, in which God is the focus (and hero).

Illustrating the Text

To confess Jesus to be the Messiah, the Son of the living God, is to demonstrate a right understanding of who Jesus is.

Biography: Theodulf, a ninth-century priest, had risen from humble beginnings to serve in the court of Charlemagne. Known for his articulate pen and creative mind, Theodulf distinguished himself by writing hymns and theological treatises. However, when Charlemagne died, Theodulf was banished into obscurity by one of the emperor's sons. Theodulf, who had stood before the most powerful man in the world, died in Saint-Aubin monastery. Yet it was in this place of obscurity that Theodulf wrote his best-known hymn, "All Glory, Laud, and Honor," traditionally sung on Palm Sunday, which includes this confession about Jesus' identity:

> Thou art the King of Israel,
> Thou David's royal Son,
> Who in the Lord's Name comest,
> The King and Blessed One.

Although Peter and the rest of the Twelve confess Jesus' true identity, they do not provide an exemplary portrait of discipleship.

Poetry: "Trembling Limbs," by Jeannine Brown. Preaching about Peter and the other disciples should include the ways in which they are exemplary for discipleship (as in their right confession here) as well as the ways that they fall short of discipleship ideals. Preaching both sides of the picture requires us to explore how Jesus meets them in their weaknesses. The following lyric, based on Hebrews 12:1–3, expresses how Jesus remains with us even as we fall short of the mark.

> Trembling limbs as the race begins
> I wonder if I'll finish this course I've
>   begun;
> Looking in I see all my sin,
> And it drags me down, keeps me from
>   moving ahead.

But far, far in the distance I see him
He is there holding out his hand;
He's the one who's started this race
     before me,
And he's promised to see me to the end.

Take courage, my soul
There are many who've gone before,
And the author and finisher of faith
Cheers you on—Jesus cheers you on.

Far, far in the distance I see him
He is there holding out his hand;

He's the one who's started this race
     before me,
And he's promised to see me to the end.

Cultural Institution: An analogy that we might offer for "binding and loosing" is the function of the judicial branch in the United States. This branch of government neither creates nor enforces laws; rather, it interprets if and how various laws apply in specific circumstances.

Summary: 4:17–16:20. Matthew narrates Jesus' ministry to Israel, showing Jesus teaching and doing miracles with authority all the while including seekers, sinners, and even Gentiles in his kingdom ministry. As Matthew clarifies Jesus' identity as the healing and compassionate Messiah, he also illustrates a variety of responses to Jesus and the hiddenness of the kingdom that Jesus inaugurates: the unbelief of the Jewish leaders and Jesus' hometown, the little faith and frequent misunderstanding of the twelve disciples, and the faith of various ones who come to Jesus for healing and ministry. At the climax of this part of the story, Peter and the other disciples confess Jesus to be the Messiah.

Looking Ahead: 16:21–28:20. To Jerusalem: kingdom enactment through death and resurrection.

1. Journey to the cross and teaching on discipleship (16:21–20:28)
   a. Jesus predicts the cross and defines discipleship (16:21–17:27)
   b. Jesus' fourth discourse: the Community Discourse (18:1–35)
   c. Nearing Jerusalem: illustrations of discipleship (19:1–20:28)
2. Final proclamation, confrontation, and judgment in Jerusalem (20:29–25:46)
   a. Jesus' royal arrival and controversies with Jerusalem leadership (20:29–22:46)
   b. Judgment announced on Jewish leadership (23:1–39)
   c. Jesus' fifth discourse: the Eschatological Discourse (24:1–25:46)
3. Jesus' execution by Rome and resurrection/vindication by God (26:1–28:20)
   a. Prelude to the cross: betrayal and desertion (26:1–56)
   b. Jesus on trial (26:57–27:26)
   c. Jesus' crucifixion, death, and burial (27:27–66)
   d. Resurrection as vindication and the commissioning of disciples (28:1–20)

Jesus Announces His Impending Suffering and Death

Big Idea *Though they have just confessed Jesus as the Messiah, the disciples struggle to understand his revelation that he will suffer, die, and be raised, and that they are to follow in his cruciform footsteps.*

Understanding the Text

The Text in Context

This passage begins a new section, signaled by the formula "From that time on Jesus began to [explain]" (16:21 [as in 4:17]), narrating Jesus' journey to Jerusalem (16:21–20:28). Jesus and his disciples travel from Galilee to Jerusalem, with Jesus teaching the Twelve along the way about his mission and their vocation as his followers. Jesus predicts his impending death and resurrection at 16:21—the first of three such predictions in this section of Matthew (17:22–23; 20:17–19). The focus on discipleship in this section of Matthew includes themes of self-denial (16:24–26; cf. 10:37–39), renunciation of status preoccupation (18:1–5; 19:30; 20:16, 25–28), and valuing those most on the margins (18:6–14; 19:13–15; cf. 10:42; 25:40, 45). Yet the Twelve struggle to understand the ways of discipleship that Jesus proclaims, often showing an inordinate concern for status categories and their own elevated position

in the kingdom (e.g., 18:1; 19:13–15, 27; 20:20–28).

Interpretive Insights

16:21 *From that time on Jesus began to explain to his disciples.* Matthew draws on a twofold formula here and at 4:17 to emphasize the narrative contours of his account of Jesus' ministry. At 4:17 the formula signals the inception of Jesus' kingdom ministry in Galilee: "From that time on Jesus began to preach [the kingdom]" (*apo tote ērxato ho Iēsous* + infinitive). At 16:21 the formula turns the story line toward Jesus' passion, as he begins to teach his disciples of the divine necessity for his death in Jerusalem.

he must go to Jerusalem. The necessity of Jesus' coming death is expressed in the form of four Greek infinitives specifying that Jesus must go to Jerusalem, suffer, be killed, and be raised. The use of *dei* ("must") expresses this divine necessity. This is the first of three passion predictions in the account of Jesus' journey to Jerusalem in 16:21–20:28. All three predictions are spoken to Jesus' twelve disciples, who struggle to understand what he is anticipating in Jerusalem.

the elders, the chief priests and the teachers of the law. In this passion prediction Jesus speaks of his suffering at the hands of the Jewish leadership. The subsequent passion predictions indicate the breadth of agency for Jesus' death; he will be delivered into human hands (17:22) and will be crucified by Gentiles (20:19).

and on the third day be raised to life. Each of Jesus' three passion predictions references his resurrection. Yet it is unclear that the disciples comprehend or would be able to comprehend what this means. Jewish eschatological expectations often included the hope for resurrection understood as a general resurrection of all believers at the time of final judgment. Jewish expectations did not include an individual's resurrection

Key Themes of Matthew 16:21–28

- Jesus is the suffering Messiah.
- The disciples lack understanding.
- Discipleship is patterned after Jesus crucified.

at a different point in time from the rest of humanity. So any words of Jesus about his resurrection would likely have been absorbed as reference to that final, general resurrection (cf. John 11:23–24; 1 Cor. 15:20–23). The phrase "on the third day" could easily have been heard by the disciples as referring to a more general timeframe of

Jesus explains to his disciples that "he must go to Jerusalem and suffer many things at the hands of the elders, the chief priests and the teachers of the law" (16:21). Representatives of these leadership groups could be found serving and teaching in the various courts of the temple complex in Jerusalem. The porticoes at the perimeter of the court of the Gentiles were shaded locations where Jewish teachers would conduct their classes. The royal stoa was at the southern end. This model of the temple complex is part of the 50:1-scale reproduction of the first-century AD city of Jerusalem now on display at the Israel Museum in Jerusalem.

royal stoa

court of the Gentiles

completion as in Hosea 6:2: "After two days he will revive us; on the third day he will restore us."

16:22 *Peter . . . began to rebuke him.* Matthew uses strong language here to show that Peter, while knowing Jesus to be the Messiah (16:16), cannot integrate Jesus' passion prediction with his view of what the Messiah was supposed to do.

16:23 *Get behind me, Satan! You are a stumbling block to me.* Jesus uses strong language to counter Peter's rebuke. Matthew uses his thematic *skandalon* ("stumbling block") to indicate that Peter unwittingly provides a significant temptation for Jesus. While many people stumble over Jesus and his teachings (e.g., 13:57; 15:12; cf. 26:31), Matthew also uses the term *skandalon* or its verbal form, as he does here, to refer to a source of temptation (cause of stumbling; see 5:29–30; 13:41; 18:6–9).

Using "Satan" to identify Peter evokes the temptation narrative, in which Jesus is tempted to be less than fully faithful to his God and his mission (4:1–12; see comments on 4:1–2). The temptation for Jesus to avoid his mission to the cross sits at the center of Peter's rebuke and will cost Jesus much anguish in Gethsemane (26:39, 42, 44).

you do not have in mind the concerns of God, but merely human concerns. In this context, with Jesus' reference to Satan, it is clear that "merely human concerns" are not neutral but rather are leveraged against "the concerns of God."

16:24 *Whoever wants to be my disciple.* Jesus turns from predicting his own death to describing discipleship in comparable terms. Jesus' teaching on self-denial and

Peter once again plays a prominent role in Matthew's narrative. This icon of Simon Peter is from a larger piece titled *Christ and Twelve Apostles* taken from a nineteenth-century Orthodox church in the Antalya region of Turkey.

on bearing one's cross as the way to follow him will be further elaborated as involving tangible actions (16:27). Self-denial, defined in subsequent chapters, involves (1) setting aside self-interest and self-promotion to care for others in the community of faith (18:1–14); (2) extending unlimited forgiveness (18:21–35); and (3) renouncing status concerns to follow the path of Jesus, the model Servant of the Lord (19:30; 20:16, 25–28).

16:25–26 *life . . . life . . . soul . . . soul.* All four of these words render the Greek *psychē*, which can refer to earthly or transcendent life (often rendered "soul" for the latter). A play on the word is used in these two verses, with *psychē* referring to earthly life in 16:25 and to transcendent life in 16:26. To focus on preserving earthly life means losing one's soul; to give up one's earthly life actually results in finding transcendent life. Both occurrences of *psychē* in 16:26 refer to the soul or transcendent life, with the idea being communicated that nothing can compare to it.

16:27 *For the Son of Man is going to come in his Father's glory.* Jesus alludes to Daniel 7:13–14 for a second time (see comments on 10:23). In Daniel 7:13–14 the picture is of "one like a son of man, coming on the clouds of heaven," enthroned and given authority over all things for an everlasting kingdom. Jesus implicitly claims his future vindication by God. The same phrasing of "Son of Man" and "coming" (*erchomai*) is repeated in 16:28.

he will reward each person according to what they have done. In Matthew, Jesus frequently references final judgment, as he does here. In line with his use of Daniel 7, Jesus claims that he ("the Son of Man") will be the one to judge all peoples. People's actions will matter in that final day, as has already been emphasized at 7:24–27; 13:41–42 (also 25:31–46). For Matthew, this truth does not negate the reality of God's grace and forgiveness in believers' lives, since human covenant loyalty is always in response to the reality of God's initiating covenant loyalty and grace.

16:28 *some who are standing here will not taste death before they see the Son of Man coming.* If this refers to Jesus' second coming or reappearing (his *parousia*), as often argued, then Jesus was simply wrong (as some have asserted). But, as noted at 10:24, Matthew does not use *parousia* except in chapter 24; instead, he uses *erchomai* as in Daniel 7:13 (also 16:27). In line with Daniel, Jesus refers to his own vindication by using the language of the coming of the Son of Man. In Matthew's

perspective, Jesus' vindication occurs both at his resurrection (26:64; 28:18) and at the fall of the temple as vindication of his prophetic warnings (see 24:3, 30–31). If Jesus is referring to either of these events, then it is true that some of the disciples live to see them. In literary context, it is also plausible that Matthew understands the transfiguration (17:1–13) as prefiguring Jesus' resurrection, in which case he wants his readers to understand 16:28 in light of 17:1–13.

Teaching the Text

1. *Jesus is truly Israel's Messiah, but his way of being the Messiah is marked by cruciformity;*[1] *he will die and be raised to inaugurate God's reign in this world.* Though the disciples rightly confess Jesus to be the Messiah (16:16), they do not understand the nature of Jesus' messianic mission, which will lead him to the cross, to his death. Given that there is little evidence in Judaism of the time that messianic expectation included suffering and death, it is not surprising that Peter pushes back when Jesus announces his coming passion in Jerusalem. But as Matthew makes clear, Jesus as the Messiah comes to "give his life as a ransom for many" (20:28). The shape of the Gospel story itself makes it impossible to separate Jesus as Messiah from the climactic arc that moves from his ministry to his passion and death. Preaching the cross continues to be an unexpected and, in many ways, unfathomable message. The one who is expected to come to conquer Israel's enemies and reign in God's stead will, instead, be crucified. The shape of the story tells us something profound about the God who acts and works in Christ.

When we speak of "following Christ," it is the crucified Messiah we are talking about. His death was not simply the messy bit that enables our sins to be forgiven but that can then be forgotten. The cross is the surest, truest and deepest window on the very heart and character of the living and loving God.[2]

2. *The nature of Jesus' role as Messiah necessarily and profoundly shapes Christian discipleship as cruciform.* The shape of Jesus' story is to be the shape of our own. As we discover in 16:21–20:28, discipleship is cross-shaped through and through. This means that those who follow Jesus are to turn away from self-promotion and status acquisition and take the role of a servant just as Jesus does (20:25–28). It also means participating in and shaping a Christian community that is known for the way it restores relationship, forgives, and seeks out those who have strayed or are most vulnerable in the believing community (18:1–35). Bearing one's cross, or self-denial, is not about holding a certain attitude; it is about doing actions (16:24–27), and, specifically, doing actions on behalf of others. It is not about self-loathing or eliminating the self from view; instead, it follows Jesus in mission and ministry wherever he leads.

Illustrating the Text

Jesus is truly Israel's Messiah, but his way of being the Messiah is marked by cruciformity; he will die and be raised to inaugurate God's reign in this world.

Nature: Hold up a single corn seed. Talk about the value of the seed. From this one seed can come a plant that produces not only nourishment but also many more seeds. Yet the seed will not reproduce if it is placed in a jar, or set in a frame, or displayed for all to see and appreciate. It must be buried in the ground, going the way of death. And as the seed goes into the soil and dies, it makes new life. In John 12:23–26 Jesus uses this illustration of a dying seed producing life to speak of his own coming death and the way to life for his own followers. Life emerges from the other side of death.

The nature of Jesus' role as Messiah necessarily and profoundly shapes Christian discipleship as cruciform.

Quote: Miroslav Volf, in *Exclusion and Embrace*, writes of dying to self in this way: "The Spirit enters the citadel of the self, de-centers the self by fashioning it in the image of the self-giving Christ, and frees its will so it can resist the power

Jesus says that to be his disciple, one must take up one's cross and follow him, even to death. Carrying a cross evoked images of those destined for crucifixion being forced to carry the horizontal beam on which they would hang. Only John's Gospel records Jesus carrying his own cross. This ivory panel contains one of the earliest depictions of that event (Rome, AD 420–30).

of exclusion in the power of the Spirit of embrace."[3]

Scripture: The image of denying self and taking up one's cross is embodied communally in the early chapters of Acts, as the members of the church, from its inception, live life together with the needs of others in view. We see them leave behind comfort, security, and individual needs to pursue authentic worship and growth, ministry and mission, and the common good. This vision of communal cruciformity is portrayed in Acts 2:42–47:

> They devoted themselves to the apostles' teaching and to fellowship, to the breaking of bread and to prayer. Everyone was filled with awe at the many wonders and signs performed by the apostles. All the believers were together and had everything in common. They sold property and possessions to give to anyone who had need. Every day they continued to meet together in the temple courts. They broke bread in their homes and ate together with glad and sincere hearts, praising God and enjoying the favor of all the people. And the Lord added to their number daily those who were being saved.

Church History: *Acts of Peter*, an early Christian writing from about AD 200, portrays Peter's courage as he heeds the words of Jesus that he must be ready to suffer for him, even submitting to crucifixion and choosing to die upside down.

Jesus Transfigured as a Foreshadowing of Future Glory

Big Idea *Matthew indicates that Jesus will suffer in the pattern of his predecessor, John the Baptist, but also foreshadows Jesus' resurrection glory, which will follow his suffering.*

Understanding the Text

The Text in Context

Matthew's account of the transfiguration, following directly on the heels of Jesus' first passion prediction, highlights Jesus' (future) resurrection glory. As Peter has been prominent in the confession of Jesus as Messiah in 16:16–20, so here too he plays the key, supporting role in this

> Mountains are important settings in Matthew (5:1; 28:16). The transfiguration narrative is set on a "high mountain" (17:1). This photo is of Mount Tabor, located in Galilee.

narrative (emphasis on Peter in 4:18–22; 8:14–15; 14:22–32; 17:24–27; 26:69–75). Peter is the recipient of the divine words affirming Jesus as the beloved Son of God (17:5; cf. 3:17). Jesus, in this passage, clarifies his relationship to John the Baptist (see 4:12; 11:2–5, 11–19; 14:1–12). Although John is the forerunner of Jesus the Messiah, they are united in the persecution and suffering that they endure to bring God's kingdom to this world (17:12).

Interpretive Insights

17:1 *After six days.* Matthew provides few specific temporal connections in his narrative, so it is likely that this reference

ties 17:1–13 closely with the previous passage, which concludes with a reference to some of Jesus' followers not experiencing death before seeing "the Son of Man coming in his kingdom." Matthew likely understands the transfiguration as a (at least partial) fulfillment of these words of Jesus about some of his disciples seeing "the Son of Man coming in his kingdom" (see comments on 16:28).

Jesus took with him Peter, James and John. These three disciples are portrayed as the closest of Jesus' followers. Peter, James, and John are three of the four disciples first called by Jesus in Matthew (4:18–22). James and John also receive special focus in 20:20–23. Peter is the most prominent of the twelve disciples in Matthew (e.g., 14:28; 15:15; 16:16; 17:4, 24; 19:27; 26:33).

17:2 *There he was transfigured before them. His face shone like the sun.* Jesus' transfiguration has storied evocations with Moses at the giving of the Torah. Moses, coming down from the mountain with the covenant tablets, strikes fear in the hearts of the Israelites because his face is radiant. The face of Jesus, who is transfigured on a mountain (17:1), shines like the sun. Yet, as Matthew will indicate in this account, Jesus is greater than Moses (and Elijah). He is the beloved Son of God.

17:3 *Moses and Elijah, talking with Jesus.* The significance of the appearance of Moses and Elijah with Jesus involves their representative roles in Israel's salvation history, with Moses representing the Law and Elijah representing the Prophets (see "the Law and the Prophets" in 7:12; 22:40). Both figures are referenced in Matthew a number of times, and some have

Key Themes of Matthew 17:1–13

- Jesus' resurrection glory is foreshadowed.
- John the Baptist was the precursor of the Messiah.
- Jesus is the suffering Messiah.

argued for a Moses typology as a significant christological category.[1]

17:4 *Lord, it is good for us to be here.* Peter responds to Jesus' changed appearance and the vision of Moses and Elijah by offering to set up three shelters for them, presumably to prolong the experience. Peter is portrayed elsewhere in Matthew as rash and impulsive (14:28–29; 16:22; 26:33); this characterization seems to fit here as well, with Peter getting caught up in the moment.

17:5 *While he was still speaking, a bright cloud covered them.* Matthew indicates that the heavenly voice interrupts Peter's babbling midstream, turning the focus back to Jesus and his identity as God's son. The whole of the transfiguration scene has the marks of a theophany, with the bright cloud and the voice of God coming from it signaling a divine appearance. The disciples in the story and Matthew's audience are prepared for the divine commendation that follows.

This is my Son, whom I love . . . Listen to him! The words spoken from the cloud are identical to those spoken by the voice from heaven in 3:17, with the addition here of "Listen to him!" (cf. Deut. 18:15). This echo signifies Jesus as the prophet like Moses who would come to teach Israel. The command to listen also fits the focus on discipleship in 16:21–20:28, since the disciples are the primary narrative characters who interact with Jesus and receive his many teachings on discipleship in this section of Matthew. As already noted (see comments on 3:17; 12:18), there is a likely textual allusion to Isaiah 42:1 here and in the baptism scene. Matthew has drawn on the verbs "I love" and "I am well pleased" here and in 3:17 and used them in his citation of Isaiah 42:1 at 12:18. By doing this, he clearly indicates that he wants his reader to hear Isaiah 42:1 in the divine words at Jesus' baptism and transfiguration. For Matthew, Jesus is the Isaianic servant. Jesus' ministry has been characterized by justice and mercy (12:18–21; cf. Isa. 42:1–4), and his death will fulfill the servant's mission (see comments on 20:28; cf. Isa. 53:12). For more about the Isaianic servant figure in Matthew, see the sidebar "Jesus as Isaiah's Servant Figure" in the unit on 12:15–21.

17:6 *they fell facedown to the ground, terrified*. As befits a theophany, the disciples fall on the ground in abject fear. Jesus will speak words drawn from the Old Testament used to assure and comfort people when they have encountered the divine presence: "Don't be afraid" (e.g., Dan. 10:12).

17:7 *Jesus came and touched them*. Matthew portrays Jesus touching someone for healing in the case of a leper (8:3); Peter's mother-in-law, who has a fever (8:15); and in the pair of stories about two blind men (9:29; 20:34). Here Jesus touches his disciples to provide comfort and alleviate their fears.

17:9 *Don't tell anyone what you have seen, until the Son of Man has been raised from the dead*. In all three synoptic Gospels the transfiguration account prefigures Jesus' resurrection by providing a glimpse of his coming glory (Matt. 17:2; 28:18; cf. Mark 9:2–8; Luke 9:28–36). The warning in 17:9 ties the two together explicitly.

17:10 *Why then do the teachers of the law say that Elijah must come first?* Presumably, the disciples are responding to Jewish rumination on Malachi 4:5–6, which refers to Yahweh sending Elijah "before that great and dreadful day of the LORD comes" (4:5). In various strands of Jewish reflection based on Malachi, Elijah had become an eschatological figure who would presage the final day of the Lord. The Jewish book of Sirach (see Sir. 48:1–11), for example, ties together Malachi and Isaiah 49:6 to portend Elijah's return.

> At the appointed time, it is written, you
>   are destined
>   to calm the wrath of God before it
>   breaks out in fury,
> to turn the hearts of parents to their
>   children,
>   and to restore the tribes of Jacob.
>   (Sir. 48:10 NRSV)

Given that the disciples have confessed Jesus as the Messiah (16:16) and have now witnessed something of his future glory with Elijah in attendance (17:2–3), it is not surprising that they are asking Jesus about the coming "day of the Lord" (often signaled in Matthew by "end of the age" language [e.g., 13:39; 24:3; 28:20]).

17:12 *Elijah has already come*. Jesus' words likely would have taken the disciples by surprise. They have given no indication of understanding that an Elijah figure had already come on the scene. In fact, their question in 17:10 implies otherwise. If Jesus is the Messiah, as they understand him to be, they appear to be wondering what this does to the expectation that Elijah would precede the Messiah. But as Matthew has narrated it, John the Baptist is Malachi's

Elijah figure. John dresses like Elijah (3:4; cf. 2 Kings 1:8), and Jesus speaks of John as "the Elijah who was to come" (11:14). So Elijah has already come, as Jesus affirms here.

In the same way the Son of Man is going to suffer at their hands. Jesus compares John's treatment (by Herod) with the way he himself will suffer at the hands of the authorities when he comes to Jerusalem. This verse functions as a brief passion prediction, corresponding to the three more-formulaic predictions at 16:21; 17:22–23; 20:17–19.

17:13 *Then the disciples understood that he was talking . . . about John the Baptist.* After Jesus refers to John's death ("they did with him what they wished"), the disciples understand that he has been talking about John in his references to Elijah's coming. Although they understand this particular connection after Jesus explains it, 17:13 does not support the notion that Matthew's portrayal of the disciples involves understanding as a character trait. They continue to misunderstand much of Jesus' teaching, as Peter has just done at 16:22.[2]

Teaching the Text

1. *Disciples should listen well to the teachings of Jesus, who is God's authorized*

"Elijah has already come, and they did not recognize him, but have done to him everything they wished" (17:12). This reference evokes the story of John's death by beheading (14:1–12). Depiction of the head of John the Baptist on a platter, like this oak carving from AD 1430, became a common motif during the Middle Ages.

servant and son. The climactic moment of the transfiguration account is the affirmation of Jesus by God in 17:5. The confirmation of Jesus as God's beloved and pleasing son echoes the same words at Jesus' baptism and connects closely to Jesus' ministry as the Isaianic servant expressed at 12:18 (cf. Isa. 42:1). In this way, Jesus is shown to be God's chosen and authorized servant. The command to "listen to him" coheres with this christological affirmation and certainly expresses Matthew's exhortation to his own audience. All believers in Jesus should listen and follow what he says. And what we hear from Jesus in these "discipleship chapters" of Matthew sometimes involves teachings that challenge our cherished understandings, much like they did Jesus' disciples, who struggled to comprehend his expectations for them. For example, Jesus teaches about a way of discipleship that is cross-shaped, as is his own mission (16:21–28). This cruciformity pushes Jesus' disciples away from their preoccupation with their own interests and status in the coming kingdom and draws them to service toward others (18:1–35). Teaching these truths from Jesus continues to be important and may cause consternation for our own audience today, given the

This icon depicts Christ's glory at his transfiguration, while the disciples cower in fear (ca. AD 1200).

human propensity toward self-preservation and cultural concerns for "our rights."

2. *Jesus as God's Messiah is unique and glorious.* The transfiguration account provides a glimpse of Jesus' postresurrection exaltation and glory (26:64; 28:18), even as he turns toward Jerusalem and his anticipated passion and death. Given that we in the contemporary church still sit at the place of the "already and not yet" of the kingdom, we too experience the hiddenness of the kingdom as well as its present reality. Even our experiences of Jesus in the present, powerful though they may

be, are muted compared to how we will someday know him fully. As Paul puts it, we still "see only a reflection as in a mirror" (1 Cor. 13:12). So we need and long for the fuller picture of Jesus in all his glory. To have glimpses of Jesus' glory and his unique identity in this "in between time" can strengthen our faith and draw us into deeper loyalty. Preaching this passage provides us with an opportunity to do just that—to portray with Matthew the glory and uniqueness of Jesus and to call people to trust in this glorious Messiah.

Illustrating the Text

Disciples should listen well to the teachings of Jesus, who is God's authorized servant and son.

Human Experience: Literary theorist Roland Barthes distinguishes between hearing and listening: "Hearing is a physiological phenomenon; listening is a psychological act."[3] This distinction makes good sense of the disciples and discipleship in Matthew. The disciples do hear Jesus' teachings, but they struggle to understand them. In Barthes's terms, we might say that they hear but do not listen. In this passage God commends Jesus' teaching to the disciples: "Listen to him!" (17:5). This call to listen well fits Jesus' own repeated exhortation to the disciples and the crowds earlier in the narrative: "Whoever has ears, let them hear" (i.e., move beyond hearing to listening).

Jesus as God's Messiah is unique and glorious.

Literature: *The Lord of the Rings*, by **J. R. R. Tolkien.** The theme of hidden glory is one of the themes running through

Tolkien's masterpiece. Consider the various characters. Strider, the Ranger, is in fact the King of Gondor. The elves, usually cloaked in human form, occasionally show their true radiance. And Gandalf the Grey, whom the Hobbits mostly appreciate for his fireworks displays, is much more than they can imagine in his person and power.

Film: *Star Wars*. We also see the theme of hidden glory in the Star Wars series. In the first movie, Luke Skywalker and his newly acquired protocol droid, C3PO, are forced into a miniadventure, chasing after R2D2, who has escaped on a search for Obi-Wan Kenobi. Obi-Wan is in reality a great Jedi, yet he has been living on Luke's desert home planet for years. This general, who fought in one of the greatest wars in Galaxy history, has willingly worn the cloak of a strange desert hermit. Luke's uncle calls him a "crazy old man." When we first meet him, we have no idea how hugely important Obi-Wan really is.

Quote: The transfiguration as the foreshadowing of Jesus' postresurrection glory implicitly points to the cross, which will be a necessary part of the journey for Jesus. And the immediate context (17:10–13) makes this connection explicit: glory and the cross go together. As N. T. Wright puts it,

> Learn to see the glory in the cross; learn to see the cross in the glory; and you will have begun to bring together the laughter and the tears of the God who hides in the cloud, the God who is to be known in the strange person of Jesus himself. This story is, of course, about being surprised by the power, love and beauty of God. But the point of it is that we should learn to recognize that same power, love and beauty in Jesus, and to listen for it in his voice—not least when he tells us to take up the cross and follow him.[4]

The Disciples' Insufficient Faith to Heal as Jesus Heals

Big Idea *Jesus, now revealed as the suffering Messiah, continues his kingdom ministry of healing, while his disciples demonstrate their "little faith" by their inability to heal as he does.*

Understanding the Text

The Text in Context

Matthew's emphasis in the account of the healing in 17:14–20 is on the disciples' inability to heal (17:19–20) in spite of the authority given them by Jesus to do so (see 10:1, 8). Their inability is tied to their little faith (17:20), already attributed to the disciples at 6:30; 8:26; 14:31; 16:8. Matthew continues the story by including Jesus' second prediction of his coming death and resurrection (17:22–23; see also 16:21; 20:17–19), followed by the story of Jesus and the temple tax. The latter account highlights the freedom of the children in the kingdom of God (17:26), while also exhorting followers of Jesus to avoid causing stumbling or offense (17:27), a theme that will be taken up in chapter 18 (18:6–9).

Interpretive Insights

17:15 *Lord, have mercy on my son.* Matthew tells of numerous supplicants who come to Jesus for healing for themselves or those in their care (8–9; 15:21–28; 20:29–34). And as they ask for mercy, they receive healing from Jesus, the compassionate Messiah.

He has seizures and is suffering greatly. In 17:18 it becomes clear that a demon causes the boy's suffering, but initially Matthew shapes the story as an account of a healing. This fits Matthew's tendency to categorize exorcisms within the overarching category of healings (4:24; 12:22; cf. Matt. 17:15 // Mark 9:17–18; see also Matt. 15:28 // Mark 7:30).

17:16 *I brought him to your disciples, but they could not heal him.* Since the twelve disciples have been given authority by Jesus "to drive out impure spirits and heal every disease and sickness" (10:1), their inability to do so here is revealing. As Jesus will diagnose it, their inability to heal is a sign of their "little faith" (17:20).

17:17 *You unbelieving and perverse generation.* Jesus' language evokes Deuteronomy 32, which laments the "perverse generation" of Israelites who were unfaithful to Yahweh in their wilderness wanderings

(Deut. 32:5, 20). Matthew draws directly from Deuteronomy 32 in his language of "unbelieving" (*apistos*; Deut. 32:20 LXX: *ouk estin pistis*) and "perverse generation" (*genea . . . diestrammenē*; likewise Deut. 32:5 LXX). Jesus' words compare the current generation to the wilderness generation that strayed from loyalty to Yahweh (see comments on 12:39). Whereas previous uses of "[this] generation" have focused on the Jewish leaders and/or the crowds, here the referent for Jesus' lament about this "generation" seems to be the disciples who are unable to heal this boy. In their inadequate faith, the disciples are looking much like the current generation in its faithlessness.

17:18 *Jesus rebuked the demon, and it came out of the boy.* The placement of a pronoun in the Greek sentence has given rise to different renderings of this verse. The word *daimonion* does not occur until the second clause of the verse, with the pronoun *autō* ("it" or "him") providing the object of Jesus' rebuke in the first clause. The dative pronoun *autō* can be either masculine or neuter and so could indicate either the demon (a neuter noun, "it") or the

boy (a masculine noun, "him"). Thus, the NASB reads, "And Jesus rebuked him [the boy], and the demon came out of him," whereas the NIV's "rebuked the demon" reads the pronoun as a neuter, referring forward to the demon (a proleptic use of the pronoun). Jesus' power over the demonic realm has already been narrated at 4:24; 8:32; 9:33; 12:22; 15:22.

he was healed at that moment. This phrase occurs elsewhere in Matthew to

In a culture where illness or abnormal behavior was often attributed to supernatural causes, successful healers and exorcists were sought out. Amulets were commonly worn to ward off demonic activity, and freeborn Roman boys were given pendants (bullae) to wear to provide protection against evil spirits. The young boy standing between his parents in this funerary relief wears a Roman bulla (first century AD).

Jesus Teaches His Disciples about the Nature of True Discipleship

[a] J. K. Brown, *Disciples in Narrative Perspective*, 48–49.

express Jesus' power to heal instantly. The accounts of the healing of the centurion's servant (8:13), the woman with a bleeding disorder (9:22), and the Canaanite woman's daughter (15:28) conclude with this phrase.

17:19 *the disciples came to Jesus in private.* The turn from Jesus' interaction with the crowds (17:14) to a conversation "in private" between Jesus and his twelve disciples provides one of many "debriefing moments" in the road to Jerusalem narrative (16:21–20:28).[1] Throughout this section the disciples are the most prominent character group that interacts with Jesus. And even passages that initially focus on Jesus in his interaction with nondisciples typically end with such debriefing moments with the Twelve, as in 17:19–20. The upshot of this arrangement is that Matthew emphasizes discipleship teachings in this

section of his Gospel (see the sidebar "Jesus Teaches His Disciples about the Nature of True Discipleship").

17:20 *Because you have so little faith.* This is Matthew's final use of "little faith" to describe the disciples (see also 6:30; 8:26; 14:31; 16:8). Jesus provides this answer when the disciples ask him why they could not cast out the demon from the boy. In spite of being empowered to do this kind of healing, the disciples fall short of Jesus' expectations due to their little faith (already at 14:15–16; 15:32–33).

if you have faith as small as a mustard seed. Given that Jesus has already referred to the mustard seed as "the smallest of all seeds" (13:32), this statement is quite amazing. Their amount of faith need not be large to do all that Jesus expects the disciples to do and what they have been empowered to do (10:1). Yet the disciples—those consistently portrayed as having "little faith" (*oligopistos, oligopistia*)—do not even possess faith the size of a mustard seed; otherwise, they would have been able to perform this miracle. So although mustard-seed faith is small, it is clearly more "adequate" than the faith that the disciples possess at this point in the narrative. For a parallel passage on faith that can move mountains, see 21:18–22.

Nothing will be impossible for you. The gap between 17:20 and 17:22 represents a sentence included in some Greek manuscripts: "But this kind does not go out except by prayer and fasting." Given that this line is missing from quite a number of reliable Greek manuscripts, and that something quite like it occurs in the parallel account in Mark 9:29, the sentence is not likely original to Matthew. Particularly in the Gospels, copyists often added words to one Gospel that they recalled from another in its parallel account.

17:22 *When they came together in Galilee.* Rather than assuming that the disciples were somehow scattered prior to 17:22, Donald Verseput helpfully sets this verb ("come together," *systrephō*) in the context of Jewish pilgrimages to Jerusalem, in which whole groups of people would set out for an approaching festival in Jerusalem (e.g., Luke 2:44).[2]

The Son of Man is going to be delivered into the hands of men. This is the second passion prediction that Jesus makes in 16:21–20:28. Unlike the first and the third (16:21; 20:17–19), this prediction provides a more general reference to those who bring about Jesus' death. Jesus speaks of being delivered into "human hands" (*cheiras anthrōpōn*). This phrase can be rendered as "the hands of men" (NIV) to indicate the probability that only men were directly responsible for the specific events of Jesus' arrest, trial, flogging, and execution. Yet given Matthew's care to highlight both Jewish and Gentile culpability (16:21; 20:17–19), it is more likely that this phrase is meant to signal the generic sense of *anthrōpōn* rather than its particular referent. As such, the phrase implicates all humanity in the question of "who kills Jesus" in Matthew (see comments on 27:25).

17:23 *And the disciples were filled with grief.* Upon hearing about Jesus' coming death, the disciples are filled with grief, even though Jesus predicts his resurrection as well. That they do not catch the import of Jesus' statement about resurrection is understandable in their setting. The Jewish belief in bodily resurrection was not individual but corporate; it was an expectation of the resurrection of all of God's faithful people at the time of final restoration (Dan. 12:1–3; cf. 2 Macc. 7:13–14, 20–23). "So Jesus' reference to his resurrection here was not likely heard as Christian readers of Matthew have (rightly) heard it since: as referring to Jesus' resurrection ahead of the final, general resurrection (cf. 1 Cor. 15:20–23)."[3]

The disciples' responses to each of the three passion predictions indicate a lack of comprehension about the nature of Jesus' messianic mission (16:22; 17:23; 20:21–22).

> To pay the temple tax, Jesus directs Peter to find a four-drachma coin in the mouth of a fish. Shown here is a silver tetradrachm from Qumran (145–140 BC).

17:24 *the collectors of the two-drachma temple tax.* These Jewish collectors of the temple tax are not the same group working on behalf of Rome to collect its taxes (e.g., those in 9:9–12). The temple tax, traditionally levied on all adult Jewish men annually, amounted to two drachmas (essentially equivalent to the half shekel in Exod. 30:11–16).

17:27 *But so that we might not cause offense.* Although Jesus has exempted the children of the kingdom from the requirement of payment (17:25–26), he now qualifies that freedom. The provision of a four-drachma coin to pay for Jesus and Peter avoids putting a cause for stumbling (*skandalizō*) before the temple-tax collectors. The theme of avoiding causing stumbling will recur in 18:6–9.

Teaching the Text

1. *Matthew, drawing on the picture of the disciples as those of little faith, encourages his readers to trust fully in Jesus and his authority for doing what he has called them to do.* By providing the disciples as a foil for exemplary or even adequate faith, Matthew implicitly calls his readers to trust Jesus and his power. In this passage the disciples fall short of trusting Jesus for the power to fulfill the mission that he has already given to them (10:1). Matthew's readers are encouraged to trust that Jesus will provide them with what they need to accomplish the mission that he has entrusted to them. And that mission is focused on participation in Jesus' kingdom ministry. It is sometimes the case, in our own contexts, that people are comfortable leaving the work of ministry to the "professionals." Yet participation in the kingdom ministry of Jesus is the job description of all who follow him. So we can encourage people with a text like this one, since it shows that the first disciples struggled to trust Jesus to empower them for ministry and also shows Jesus promising power for ministry to his followers.

2. *Jesus continues to affirm that his death and resurrection are necessary for his mission and for the divine plan to be fulfilled.* Matthew has made it clear that Jesus in his life and ministry is bringing near God's kingdom (e.g., 4:17; 5:3–10). And as he turns the story toward Jesus' final days, Matthew emphasizes the necessity for Jesus to go to Jerusalem, declare himself to

Jesus once again tells his disciples that he will be killed and then raised to life. This intricate ivory bookbinding plate from the ninth century AD tells the story of Jesus' passion, resurrection, and ascension.

be the Messiah, and suffer the consequences of making this claim. Jesus will be handed over to be killed, but after three days he will be resurrected from the dead. Preaching Jesus from Matthew is about telling the story and meaning of both his life and his death. The whole of Jesus' story is important for the meaning of the arrival of the kingdom. The kingdom comes to this world both in Jesus' teaching and healing ministry and in his culminating act of service at the cross. His death brings about forgiveness of sin (1:21; 26:28), and his resurrection demonstrates that God has truly vindicated him as the Messiah and the servant of the Lord. Whether we come from ecclesial traditions that tend to emphasize the arrival of the kingdom in Jesus' life and ministry or those that focus more exclusively on his death as the key point of meaning for understanding Jesus, we would do well to lean into a more holistic way of preaching Jesus. Matthew does not begin with the cross, so preaching Jesus as inaugurator of the kingdom through his compassionate healing ministry is an important task. Yet the pallor of the cross falls across the latter half of Matthew's narrative, so preaching the cross and resurrection as climactic kingdom actions is also crucial.

Illustrating the Text

Matthew, drawing on the picture of the disciples as those of little faith, encourages his readers to trust fully in Jesus and his authority for doing what he has called them to do.

Popular Culture: We live in a "vending machine" culture built on a service economy. At most places we visit, there are people willing to meet our needs and desires for a dollar amount. If they do not, we can simply take our money elsewhere. It is easy to adopt this kind of consumer mentality in our understanding of discipleship. This often works itself out in people regularly wondering, "How is the church meeting my needs?" In the kingdom, however, we are called to be people who give, not people who simply consume. And it is when we are called to give beyond our comfort level that our faith is tested and strengthened. And it is in these situations of discomfort that Jesus proves himself faithful to empower us as we press into trusting him for all that we need.

Jesus continues to affirm that his death and resurrection are necessary for his mission and for the divine plan to be fulfilled.

Sports: It is common for a football team to be famous for its stellar offense or noted for great defense. Football teams might even place a special focus on one or the other of these elements of the game. But no team can become a championship team without paying attention to both elements, because each is essential for a winning team. While different theologians might emphasize one aspect of Jesus' work on our behalf more than others, we should listen to Matthew's priorities in this regard. Matthew holds together Jesus' compassionate ministry of teaching and healing along with his death and his resurrection. All are cut from one cloth and are necessary within his representative work for Israel and the nations.

Popular Culture: In our cultural milieu the rights of the individual are highly prized, so the call to put aside rights willingly probably sounds strange to many. We speak regularly of our rights (the Bill of Rights, constitutional rights, human rights, civil rights, Miranda rights, patient's rights). We live with an expectation that our rights will be honored and protected. Listing the rights that we cherish and then reading through them in light of a cruciform discipleship described in this text (specifically, 17:24–27) would create a rich point of reflection and discussion among contemporary disciples.

Community Discourse

Care for Others in the Kingdom

Big Idea *Jesus confronts the disciples about their preoccupation with status and teaches that the kingdom community is to be not status focused but other focused, with Jesus in their midst, caring for the vulnerable and addressing sin that might harm the community.*

Understanding the Text

The Text in Context

Chapter 18 is the fourth of five major teaching discourses in Matthew (chaps. 5–7, 10, 13, 18, 24–25) and is often referred to as the Community Discourse. The first half of the discourse (18:1–20) focuses on Jesus' teaching about status in God's kingdom (18:1–5; cf. 20:20–28), the harmful effects of sin within the faith community (18:6–9), and the importance of restoration of a fellow believer who sins (18:10–20; cf. 7:3–5). The latter emphasis leads seamlessly into the admonitions to forgive in 18:21–35. This section of chapter 18 concludes with a saying of Jesus promising his presence with his people, connecting this chapter to the affirmations that form bookends in Matthew: Jesus as "God with us" (1:23), and he declares "I am with you always" (28:20).

Interpretive Insights

18:1 *the disciples came to Jesus.* The disciples are the audience of the Community Discourse, as well as three of the four other Matthean discourses (chaps. 5–7, 10, 24–25). Yet Matthew's audience will also hear this Community Discourse as directed to them—to the church (18:17) looking to Matthew's Gospel for guidance for their life together.[1]

To emphasize the seriousness of causing vulnerable believers ("little ones," 18:6) to sin, Jesus says it would be better to be thrown into the sea with a millstone around one's neck. Millstones were quite heavy, some needing donkeys to turn them. Shown here are several millstones on display at Capernaum.

Who, then, is the greatest in the king-dom of heaven? As in each of the Matthean discourses, Jesus' teaching focuses on the kingdom. Here the disciples ask an initial question about kingdom greatness—a question about status. In chapters 18–20 Matthew will emphasize status issues by using "great" and "first/last" language (19:30; 20:16, 26–27) as well as by drawing upon positive discipleship examples from those of low status in the first-century world: children and slaves (18:2–5; 20:26–27).

18:2 *He called a little child.* Jesus draws in a child to provide an object lesson, as he answers the disciples' question about greatness. Given that their question is about status (18:1), it is most likely that the child is meant to illustrate someone of low status (as 18:4). In ancient perspectives, children were viewed as lacking *logos* (the full measure of rationality) and so were considered irrational and lacking in judgment.[2] Additionally, they were viewed as weak and vulnerable, given their suscep-tibility to illness and abuse. As William Davies and Dale Allison conclude about 18:2, "The point . . . is not that children are self-consciously humble but that they are, as part of society at large, without much status and position."[3]

18:3 *unless you . . . become like little children, you will never enter the kingdom.* Jesus first draws the analogy of a child to speak of kingdom entry, not kingdom greatness, which is what the disciples have asked about. This is a narrative clue that their question might not have been an ap-propriate one. If Jesus so redefines kingdom status that those of lowest status are to be emulated, then the question about who is greatest is utterly misguided.

18:4 *whoever takes the lowly position of this child is the greatest.* Jesus answers the disciples' question about kingdom greatness by pointing to a child who has little status. The NIV's "lowly position" reflects the Greek word *tapeinoō*, which can indicate internal disposition or exter-nal situation (BDAG 990). In this context, the latter is most likely. Jesus uses a child to demonstrate that the disciples are mis-guided in seeking greatness in the kingdom. They should instead assume the position of those who are lowest in status within the kingdom community (also 20:26–27).

18:5 *And whoever welcomes one such child in my name welcomes me.* There is a shift here from a child as exemplar to the call to welcome "one such child." This might mean welcoming actual children (as at 19:13–15), or Jesus might be referenc-ing those like children (18:3), who will be referred to as "little ones" in 18:6–14. Jesus has already taught about welcoming a prophet, a righteous person, and "one of these little ones who is my disciple" at the conclusion of the Mission Discourse (10:40–42).

18:6 *little ones.* In this section of the Community Discourse (18:6–14) the focus of Jesus' teaching moves from a child (*teknon*) to "little ones" (*mikros*; with *adelphos* used in 18:15–35). For Matthew, "little ones" is a status term that indicates those most vulnerable within the believing community. The term likely refers to believers of lowest status—those valued least (see 18:10).[4]

stumble. Matthew's thematic *skandalizō* is used here to indicate something that causes another person to sin. The verb or its cognate noun occurs six times in 18:6–9 (also 17:27).

18:8 *If your hand . . . causes you to stumble . . . cut it off.* Jesus' warnings turn to someone causing their own stumbling. The hyperbole in 18:8–9 is powerful. As Robert Stein helpfully notes, we read these words as hyperbolic because we know that obedience in any literal fashion would not actually remove the temptation to sin.[5] Hands and eyes are not the root of the problem. The point is clear. Sin is so serious that cutting off a hand or gouging out an eye is preferable to allowing the cause of sin to remain.

18:10 *See that you do not despise one of these little ones.* Jesus' statement helps the reader to define *mikros*, since the implication is that "little ones" are easily despised. This points to little ones as those of low status, who are easily seen as less valuable.

their angels in heaven always see the face of my Father. The face of someone who is a ruler indicates favor, while the ruler's back typically signals displeasure. So the "little ones," though considered less important, are actually favored by God (with the point emphasized again at 18:14). The reference to "their angels" has raised much speculation (e.g., guardian angels), but the presence of angels in the heavenly court fits well such biblical portraits of God's throne room and should not be pressed further.

Father in heaven. Some later manuscripts include 18:11, which reads, "For the Son of Man came to save the lost" (derived from Luke 19:10). Copyists very likely added this line, possibly to smooth the transition from 18:10 to the parable in 18:12–14.

18:12 *If a man owns a hundred sheep.* The parable of the wandering sheep receives a similar rehearsal in Luke 15:3–7, though there with an emphasis on a lost sheep. In Matthew, the parable highlights the value of pursuing a single sheep that has wandered away, fitting nicely between teachings on those vulnerable to stumbling (18:6–7) and on restoration of those who have sinned in the community (18:15–20).

18:15 *If your brother or sister sins.* The focal point of Jesus' teaching moves from a child (*teknon*) to little ones (*mikros*) to a brother or sister (*adelphos*). The inclusion of "against you" is debatable from the manuscript evidence. It is likely that it was not included originally in Matthew but was added by scribes due to auditory confusion and elision (*hamartēsē* = sins; *hamartē eis se* = sins against you).[6]

you have won them over. The goal of going to an erring person privately is restoration. This same goal of restoration should also be presumed for the rest of the process (already emphasized at 18:10–14).

18:16 *testimony of two or three witnesses.* This citation from Deuteronomy 19:15 provides protection for the one being accused of wrongdoing by requiring more than a single witness. This context provides a helpful corrective to understanding the witnesses as simply present to provide a "rubber stamp" for the charge of wrongdoing.

18:17 *tell it to the church.* Reference to the church (*ekklēsia*) occurs only twice in all the Gospels (Matt. 16:18; 18:17). The use of the term in Matthew fits Old Testament references to the "assembly" of Israel (Heb. *qāhāl*), with the Septuagint translators using *ekklēsia* routinely to translate *qāhāl*. The whole community is to work for restoration of a brother or sister who has sinned.

treat them as you would a pagan or a tax collector. It is true that Matthew often portrays Gentiles (*ethnē*; here "pagan" [*ethnikos*]) and tax collectors positively responding to Jesus' ministry (e.g., 8:10; 21:32). Yet Matthew also uses these categories, in more or less offhand fashion, as examples of outsiders, as in popular Jewish parlance (see 5:46–47). Although not explicitly stated, this action of treating an erring member as an outsider could be understood as furthering restoration, especially in Matthew's social context (cf. 1 Cor. 6:9–12).

18:18 *whatever you bind . . . whatever you loose.* For discussion of the same promise, see comments on 16:19.

In the rugged terrain of Israel, a sheep that wandered away, like the one shown here heading farther up the hill, could be in grave danger. As a shepherd searches diligently for a sheep that has wandered, so Matthew's community is to pursue restoration of those who have gone astray.

18:20 *where two or three gather in my name, there am I with them.* The "two or three" draws from the language of Deuteronomy 19:15 but also reflects the nature of Matthew 18 as providing community regulation and teaching. As such, it is not simply a cap to the "church discipline" section (18:15–20) but provides a culminating word for the first half of the Community Discourse. "At the thematic center of the Community Discourse, Matthew emphasizes Jesus' presence with his people as the hope for their common life" (1:23; 28:20).[7]

Theological Insights: Renunciation of Status

Establishment and preservation of status and position were fundamental values in the first-century world. So it is not surprising that Jesus in Matthew addresses issues of "greatness." His answer would have been a surprising one for people of the Greco-Roman world, who assumed the value of maintaining status distinctions. Luke's Gospel also provides examples of Jesus' teachings that subvert usual practices of seeking to gain honor and prestige (14:7–11) and of inviting one's peers or betters to meals (14:12–14). Instead, Jesus' followers are to humble themselves (14:11) and invite to meals those who cannot repay the favor (14:13–14). In 1 Corinthians Paul takes that church to task for falling prey to valuing the status that accrues from contests of oration (1:12, 20–25). Instead, he reminds them of God's decision to "chose the lowly things of this world" to eliminate all boasting (1:28–29). And the Epistle of James reminds readers that their favoritism toward the rich actually belies God's decision to choose "those who are poor . . . to be rich in faith" (2:5).

Teaching the Text

1. *Becoming like children involves turning away from preoccupation with status concerns and self-promotion to care for others.* Views of children were substantially different in the first-century world than in our contemporary Western context, so we are prone to import into this passage qualities of children as we perceive them. We might, for example, highlight the innocence of children, when in a first-century Greco-Roman context children were viewed as less reliable than adults, who had the full measure of *logos* or rational capacity. We might also emphasize that children are humble in attitude, as the language of Matthew 18:4 in some English versions suggests (e.g., "whoever becomes humble like this child" [NRSV]). Yet children are not necessarily humble in the sense of holding an attitude of selflessness. Instead, as we have seen above, children are an example in the first-century world of those with little status. As the NIV reads, "Whoever takes the lowly

"Unless you change and become like little children, you will never enter the kingdom of heaven" (18:3). Jesus summons a child to teach about status renunciation in the kingdom of heaven. This scene is carved into this tenth-century AD ivory plaque from the Magdeburg Cathedral, Germany.

position of this child is the greatest in the kingdom of heaven." We can teach this text well by helping people to understand that they should renounce status preoccupation in favor of taking care of those most vulnerable and marginalized in the community of faith. This is the focus of Jesus' message using the example of a child.

2. *Addressing sin in the believing community and with fellow brothers and sisters is always for the goal of restoration.* This section of chapter 18 includes the famous "church discipline" passage (18:15–20), which provides guidance for addressing serious sin in a fellow believer. This passage is misapplied and misused when it is not used in service of restoration of the Christian community and of its members. Attention to context is crucial for its proper understanding and application (see comments above). It is also instructive that guidance on "church discipline" is surrounded by Jesus' teachings about restoration and forgiveness. The parable of the wandering sheep teaches that God rejoices over a single wandering or erring believer who is restored (18:10–14). In fact, the parable encourages believers to go in search of those who have wandered or strayed. In 18:21–35 Jesus teaches that unlimited forgiveness should

characterize the church, just as extravagant forgiveness defines God and God's reign. This contextual frame should caution us to avoid any kind of casual or facile application of this passage within our communities. Instead, a prayerful and sober attitude should lead the way to assess whether a situation calls for direct (and private) intervention and whether we have rightly assessed if serious sin is present (versus conflict or difference, for instance). In teaching this passage, we will want to emphasize that the goal of pointing out sin is restoration of relationship and not to cause harm.

Illustrating the Text

Becoming like children involves turning away from preoccupation with status concerns and self-promotion to care for others.

Literature: *Of Mice and Men*, by John Steinbeck. This well-known novel traces the story of George and Lennie, migrant workers during the depression. Lennie is developmentally disabled, and his aunt, before she died, had made George promise to look after him. Yet George cares for Lennie and watches out for him not simply out of obligation but because of the friendship and companionship that they share. Lennie, always good-natured, sometimes exasperating, listens to George's dreams of the future. And they dream together of a place of their own someday where Lennie can care for his beloved rabbits. Up to the very end, when he has to make an excruciating decision in a tragic situation, George serves as an example of what it means to care

for "little ones" who, as Matthew portrays them, are marginalized and vulnerable.

News Story: Shortly after being elected to office (2013), Pope Francis distinguished himself as a "different kind of pope." This was signaled, first, by his choice of papal name, embracing the name of the humble, often homeless St. Francis of Assisi. Pope Francis has demonstrated an unusual willingness to forgo titles of honor and the bubble of dignified distance that usually surrounded his predecessors. This was captured well in October 2013, as Francis spoke about family in St. Peter's Square. In the middle of this official event, a young boy came up on stage and interrupted the proceedings. Security guards attempted to intervene, but Pope Francis embraced the child and smiled at him, showing patience and kindness.

Addressing sin in the believing community and with fellow brothers and sisters is always for the goal of restoration.

Human Metaphor: Restoring a piece of furniture is a painstaking process (if your context allows, display an item that has been restored). It involves work, careful choice of materials, and very often a love and appreciation for what is being restored. From a practical standpoint, it certainly would be easier to simply buy a replacement piece. But a family heirloom or a favorite chair is nearly impossible to replace. So we go about the work of restoration. Church discipline is for the purpose of restoration, bringing back the beauty of the Christian community and the relationships that have been marred by sin. In Jesus' instructions, we must remember the goal; it is restoration of relationship and healing of community.

Community Discourse

Lavish Forgiveness in the Kingdom

Big Idea *Jesus stresses that the kingdom community is characterized by unlimited forgiveness based on God's prior and lavish forgiveness, warning those who are not persistent in offering forgiveness that they will not receive it in the end.*

Understanding the Text

The Text in Context

In the second half of the Community Discourse (chap. 18) Jesus highlights the necessity of forgiving others in the Christian community, a theme already introduced in the Sermon on the Mount (6:12–15). As in the first half of the discourse, a question by the disciples provides the opportunity for Jesus to teach on discipleship (18:1, 21). Jesus' teaching about forgiveness is an important contextual requisite for any confrontation of a sinning community member (18:15–20). The chapter's twin emphases on taking sin seriously and forgiving without limit balance each other, as the members of the community seek to live well with Jesus and with one another.

Interpretive Insights

18:21 *Peter came to Jesus.* Peter often functions as the representative of the twelve disciples in Matthew (14:28; 15:15; 16:16; 17:24–27; 18:21; 19:27).

Lord, how many times shall I forgive my brother or sister . . . ? This verse introduces the last half of the Community Discourse, which focuses on forgiveness in the believing community. Peter's question leads to Jesus' statement about unlimited forgiveness, and the parable that follows provides the basis for kingdom forgiveness, expanding on the saying about forgiveness in 6:14–15. The reference to forgiving "my brother or sister" (*adelphos*) picks up the referent of 18:15–20 (also 18:35).

18:22 *not seven times, but seventy-seven times.* Jesus' response to Peter's question indicates that Peter does not think broadly enough about the nature of forgiveness in the kingdom community. As magnanimous as Peter might view his allowance of forgiveness (seven times), Jesus is conceiving of forgiveness in much more expansive terms. The number "seven" and its variations connote fullness or perfection, so Jesus' use of these numbers implies that unlimited forgiveness characterizes the kingdom. Moreover, the use of "seven" and "seventy-seven" evokes Genesis 4:24: "If Cain is avenged seven times, then Lamech seventy-seven times." This allusion signals a reversal based on the coming kingdom. As unlimited revenge characterized the entry of sin into human existence, so the restoration of God's ways and God's kingdom brings the possibility of unlimited forgiveness.[1]

18:23 *the kingdom of heaven is like a king who wanted to settle accounts.* Reference to the kingdom in both halves of the chapter and at key moments (18:1, 23) alerts the reader to its thematic nature in the Community Discourse. Jesus in Matthew tells numerous parables that provide comparisons to "the kingdom of heaven" (13:24, 31, 33, 44, 45, 47; 20:1; 22:2; 25:1). Here the comparison is to a king who wants to settle accounts with those servants who owe him money, setting up the context for Jesus' teaching on forgiveness.

18:24 *ten thousand bags of gold.* The component amounts used in the story for the first servant's debt are the highest possible. "Ten thousand" is

the highest number of reckoning, and the *talanton* ("bags of gold") is the largest measure of currency, with a single talent being worth about six thousand denarii or day's wages (so the NIV footnote of "20 years of day laborer's wages"; cf. 18:28). Some have argued that this is an unrealistic amount of money for any servant to owe a master, but its exorbitant nature is precisely the point (approximately two hundred thousand years' wages!). Jesus' parables often contain unrealistic, striking elements that contribute to the parable's effect on the

In this parable, the king shows great mercy and cancels his servant's unpayable debt. At various times in Roman history, the government extended tax-debt relief by destroying the debt records. This frieze found in the Roman Forum shows tax records being placed on a pile to be burned (early second century AD).

hearers and readers. In this case, it would be like someone speaking of a "zillion" of a particular currency. Paying off this kind of debt is an impossible feat and thus magnifies the graciousness of the forgiveness.

18:25 *the master ordered that he and his wife and his children and all that he had be sold.* The practice of being sold to pay back a debt or having one's children sold for the same purpose is attested in the Old Testament (2 Kings 4:1; Isa. 50:1). That there is no way that a family's indentured servitude could earn the huge amount owed only heightens the servant's plight in the story line.

18:26 *Be patient with me . . . and I will pay back everything.* Given the magnitude of his debt, the plea for patience to allow time to pay back "everything" comes across as rash. This quality of the servant will be confirmed when another servant who owes him money will use the same plea but without its reference to "everything" (18:29).

18:27 *took pity on him, canceled the debt.* This is the first of two points in the parable at which the master is moved to act toward the servant. Here the master is motivated by pity or compassion (*splanchnizomai*). The other occurrences of *splanchnizomai* in Matthew describe Jesus' compassion toward the crowds or particular people who come to him seeking healing (9:36; 14:14; 15:32; 20:34). At 18:34 the master will be moved by anger (*orgizō*).

18:28 *he found one of his fellow servants.* The second scene of the parable provides a powerful contrast to the first. In spite of receiving mercy, the first servant searches for and finds a fellow servant who owes him a fraction of what the first servant owed the king. The imagery of the scene is graphic: "He grabbed him and began to choke him. 'Pay back what you owe me!' he demanded."

a hundred silver coins. The second servant owes the first servant one hundred silver coins or denarii, with a *dēnarion* being equivalent to about one day's wage for a day laborer. So the amount owed is about a third of a year's wages, a fraction of the first servant's debt.

18:29 *Be patient with me.* The action of the fellow servant falling to his knees and the content of his plea are cast in language virtually identical to that of the first servant in 18:26. The telling difference is the second servant's omission of "everything."

18:30 *he . . . had the man thrown into prison.* On being put in prison to repay a debt, see 5:25–26 (see also 2 Kings 4:1; Isa. 50:1).

18:33 *Shouldn't you have had mercy on your fellow servant . . . ?* This question by the king provides the core of the parable's meaning. The point has been made obvious in the telling of the story: one who had received so much compassion and forgiveness of debt should have shown mercy to his fellow servant and forgiven his debt. For the importance of showing mercy as part of Matthean discipleship, see 5:7; 9:13; 12:7; 23:23.

The second servant in the parable owes one hundred denarii to the first. A denarius was about a day's wage. Here are two examples of Roman denarii from the first century BC.

18:34 *handed him over to the jailers to be tortured.* The first judgment of the master toward the servant was to sell him and his family into servitude to repay the debt (18:25). This last judgment is far worse. The imagery of torture in prison is a detail of the parable meant to heighten its impact (for an example of Herod the Great torturing a prisoner, see Josephus, *J.W.* 1.548).

18:35 *This is how my heavenly Father will treat each of you.* Now the comparison of the parable is made explicit. The kingdom is characterized by an imperative of forgiveness based on the action of God as the one who has forgiven the largest of debts. Those who refuse forgiveness to their fellow believers demonstrate as little gratitude for God's forgiveness of them as the unforgiving servant has shown. The power of the parable is to create a sense of disgust in the hearers or readers toward the behavior of that servant, motivating them toward mercy and forgiveness toward others. Some interpreters have complained that if God is the king in this analogy, then even God does not live out Jesus' exhortation to unlimited forgiveness (18:22). Presumably, the king in this parable does not even forgive the servant up to seven times, much less seventy-seven, so the logic goes. However, the purpose of the parable is to provide the basis for forgiveness—God's forgiveness of the greatest of debts—not to provide an example of unlimited forgiveness. This basic analogy between the parable and the kingdom stands without requiring all details to be analogous.

unless you forgive your brother or sister from your heart. The parable's application mirrors Jesus' teaching at 6:14–15: "If you do not forgive others their sins, your Father

will not forgive your sins" (6:15). The parable provides additional teaching about this conditional statement by demonstrating that a lack of forgiveness betrays a lack of gratitude and true acknowledgment of God's prior forgiveness. In this way, the parable of the unforgiving servant clarifies that forgiving others from one's heart is predicated on having received God's forgiveness deeply into one's heart and life. In the end, the parable is meant to encourage a powerful and ongoing pattern of forgiveness among the family of God.

Teaching the Text

1. *Jesus teaches that the community of his followers should be marked by extravagant and unlimited forgiveness.* Peter seems to think that his offer to forgive seven times is quite magnanimous, but Jesus raises the bar exponentially. By drawing on an allusion to the story of Cain and Lamech (Gen. 4:17–24), Jesus calls his followers to unlimited forgiveness in place of the cycle of unlimited revenge that is pictured in Genesis after the fall of humanity. This reversal is rooted in the arrival of God's kingdom that formatively shapes the Christian community. Preaching this extravagant forgiveness involves impressing upon the church that such forgiveness is a marker of who they are; extravagant forgiveness is a sign of communal covenant faithfulness. Those who see the church in its particular manifestations should be able to identify forgiveness as its hallmark. "They are the people who forgive," should be what is said of the church both from within and from without.

When we preach the imperative of forgiveness, we should also be aware that some in our audience might have experienced abuse, violence, or other patterns of serious betrayal. In these situations, preaching forgiveness without addressing the contours of perpetual violence could be not only damaging but also dangerous. A helpful course can be to distinguish between forgiveness of and reconciliation with an abuser.[2] We ought to help victims of abuse seek the help that they need to learn what forgiveness looks like in their particular situations (and what it does not look like).

2. *According to Jesus' parable, if we have received and understood the extravagant forgiveness of God, it will lead organically to practicing forgiveness in our relationships with our Christian brothers and sisters.* In the parable of the unforgiving servant, the fundamental problem is a disconnect between the mercy that the servant receives from his master that cancels an astronomical debt and the lack of mercy that he shows his fellow servant for a much smaller amount owed. The details of the parable heighten the callous and casual nature of the servant's disregard for mercy received. The thrust of the parable in its metaphor is to question how someone who has truly experienced and received God's overflowing forgiveness could pursue a life of retribution and revenge for wrongs that he or she has suffered. The reality of God's forgiveness changes our perspective on wrongs that we experience. Part of preaching this theme is about helping our audience understand the extravagant forgiveness of God. Sometimes this truth has difficulty penetrating through to the core of our selves. If we have difficulty letting go of our sin, we often imagine that God, though forgiving in some way, still holds our sin against us. But Israel's covenant God always has been and continues to be a forgiving God (see Ps. 103:12; Isa. 43:25). And in line with kingdom values, God's people are called to live out this way of forgiveness with one another.

Illustrating the Text

Jesus teaches that the community of his followers should be marked by extravagant and unlimited forgiveness.

Scenario: An employee has been invited to a work party at his employer's home. While there, he accidentally bumps an end table, knocking an egg-shaped decoration to the floor, which cracks down the center. He apologizes profusely, and the boss graciously says, "That's all right, I forgive you." This "egg-shaped decoration" is in fact a Fabergé egg—a work of art worth millions.

Do you think that the employee will value the employer's gracious forgiveness more if he realizes the value of the egg? When we do not understand the true depth of our debt to God, forgiveness will be accepted but possibly not fully appreciated. Matthew's use of such an excessive monetary amount ("ten thousand bags of gold") highlights the depth of that debt from which God has released us.

According to Jesus' parable, if we have received and understood the extravagant forgiveness of God, it will lead organically to practicing forgiveness in our

relationships with our Christian brothers and sisters.

Science: In 1952 the first polio vaccine was tested. In a relatively short time the world has drawn closer to eradicating this terrible disease, which has left many people paralyzed. Through exposure to the vaccine, humans are no longer capable of catching or transmitting this disease. The poliovirus cannot live for very long outside the human body, and experts argue that the key for defeating the disease is global vaccination.

According to Jesus' parable, encountering the depth of God's forgiveness will change us on the deepest levels. God's forgiveness organically leads to human forgiveness. We should be people who, rather than spreading vengeance and retribution, extend the grace that we have received.

Art: What is the first thing that people notice when they see the *Mona Lisa*? The smile, right? (Though many who see it firsthand notice first how small the canvas of this masterpiece is.) When we hear the name "O'Keefe," most people probably think of gigantic flowers. "Van Gogh"—a night sky filled with stars. Art and artists have their own distinctive style and characteristics. They have a "brand," to put it in marketing terms. So what defines the church? It should be the way we extend grace. Extravagant forgiveness should be what comes to mind when people think of the church.

Matthew 18:21–35

Jesus Demonstrates Status Inversion in the Kingdom

Big Idea *Matthew illustrates the inversion of status in God's kingdom by narrating Jesus' protection of women in his teaching on divorce, his valuing of children, and his stringent call to a rich man who would follow him.*

Understanding the Text

The Text in Context

Following Jesus' fourth major teaching block (chap. 18), Matthew provides his usual formula to transition to a narrative section (19:1; also 7:28–29; 11:1; 13:53; 26:1). Themes accentuated in the previous discourse are illustrated narratively in 19:1–26. The disciples' concern for status categories is conspicuous in their treatment of children (19:13–15; cf. 18:1–5) and their assumptions about marriage (19:10) and about the status of the wealthy before God (19:16–26). Although the disciples and Jesus have been focal characters in the narrative since 16:21, in 19:3 a group of Pharisees makes an appearance in the story (last seen at 16:1–4), testing Jesus on his teaching about divorce (19:3–12; see also 12:1–14; 15:1–20).

Interpretive Insights

19:1 *When Jesus had finished saying these things.* This is the fourth occurrence of this formulaic conclusion to the Matthean discourses (also 7:28 [see comments there]; 11:1; 13:53; 26:1). In this instance it transitions from Jesus' teaching about kingdom expectations for his disciples to their continuing journey to Jerusalem

Jesus tells the Pharisees that the teachings of Moses permitted divorce only because of human hardness of heart. Shown here is a Jewish bill of divorce from AD 72. It is written in Aramaic and was found in one of the caves located within the high walls of the Wadi Murabba'at.

and his ongoing teaching through example about discipleship.

he left Galilee. At the beginning of Jesus' public ministry Matthew indicates that Jesus focuses his ministry to Israel in Galilee (4:12, 23–25), providing the setting for all of chapters 4–18. Now Jesus leaves the confines of Galilee and approaches Jerusalem, the setting of 19:2–28:15.

19:3 *Some Pharisees came to him to test him.* The Pharisees appear only here in 16:21–20:28. Their test here concerns Jesus' interpretation of the Jewish law regarding divorce. Matthew has already provided Jesus' teaching on divorce at 5:31–32 in response to Deuteronomy 24:1; here he expands that teaching to provide Jesus' rationale for his interpretation.

Is it lawful . . . for any and every reason? The Pharisees ask Jesus about the Torah's provision for divorce. From later Jewish sources, first-century Jewish views on divorce seem to be quite diverse, with some rabbis limiting divorce to cases of adultery (school of Shammai) and others allowing quite a wide set of allowable reasons (school of Hillel) (see, e.g., Josephus, *Ant.* 4.253). The Pharisees' test that mentions "any and every reason" seems aimed at aligning Jesus with the latter, broader set of allowances for divorce and showing him to be less scrupulous with Torah interpretation than he has suggested.

19:4 *Haven't you read . . . ?* Jesus answers the question about legitimate reasons for divorce with two citations from Genesis (1:27; 2:24). These citations are brought together "to demonstrate the intention of God as creator of humanity for lifelong marriage or monogamy."[1]

19:7 *Why then . . . did Moses command . . . ?* In response to Jesus' citation of the Genesis creational texts, the Pharisees refer to Deuteronomy 24, which prohibits a man from remarrying the same woman after a divorce (24:4) and indicates the possibility of a man writing his wife "a certificate of divorce" if he "finds something indecent about her" (24:1). The Hebrew word underlying "indecent" is not fully clear, and the rabbinic debates reflect the ambiguity.

19:8 *Moses permitted you to divorce your wives because your hearts were hard.* Jesus counters the use of Deuteronomy 24 by clarifying that this text permits rather than commands divorce. He attributes the need for such an allowance to the hardness of human hearts and contrasts this allowance with the creational mandate ("from the beginning"). Matthew shows Jesus to be interpreting the Torah (Deuteronomy) in light of the Torah (Genesis), as he has done elsewhere (e.g., 12:7; 22:40; 23:23).

19:9 *except for sexual immorality.* Only Matthew has this exception clause included in Jesus' teaching about divorce (here and in slightly different grammatical form at 5:32). Although here Matthew uses not *moicheia* ("adultery") but rather *porneia*, which is a more general term for sexual sin, it is likely that Jesus is forbidding divorce except when a wife is sexually unfaithful.[2] Women in first-century Judaism, for the

Matthew 19:1–26

Jesus demonstrates that the kingdom of heaven values those of lower status when he welcomes children. This relief fragment shows children playing with balls (second century AD).

most part, would have lacked the social power or sanction to initiate divorce, which would explain why the man is addressed in this saying.[3]

19:10 *it is better not to marry.* The disciples are portrayed as misconstruing Jesus' teachings. His words about the permanence of marriage and the prohibition against casually divorcing one's wife sound so difficult that they think singleness is preferable. Yet Matthew has indicated that Jesus' way of teaching the Torah is not burdensome to follow (11:28–30).

19:11 *this word.* The referent of "this word" is ambiguous; it could refer to Jesus' prohibition against divorce (19:9) or the disciples' statement about singleness (19:10). From what follows, it seems more likely that Jesus refers to the disciples' "word" about singleness or celibacy.[4] Avoiding marriage is not the answer to Jesus' strictures on divorce, since celibacy is only for those "to whom it has been given."

19:12 *eunuchs for the sake of the kingdom of heaven.* This statement and call for some to choose celibacy and singleness over marriage has countercultural overtones in Jewish society, which valued and prized marriage and childbearing. Jesus confirms that some will follow God's leading to be unmarried because of the kingdom, a path that Jesus himself has taken.

19:13 *the disciples rebuked them.* In spite of Jesus' earlier words to the disciples about welcoming children (18:5), the disciples rebuke those who would bring children to Jesus for prayer. Children, as those with less status than adults in the first-century world, are of great importance to Jesus, as he demonstrates in his correction of the disciples (19:14).

19:14 *the kingdom of heaven belongs to such as these.* This language evokes Jesus' earlier words and actions at 18:1–5, in which he makes a child an example for entering the kingdom. There he uses the lowly status of a child to correct the disciples' concern over who would be greatest in the kingdom.

19:16 *Teacher, what good thing must I do to get eternal life?* As at 18:1–5, Jesus initially responds to this question with an indirect answer, indicating that the question may not adequately express the nature of things. In this case, Jesus turns the focus from the "good thing" to be done to the "only One who is good" (19:17; as at 19:26).

19:17 *keep the commandments.* Jesus'

answer fits Matthew's view of the law, in which human covenant faithfulness (e.g., doing "the will of my Father" [7:21; 12:50]) fits within the broader context of God's initiating and ongoing covenant faithfulness and acknowledges the human need for God's power and grace (19:26).

19:21 *If you want to be perfect.* Matthew's use of *teleios* (rendered "perfect" [also 5:48]) is helpfully clarified in context by its antonym, "lack" (*hystereō*), in the preceding verse. This points to the sense of *teleios* as complete, whole or fully mature, not lacking anything. In 5:48 the word is used to express the moral perfection that God has and so the complete covenant loyalty that should characterize Jesus' followers.

sell your possessions and give to the poor, and you will have treasure in heaven. Jesus' specific command and promise of "treasure in heaven" evokes his teaching at 6:19–24, where he calls his followers to full allegiance to God and not to one's money or possessions (also 13:22).

19:24 *it is easier for a camel to go through the eye of a needle.* Although some have fabricated a referent for Jesus' language (e.g., a purported gate in Jerusalem called the "eye of the needle"), the hyperbole that Jesus uses is eminently effective to indicate how difficult it is for those who are rich to enter the kingdom. Jesus' call for this man to sell his possessions proves too great a cost, and he does not follow Jesus (19:21–22). This statement likely sounded odd to the disciples, since the wealth of a person (who was faithful to the law, as here) could easily have been viewed as a sign of God's blessing. Jewish wisdom literature warns of inappropriate reliance on riches

(Prov. 11:28), but it also shows that wealth comes from living wisely in the fear of the Lord (Prov. 8:18–21; 22:4). Jesus turns the latter notion on its head. The disciples' response confirms the surprising quality of Jesus' teaching.

19:25 *Who then can be saved?* The disciples' question implies incredulity at anyone being saved if this rich person cannot. Their question implicitly raises the issue of status, since a wealthy person would have greater status and so be granted greater honor in their world (e.g., James 2:1–4).

19:26 *with God all things are possible.* This final saying highlights the basis of salvation as God's work in redemption. In relation to the status issues that have been raised by Jesus' teaching that a rich person does not have greater access to and blessing from God than the poor, Matthew highlights that God's power and grace to save are the great equalizer (and means of status reversal; see 20:1–15).

Teaching the Text

1. *Matthew indicates that Jesus embodies and teaches that his followers should not be preoccupied with status concerns, since the kingdom is not about status but about service.* Throughout this section of Matthew the disciples have been portrayed as being preoccupied with status in God's coming kingdom and their own place in it (e.g., 18:1; 19:13–15, 24–26; also 19:27; 20:20–28). In contrast, Jesus' teachings on the kingdom have both hinted and highlighted that God's reign will be characterized by concern for those with lower status, such as children, "little ones," women, and the poor (18:1–14; 19:1–26). Jesus points

to children, for instance, as examples for the disciples to emulate. In the first-century Greco-Roman world, with its clear levels of status and codes of honor for relationships, Jesus' teachings offer a different view of reality. The kingdom is not defined by status categories; in fact, it is defined by a surprising equality among those who belong to it (see 20:12).

Those of us who live in a democracy might be tempted to think that this will be easy to preach. After all, equality of persons is one of our fundamental values. Yet the practical reality is that we live within implicit hierarchies that provide status, access, and honor to some people and virtually ignore others deemed less important. As Brennan Manning puts it, more often than not "the Christian community resembles a Wall Street exchange of works wherein the elite are honored and the ordinary ignored."[5] So preaching this theme from chapters 18–20 may mean confronting both explicit and implicit status systems in which we participate and calling people to follow Jesus in service toward and care for the "little ones" and those who are perceived as expendable.

2. *Wealth, rather than being a sign of God's favor, can be a barrier to following Jesus.* The disciples in this passage seem to view wealth as a sign of God's favor since they presume that a rich person (like the man in 19:16–22) is a most likely candidate for kingdom entry (19:25). Jesus corrects their misperception. Wealth is a stumbling block to following Jesus because it presents

> Jesus says, "It is easier for a camel to go through the eye of a needle than for someone who is rich to enter the kingdom of God" (19:24). These bone needles from the Roman period were found at Sepphoris.

an alternate allegiance to wholeheartedly committing to and following him. This idea is already present in Matthew in Jesus' earlier teachings. Disciples cannot serve both God and money because allegiance is always singular (6:24). And the message of the kingdom can easily be strangled and made unfruitful by the "deceitfulness of wealth" (13:22). In many Western contexts where the church is wealthy, preaching these words of Jesus will pose an incisive critique to us and to our hearers. We will want to be sure that we do not remove the sting of that critique by muting the message (say, by noting that Matthew's Jesus does not call everyone in the Gospel to sell their possessions and give all to the poor [19:21]). If anything, we need to hear afresh and with conviction this Matthean theme of the dangers of wealth.

Illustrating the Text

Matthew indicates that Jesus embodies and teaches that his followers should not be preoccupied with status concerns, since the kingdom is not about status but about service.

Biography: In his book *Johnny Carson*, Henry Bushkin, the lawyer and close friend of the star, offers a glimpse of the social politics that often swirled around one of the most popular figures in television history. For instance, seating arrangements at the

Reagan inauguration nearly cost Bushkin his job as Carson's attorney. Apparently, Carson's wife, Joanna, was infuriated at being seated slightly farther away from the main stage than the McMahon family. Bushkin, who had been responsible for overseeing arrangements, was raked over the coals for this breach of status etiquette. This illustration suggests that our democratic society is far from immune to status preoccupation.

Mission: In his book *Too Small to Ignore: Why the Least of These Matters Most*, Wess Stafford argues convincingly that we are called to invest heavily in children as prime examples of the "least of these." As the president of Compassion International, Stafford advocated for children in poverty, and his book contains numerous examples of what true compassion for children looks like. This might be an opportunity to encourage your listeners to consider supporting a child through an organization like Compassion International.

Wealth, rather than being a sign of God's favor, can be a barrier to following Jesus.

Scripture: The story of Ananias and Sapphira (Acts 5:1–11), who die as a result of secretly withholding money that should have gone to the community, captures how seriously the early Christian community embraced Jesus' words about the dangers of wealth and the power of giving. They were a community that sought a path of self-sacrifice, rejecting the mode of acquisition that so many around them embraced. Rather than seeking social standing, community status, or personal wealth, the disciples were called to be willing to give sacrificially.

Film: *Wall Street*. In this 1987 film, Gordon Gekko, the central antagonist, makes no bones about his unrestrained greed. Everything about this character is driven by self-centered acquisition. At one point in the film Gekko proclaims, "Greed is good. Greed works. Greed clarifies, cuts through, and captures the essence of the evolutionary spirit."

Jesus Warns of Presuming Reward and Status

Big Idea *While promising eternal reward to the first who have followed him, Jesus also warns against presumption of reward and status by telling a parable about the equalization of status that will occur in God's kingdom.*

Understanding the Text

The Text in Context

Peter's initial question in this passage about the rewards that he and the rest of the Twelve will have for leaving everything to follow Jesus (19:27) connects directly with the previous passage, in which a rich man chooses his wealth over the chance to follow Jesus (19:21–22). Although Jesus answers that there will be reward for leaving all to follow him (19:28–29), his words turn to warning at 19:30–20:16. His admonitions against status presumption echo across this section of Matthew (see 18:1–5; 20:20–28). The dual refrain about the inversion of the first and the last frames the parable of the first and last day laborers (19:30; 20:16) and will find an echo in 23:12, where the places of the humble and the exalted are reversed.

Interpretive Insights

19:28 *at the renewal of all things.* Matthew uses a word (*palingenesia*) that would be generally understandable in the Greco-Roman world but in a Jewish context would signal the eschatological time of the Messiah, when all things would be made new.

sit on twelve thrones, judging the twelve tribes of Israel. Jesus indicates that the Twelve, whose number signals the twelve tribes of Israel and so represents the reconstitution of Israel, will have a role alongside Jesus at the final judgment.

19:29 *or wife.* Some early manuscripts do not include "or wife" (*ē gynaika*), and so a number of translations omit it (e.g., CEB, NRSV, NASB). Since the parallel text in Luke 18:29 has *gynaika*, it may be that its inclusion in Matthew is due to scribal harmonization with Luke. Yet it was relatively easy for scribes to omit an item in a list, so it might be that *ē gynaika* was inadvertently left out and is therefore original to Matthew.

a hundred times as much. This descriptor hints at the metaphorical nature of the previous list, since receiving a hundred times as many fathers or children, for example, makes little sense literally. Although he may be signaling the reward of being part of God's family, Matthew likely uses this list to express metaphorically what inheriting eternal life will look like; it will truly be life abundant. According to R. T. France, it is likely that "the hundred-fold receipt and the inheriting of eternal life . . . are effectively synonyms."[1]

19:30 *But many who are first will be last, and many who are last will be first.* This saying is repeated (with inverse order) at 20:16, forming an inclusio around the parable of 20:1–15. The language of "first" and "last" is status language and will be used again at the climactic moment of the road to Jerusalem section to highlight the ways of the kingdom as contrasted with ancient status categories (20:25–27). The saying functions to qualify discussion of reward and to warn the twelve disciples against presumption of their own status and importance in the kingdom. The parable that follows provides a different picture about

Key Themes of Matthew 19:27–20:16

- Jesus promises reward to the Twelve.
- Jesus warns against presumption of status in the kingdom.
- Status equalization will occur in the kingdom.

the kingdom, in which equality based on God's generosity is highlighted.

20:1 *For the kingdom of heaven is like a landowner who went out . . . to hire workers.* Once again, Jesus provides a parabolic comparison to "the kingdom of heaven" (13:24, 31, 33, 44, 45, 47; 18:23; 22:2; 25:1). This parable draws on the scenario of day laborers during harvest time hired to work in a vineyard.

20:2 *a denarius.* The offer of a denarius is equitable, given that a denarius is a day's wage for a day laborer.

Jesus tells his disciples that one day they will sit with him, "judging the twelve tribes of Israel" (19:28). In this fourteenth-century AD fresco depicting the last judgment, the twelve apostles are seated in the front row on both sides of Jesus.

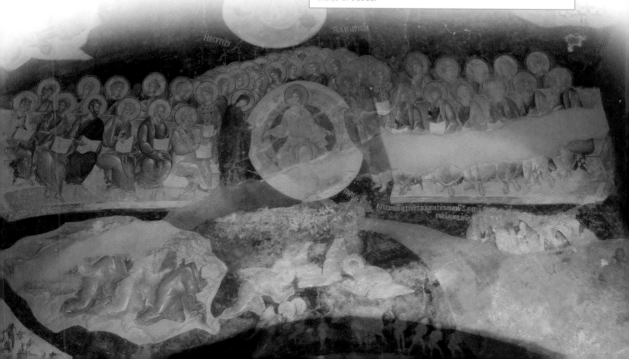

20:3–6 *About nine in the morning . . . about noon and about three in the afternoon.* The workers hired "early in the morning" (20:1) are followed by those hired at three-hour intervals, from nine in the morning to three in the afternoon. These workers fill in color for the story but are not the focus of the parable when it comes time for distribution of payment. There it will be the "first" and "last" workers who contribute to the meaning of the parable.

I will pay you whatever is right. The promise of a fair wage is important for the parable, since the original workers hired will accuse the landowner of being unfair (20:12), which the landowner will dispute (20:13).

About five in the afternoon. A final group of workers is hired when there is only one more hour left in the workday, which stretched from 6 a.m. to 6 p.m. (sunrise to sunset [see 20:12]).

20:8 *beginning with the last ones hired and going on to the first.* There is no historical reality that would account for the reversal of the order of payment. Rather, this detail is necessary for the story to work. The full-day workers must observe the payment of the single-hour workers to be able to respond to the perceived injustice of identical payment for different amounts of work.

20:10 *they expected to receive more.* The full-day workers, having observed those who worked only one hour being paid a denarius—the amount that they themselves were originally promised—now expect to receive more than a denarius.

20:12 *you have made them equal to us.* The full-day workers grumble (20:11) and complain about unequal amounts of work with equal pay. At this point in the parable readers often resonate with the complaint. Equal payment for those who have worked only one-twelfth the time does seem unfair. In fact, when the landowner claims that he is not being unfair (20:13), readers might struggle to agree.

20:13 *I am not being unfair to you.* The landowner claims that he has been fair precisely because he has kept his contractual obligation; he has paid the full-day workers what he had originally promised and what they had agreed to by coming to work in his vineyard. Fairness in this case is assessed not by comparison with other

In this parable of Jesus, a landowner hires workers throughout the day to work in his vineyard. This photo from 1930s Palestine shows workers gathering grapes in a vineyard.

workers (as the full-day workers have done) but rather by the promised wage.

20:15 *Or are you envious because I am generous?* This rhetorical question provides the surprising twist to the parable and shifts the focus from the question of parity to the issue of generosity. The word "envious" appropriately renders the Greek idiom *ponēros ophthalmos* ("evil eye" [see 6:22–23]). According to the landowner, the problem for the full-day workers is not his fairness (as they have framed it), but his extravagant generosity to the single-hour workers. This reorientation of the issue signals the thrust of the parable for Matthew's readers and Jesus' hearers. God is generous to a fault, and this generosity to those who seemingly do not deserve it can prove offensive to those who think they do. The parable's central teaching focuses on God's extravagant generosity, without reference to human earning.

20:16 *So the last will be first, and the first will be last.* The saying that introduces the parable (19:30) is inverted here for the sake of the story, in which the last workers are paid first. As noted at 19:30, "first" and "last" are status terms and would have been heard as such in the highly status-conscious Greco-Roman world.

With this repeated saying as an inclusio (19:30; 20:16), Matthew signals that the parable and the proverbial saying are mutually interpretive. The parable's emphasis on the unsettling equality of the kingdom ("you have made them equal to us") combines with the sense of the saying as a warning against presumption of reward and status (see 19:27–29) to communicate that the kingdom will upset human status

categories and assumptions. God's grand generosity may prove offensive to human sensibilities about fairness and worthiness.

Interpreting Parables

In the history of biblical interpretation parables have proven a difficult genre to interpret. From early and ongoing attempts to allegorize parables (e.g., Origen, Martin Luther, some contemporary preaching) to claims that parables do not say things but only do things, parables have generated much hermeneutical energy. The following are some general guidelines for interpreting parables.

1. At their center, parables are comparisons, indicating how one thing (e.g., the kingdom) is like another (e.g., a mustard seed). So it is helpful to seek the central point of comparison between the story-picture and the reality, although this does not limit a parable to a single point.
2. In longer parables the story-picture typically corresponds to more than one point of reference, so it is fair to try to identify these referents. For example, in the parable of the workers (20:1–15) the landowner refers to God; the full-day workers correspond to those first responding to the kingdom message (in literary context, the Twelve [19:27–30]); and the single-hour workers refer to those who are "latecomers" to faith (in Matthew's historical setting, likely Gentiles).
3. There are usually quite a few details in a parable that are not intended to have significance outside the metaphor; instead, they provide color within the story. Discerning the central point of comparison helps to navigate the metaphorical importance of any particular detail of the parable.
4. Parables are speech-acts: they do things as well as say things. So it is important to ask about a parable's intended effects. This has typically been asked on the level of the historical Jesus: What did a parable do in its original setting? But since we have parables in their literary settings, we should also ask about the effect intended by the evangelist. In 20:1–15, for instance, the reader/hearer is warned about resenting God's generosity toward others.

Teaching the Text

1. *The parable of the workers highlights the surprising equality of the kingdom.*

Matthew has been highlighting the reality of status categories in this part of his Gospel. Jesus' teachings have emphasized that his followers, instead of presuming the same status categories that they are familiar with in their current experience, should renounce status concern, since the kingdom is not about status presumption and acquisition. This parable clarifies that the kingdom has a surprising and potentially disturbing equality to it. The central complaint of the full-day workers captures this affront: "You have made them equal to us."

2. *The parable of the workers confronts its hearers with the deep and potentially disturbing generosity of God*. In the story of this parable the concluding words of the landowner signal the message of the parable in its metaphor: "Are you envious because I am generous?" (20:15). Biblical theology rightly emphasizes God's generous nature. God's self-revelation in the covenant with Israel is marked by grace from the start: "The LORD, the LORD, the compassionate and gracious God" (Exod. 34:6). This parable emphasizes that same quality and indicates that God's deep generosity toward others can actually trip us up if we think of the kingdom in terms of limited amounts of grace being distributed based on "deservedness." Moving beyond the details of the parable (which should not be pressed into service for its metaphorical meaning), we learn that God's grace is effusive and is based

not on what humans deserve but on God's own nature.

If the parable proves troubling, we would do well to capitalize on that response for our preaching and teaching of it. It disturbs us probably because we have identified in some way with the full-day workers, and we feel the affront of the landowner's generosity to those who seem less deserving. We, and our audience, will likely feel a certain lack of fairness in this scenario (as the full-day workers did). We might helpfully use the question of the landowner at the end of the story recast for ourselves and our audience: "Are we envious of God's great generosity when it is given to others who seem to deserve it less than we do?" By casting the question in this way, we might help people to hear the ways in which we, against the theology that we claim to hold, actually think we have earned God's goodness and generosity to us. But, as Scripture

In this parable of Jesus, workers are hired at different times of the day: 6 a.m., 9 a.m., noon, 3 p.m., and 5 p.m. Sundials, like this one from the first century AD, were used to tell time during the Roman period.

affirms, God's grace and mercy always initiate relationship and covenant.

Our responses to God are truly that—responses. We respond to God's prior work of covenanting by returning to that relationship. We respond to God's saving work of redemption by participating in salvation in Christ. We respond to God's daily leading with dependent discernment. And in those moments when we more fully realize all that God has worked to return us and love us, we fall on our knees in gratitude for such goodness and grace.[2]

Illustrating the Text

The parable of the workers highlights the surprising equality of the kingdom.

Children's Book: *Charlie and the Chocolate Factory*, **by Roald Dahl.** This popular book tells of a fantastical world of trained squirrels and chocolate waterfalls. When factory owner Willy Wonka announces that he is opening up his factory to five lucky children, people begin snatching up Wonka chocolate bars in hopes of winning one of the five golden tickets. Each of the winning children, except for Charlie, comes with some particular sense of entitlement that ends up disqualifying him or her from Willy Wonka's true purpose, which is to give his factory away to a deserving child. He is looking for a child without any such entitlement because he wants to give his factory to someone who will simply respond in wonder and joy at a gift freely given.

The parable of the workers confronts its hearers with the deep and potentially disturbing generosity of God.

Reflection: We can claim that we, as believers, are saved only by the grace of God, but our true assumptions are exposed by this parable. You might ask the people in your audience to think about the most unworthy person they can imagine. Then have them imagine God ushering that person into the kingdom side by side with the most faithful of saints. How would it feel to see that unworthy person being showered with God's grace apart from doing anything to earn it?

Quote: Brennan Manning, in *The Ragamuffin Gospel*, speaks of God's lavish grace that neutralizes human distinctions of "first" and "last" in the kingdom.

The gospel of grace nullifies our adulation of televangelists, charismatic superstars, and local church heroes. It obliterates the two-class citizenship theory operative in many American churches. For grace proclaims the awesome truth that all is gift. All that is good is ours, not by right, but by the sheer bounty of a gracious God. While there is much we may have earned—our degree, our salary, our home and garden, a Miller Lite, and a good night's sleep—all this is possible only because we have been given so much: life itself, eyes to see and hands to touch, a mind to shape ideas, and a heart to beat with love. . . . My deepest awareness of myself is that I am deeply loved by Jesus Christ and I have done nothing to earn it or deserve it.[3]

Jesus Is the Example of Service for His Followers

Big Idea *Jesus' disciples are exhorted to renounce their concern for status, following the example of Jesus himself, who willingly suffers and dies to ransom people.*

Understanding the Text

The Text in Context

This passage narrates a final teaching opportunity for Jesus' disciples before arriving in Jerusalem (20:29–21:11). The passage begins with a third passion prediction by Jesus (20:17–19; cf. 16:21; 17:22–23) and ends with the first explicit purpose statement that Jesus provides for his coming death: to be "a ransom for many" (20:28). In this way, the whole of 16:21–20:28 is framed by the anticipation of Jesus' coming death in Jerusalem. As has been the case throughout 16:21–20:28, the disciples are portrayed as seeking their own interests and status rather than following the pattern of self-denial set by Jesus himself (20:28). In this passage they argue about the highest positions of status in the coming kingdom (20:2–24; see 18:1; 19:27). So Jesus continues to teach the Twelve about the importance of renouncing status concerns and of emulating those who have little or no status in their world: slaves (20:25–27) and children (18:3–4).

Interpretive Insights

20:18 *the Son of Man will be delivered over.* This is Jesus' third passion prediction in 16:21–20:28, with the other two included at 16:21 and 17:22–23 (see 26:2 for a final one in Matthew).

20:19 *will hand him over to the Gentiles.* This passion prediction is the first to mention the culpability of Gentiles in Jesus' death. As Matthew will narrate it, Jesus' death comes about when the Jewish chief priests and elders convince the people to ask Pilate, the Roman governor, for Jesus' death (27:1–2, 20). It is Pilate who, in the end, delivers Jesus to be crucified (27:26). Yet Matthew also speaks of Jesus' death coming about by "human hands" (17:22).

20:20 *the mother of Zebedee's sons.* Matthew has already identified James and John as the sons of Zebedee (4:18–22; 10:2). Here their mother comes with a request on their behalf (cf. Mark 10:35–36, where they make the request themselves).

20:21 *sit at your right and . . . at your left in your kingdom.* The request consists in James and John ruling as second and third authorities in the kingdom. This is quite a bold and presumptuous request. That the brothers might presume a ruling role could be derived from 19:28, where Jesus has promised the twelve disciples an eschatological judging role, though judging does not necessarily imply ruling.[1] The disciples' ongoing presumption of positions of power and status is clear at 18:1, in their question about who will be greatest in the kingdom. Jesus' teaching there and here contradicts such presumption about status acquisition in the kingdom.

20:22 *Can you drink the cup I am going to drink?* Matthew indicates that Jesus' response is directed at James and John by using a plural "you" (in three Greek verbs in 20:22). In the Old Testament, reference to "cup" often refers to God's wrath or judgment (e.g., Jer. 25:15; 49:12). The two brothers do not seem to catch this connotation in their affirmative answer.

We can. The brief answer by James and John again highlights their bold request and lack of understand-

Key Themes of Matthew 20:17–28

- Jesus, as the suffering Messiah, serves others and gives his life as a ransom.
- James and John make a presumption of status.
- The renunciation of status is essential in the kingdom.

light, in line with a few Old Testament texts that connect "cup" with salvation or provision (e.g., Pss. 16:5; 116:13; cf. Zech. 12:2, where Israel becomes the cup of judgment upon surrounding nations). Their answer is particularly incriminating in light of the passion prediction that has immediately preceded their request.

20:23 *You will indeed drink from my cup.* Jesus' statement that James and John will drink from the same cup of suffering that Jesus will experience finds no resolution within the story line of Matthew. In Acts, however, we read about the death of James at the hand of Herod Agrippa I (AD 41–44).

These places belong to those for whom they have been prepared by my Father. At a few places in Matthew the reader hears Jesus refer

As they travel to Jerusalem, Jesus tells his disciples that he will be handed over to the Gentiles "to be mocked and flogged and crucified" (20:19). These fourteenth-century AD marble statuettes depict the flogging of Christ.

ing about the nature of Jesus' mission in Jerusalem, which will involve suffering and death. It may be that they understand his picture of sharing a cup in a more positive

to God's authority that stands above and beyond his own. For example, this idea is implicit in the centurion's comparison of his own situation with that of Jesus;

Matthew 20:17–28

the centurion states that he "also" (*kai*) is under a higher authority (8:9). Here Jesus indicates that the request for positions of honor is the prerogative of his Father. Yet Matthew also signals that Jesus is granted authority by God (11:27) and will be given all authority after his resurrection (28:18).

20:24 *they were indignant with the two brothers.* Given the frequent misunderstanding of the disciples and their preoccupation with status across this section of Matthew, it is likely that their indignation with James and John has something to do with competition for these "greatest" positions in the coming kingdom. Rivalry, not altruism, is most likely the motivation.

20:25 *You know that the rulers of the Gentiles lord it over them.* Matthew has been evoking the status consciousness of the Greco-Roman world in this section of his Gospel by means of status language, such as "greatest" and "first" and "last" (18:1; 19:30; 20:16) and by attention to those with lower and higher status, such as children and women (19:1–15) and, alternately, the rich (19:16–26). In 20:25 Jesus' comment makes this status-conscious context explicit by referencing practices of Gentile rulers in contrast to servants and slaves (20:26–27). In Jesus' comparison these rulers "lord it over" and "exercise authority over" others. The first verb, *katakyrieuō*, can indicate absolute mastery or domination (Acts 19:16; 1 Pet. 5:3). The image evoked is that of acting as a master over a slave. Jesus inverts this paradigm by calling his followers to take the position of a slave or servant in the community of believers. "As opposed to the role of absolute masters, which characterizes Gentile rulers, Jesus' disciples are to be characterized by service with no regard for position."[2]

20:26 *whoever wants to become great . . . must be your servant.* Jesus has already responded to the disciples' query about greatness, clearly a status question (18:1). Here he defines greatness in such a way as to derail all attempts to assume or claim status prerogatives. As Ulrich Luz suggests, "The issue . . . is not to present a new way to greatness—a more noble way than that of authority and power; it is rather that the desire to be great is itself to be eliminated, since even the most subtle desire for greatness for oneself corrupts genuine service."[3]

20:27 *whoever wants to be first must be your slave.* "First" and "last" language has been used to frame the parable of the workers to

In contrast to pagan rulers who used their positions of leadership to "lord it over [others]" (20:25), Jesus calls his followers to be servants in his kingdom. Shown here is a statue of Tiberius, the Roman emperor during the time of Jesus' ministry. He is depicted sitting in a Zeus-like pose and holding a scepter, a symbol of power and authority.

indicate the reversal (and more particularly, equalization) of status in the kingdom. Here Jesus picks up this motif again to highlight the same point: his disciples should renounce status concerns and embrace service and care for others.

20:28 *just as the Son of Man did not come to be served, but to serve.* Jesus points to his own mission as the analogy for his disciples' service on behalf of others. As the Messiah-King (which he will "announce" in action in 21:1–11), he could expect to be served, like the Gentile rulers he has just referenced. Yet his way of ruling as king is utterly different from what was expected. His defining action as the Messiah is to stand in as representative for Israel (and so for the nations); he will serve rather than require others to serve him. In this way, Jesus provides the example for true discipleship.

give his life as a ransom for many. At this climactic point in Jesus' journey to Jerusalem (16:21–20:28), he provides the reason for his coming death, which he has predicted three times (16:21; 17:22–23; 20:17–19). The language and themes of 20:28 evoke Isaiah 53, which Matthew has already cited in 8:17 (Isa. 53:4). First, the picture of Jesus as one who serves connects with Isaiah's servant figure, and Matthew has made this connection explicit earlier in his narrative (12:18–21). Second, Isaiah 53:12 appears to sit behind Jesus' words of giving his life for many: "He poured out his life unto death, and was numbered with the transgressors. For he bore the sin of many, and made intercession for the transgressors." Jesus will draw on these words and ideas at the Passover meal as well: "This is my blood of the covenant, which is poured out for many for the forgiveness of sins" (Matt. 26:28).

Theological Insights: Jesus as Suffering Servant

Matthew connects his portrait of Jesus with the Suffering Servant of Isaiah 53 (see the sidebar "Jesus as Isaiah's Servant Figure" in the unit on 12:15–21). He is not unique among New Testament writers in doing so. Luke narrates Jesus citing Isaiah 53:12 in reference to his coming death (Luke 22:37). And John's reference to Jesus as "the Lamb of God" (John 1:29, 36) may allude to Isaiah 53:7 ("he was led like a lamb to the slaughter"). In Acts Philip explains to the Ethiopian eunuch that Jesus is the referent for the Isaianic lamb (Isa. 53:7–8 in Acts 8:32–33). And in 1 Peter 2 Jesus as the righteous suffering one is the model for believers experiencing mistreatment (Isa. 53:9 in 1 Pet. 2:22) and is the bearer of sins (Isa. 53:4–6 in 1 Pet. 2:24–25). These New Testament uses portray Jesus as the Isaianic servant in his suffering and death, who brings healing (Matt. 8:17; 1 Pet. 2:24), gives his life as a ransom (Matt. 20:28), and exemplifies remaining faithful through suffering (1 Pet. 2:21–22).

Teaching the Text

1. *Jesus calls his followers to service for others modeled after his own example and not that of Gentile rulers.* This passage brings together themes from across 16:21–20:28. One of these is Jesus' expectation that his followers focus on service to others (e.g., 16:24–26; 18:1–14). In this passage Jesus grounds that call to service in

his own mission and model. Jesus, as the exemplar of Isaiah's Servant of the Lord, is the model we ought to follow. He sets the standard by turning away from self-focus and status maintenance or acquisition; we are to follow in his footsteps. It is common enough to speak about "servant leadership" in our churches, and this notion has the ability to transform our ministry values and practices. Yet the analogy provided in 20:25–27 is even more potent. The contrast that Jesus draws is between acting as master over slave and the complete inverse of this picture. Those who lead should renounce status as if they were in the position of slave in relation to their master (20:27). While it is possible that we have become inoculated to the language of "servant leadership," we can hear Jesus afresh if we suggest that "slave leadership" is his proposed path for us. And this message applies first and foremost to ourselves and others who lead with us.

2. *Matthew reveals that Jesus' mission is to act as the representative of Israel to bring redemption to Israel and to the nations.* After providing predictions of Jesus' coming death, Matthew now states its purpose: "to give his life as a ransom for many." This language draws from Isaiah 53 and Isaiah's portrait of the Servant of the Lord to highlight Jesus' representative role in salvation. He will die on behalf of his people (1:21), and, as Matthew will make clear, his death will usher Gentiles into the people of God (28:19). These corporate contours of Jesus' mission are important to highlight in preaching, especially in our

Jesus tells his disciples, "Whoever wants to become great among you must be your servant" (20:26). John 13 narrates how Jesus demonstrates this for his disciples when he washes their feet the evening before his death. Here is a tenth-century AD ivory icon from Constantinople depicting the event, showing Christ as servant.

contexts, which are often highly individualistic. I recall a statement often made in my childhood Bible camp days: "If you were the only person in the world, Jesus would have died just for you." This refrain, though perhaps lovely and pietistic, finds little purchase in the New Testament. The power of Jesus' representative role in Matthew is his mission to suffer and die on Israel's behalf to bring about their redemption (cf. Isa. 53:4–6) and his role on behalf of Israel to fulfill their mission to the nations (cf. Isa. 49:6). That Jesus comes to "save his people from their sins" (1:21) certainly means that individuals are included. Yet by helping people to see the corporate nature of Jesus' actions and mission, we invite them to recognize that they are part of God's cosmic drama of salvation. The scope of God's work in Jesus is not the small stage of my individual life; instead, it is the broad canvas of the redemption of Israel, the nations, and ultimately the whole of creation (Rom. 8).

Illustrating the Text

Jesus calls his followers to service for others modeled after his own example and not that of Gentile rulers.

History: Conduct an image search for historical figures known as great and powerful rulers. For example, you might search for images of Alexander the Great, Marcus Aurelius, and Napoleon. Paintings and statues of these famous rulers often depict them in strength and power—astride a horse, hand held out in a gesture of divine authority. If appropriate for your setting, you could visually contrast these rulers with Jesus' teachings about discipleship in this passage as exhibited by other historical figures (e.g., Mother Teresa in the next illustration).

Biography: Consider providing a brief overview of how the simple, humble vision of Mother Teresa grew from one person's caring service to an organization, the Missionaries of Charity, with more than one million workers in more than forty countries. The Nobel Prize website provides a summary of her life and ministry.[4]

News: In October 2013 Bishop Franz-Peter Tebartz-van Elst met with Pope Francis. The meeting probably was not a comfortable one. Francis, who took his papal name from a man noted for his rejection of worldly wealth and embrace of simplicity, required an explanation from Tebartz-van Elst about the $20,000 bathtub and plans for a 800-square-foot fitness room for the bishop's personal residence, as well as $1.1 million in church funds for a landscaped garden on the church's property. This situation might be used as an example of priests or pastors acting more like rulers than servants.[5]

Matthew reveals that Jesus' mission is to act as the representative of Israel to bring redemption to Israel and to the nations.

Art: The Bayeux Tapestry is a wonder of history. This tapestry, created in the eleventh century, illustrates epic events during the Norman invasion of England under William, Duke of Normandy. Fifty scenes woven of fabric and thread and stretching nearly seventy-five yards capture historical events with artistic genius (if your context allows, you might display images of the tapestry). It would be the height of folly to cut out any one piece of this great tapestry and try to let it stand alone as the point of the whole. Similarly, when we make Jesus' life, death, and resurrection a purely personal (individual) matter, we run the risk of missing the big picture. Statements like "If I was the only person on earth, Jesus would have died for me" might make us feel good, but they miss the grand sweep of God's amazing plan for history and our identity within God's redeemed people—the church.

Matthew 20:17–28

Jesus Enters Jerusalem as a Peaceable and Humble King

Big Idea *After mercifully healing two blind men, Jesus enters Jerusalem as a peaceable and humble king in concert with Zechariah's vision of Israel's king who comes to bring salvation.*

Understanding the Text

The Text in Context

This passage, which narrates Jesus healing two blind men outside Jericho (20:29–34) and thereafter entering Jerusalem in kingly fashion (21:1–11), introduces a new section of Matthew focused on Jesus' ministry to crowds and confrontations with Jewish leaders in Jerusalem (chaps. 21–23). Matthew ties the healing account and Jerusalem entry stories together by emphasizing Jesus as the "Son of David" in both (20:30–31; 21:9). After an extended section featuring Jesus and his disciples (16:21–20:28), the crowds reappear in these two passages (20:29; 21:9, 11; though see 19:2). Matthew distinguishes the Jerusalem crowds that ask about Jesus' identity from the Galilean crowd that accompanies Jesus into the city. In terms of that identity, Matthew emphasizes that Jesus' kingship (explicated by Zech. 9:9) promotes a peaceable and humble reign (21:5).

Interpretive Insights

20:29 *Jericho.* Jericho sits approximately fourteen miles to the northeast of

Jesus encounters two blind men as he leaves Jericho. The first-century town has not been extensively excavated because the modern town lies over any remains. However, archaeologists have uncovered the ruins of Herod the Great's elaborate winter palace, shown here.

Jerusalem. The last geographic reference was in 19:1, where Matthew indicated that Jesus "left Galilee and went into the region of Judea to the other side of the Jordan." Jesus' journey to Jerusalem is now nearly complete.

20:30 *Lord, Son of David, have mercy on us!* These two blind men call Jesus "Son of David" and call out for mercy, as do other supplicants in Matthew's story (9:27; 15:22). The motif of Jesus as the Son of David occurs here and in 20:31, preparing the way for Jesus' entry into Jerusalem, where the crowds escort him into the city acclaiming him "Son of David." Children will also join this refrain in the temple courts in 21:15.

20:34 *Jesus had compassion on them and touched their eyes.* Jesus' compassion is thematic in Matthew. Jesus has healed people because of his compassion already at 9:35–36; 14:14 (see also 15:32). This passage provides a fitting conclusion to Jesus' compassionate healing ministry in Galilee.

they . . . followed him. Matthew notes that these two people healed by Jesus follow him. The word *akoloutheō* is frequently used to signal following in discipleship (e.g., 4:20, 22; 8:22; 9:9; 10:38; 16:24; 19:21, 27, 28). So although its use here could simply mean that the two men join the crowd as Jesus enters Jerusalem (20:29), it may be that Matthew is subtly signaling a discipleship motif.

21:1 *Bethphage on the Mount of Olives.* Bethphage was located near Jerusalem in close proximity to Bethany (see Mark 11:1). The Mount of Olives will be the scene of Jesus' predictions about the fall of Jerusalem (24:3) and about Peter's denial (26:30–35).

21:2 *at once you will find a donkey tied there.* Matthew has portrayed Jesus as knowing people's thoughts (12:25), so it is possible that he is portraying Jesus as knowing through divine provision the location of this donkey and colt. It is more likely, however, that prearrangement of these details is to be inferred. As R. T. France suggests, "The brief formula 'The Lord needs them' [21:3] would serve well as an agreed upon password, but would not persuade any but a very gullible villager to part with his animals to two strangers if he had not been forewarned."[1] We see such signs of prearrangement at 26:18–19, where Jesus has his disciples connect with a particular person to arrange their celebration of Passover.

21:3 *he will send them right away.* The Greek is ambiguous regarding the subject of the verb "send." It might be "the Lord" (the closest referent), but this makes little sense in context. The more likely referent is the "anyone," who could quite likely be the owner of the animals.

21:4–5 *This took place to fulfill what was spoken through the prophet.* This is one of the ten fulfillment quotations that Matthew uses across his Gospel. Here, Zechariah 9:9 is used to provide the royal significance of Jesus' entry into Jerusalem.

See, your king comes to you, gentle and riding on a donkey. Zechariah's prophetic picture is of Israel's king riding into Jerusalem on a donkey, the mode of transportation of a king during times of peace (e.g., 1 Kings 1:33, 38; cf. 1 Kings 20:1, where kings ride horses into battle). So Matthew highlights Jesus as a peaceable Messiah, one who is gentle or humble (*praus* [21:5]). Jesus has described himself in this way at 11:29: "I am gentle [*praus*] and humble in heart."

21:8 *others cut branches from the trees and spread them on the road.* The crowds that enter with Jesus into Jerusalem, presumably pilgrims from Galilee for Passover, celebrate his arrival (21:9). The use of branches to pave Jesus' way recalls the people of Israel waving palm branches in celebration at the expulsion of Israel's enemies from Jerusalem during the Maccabean revolts (1 Macc. 13:51; cf. John 12:13) and suggests the political ramifications of first-century messianic hopes.

21:9 *Hosanna to the Son of David!* "Hosanna" is a Hebrew/Aramaic word meaning "save," used as an expression of praise (see Ps. 118:25). The acclamation of Jesus as "Son of David" confirms the (Galilean) crowd's perception that Jesus is the Messiah. Although they will describe him as a prophet in 21:11, the latter is presumably how he has been designated and known by reputation throughout his Galilean ministry and does not conflict with understandings of Jesus' messianic identity (e.g., Matthew holds both to be true [see 13:57; 23:29–39]).

Blessed is he who comes in the name of the Lord! Matthew narrates that the crowds shout acclamations with the words of Psalm 118:26. This psalm references procession to the temple (Ps. 118:19–20, 26–27). It may be that in Jesus' time Psalm 118 was used during festival processions. Rabbinic sources note its (later) use during the Feasts of Passover, Tabernacles, and Hanukkah (b. 'Arak. 10a).[2]

Jesus enters Jerusalem riding on a donkey and surrounded by pilgrims shouting "Hosanna to the Son of David!" (21:9). The route Jesus followed would have brought him down the western slopes of the Mount of Olives, across the Kidron Valley, and up through the city gates into Jerusalem. This is the view from the Mount of Olives into the Kidron Valley with the walls of the Old City of Jerusalem and the modern Temple Mount in sight.

This connects Jesus' entry into Jerusalem with his action in the temple in 21:12–17, both of which are messianic actions (see 21:12). Later in the chapter a citation from Psalm 118:22–23 will be used by Jesus to explain the rejection of the son in the parable of the tenants—that is, his own rejection (21:42).

21:11 *The crowds answered, "This is Jesus, the prophet from Nazareth in Galilee."* The Galilean crowds that have accompanied Jesus into Jerusalem answer the people of the city who ask about the identity of this one who rides into Jerusalem as a peaceable king (21:10). The Galilean crowds answer that it is Jesus, the Galilean prophet (for their messianic acclamations, see 21:9). Although the "crowds" (*ochlos*; sometimes *laos* ["people"]) have been portrayed so far as a single character group, here Matthew makes it clear that the people of Jerusalem are not identical to the many Jewish people from Galilee who have followed Jesus in his ministry and to Jerusalem. This distinction will be important when it comes to understanding the portrayal of the people (*laos*) at 27:25. For the distinction presented here between Jews from Galilee and those from Judea/Jerusalem, see comments on 4:12.

Teaching the Text

1. *Matthew shows Jesus to be the true king of Israel, the Son of David, who brings restoration.* On the story level of Matthew, Jesus now openly demonstrates his claim to be Israel's king. For Matthew, chapter 21 provides a fitting climax to Jesus' Galilean ministry and his turn toward Jerusalem. Now Jesus as king will assert and prove

Jesus' Entry into Jerusalem as First Public Messianic Claim

Although Matthew has clearly identified Jesus as the Messiah from the start of his Gospel (1:1), on the narrative's story level Jesus' public preaching has not made this truth explicit. And although Jesus has announced the arrival of the kingdom (4:17; 5:3–10) and even intimated his role in it (12:28), he has not publicly proclaimed himself as king. For any would-be messiah in the first-century world, this would be a wise course, since Rome did not look kindly on contending kings from its subjugated peoples. There was one Roman king, and that was Caesar. And regardless of the ways in which Matthew indicates that Jesus defies or transcends some Jewish expectations for the Messiah, it is clear that "messiah" carried connotations of king in public parlance (see 27:11, 17).

It is true that Jesus has already confirmed that the disciples rightly identify him as the Messiah (16:16), but this is not a public proclamation, and according to Matthew, Jesus immediately warns them to keep his identity to themselves (16:20). So when Jesus enters Jerusalem, intentionally setting the stage by riding a donkey so that the crowds will recognize the connection to the royal promises in Zechariah 9, this is the first public claim that he makes regarding his messianic identity. It is a claim made by action rather than words, but it is clearly a kingly claim, as the people's acclamation of the "Son of David" demonstrates (21:9). It is not surprising, then, that less than a week after Jesus' public declaration of his messiahship, he is crucified by the Romans. Messianic contenders were not tolerated by Rome.

his messianic authority in contest with the temple leaders and Jerusalem establishment. We see in this scene Jesus declaring his kingship and receiving acclaim as Messiah-King.

What does it mean to preach and teach Jesus as Messiah-King? First, it means proclaiming that Jesus is the one who brings God's salvation and restoration to his people, Israel (1:21), and to all nations (28:19). Jesus acts on God's behalf to bring God's salvation in line with the Old Testament promises about a coming son of David (e.g., Isa. 11:1). Second, it means highlighting Jesus' authority as king.

Matthew has told the story of Jesus focused on his authority. Jesus is the rightful king, even as a child in contrast with King Herod (2:1–23); Jesus' teaching and healing demonstrate his messianic authority (7:28–29; 8:9; 9:8); and Jesus will be shown to have all authority in heaven and earth in the final scene of the Gospel (28:18). And Jesus' kingly authority provides comfort and promise that in his death and resurrection he has conquered all powers and enemies, including death (e.g., 27:53). So Jesus' followers can trust that in time Christ as king will destroy all contending powers, including death (1 Cor. 15:24–26), to reconcile all things to God (Col. 1:20). Even when circumstances in life suggest that things are out of control, we can trust that Jesus is Lord, king over all. This is Matthew's message of Jesus as Messiah-King here and throughout his Gospel.

2. *Matthew shows Jesus to be the merciful and peaceable king of Israel.* Matthew indeed shows Jesus to be Lord and king, but there is also an unexpected turn in his messianic portrayal. He has already characterized Jesus as healer who enacts Isaiah's vision of restoration (8:17; 12:18–21). We see this again at 20:29–34, where Jesus is compassionate healer of two blind men. Even in Jesus' triumphal entry into Jerusalem, Matthew portrays him as humble and peaceable, in line with Zechariah's vision (21:5). As we preach Jesus as king, we must also pay attention to these facets of his kingship. Just as those in Matthew's first-century audience could have had views of royal power that emphasized its absolute and violent use, we too might picture kingship in ways that do not fit Matthew's royal portrait of Jesus. Matthew portrays Jesus as the humble Messiah-King, who comes with peaceful intentions. This is an essential part of how we are to preach and teach Jesus as king.

Illustrating the Text

Matthew shows Jesus to be the true king of Israel, the Son of David, who brings restoration.

Cultural Institution: For political junkies, election night is like the Super Bowl. Especially in close elections, the evening can progress with nail-biting excitement. Hour by hour, a trend begins to emerge, and the picture of the next officeholder is slowly clarified. In a close election, the outcome may not be clear until late into the evening. Analogously, as Jesus' ministry progresses in Matthew, his true identity emerges slowly; it is here in 21:1–11 that Jesus most clearly reveals to the crowds his messianic identity.

Matthew shows Jesus to be the merciful and peaceable king of Israel.

Human Experience: The best books often have endings that you do not see coming. But even the most surprising endings fit with what has happened up to that point. And after the fact, it is difficult to imagine them unfolding any other way. The plot twists of a Charles Dickens novel, for instance, usually bring a happy ending to a hopeless situation. However surprising, they are always connected to and build upon what came before. In a similar way, not all facets of Jesus as the Messiah fit Jewish expectations. Jesus' peaceable way of being king is one such facet; he lives out a countercultural kingship that gives up rather than garners power.

Scripture: In the book that bears her name, Esther, along with her uncle Mordecai and all the Jews in the Persian Empire, appears to be at the mercy of King Xerxes. This ruler exercises his power by commanding the affairs of a kingdom. He demonstrates his might by holding the power of life and death over every person in his empire, and at one point he declares that all the Jews be put to death. Mordecai appeals to Esther, as queen, to intercede on behalf of their people. In her reply she reminds him, "All the king's officials and the people of the royal provinces know that for any man or woman who approaches the king in the inner court without being summoned the king has but one law: that they be put to death unless the king extends the gold scepter to them and spares their lives" (Esther 4:11). Matthew shows that Jesus' kingship is diametrically opposed to such displays of despotism.

Jesus Demonstrates Messianic Authority over the Temple

Big Idea *Matthew emphasizes Jesus' authority as Messiah over the temple and his critique of its leadership as well as the importance of unwavering faith in following Jesus.*

Understanding the Text

The Text in Context

In Matthew the account of Jesus in the temple immediately follows his entry into Jerusalem. Both stories highlight Jesus' identity and authority as Israel's Messiah, with the acclamation of Jesus as the "Son of David" by the crowds and by children (21:9,

15). In 21:12–17 Jesus acts with messianic authority by denouncing current practices in the temple that have distorted its purposes (21:12–13), as in the analogous and parabolic cursing of the fig tree (21:18–22). This denunciation fits a broader pattern of critiques of the temple and its leaders by Jesus in this part of Matthew (23:38; 24:1–35; see also 26:60–61). This passage

This map shows the city of Jerusalem and the surrounding area during the time of Jesus. Buying and selling animals for sacrifice and changing money for acceptable temple currency most likely occurred in the court of the Gentiles or under the roof of the royal stoa. It was here, too, that the blind and the lame could come. After his arrival in Jerusalem, Jesus teaches in the temple courts by day and stays in Bethany by night (about two miles away; 21:17; see 26:6).

also begins a series of conflicts between Jesus and the Jerusalem leadership (21:23, 45; 22:15–46). In contrast to this conflict, Matthew highlights praise (21:15–16) and faith (21:21–22) as appropriate responses to Jesus' deeds.

Interpretive Insights

21:12 *Jesus entered the temple courts and drove out all who were buying and selling there.* According to Matthew, the sale of sacrificial animals and the transactions of changing money were happening in the area of the temple courts. The former would have been necessary for pilgrims traveling significant distances to Jerusalem for the various Jewish feasts, including Passover (26:2). Greek and Roman currencies had to be exchanged for the prescribed temple currency—coins from Tyre in Phoenicia, whose weight and value were considered close to the prescribed half shekel required from Jews for temple support (Exod. 30:11–16).

It is unlikely, given that the functions of selling animals and changing money were necessary, that Jesus is protesting these per se. Rather, Matthew is likely indicating that Jesus protests the locating of these transactions within the temple courts, which obscures the temple's true purpose as "a house of prayer" (21:13; cf. Isa. 56:7). In spite of Matthew's omission of the descriptor "for all nations" for "house of prayer" in Mark 11:17, the specific temple area probably in view is the court of the Gentiles, which would have had the space to accommodate the large festival crowds. By bringing these commercial activities into the temple courts, the temple leadership

Key Themes of Matthew 21:12–22

- Jesus has messianic authority over the temple.
- The current administrators of the temple have distorted its purpose.
- Disciples are exhorted to be unwavering in their faith.

was directing the focus of the temple away from its true purposes.

In terms of broader purposes, was Jesus cleansing the temple and restoring it to its proper use (21:13; cf. Isa. 56:7; Mal. 3:1–4)? Or was he enacting God's judgment prophetically and symbolically on the temple and on the temple leadership (21:13; cf. Jer. 7:11)? It may be that Jesus' action signals both a purifying of the temple by protesting abuses in it and a judgment of its leadership and practices.[1] The latter will be clarified in 24:3–35, where Jesus announces future judgment on the temple and predicts its destruction. Additionally, Jesus' actions in the temple most certainly had revolutionary overtones, whether these were intended or not.[2] Within a week, he is crucified as a threat to Rome.

He overturned the tables of the money changers. Jesus' action in the temple functions as an assertion of his messianic authority. This is certainly how the Jewish leaders perceive it, since they come to Jesus to ask about his authority to do this (21:23). Matthew also, by having Jesus' temple action follow directly upon his entry into Jerusalem as its Messiah-King, signals that Jesus draws on his messianic authority to critique these particular practices within the temple.[3] Within at least some strains of Jewish thought there was an expectation that the Messiah would purify the temple: "He [the Davidic king] will purify

Jerusalem in holiness as it was at the beginning" (*Pss. Sol.* 17:30).

21:13 *It is written . . . "My house will be called a house of prayer."* Jesus draws on Isaiah 56:7 to indicate the true purpose of the temple as a place of prayer rather than commerce. The passage from Isaiah (56:1–8) is a powerful picture of the inclusivity of the temple in a future day: eunuchs and Gentiles will be welcomed into Yahweh's temple (a reversal of Deut. 23:1). This inclusive vision coheres with Matthew, who portrays the blind and the lame being healed by Jesus at the temple and children shouting acclamations in the temple courts (21:14–15).

a den of robbers. In contrast to the true purpose of the temple, Jesus accuses the sellers and money changers (and so the temple authorities) of making the temple into a "den of robbers." This language comes from Jeremiah 7:11, from a passage in which Yahweh warns the people of Judah that their lack of covenant faithfulness will follow them into the temple. So they will not find safety and protection in the temple; instead, their trust in the temple will prove misplaced when God judges them for their idolatry and injustice (Jer. 7:4, 10, 14).

21:14 *The blind and the lame.* The portrait of Jesus healing in the temple is unique to Matthew but fits the various summaries of his healing ministry in Galilee (e.g., 4:23–25; 9:35; 12:15; 14:34–36; 15:29–31). The specific reference to the blind and the lame (*typhloi kai chōloi*) may be an evocation of either Leviticus 21:18 or 2 Samuel 5:6–8. The former is found in the prohibition against any priest who is "blind or lame" serving in the temple (Lev. 21:17–18), although this says nothing of strictures

about who may worship at the temple. A type-scene parallel to 2 Samuel 5:6–8 seems likely. There King David (note Jesus in Matt. 21:15 as "Son of David") fights to claim Jerusalem and is taunted that "even the blind and the lame" could keep him out (5:6 LXX: *hoi typhloi kai hoi oi chōloi*). David, in turn, calls his enemies defending Jerusalem "those 'lame and blind'" (5:8). The narrator of 2 Samuel then indicates that this is the origin of the saying "The 'blind and lame' will not enter the palace [house]" (5:8). As R. T. France suggests, "Here, in 'the house,' Jesus the Son of David is approached by the blind and the lame, and, far from dismissing them [as David does], he heals them."[4]

21:15 *children shouting in the temple courts, "Hosanna to the Son of David."* Matthew again highlights Jesus as the messianic "Son of David," this time through the words of children's praises. Earlier in the narrative, children have signified those of low status (18:1–5; 19:13–15). Here they are paired with the blind and the lame to exemplify the audience of Jesus' ministry as those with little to offer, when perceived in terms of value and status in the first century.

the chief priests and teachers of the law . . . were indignant. With his reference to the chief priests, Matthew introduces the central antagonists to Jesus in Jerusalem. While Galilean teachers of the law have been paired with Pharisees during Jesus' ministry there (e.g., 5:20; 12:38; 15:1), here such teachers join with the temple leaders—the chief priests—to challenge Jesus (see 2:4). The chief priests will also collude with the elders of the people (e.g., 21:23; 26:3; 28:12) and the Pharisees (21:45–46; 27:62) to plot Jesus' demise.

A fig tree with no fruit, like the one shown here, receives a curse from Jesus, as a symbolic warning of the judgment coming on the temple and its leadership.

21:16 *From the lips of children and infants.* Jesus' reply to the complaint of the chief priests and elders derives from Psalm 8:2 and accents the unlikely source of praise for Israel's Messiah: not from the leaders of Israel, but rather from children and even infants.

21:19 *May you never bear fruit again!* Jesus' cursing of this tree is another symbolic action, corresponding to his action of judgment upon the temple (21:12). The fruitlessness of this tree is an analogy to the temple that should be bearing fruit (prayer and worship [21:13–16]) but whose purpose is being obscured by commerce.

21:21 *if you have faith and do not doubt.* Matthew has highlighted the importance of faith for Jesus' followers already at 17:20 and through the portrayal of various supplicants who trust Jesus for their healing (e.g., 9:2, 22, 29). The disciples, on the other hand, have been characterized by "little faith," which has been tied to doubt or wavering at 14:31.

say to this mountain. That this story of the fig tree points back to Jesus' judgment upon the temple is confirmed by this reference to a mountain. As they return to Jerusalem from Bethany, the obvious referent of "this mountain" would be the Temple Mount itself, further underscoring its coming judgment.[5]

21:22 *If you believe, you will receive whatever you ask for in prayer.* Prayer has been highlighted as the purpose of the temple at 21:13. Here Jesus ties prayer to trust in God and indicates that such trust will result in efficacious prayers. Jesus has already indicated that believers can trust God to answer their prayers (7:7–8), grounding their trust in the covenantal goodness of God. Matthew does not qualify this promise of Jesus, but the whole of his story does caution against applying this teaching in absolute fashion. Jesus himself prays (presumably in faith) to be rescued from his coming death (26:39), but he recognizes that God's plan for him should take precedence over his own wishes (26:42).

Theological Insights: Temple Theology

Jesus was not the first Jew to critique the temple's practices and leadership, as the Jeremiah text cited by Matthew attests (Jer. 7:1–20; see also Ezek. 8; Mal. 1:6–14). In his critique Jesus and his Jewish audience could well have been aware of the Jewish expectation for a "final temple wrought not by human hands" (cf. Heb. 9:24).[6] This eschatological hope within Judaism gives context to Jesus' critique without assuming that he was rejecting the temple outright. Instead, he and his contemporaries likely were assuming that the physical temple would one day be obsolete when God established the heavenly temple. This picture fits well with other New Testament writers who present (1) Jesus as the manifestation of the eschatological temple (John 2:19–21); (2) the church—Christ's body—as the temple (1 Cor. 3:16–17; Eph. 2:19–22; 1 Pet. 2:4–5); (3) the vision of a "new Jerusalem" that has no temple "because the Lord God Almighty and the Lamb are its temple" (Rev. 21:2, 22).

Teaching the Text

1. *Jesus shows his messianic authority over the temple by critiquing the Jerusalem temple administration.* Matthew seems to draw on expectations for the Messiah to purify the temple in this scene, in which Jesus emphasizes God's intention for the temple as a place of prayer and worship. This is the first of a number of indicators in chapters 21–28 that God's judgment will come upon the temple in Jerusalem. Jesus will predict the temple's destruction (24:3–35) and lament its desolation (23:37–39). And immediately after Jesus dies, the temple curtain is torn from top to bottom (27:51). Matthew communicates Jesus' authority over the temple and also seems to point to him as the center of Jewish worship (21:15–16) and as the eschatological inaugurator who

will make temple-focused faith obsolete (27:51).

As we preach this passage, we can highlight Jesus' relation to the temple as messianic authority, as prophetic voice, and as inaugurator of the kingdom. We should be careful, however, not to overreach on this front. It can be easy to move from Jesus' critique of the temple and its leadership and his announcement of judgment on the temple to claims that he is issuing judgment on Israel as a whole in this passage and elsewhere. This conclusion would not fit Matthew's portrayal of the people (*laos*) or the crowds (*ochlos*); the people remain open to Jesus even at the end of the Gospel (see 27:64). It has become all too easy in Christian sermons and reflection to castigate all of Judaism, in spite of Matthew's portrayal of Jesus as the (Jewish) Messiah and as savior of Israel (1:21). We would be wise to consider carefully how our preaching characterizes first-century Judaism in this regard. For Matthew, Jesus is the center of the good news not because Judaism offered bad news but because he is the fulfillment of Israel's hopes and the completion of Israel's story.

This painting by Balage Balogh illustrates the scene recorded in Matthew 21:12.

2. *Jesus calls his disciples to unwavering faith.* As Matthew has already emphasized, followers of Jesus can and should trust in him and his authority in their lives (e.g., 6:25–34; 17:20). Here Jesus calls his followers to have faith and not doubt. The disciples are not models of this kind of unwavering faith; in fact, they are characterized by "little faith" across the Gospel (6:30; 8:26; 14:31; 16:8; 17:20). But there are other models of faith in Matthew that can help us as we preach and teach this theme, such as the seekers who come to Jesus for healing (8:5–13; 9:1–8, 18–26, 27–31; 15:21–28).

Illustrating the Text

Jesus shows his messianic authority over the temple by critiquing the Jerusalem temple administration.

Quote: Stanley Hauerwas provides helpful context for understanding Jesus' temple action:

> It is tempting for us—for people who have learned to distinguish between politics and religion—to describe [Jesus'] entry into Jerusalem as political and his entry into the temple as religious. But his going to the temple is perhaps even more politically significant. . . . The temple defines Israel. The worship of God and political obedience are inseparable. The abuses surrounding the temple and Israel's political subjugation are but aspects of the same political reality.
>
> To call Jesus' entry into Jerusalem and his cleansing of the temple politics challenges the dominant understanding of politics in modernity. We normally do not associate questions of truth and worship with politics. But I am suggesting that

> When Jesus overturns the money changers' tables, he asserts that the temple should be a place of prayer, not a place of commerce. Temple currency was the Tyrian shekel. Two first-century AD silver Tyrian shekels are shown here.

Jesus' drawing on the promise of God to Israel refuses to let Rome determine what counts or does not count for politics. Politics, for Jesus, is about power. But the power that Jesus exercises is that which is life-giving, drawing as it does on the very source of life itself.[7]

Jesus calls his disciples to unwavering faith.

Scripture: Examples of faith can be found all around us. You might ask someone who has trusted God in difficult circumstances in recent days to share their journey of faith—both the difficulties of trusting and the ways God answered that person's prayer and gave him or her strength to keep on trusting. The author of Hebrews looks to the Old Testament Scriptures when thinking of examples of faith and faithfulness. In Hebrews 11 the author provides a litany of believers who trusted God for their futures and the future of God's redemptive work in this world. The list begins with Abel, Enoch, Noah, Abraham, and Sarah and concludes with untold others who faced death and were "destitute, persecuted and mistreated—the world was not worthy of them" (11:37–38). The author concludes this renowned "faith chapter" with these words (11:39–40):

> These were all commended for their faith, yet none of them received what had been promised, since God had planned something better for us so that only together with us would they be made perfect.

Matthew 21:12–22

Three Parables about the Unfaithfulness of the Jewish Leaders

Big Idea *When his authority is questioned by the Jerusalem leaders, Jesus, the faithful Son of God, tells three parables contrasting those who are faithful and do God's will (even supposed sinners) and those who disbelieve and disobey (the Jerusalem leaders).*

Understanding the Text

The Text in Context

Two symbolic actions of Jesus—his entry as king into Jerusalem and his temple critique (21:1–22)—provoke a contest of authority with the chief priests and Jewish elders (21:23–27). Jesus refuses to answer their question about the source of his authority directly; instead, he tells three parables that provide an implicit claim of his messianic identity and implicate the Jewish leaders in their rejection of his identity and authority (21:28–22:14). In their rejection, Jesus contrasts them to those who have believed his message (and John's): tax collectors and prostitutes (21:31–32; cf. 9:9–13) and people who produce fruit (21:43; cf. 3:8; 7:15–20; 12:33). It is at this point in Matthew's story that the Jerusalem leaders begin the final plot to arrest and execute Jesus (21:46; see 26:3–4).

Interpretive Insights

21:23 *By what authority are you doing these things?* The challenge issued by the chief priests and elders sets the stage for the rest of chapters 21–22. The question of authority is at the heart of the conflict between Jesus and various groups of Jewish leaders that challenge him. But Jesus will confound them and evade their "traps" (22:15, 23, 34). His wisdom amazes those listening (22:22, 33), and his final riddle silences their interrogations (22:46). We can outline this as follows:

- A. Jesus' authority is challenged by chief priests and elders (21:23–27).
- B. Jesus tells three parables to challenge the Jewish leaders: they will miss out on the kingdom because they reject him (21:28–22:14).

C. Pharisees and Herodians test Jesus on the imperial tax (22:15–22).
D. Sadducees test Jesus on resurrection (22:23–33).
E. Pharisees test Jesus on Torah (22:34–40).
F. Jesus confounds the Jewish leaders with a riddle (22:41–46).

21:25 *John's baptism—where did it come from?* Wisely, Jesus counters with a question not directly about his own authority (21:23) but about the origin (i.e., authority) of John's baptism. Jesus is asking if the Jewish leaders in Jerusalem recognized that John's baptizing ministry was authorized by God. By focusing his question on John, Jesus situates the contest between the crowds and the leaders, since the crowds honor the martyred John as a prophet (21:26).

21:26 *we are afraid of the people.* The chief priests and elders betray a fear of the crowds that causes them to back down from

Jesus uses the setting of a vineyard, perhaps similar to the one shown here, as he tells the parable of the two sons and the parable of the tenants, both recorded in Matthew 21.

their confrontation with Jesus. Inappropriate fear has been shown to be a trait of other leaders in Matthew. Parallel to 21:26, Herod fears the people's reaction (if he kills John) because they consider John to be a prophet (14:5). And after Jesus tells a parable indicting the Jewish leadership for neglecting care for Israel, the chief priests and Pharisees want to arrest him, but their fear of the crowds (who hold Jesus to be a prophet) keeps them from doing this immediately (21:46).

21:28 *There was a man who had two sons.* The parable of the two sons highlights the importance of responding to Jesus in covenant loyalty by juxtaposing a son who obeys his father after saying he will not and a son who does not obey in spite of saying he will. Jesus makes the correspondences clear (21:31–32): the Jewish leaders are like the son who, in the end, does not obey, and tax collectors and prostitutes are like the obedient son. It is the latter's proper response of repentance and faith to John's call to righteousness that constitutes and produces their obedience.

21:31 *The first.* The parable's thrust is about the importance of action, although not necessarily in contrast to words—as if the point were that the promise made is unimportant (cf. 5:33–37; 12:36–37). Some Greek manuscripts, instead of reading "the first" here, have the word *eschatos* ("the last"; or *deuteros* ["the second"]). This reading makes little sense for the parable's purpose and also contravenes Matthew's strong emphasis on doing God's will (in this section, see 21:43; 22:11–12).

tax collectors and prostitutes are entering the kingdom of God ahead of you. The affront of Jesus' parable is that those who are scorned and despised for their moral compromise will enter the kingdom "ahead of" (i.e., instead of [see 23:13]) those considered Israel's leaders.

21:33 *There was a landowner who planted a vineyard.* Any Jewish reader from Matthew's world would recognize the parable's allusion to Israel. In Isaiah 5:1–7 Israel is compared to a vineyard belonging to Yahweh that does not produce good fruit. In Jesus' parable the Jewish leaders

Jesus ends his parable of the vineyard tenants by quoting Psalm 118:22, which speaks about a rejected stone becoming a cornerstone. This imagery, for Matthew, seems to be a reference to the foundation stone at the corner of the temple. In this photograph, Herodian cornerstones hold up the southeast corner of the Temple Mount platform. They average over seven feet long and three feet wide and weigh approximately eighty tons.

correspond to the tenants who mistreat the landowner's servants and son. This connection becomes clear at the end of the parable (21:45).

21:37–39 *Last of all, he sent his son to them . . . they . . . killed him.* The referent for the landowner's son is Jesus himself, who will also be the "son" referent in the subsequent parable of the wedding banquet (22:1–14) as well as in the climactic riddle that Jesus tells (22:41–42).

21:42 *The stone the builders rejected has become the cornerstone.* Jesus draws on Psalm 118 to explain the rejection that he experiences from the temple authorities. Implicitly, Jesus compares himself to the temple cornerstone, placing himself at the center of Jewish eschatological hopes (21:44).

21:43 *the kingdom of God will be . . . given to a people who will produce its fruit.* Although there is some debate about whether this judgment by Jesus indicts all of Israel, the focus of the parable (on tenants who mismanage the vineyard [21:41]) and the response of the leaders who hear the parable ("they knew he was talking about them" [21:45]) argue for a narrower referent. The kingdom will be given to a "people" (*ethnos*) who will produce fruit, in contrast to the Jewish leaders. The fact that *ethnos* is used here does not necessarily refer to Gentiles rather than Jews, since *ethnos* can denote a people (or nation) "united by kinship, culture, and common traditions" (BDAG 276).

21:46 *They looked for a way to arrest him.* Jesus has been perceived as a threat from the time of his Galilean ministry (12:14), and now the Jerusalem leaders seek a way to arrest Jesus (also 26:3–5). Presumably, they are looking for particular evidence to level a charge against him. In the end, they will accuse him of blasphemy (26:65) and bring him to Pilate as a royal pretender (27:11).

22:2 *a king who prepared a wedding banquet.* This parable compares the kingdom to a banquet, with invitations offered but rejected by expected guests (22:5). Given that the previous two parables have focused on the Jerusalem leaders' rejection of Jesus, the reader will be anticipating that this third (final) parable will also indict them. Although this parable seems more general, there are clues that it too addresses the leaders: (1) they are Jesus' audience as he tells the parable; (2) the extreme action of the first to be invited (they mistreat and kill those sent with the invitation) fits the previous parable's indictment of the Jewish leaders (21:35–39); and (3) the reference to the burning of "their city" (22:7) may evoke for Matthew's audience Jesus' prophetic action of judgment on the temple and so its leaders (21:12–17; 24:1–35).

22:3 *invited to the banquet . . . but they refused to come.* The center of the parable is the invitation that goes out to expected, and then unexpected, guests. In the story the rejection of the invitation escalates quickly from ignoring it (22:5) to killing the slaves who bring it (22:6). This rather odd detail encourages the reader to move outside the parable and identify this action with the extreme action of the tenants in the previous parable (21:35–39). It is rejection of God's invitation through Jesus that is the central thrust of this parable.

22:7 *The king . . . sent his army . . . and burned their city.* Some have understood this part of the parable to refer to the fall of Jerusalem in AD 70, likely a past event for Matthew's audience (see the section "Date and Provenance" in the introduction).

22:10 *the servants . . . gathered . . . the bad as well as the good.* This detail of the parable prepares for the presence in the next verse of a man who lacks the proper wedding clothes—that is, good deeds.

22:11 *he noticed a man there who was not wearing wedding clothes.* The referent of "wedding clothes" (not included in Luke's version [Luke 14:15–24]) has been variously identified. Given Matthew's emphasis on doing God's will (e.g., 7:16–23; 12:33–37, 48–50) and the preceding reference to people producing fruit who will inherit the kingdom (21:43), it is likely that the wedding clothes represent obedience or covenant faithfulness (see 25:1–46, where the way for Jesus' followers to prepare for final judgment is by pursuing acts of justice and mercy).

22:14 *For many are invited, but few are chosen.* This concluding aphorism derives its meaning from the parable. The many who are invited are portrayed as expected and unexpected, good and bad (22:10), so the "many" represent the scope of the invitation's audience. The few who are chosen are those who are not necessarily expected in the kingdom but who are prepared for the coming kingdom by their covenant faithfulness. This "chosen few," surprisingly in Matthew's story, does not include the esteemed Jerusalem leaders, whom Jesus' audience would have expected to be first in line for the kingdom (cf. 21:31, 43).

Teaching the Text

1. *These three kingdom parables indicate that covenant faithfulness, not rank or status, is central to kingdom participation.* While the Jewish leaders, specifically in this passage the chief priests, Jewish elders, and Pharisees (21:23, 45), could be expected to be first in line for the kingdom, given their status as Israel's spiritual leaders, Jesus' parables illustrate that these leaders will not enter the kingdom without repentance and faith (21:32). In fact, Jesus commends those who were considered least worthy or likely to make it into the kingdom: tax collectors and prostitutes (21:31). The parable of the wedding banquet illustrates the wide-open nature of the kingdom invitation ("invite to the banquet anyone you can find" [22:9]). Preaching and teaching this message of invitation for all persons is relatively easy, but we need to back up our words with actions. We can speak of God's wide-open invitation, but people will judge our message by our actions of inclusion or exclusion. Are we ready and willing to open our doors and hearts to the most unlikely and, seemingly, most unworthy of candidates? Are we ready to see covenant faithfulness in the repentance and faith of those who do not fit our community profile?

2. *Jesus as the faithful Son of God in the final two parables is the fulcrum of people's response: covenant faithfulness centers on their response to him.* Whereas Jesus' interpretation of the first parable (the parable of the two sons) identifies people's response to John's message as repenting and believing, the final two parables indicate that the center point of proper response is to Jesus himself (21:37; 22:2). Covenant loyalty—bearing fruit (21:43; 22:11)—is framed in terms of proper response to Jesus and his teachings (see 7:24–27; 28:20). The Jewish leaders fail in their task of leading the people because they reject Jesus as the Messiah and refuse his message. They prove themselves unfaithful to lead Israel and will not receive the kingdom (21:43). But all who respond to Jesus in repentance, trust, and covenant loyalty will be welcomed into God's kingdom.

So does our preaching center on Jesus and his teachings? Does it illuminate who Jesus is, so that people have a clearer picture of him after hearing what we have to say? It is easy to preach about all sorts of things besides Jesus—life lessons, how-to sermons, and the like. These topics have their place, but the text of Matthew compels us to preach Jesus and provides us with all sorts of ways to do so. Jesus the Messiah should be the centerpiece of what people hear from us, as he was for Matthew. And we can offer the invitation to respond to Jesus, inviting people to turn to him in faith and faithfulness, worship, and allegiance.

Illustrating the Text

These three kingdom parables indicate that covenant faithfulness, not rank or status, is central to kingdom participation.

Cultural Experience: If these parables indicate God's wide-open invitation to people and the importance of inclusion of those outside our community profile in the welcome of the church, then a look at cultural propensities to limit our welcoming reach and put up dividing walls could be helpful. Professor and researcher Setha Low, in her social analysis of the increasingly popular gated communities, has this to say based on interviews conducted with this population:

> Whether it is Mexicans, black salesmen, workers, or "ethnic changes," the message is the same: residents are using the walls, entry gates, and guards in an effort to keep perceived dangers outside of their homes, neighborhoods, and social world. Contact incites fear and concern, and in response they are moving to exclusive, private, residential developments where they can keep other people out with guards and gates. The walls are making visible the systems of exclusion that are already there; now the walls are constructed in concrete.[1]

Jesus as the faithful Son of God in the final two parables is the fulcrum of people's response: covenant faithfulness centers on their response to him.

Children's Games: Juxtaposing two childhood games might illuminate the importance of focusing people's attention on Jesus as the center of human response.

In the parable of the wedding banquet, Jesus illustrates that the kingdom is open to all. When the wedding guests who were initially invited refuse to come, the king sends his servants to invite anyone they find in the streets to the banquet. This frieze from the Nereid monument shows a banquet scene (400 BC).

A "treasure hunt" consists of following various clues to locate a prize at the end of the game. Players begin with a single clue that leads them to the next clue and to the next, with the final clue leading to the treasure. This kind of game has a transactional quality to it. The person who finds all the clues first wins the prize. The game "follow the leader" is quite different. In it, the leader is the focus throughout. There is no mapping of clues to get to a prize; instead, to be successful, the players must keep their focus on the leader and do what that person does. This game has a more relational quality to it and provides a better illustration of what Matthew calls his readers to do in relation to Jesus. Discipleship for Matthew is about people's responses to Jesus the Messiah and his direction and teachings.

Quote: John Stott, in *Authentic Christianity*, points to Jesus as the centerpiece of our corporate life and witness.

> The words "witness" and "testimony" have been much devalued, and are sometimes employed to describe what is little more than an essay in religious autobiography. But Christian witness is witness to Christ. And the Christ to whom we have a responsibility to witness is not merely the Christ of our personal experience, but the historic Christ, the Christ of apostolic testimony. There is no other Christ.[2]

Jesus, Messiah and Lord, Is True Interpreter of the Torah

Big Idea *When his authority is tested, Jesus is shown to be the true interpreter of the Torah, amazing people with his answers, calling people to absolute loyalty to God and love of neighbor, and showing himself to be Messiah and Lord.*

Understanding the Text

The Text in Context

In response to Jesus' three provocative parables, various groups of Jewish leaders initiate confrontations with Jesus (see 22:15, 23, 34). These revolve around Torah adherence and how to live out faithful allegiance to Yahweh, similar to earlier disputes with Jewish leaders in Matthew (e.g., 12:1–14; 15:1–20). As in Jesus' earlier teachings, love is shown to be central to proper interpretation of the law (22:34–40; see 5:43–48; 19:19). This series of encounters culminates in a final riddle by Jesus regarding his identity and authority, which silences all his opponents (22:41–46) and leads into a series of judgments on the Jewish leaders (chap. 23).

Interpretive Insights

22:15–16 *Then the Pharisees . . . laid plans to trap him.* Following the initial question about Jesus' authority from the chief priests and elders (21:23–27), the Pharisees, teaming up with the Herodians (22:16), try to trap Jesus with a question about paying the imperial tax. Although the exact identity of "the Herodians" is unclear (not known from other primary sources), we may presume that they are associated with and supporters of the Herodian dynasty. If so, they provide an unlikely pairing with the Pharisees (though united in their antagonism toward Jesus), who were more likely to critique Herodian leadership and practices as lax concerning the law.

You aren't swayed by others, because you pay no attention to who they are. This description of Jesus by his opponents helps to define their reference to him as "a man of integrity." As such, Jesus is quite different from his opponents, whom he describes as "hypocrites" (22:18), those who are swayed by others (21:46) and lack integrity between their thoughts and actions (e.g., 6:1–18; 23:25–28).

22:17 *imperial tax.* The tax in view here is the Roman census tax (*kēnsos*) that required an annual payment of a denarius per person.

22:20 *Whose image is this? And whose inscription?* Although Matthew makes no explicit mention of it, Jesus' reference to his opponents' hypocrisy may derive in part from the ease with which they have in their possession a denarius with Tiberius's image within the confines of the temple, a transgression of the second commandment, concerning images (Exod. 20:4). The denarius that they provided would have borne the inscription "Caesar Augustus Tiberius Caesar, son of the Divine Augustus" on the image side and the words "High Priest" on the other.[1]

22:21 *So give back to Caesar what is Caesar's, and to God what is God's.* This saying has a riddle-like quality because it plays on more than one possible configuration of lordship. On its surface, it seems to divide the world neatly into two categories of authority: Caesar's authority as Roman emperor (presumably the political sphere) and God's authority over the rest (presumably the spiritual realm). Yet this division sounds much more like Martin Luther's two-kingdom theology than Jesus' preaching of the inauguration of God's reign over both heaven and earth (4:17; 6:10). Given the Jewish theological assumption that everything belongs to God (e.g., Pss. 24:1–2; 50:9–12), it is likely that Jesus does not provide a neat and tidy division between what God owns and what Caesar owns. If not, then his answer is both evasive and

Since Tiberius is the Roman emperor ruling during the time of Jesus' ministry, the coin the Pharisees show Jesus is most likely a denarius struck with the image of Tiberius, like the one shown here.

suggestive. Without indicating that Jews should not pay the imperial tax (a revolutionary assertion), it questions Roman imperial absolutist claims. For other riddles in Matthew, see comments on 12:39–40; 22:42–45.

22:23 *the Sadducees, who say there is no resurrection, came to him with a question.* The Sadducees approach Jesus with a trick question about the hope of resurrection (which, as Matthew indicates, they do not embrace). The scenario is based on a woman who outlives her husband as well as his six brothers, who remarry her in line with the Jewish practice of levirate marriage.

22:24 *Moses told us.* The Old Testament reference is Deuteronomy 25:5: "If brothers are living together and one of them dies without a son, his widow must not marry outside the family. Her husband's brother shall take her and marry her and fulfill the duty of a brother-in-law to her." The Deuteronomy regulation commanding levirate marriage evokes the story in Genesis 38 of Onan and Tamar (38:8).[2]

22:28 *whose wife will she be of the seven . . . ?* The Sadducees conclude the scenario with this question. Apparently, they think that they have provided an unanswerable

The Pharisees identify the Messiah as the son of David, but they cannot answer the follow-up question Jesus raises from Psalm 110:1. Shown here is an Aramaic inscription from 840 BC that refers to "the house of David." It is the only ancient text outside the Bible that mentions David and his dynasty.

quandary. Implicit in this extreme scenario is that future (bodily) resurrection is an unfounded belief.

22:29 *you do not know the Scriptures or the power of God.* Jesus' reply critiques the Sadducees on two fundamental levels: their understanding of the Scriptures and their understanding of God. Jesus draws his scriptural argument from the part of the Old Testament canon that would have been accepted as authoritative by the Sadducees, the Pentateuch (Exod. 3:6; see Matt. 22:32). Jesus implies that the Jewish belief in resurrection is based on God's power to change (and not merely reanimate) human bodily existence.

22:30 *they will be like the angels in heaven.* Jesus provides an analogy to help make his point. Those who will be raised in the eschaton will be like angels in that they will not marry. How does this analogy further Jesus' argument? N. T. Wright helpfully suggests that as angels do not experience death and thus have no need for progeny, so too resurrected humanity will have no need of marriage, which in Jesus' context has strong associations with procreation. In fact, levirate marriage, which provides the basis of the Sadducees' improbable scenario, assumes the necessity of marriage for procreative purposes. Without death, there is no need to produce offspring.[3]

22:32 *He is not the God of the dead but of the living.* Jesus argues for resurrection from the language of Exodus 3:6. If Israel's God can be referred to as "the God of Abraham, the God of Isaac, and the God of Jacob" even after the death of the patriarchs, then the implication is that this God is able to raise them to life on the final day.

22:34 *the Pharisees got together.* The Pharisees bring a question from the law that provides the final challenge of the Jewish leaders to Jesus.

22:37–39 *"Love the Lord your God" . . . "Love your neighbor."* Jesus cites Deuteronomy 6:5 and Leviticus 19:18 to answer the question of which commandment is greatest. Love of God is "the first and greatest command" and formed part of the Shema (Deut. 6:4–5), regularly recited by faithful Jews. Love of neighbor is expressed as being like the command to love God, giving it equal status by all accounts.[4] The combination of these two commands is not unique to Jesus. For example, *Testament of Issachar* (second century BC) reads, "Love the Lord and your neighbor" (*T. Iss.* 5:2). What is distinctive is the way Jesus (in Matthew) draws on these two commandments to understand all the rest of the Torah. Gary Burge refers to Jesus' understanding of the centrality of these two commands as a "first principle" of the Torah.[5]

22:40 *All the Law and the Prophets hang on these two commandments.* Jesus is not negating the rest of the Jewish law, or even moving to the law's lowest common denominator. Instead, he is prioritizing love of God and neighbor as an interpretive lens for viewing the rest of the Torah.[6] The rest of the Torah, which retains validity and applicability for Jesus, hinges upon these two central commands.

22:41–42 *Jesus asked them, "What do you think about the Messiah? Whose son is he?"* In the final scene of this series of confrontations Jesus provides a riddle that confounds his hearers (22:46). The riddle revolves around his own identity, so that this riddle, if understood properly, actually answers the initial question of the chief priests and elders about the source of his authority for his temple action (21:23–27).

the son of David. Their answer that the Messiah is expected to be a "son of David" is accurate but, in the end, inadequate. Jesus exceeds the typical understandings of the Messiah-King. Jesus, while being a son of David, is also somehow David's lord as well.

22:43 *How is it then that David . . . calls him "Lord"?* Jesus cites Psalm 110:1, in which David (according to the psalm title) refers to another personage who is his own "lord" (*'adōnāy*). God gives to this "lord" power and position over his enemies. Jesus' riddle depends on the idea that David could be addressing no one other than his own descendant, the Messiah (note Ps. 110:2: "The LORD will extend your mighty scepter from Zion").

22:46 *from that day on no one dared to ask him any more questions.* After answering with wisdom, and some opacity,

the questions and tests of various Jewish leaders, Jesus poses a climactic question that silences them all. This provides a fitting conclusion to the questioning of Jesus' authority in 21:23–27. Matthew has portrayed Jesus as ably answering tests through his superior knowledge of the Torah and the Prophets (Exod. 3; Lev. 19; Deut. 6; Pss. 110; 118).

Theological Insights: The Love Command

Jesus' teaching on the two greatest commands (from Deut. 6:5; Lev. 19:18) narrated here in Matthew (cf. Mark 12:28–31) is reiterated and expanded across the New Testament, sounding something like a musical theme with variations. In Luke 10:25–37 these two commands provide the occasion for Jesus' parable of the good Samaritan. Jesus subverts the question of "Who is my neighbor?" by telling a story about how to *be* a neighbor, even to one's enemy. John highlights the command to love one's neighbor to such an extent that it becomes "a new command" (John 13:34–35; 15:12; cf. 1 John 3:11, 23; 4:7, 11–12). The command to love abounds in Paul's letters (e.g., Rom. 12:10; 1 Cor. 16:14; Gal. 5:13; Eph. 4:2). And Paul, like Matthew's Jesus, connects acts of love to fulfillment of the Torah: "Whoever loves others has fulfilled the law" (Rom. 13:8 [cf. Gal. 6:2]). Finally, the Epistle of 1 Peter exhorts believers to love one another "deeply," because "love covers over a multitude of sins" (1 Pet. 4:8 [cf. 1:22]).

Teaching the Text

1. *Jesus is the true interpreter of the Torah and able to navigate wisely the tests of his*

opponents. Jesus has already been identified with Wisdom at 11:2, 19, 28–30 (see comments there); he is truly the embodiment of the Torah and Wisdom. In these confrontations with the Jewish leadership (chaps. 21–22) Matthew shows us Jesus as Wisdom in action. Jesus confounds his opponents, not by doing an end run around the Torah, but by interpreting it rightly and knowing in each case how to answer their tests and trick questions. In contemporary preaching there is at times a tendency to set Jesus at odds with the law or Torah—Jesus as a maverick, breaking all the rules. But this is not Matthew's portrait of Jesus (nor that of Mark, Luke, or John, for that matter). Quite the contrary, for Matthew, Jesus is the embodiment of Wisdom.

So how might this inform our preaching and teaching? In a cultural context that values knowledge we can preach Jesus as God's wisdom. Wisdom moves beyond knowledge for the sake of knowledge alone; wisdom is the appropriation of truth learned for a particular context. Jesus shows himself wise by avoiding the traps of his opponents and knowing what Scriptures apply to what situations. Yet wisdom is not mere pragmatism; it draws from a deeper well than pragmatism. The Wisdom literature of the Jewish Scriptures confirms that God's ways are often inscrutable and beyond human ways. Jesus embodies God's wisdom, which means that he may well defy our own expectations. Preaching Jesus as the wisdom

of God means that we will be less likely to domesticate him. And if Jesus is truly the wisdom of God, then preaching this could include inviting people to follow Jesus' ways rather than our own.

2. *All of the Torah hangs on the two commands to love God and love neighbor.* Jesus as the true interpreter of the Torah identifies the love commandments of the Torah as the lens through which to understand all of the Torah. By this teaching, Jesus does not make the rest of the Torah obsolete, since all the rest "hangs" on the commands to love God and neighbor. Understanding love as the center of the Torah is a teaching that is thematic across the New Testament (e.g., John 15:17; Rom. 13:8–10; 1 Cor. 13:13; 1 Pet. 4:8; 1 John 4:7–12). And for Matthew, love of neighbor extends even to one's enemies (5:43–48).

Human communities draw lines; they clarify their communal identities often by distinguishing themselves from others ("We are not like them"). Jesus' teaching has revolutionary implications for the church. If the greatest commands are to love God and neighbor, now extended to even one's enemies and persecutors, then all such lines are reconfigured. Preaching the love commands has the potential to reorient our perspective to such an extent that

Jesus is asked, "Which is the greatest commandment in the Law?" (22:36). He answers by quoting the Shema and adding Leviticus 19:18. The *Community Rule* of the Dead Sea Scrolls and later the Mishnah record that the Shema (Deut. 6:4–9) was recited twice daily. It was also during this time that the practice of wearing phylacteries seems to have begun. The Shema is one of the biblical passages housed in phylacteries. These small boxes are held in place on the head and arm by leather straps like the ones worn by this Jewish man at the Western Wall in Jerusalem.

the naturally exclusive question "Who is my neighbor?" is reconfigured to such an extent that the question becomes "How do I act as neighbor to all?" (see Luke 10:29, 36). Preaching the truth that Christians ought to cross all kinds of boundaries to become neighbors to all kinds of people may be unsettling for us as we reconsider how we have drawn boundaries between "us" and "them."

Illustrating the Text

Jesus is the true interpreter of the Torah and able to navigate wisely the tests of his opponents.

Human Experience: The following quotation is attributed to Albert Einstein: "Wisdom is not a product of schooling but of the lifelong attempt to acquire it." This definition of wisdom fits various Old Testament proverbs, where wisdom is to be gained by careful attention to God's ways, openness to correction, and, most of all, fearing or revering the Lord (Prov. 1:7). As such, the pursuit of wisdom involves a lifelong journey of discernment. Given this framework for understanding wisdom, we do not often preach about Jesus as wise (although there is nothing objectionable about this idea). This may be because we do not take to heart the truth that Jesus grew in wisdom (cf. Luke 2:52), and so grew to be a wise person who could deal with the tests from his opponents with prudence and discernment. Yet how encouraging it might be to teach Jesus in this way: both as Wisdom personified and as a human

being who learned wisdom through a life of discernment lived in reverence of and obedience to his God.

All of the Torah hangs on the two commands to love God and love neighbor.

Applying the Text: This command to love calls us to cross boundaries. To do that, we must realize that we have created boundaries in our own lives and perspectives. You might invite your audience (and yourself) to contemplate these questions: Where have I set up boundaries in my life? Are there boundaries within my family? Have I set up boundaries at my workplace? Have I erected boundaries against a whole group of people based on race, socioeconomic status, religion, or some other feature? As you prayerfully consider these questions, ask the Holy Spirit to reveal any barriers that might need to be broken down by God's redeeming love. If "perfect love drives out fear" (1 John 4:18), then we are invited to explore our fears of "the other" that might be keeping us from demonstrating love to all those whom God brings into our life.

Object Lesson: Hold up a coin and describe each side of it. Point out that it would be impossible to have only one side without the other. In a similar way, our love of God and our neighbor are inextricably linked. We cannot claim to love God, whom we have not seen, if we do not love our visible neighbor (1 John 4:20). The experience of God's amazing love for us frees us to love our neighbor and even our enemy (Matt. 5:43–48).

The Jewish Leaders as Negative Foil for Jesus' Followers

Big Idea *For Matthew, the Jewish leaders are disobedient to the Torah and pursue the honor of their positions, providing a foil to Jesus' followers, who are to renounce concern for status and live in community as brothers and sisters.*

Understanding the Text

The Text in Context

Matthew concludes his narration of confrontation between Jesus and the Jerusalem leaders with a series of judgment warnings upon the Pharisees and teachers of the law (23:1–36). The chapter begins with a call to Jesus' followers to avoid the motivation and example of these teaching leaders, while acknowledging the importance of Torah instruction (23:1–12). Jesus speaks of the heavy loads that these leaders put upon those whom they teach (through their ways of interpreting the Torah [23:4]), directly contrasting his earlier words about his own Torah instruction: "My yoke is easy and my burden is light" (11:30). Jesus' followers are to avoid the hypocrisy of seeking to gain prestige and positions of honor through religious adherence (23:5–12), a refrain already resounding in earlier parts of Matthew (6:1–18; 20:1–16, 20–28).

Jesus warns his followers to avoid the behavior of the teachers of the law and the Pharisees, who "love the place of honor at banquets and the most important seats in the synagogues" (23:6). Shown here to the left of the doorway of the second-century AD synagogue at Chorazin is an elaborately carved seat. It is thought to have been meant for someone of importance such as an elder or a synagogue official. It has also been suggested that it was the "seat of Moses," from which the teachers of the law would provide instruction.

Interpretive Insights

23:1 *Jesus said to the crowds and to his disciples.* The focus of chapter 23, coming on the heels of the series of confrontations between Jesus and the Jewish leaders in 21:12–22:46, is an indictment of the Jewish leadership, specifically those who teach the people—"the teachers of the law and the Pharisees" (23:2). Nevertheless, Jesus does not speak to these leaders directly, but rather he addresses the crowds and his disciples. In doing so, he warns them about following the teaching and practices of the Jewish leaders.

23:2 *sit in Moses' seat.* The referent of "Moses' seat" is debated. There is archaeological evidence of such "seats" or "chairs" (*kathedra*) in synagogues by the time of rabbinic Judaism, though it is not clear that there were such chairs in first-century synagogues. Whether literal or figurative, a central question is the significance of Jesus' reference to it here in Matthew. Most scholars understand Jesus to be granting some measure of authority to the Pharisees and teachers of the law in their roles as leaders, while also frequently disagreeing with their specific teachings. Yet Matthew has described the Jewish teachers of the law as lacking teaching authority (7:29) and has shown Jesus warning his followers about their teaching (16:12). Given these contextual factors, Mark Powell has argued that Jesus cannot be referring here to the authority to teach. Instead, Powell highlights the role that these Jewish teachers had in terms of access to the Torah. If most people in the first century, including Jews, were illiterate (as most scholars suggest), then these teachers provided an important point of access to Scriptures themselves. According

to Powell, it is this role as those who read the Scriptures in synagogue worship that Jesus affirms.[1] "Jesus may be simply acknowledging the powerful social and religious position that [these leaders] occupy in a world where most people are illiterate and copies of the Torah are not plentiful."[2]

23:3 *So you must be careful to do everything they tell you.* This exhortation stems from the place of authority or access that the Jewish leaders occupy (see discussion above on 23:2). As they read and express the Mosaic law, what they communicate should be obeyed. Yet Matthew has made it clear that some of their teachings are not accurate representations of the Torah (e.g., 16:5–12; also 5:21–48; 12:1–12; 23:23). It is Jesus himself who exemplifies right teaching of the law.

But do not do what they do, for they do not practice what they preach. This indictment of the teaching leaders fits other places in Matthew where Jesus critiques them for Torah disobedience. For example, in 15:3–6 Jesus accuses them of neglecting the commands of God and instead obeying their own traditions. Their disobedience springs from a misprioritizing of the law (e.g., 12:7; 23:23).

23:4 *They tie up heavy, cumbersome loads and put them on other people's shoulders.* The teaching leaders are described as putting "heavy loads" (*phortia barea*) on people. This directly contrasts Jesus' own

Honor and Shame in the Ancient World

The maintenance and acquisition of honor were fundamental values in the first-century world. Seneca, a Roman philosopher, expresses the essential nature of honor in this way: "That which is honorable is held dear for no other reason than because it is honorable" (*Ben.* 4.16.2).

Honor has two primary aspects: a self-claim of worth and a corresponding recognition by others of that worth. Negatively, shame adheres when someone performs an action that is considered dishonorable by one's community. But the threat of shame can also restrain a person from such dishonorable behavior and thus can function as a positive deterrent.

Honor can be ascribed; that is, it can be an advantage of birth or granted by patronage. Honor can also be achieved by honorable behavior or by gaining honor from a contest with another person. Such contests of honor were common occurrences in the ancient world, where honor was understood as a commodity in limited supply.

What has been described so far can be termed "honor precedence," which is "worldly honor that . . . is based on power, wealth, and other indicators of status."[a] But there is a second kind of honor, which is gained in a person's own eyes and/or in the eyes of the divine. This kind of honor has been called "honor virtue,"[b] and it makes sense of the exhortations given by Jesus in Matthew 23:1–12. The Jewish leaders seek honor precedence, but according to Jesus, his own followers are to serve others and humble themselves (23:11–12), which will not produce honor in the eyes of the wider world but will produce honor before God and (so presumably) among the community of believers.[c]

[a] Lawrence, "'For Truly I Tell You,'" 690.
[b] Ibid.
[c] Resources for this sidebar are deSilva, *Honor, Purity*, 23, 25, 28; Lawrence, "'For Truly I Tell You,'" 689–90; Neyrey, *Honor and Shame*, 18, 30.

way of teaching the Torah, described as a "light load" (*phortion elaphron* [11:30]).

23:5 *They make their phylacteries wide and the tassels on their garments long.* Phylacteries (*phylaktēria*) are the two leather boxes (Heb. *tefillin*) "containing parchment Scriptures that, since at least the second century BC, were commonly worn on the upper left arm and forehead

following the literal understanding of . . . Deut. 6.8."[3] For tassels, see Numbers 15:38 and the comments on 9:20. Jesus' critique of these Jewish leaders is that they augment their phylacteries and tassels in order to draw people's attention to them and so presumably to the leaders' piety. This connects to Jesus' earlier description of "the hypocrites," who give to the poor, pray, and fast so that others will see and honor their actions (6:2, 5, 16). Jesus will refer to the Jewish teachers as "hypocrites" repeatedly in 23:13–36.

23:6 *they love the place of honor at banquets.* The Pharisees' love of the best banquet seats begins a list emphasizing their desire for honor and prestige at meals, in synagogues, and in the marketplace (23:6–7) (see the sidebar "Honor and Shame in the Ancient World"). This kind of social ranking in meals and other situations was commonplace in Greco-Roman society. Meals in particular highlighted social disparities in the ancient world (e.g., Luke 14:7–14). In fact, Sirach, a Jewish wisdom book, gives advice about how to act at meals, warning against greed and advising deference (Sir. 31:12–18).

23:8–9 *you are not to be called "Rabbi" . . . do not call anyone on earth "father."* In these verses Jesus expresses the solidarity and equality that are to characterize the believing community, stemming from their familial relationship as siblings and their submission to one "Teacher" and "Father," references to their relationship with their God.

23:10 *Nor are you to be called instructors, for you have one Instructor, the Messiah.* Jesus grounds the solidarity and equality that are to typify his followers in their common relationship to God (23:8–9) and their relationship with him (23:10). The word for "instructor" (*kathēgētēs*) is not the more common word for "teacher" (*didaskalos*), used in 23:8. By using a different word, Matthew is likely simply distinguishing the two referents of these verses: God as "the Teacher" and Jesus as "the Messiah." The image of the Messiah as teacher corresponds to Deuteronomy 18:15, which promises a future prophet like Moses, Israel's great teacher. Matthew highlights Jesus as teacher (e.g., 4:23; 5:2; 9:35).

23:11 *The greatest among you will be your servant.* This teaching parallels Jesus' teaching about discipleship at 20:26: "Whoever wants to be great among you must be your servant." Jesus calls his followers to renounce status concerns and to live a life focused on the benefit of others in the believing community and not on self-aggrandizement.

23:12 *those who exalt themselves will be humbled, and those who humble themselves will be exalted.* This concluding statement about the relationship of Jesus' followers to one another is a proverbial statement, similar to the ones in 19:30; 20:16 (the first will be last, and the last first). These proverbial statements address inappropriate emphasis on status in the coming kingdom. Disciples are to take on the humble position of those with little status instead

To showcase their piety, the Pharisees and teachers of the law "make their phylacteries wide and the tassels on their garments long" (23:5). Shown here are the remains of a leather head phylactery box from the first century AD. Found in one of the Qumran caves, it still contains the Scriptures written on parchment.

of seeking status and position in the kingdom (see 18:3–4).

Teaching the Text

1. *Jesus uses the Pharisees and teachers of the law as a foil to teach his followers to avoid the hypocrisy of using their religious status and actions to receive honor from people.* Jesus addresses his disciples in this passage; they are not to act like the Jewish leaders he describes. Throughout chapter 23 these leaders are accused of hypocrisy: their outward actions do not cohere with their motives. They pursue religious behavior, such as the wearing of phylacteries and tassels in observance of the Torah, but they do so in order to have their piety acknowledged and to be assigned honor by others. In fact, they seek out places and titles of honor wherever they go (23:6–7). Jesus calls his followers to an utterly different way of living. To preach this text is to lean into this alternate way. It is the way of integrity—of having one's actions and motives in full alignment. This alternate way focuses on living for God's approval and not the approval and honor of people.

Of course, this is easier said than done. We long for approval from someone, and sometimes we search our entire life for this approval and honor. Jesus carefully directs the focus of that longing toward God and not honor before others. Strategies for this redirection are provided in 6:1–18, a passage parallel to 23:1–12. Of utmost importance is "practicing [one's] righteousness" secretly so that there is no opportunity for someone else to see and give that pat on the back or that place of honor. By giving to the poor, praying, and fasting "in secret," Jesus' followers will gain honor and reward from God. As we preach and teach this message, we may also have to consider whether we have designed our communal religious practices in such a way as to foster this kind of anonymity rather than as a system that actually rewards people with human honor for their spiritual practices.

2. *Instead of seeking honor and status, Jesus' followers should pursue equality in their communities through renunciation of status and recognition that they have only one Father and one Messiah-Teacher.* These themes of equality among the believing community have already been introduced in chapters 18–20 (see esp. 18:1–5; 20:1–16, 25–28). The surprising equality of the kingdom (20:12) comes about as Jesus' followers renounce the status differentials so prevalent in their world. The Christian community is countercultural in its equality in the midst of the status-conscious Greco-Roman world of the first century. To preach this message in contemporary contexts means allowing for potentially different backdrops. Yet, while most Western democratic contexts pride themselves on equality for all persons, implicit status and value differentials still exist. So the church can still fall into patterns of relationship that honor some more than others and devalue persons deemed less significant.

As you teach this passage, challenge your listeners to think of areas where they might dishonor someone because of social position or show favoritism to some above others. How would Jesus respond to such favoritism?

Illustrating the Text

Jesus uses the Pharisees and teachers of the law as a foil to teach his followers to avoid the hypocrisy of using their religious status and actions to receive honor from people.

News: Choosing to be a foster parent provides an amazing gift to children needing a loving and stable home, and the vast majority of foster parents open their homes with good intentions and with no sense of external reward. Unfortunately, the most publicized situations are those where a foster parent is abusing the system (and possibly the children) for personal financial gain. You might find such an example from the news. This kind of story illustrates what it looks like when people fake parenthood, which is supposed to be a selfless endeavor on behalf of the other, for the sake of personal gain. It gives an example of how people use something noble for supremely base purposes. Hypocrites take what should be a God-honoring act of worship and make it a means of self-promotion or gain.

Popular Culture: We live in a celebrity culture that idolizes heroes, whether in sports, entertainment, or politics. You might provide some examples of cultural heroes to illustrate this phenomenon. We also have religious heroes—famous speakers and/or church leaders who garner national followings. We certainly can learn from these "Christian celebrities," but it might be helpful to explore our cultural tendencies for creating and venerating celebrities. How have we given honor to some over others in our wider context and even in our local churches? A telling question to ask is "Who in our own communities do we view as expendable, and who do we feel compelled to honor and praise?"

Instead of seeking honor and status, Jesus' followers should pursue equality in their communities through renunciation of status and recognition that they have only one Father and one Messiah-Teacher.

Quote: *Epistulae*, **by Pliny the Younger.** Pliny illustrates the excessive nature of status divisions in the ancient world. We might do well to realize how often such excessiveness still occurs in our own world.

It would take too long to go into the details . . . of how I happened to be dining with a man—though no particular friend of his—whose elegant economy, as he called it, seemed to me a sort of stingy extravagance. The best dishes were set in front of himself and a select few, and cheap scraps of food before the rest of the company. He had even put the wine into tiny little flasks, divided into three categories, not with the idea of giving his guests opportunity of choosing, but to make it impossible for them to refuse what they were given. One lot was intended for himself and for us, another for his lesser friends (all his friends are graded) and his and our freedmen.[4]

Scripture: You might draw on the harsh words leveled against favoritism toward the rich in James 2:1–13. There James provides a scenario of a rich person entering a gathering of believers and receiving preferential treatment over someone who is poor.

> Jesus warns against emulating the teachers of the law and Pharisees who love to be seated at the place of honor at banquets. Dining Roman style meant reclining on couches or benches, usually an arrangement of three that were placed in a U around a central table. The places of honor would have been on the center couch. This arrangement, known as a triclinium, is pictured here on a third- to fourth-century AD mosaic from Sepphoris.

Warnings of Judgment on the Jewish Leaders

Big Idea *Jesus laments the rejection that he has experienced in Jerusalem and warns of judgments upon hypocritical leaders, whose actions exclude their followers from the kingdom, who prioritize their traditions over the Torah, and who ultimately reject Jesus as God's righteous one.*

Understanding the Text

The Text in Context

After exhorting his disciples to avoid the hypocrisy of the Pharisees and teachers, Jesus condemns specific hypocritical actions of these leaders (23:13–36). Matthew has collected these "woes" into seven sayings, which culminate in a final (seventh) woe that broadens to include the generation of Jesus' contemporaries (23:36; cf. 11:16; 12:39–45; 16:4; 17:17). A number of Matthean themes are highlighted in these woes, including the irony of disobeying God's commandments in order to keep various oral traditions (23:16–22; cf. 15:3–9) and the importance of interpreting the Torah by focusing on "justice, mercy and faithfulness" (23:23; cf. 9:13; 12:7). Matthew concludes chapter 23 with Jesus' lament over Jerusalem and his prediction of the temple's destruction (23:37–39; cf. 21:12–17; 24:1–2).

Interpretive Insights

23:13 *Woe to you, teachers of the law and Pharisees.* Matthew organizes this chapter by arranging seven "woes" or warnings of judgment

Jesus compares these teachers of the law and Pharisees to whitewashed tombs, beautiful to look at but full of death inside (23:27). Here is the inside of a tomb from the time of Jesus showing a collection of ossuaries, limestone boxes that contained the bones of the deceased.

into three pairs and a concluding summative oracle, followed by a lament over Jerusalem and the temple (see the sidebar "The 'Woes' of Matthew 23").

You shut the door of the kingdom of heaven in people's faces. This picture of closing off the kingdom to others coheres with Jesus' earlier portrait of tax collectors and prostitutes entering the kingdom ahead of the Jerusalem leaders. By rejecting Jesus' message and speaking against him to the crowds, the Pharisees "shut the door of the kingdom" to others (e.g., 12:22–24; cf. 16:12).

23:14 *You devour widows' houses.* This verse, a woe about mistreating widows and saying long prayers, is very likely not original to Matthew's Gospel. It has limited manuscript support (only later and less reliable witnesses include it), and it likely is an interpolation from Mark and/or Luke (cf. Mark 12:40; Luke 20:47).

23:16 *You say, "If anyone swears by the temple, it means nothing."* Matthew 23:16–22 indicts those who thoughtlessly and rashly make oaths to give weight to their words (see 5:34). Similarly, Philo, a first-century Jew, writes of persons he knows who "swear at length and make whole speeches consisting of a string of oaths and thus, by their misuse of the many forms of the divine name in places where they ought not to do so, show their impiety" (*Decalogue* 94). The practice that Jesus describes here seems to betray a view of oath taking that borders on the magical.

23:23 *the more important matters of the law—justice, mercy and faithfulness.* Jesus speaks here of the central matters of the Torah (*barytera*, a comparative, refers to what is "weightier" or "more important"),

which he defines as justice (*krisis*), mercy (*eleos*), and faithfulness (*pistis*). Mercy (*eleos*) has already been used to describe the lens through which Torah adherence is judged (9:13; 12:7). These three terms are reminiscent of Micah's rehearsal of Yahweh's requirements for humankind: "to do judgment [*krima*] and to love mercy [*eleos*] and to be ready to walk with the Lord your God" (Mic. 6:8 LXX NETS). Matthew consistently portrays Jesus as properly interpreting the Torah with reference to the Prophets (e.g., 5:17) and through the lens of mercy, justice, faithfulness, and love (5:44; 22:38–40).

You should have practiced the latter, without neglecting the former. This final comment might seem unexpected, especially since to contemporary Christians such attention to detail—tithing one's spices—seems unnecessary and even legalistic (see Lev. 27:30, where "a tithe of everything from the land" is required). Yet, for a first-century Jew, Jesus' affirmation of all that the law requires, even a tithing of spices, would be unremarkable. Jesus is again portrayed as utterly faithful to the law, even as he rightly prioritizes what is central to it.

23:24 *You strain out a gnat and swallow a camel.* The choice of "gnat" and "camel" suggests that Jesus gave this powerful image in Aramaic, his mother tongue. In Aramaic this combination forms a play on words:

qalmâ and *gamlâ* ("gnat" and "camel," respectively). Ironically, both creatures are considered unclean according to the Torah (Lev. 11:4, 20–23), which adds to the indictment of the Jewish leaders.[1]

23:25 *full of greed and self-indulgence.* The Pharisees have been characterized by disobedience to the central Torah commands (e.g., 15:1–20) and by a desire for honor (23:1–12; cf. 6:1–18). Here Jesus adds the accusation of greed and self-indulgence. The latter (*akrasia* [see 1 Cor. 7:5]) refers to a lack of self-control. Though the Pharisees in Matthew outwardly appear to be all that they should be, their insatiable desire for more defines them.

23:26 *First clean the inside of the cup.* Jesus teaches that attention to the inward life necessarily impacts what others can observe about a person, resonating with his earlier words about what enters and leaves the body (15:11–20). Yet Jesus is not saying that outward actions are unimportant. Rather, he is linking one's inner attitudes, thoughts, and dispositions with one's outwardly visible words and actions. Integrity is the consistency between the inner and outer life.

23:31 *So you testify against yourselves.*

Jesus targets the hypocrisy of purporting to honor martyred prophets (by building tombs and decorating graves [23:29]) while acknowledging lineage from "our ancestors" (*pateres*, "fathers"), the very ones who martyred the prophets.

23:33 *You snakes! You brood of vipers!* The phrase "brood of vipers" continues the image of lineage and provides an implicit accusation that the Pharisees and teachers of the law are unfaithful to their heritage (see comments on 3:7). "Here the scribes and Pharisees are portrayed as thinking of themselves as heirs of the prophets, yet describing themselves as children of those who killed them (23.30–31)."[2]

23:34 *I am sending you prophets and sages and teachers.* Matthew has readily drawn upon these categories to describe Jesus himself; Jesus is prophet (13:57; 23:29–39), wise person (11:19, 28–30; 21:23–22:46), and teacher (23:10). And those who are sent by Jesus to teach and preach will have the same reception that he has had; they will be persecuted and killed (23:34; see 10:16–18).

23:35 *from the blood of righteous Abel to the blood of Zechariah.* These two phrases illustrate the full historical scope of "the righteous blood that has been shed on earth." Abel is the first martyr in the Hebrew Bible, and Zechariah is the last (Gen. 4:8; 2 Chron. 24:20–22), with Chronicles being the final book in the ordering of the Hebrew Bible.[3] Additionally, according to Jewish legend, it is Zechariah's boiling blood that stains the temple floor.[4] And Abel's blood cries out to God from the ground (Gen. 4:10). Both require vindication (Matt. 23:35).

23:37 *Jerusalem, Jerusalem . . . how often I have longed to gather your children together.* These words provide a pronounced shift from the preceding seven woes. Jesus laments the judgment that will come upon Jerusalem and the temple. Matthew portrays Jesus as the Messiah who expresses grief over what will come upon the temple and the people of Jerusalem at the time of its destruction (AD 70). He longs instead for a different kind of relationship of protection and care. Jesus as a mother hen protecting her young under her wings evokes pictures of Yahweh caring for Israel: "He will cover you with his feathers, and under his wings you will find refuge" (Ps. 91:4 [see also Deut. 32:11; Isa. 31:5]).

23:38 *Look, your house is left to you desolate.* Jesus' language of "your house" points to the Jerusalem temple (Isa. 52:11; Jer. 7:10–11). The reference to the temple's desolation provides a prelude to chapter 24, which will focus on Jesus' predictions about the temple's destruction, which comes about in AD 70.

23:39 *until you say, "Blessed is he who comes in the name of the Lord."* It was with these words from Psalm 118:26 that crowds welcomed Jesus into Jerusalem (21:9). Here Jesus links his reappearing with these same words of acclamation. While chapter 23 has focused on the announcement of future judgment on Jewish leaders, this final word anticipates a coming day when the people of Jerusalem will once again respond favorably to Jesus. "Israel is not abandoned without hope."[5]

The "Woes" of Matthew 23

Given Matthew's careful arrangement of Jesus' teachings across his Gospel, chapter 23 likely reflects Matthean organization (cf. Luke 11:42–52, consisting of three woes to the Pharisees and three to the teachers of the law). By arranging the material into seven woes (the number of completion), Matthew intensifies the sense of prophetic judgment against these Jewish leaders.

First woe (23:13–14): For keeping others from entering the kingdom

Second woe (23:15): For converting others to follow the ways of the Jewish leaders instead of God's

Third woe (23:16–22): For commending superstitious and frivolous vows

Fourth woe (23:23–24): For neglecting weightier matters of the law for lesser ones

Fifth woe (23:25–26): For resembling cups and dishes that are clean on the outside but full of greed and self-indulgence on the inside

Sixth woe (23:27–28): For resembling a whitewashed tomb that is beautiful on the outside but full of hypocrisy and evil on the inside

Seventh woe (23:29–36): For aligning themselves with those of old who killed prophets

Conclusion to Matthew 23 (23:37–39): Lament for Jerusalem and hope for repentance

---

Teaching the Text

1. *While Jesus warns of future judgment upon Pharisees and teachers of the law for their hypocrisy, the direct audience of chapter 23 is Jesus' followers, so the "woes" provide a warning to them.* Chapter 23 is addressed to the crowds and disciples (23:1), so the many references to the judgment that Jesus warns will come upon the

Jewish leaders are meant to instruct his followers and Matthew's readers/hearers. Jesus critiques the hypocrisy of the Jewish leaders, but Matthew has included these critiques as a warning to his own community, since hypocrisy is by no means the exclusive domain of Jesus' opponents in the narrative. So as we preach and teach this text, our own focus should be on what we as believers in Jesus can learn for Christian living from these "woes."[6] The first and foremost warning of this passage is against hypocrisy, and hypocrisy is something to which all people, including Christians, are susceptible. We live in a cultural context where honesty is less important than not getting caught and where integrity is less important than looking good. Into this context of mixed-up values Matthew's message of integrity comes as a needed corrective.

2. *Jesus highlights justice, mercy, and faithfulness in order to prioritize and guide Torah interpretation and obedience.* Matthew's Jesus never devalues the Torah, but he does provide the proper lens through which to interpret and apply it. This lens centers on the "weightier" matters of the law, defined here as justice, mercy, and faithfulness (on love being essential to this lens, see 5:43–48; 22:34–40). How might we preach and teach this message? First, just like the Pharisees, we too can easily misprioritize our Christian obligations (now based on Jesus' teachings [28:20]). Keeping these values of mercy, justice, love, and loyalty at the forefront of our communities can keep our priorities in line with those of Jesus. Second, by preaching justice and mercy as kingdom values, we will be less likely to treat these as competing values. Justice, for Matthew, is fundamentally

about God coming to make all things right; included in this righting of wrongs are merciful acts on behalf of those who are disadvantaged. So we ought to adjust our definition of justice as necessary so that it includes mercy and does not oppose it. Finally, we can communicate to our congregations that these values are not new to Jesus. In 23:23 Jesus echoes Micah 6:8, where God's priorities for humanity are exactly these: acting in justice, loving mercy, and walking humbly with God (i.e., covenant loyalty).

Illustrating the Text

While Jesus warns of future judgment upon Pharisees and teachers of the law for their hypocrisy, the direct audience of chapter 23 is Jesus' followers, so the "woes" provide a warning to them.

Metaphor: "Hypocrite" springs from a Greek word that originally referred to a stage actor, someone who wore a mask and played a part. Metaphorical use of the term in Jewish writings highlights its negative connotations. In Jesus' teaching here and elsewhere in Matthew the word is applied to people who put on a false face, pretending to have virtues that they lack. At the heart of this attribution lies an inconsistency between outward actions and inward motivations.[7] While we might easily condemn the Pharisees and teachers of the law for hypocrisy, it is all too easy for us to foster, even unintentionally, such inconsistencies. So it would be helpful to ask questions of ourselves and our congregations about motivations for pious actions and religious behavior. Do we pursue religious and moral activity, certainly important in

Isaiah's cosmic language pointed at the downfall of Israel's enemies and applying it to Israel's own fortunes, Matthew emphasizes the ironic turn of events leading to the temple's destruction.

24:30 *all the peoples of the earth.* This phrase may also be translated as "the tribes [*phylai*] of the land [*gē*]" (NIV footnote). If the discussion of the fall of the temple continues through 24:35, then the latter rendering makes more sense. The people (tribes) of Israel will mourn the vindication of Jesus' prediction about the temple's destruction, as pictured in Zechariah 12:10–14.

the Son of Man coming on the clouds of heaven, with power and great glory. Here Jesus clearly alludes to Daniel 7:13–14, with its vision of "one like a son of man" entering the heavenly court and being vindicated and given authority over the nations (see comments on 10:23; 26:64). Daniel's term for this "coming" is *erchomai* (LXX), not *parousia* (the latter is the word used to refer to Jesus' return in Matt. 24). So the two "comings" should be understood as distinct, even though English translations use "coming" for both. The "coming" of the son of man in Daniel indicates an upward movement into God's heavenly court and so is an image of vindication. In the context of Matthew 24, Daniel's vision provides a portrait of the vindication of Jesus' predictions about the temple's destruction at the climactic point of those predictions.

24:32 *lesson from the fig tree.* This concluding illustration reemphasizes that there will be a forewarning of the temple's

As Jesus answers the disciples' question, "When will this happen?" (24:3), he reveals that within a generation the temple in Jerusalem will be destroyed. The Jewish revolt of AD 66–70 resulted in the destruction of the temple and the city of Jerusalem. This coin with the inscription "*Judea capta*" was a sestertius minted by Vespasian (AD 69–79) to commemorate the victory over the Jews by his son Titus. It features a figure, representing Judea in mourning, sitting under a palm tree.

destruction through particular warning signs (24:4–25).

24:34 *this generation will certainly not pass away.* If 24:34–35 provides a culminating authentication of Jesus' prediction about the temple's destruction, then "this generation" can be understood literally (as elsewhere in Matthew), since Rome destroyed the temple in AD 70, within a generation of Jesus' prediction.

Teaching the Text

Matthew portrays Jesus announcing coming judgment on the Jerusalem temple and interprets the temple's destruction as vindication of Jesus' words and so his identity claims. This passage within Matthew's Eschatological Discourse has often been interpreted to be about Jesus' return and the end of the world. Yet, as we have seen, the first question in 24:3 sets the course for 24:4–35. And even those interpreters who understand some parts of this passage to address the return of the Son of Man also see the destruction of the temple being addressed (e.g., 24:15–16). So it is important for preaching and teaching this passage to acknowledge the prophecies of Jesus spoken here that were fulfilled in

AD 70. Certainly, Matthew, likely writing after AD 70, wants to highlight Jesus as the Messiah who rightly foretells these events that have already occurred for his audience.

Additionally, given how challenging it is to provide a coherent interpretation of this notoriously difficult text, we would do well to make a commitment to reading and teaching it as holistically as possible. It is easy to use verses here and there in the chapter to tie together a kind of timeline for the end, but we must assume that Matthew intends the whole passage to read coherently. So reading holistically and with attention to Matthew's intention can only help us as we preach and teach the text. And in preaching this text it could be especially helpful to stay with Matthew throughout the sermon or lesson rather than quickly diverging to other New Testament books that we perceive fill in or clarify what we read in Matthew. The warning issued by Richard Hays is particularly apt in passages like this one: "We must let the individual voices [of the biblical authors] speak if we are to allow the New Testament to articulate a word that may contravene our own values and desires. Otherwise, we are likely to succumb to the temptation of flipping to some comforting cross-reference to neutralize the force of any particularly challenging [or confusing!] passage we may encounter."[6]

A final hermeneutical caution that we might consider regarding this passage is the need to be sensitive to the (sub)genre of this passage. As noted at 24:29, the cosmic language used to indicate cataclysmic historical events fits the broader pattern of prophetic, eschatological language from the Old Testament and other Jewish writings of the time. This sensitivity to genre is an important part of both interpretation and contextualization of Scripture. "We need to know what we are reading to interpret it properly. Yet concerted effort to identify and grasp the conventions of a literary genre will not help us if we lose sight of genre issues in the move to contextualization [e.g., preaching and teaching]."[7]

Illustrating the Text

Matthew portrays Jesus announcing coming judgment on the Jerusalem temple and interprets the temple's destruction as vindication of Jesus' words and so his identity claims.

History: Throughout history various "prophets" supposedly have predicted events hundreds of years in the future. For example, Nostradamus, born in the early sixteenth century, made various predictions, some of which his supporters have suggested presaged such events as the French Revolution and the creation of the atomic bomb. But Nostradamus's writings were vague enough to have many possible applications and just specific enough to catch the attention of certain supporters. Jesus, on the other hand, spoke quite specifically about the destruction of the temple (even if with some allusions to Old Testament language), and within four decades it happened. Matthew, likely writing after its destruction, communicates that such prophetic knowledge confirms the claims of Jesus to be Messiah.

Sports: During the 2013 Super Bowl, a loss of power caused the stadium to go dark for a full thirty minutes. The game and all other activity ceased during this time of darkness. There was no mistaking the darkness and its effects. While Jesus' predictions

of the fall of the temple indicate multiple warning signs that might be confused with the timing of the actual event, there will be no mistaking Jesus' return—his reappearing. It will be as clear and definitive as lightning in the sky (Matt. 24:27).

Quote: N. T. Wright, in *Matthew for Everyone*, ties Matthew 24 to the fall of the temple and then suggests its ongoing relevance for Christians today.

> All of this related very specifically to the time between Jesus' public career and the destruction of the Temple in AD 70. . . . But the echoes of meaning rumble on in every successive generation of Christian discipleship. We too are called to be faithful, to hold on and not be alarmed. We too may be called to live through troubled times and to last out to the end. We too may see the destruction of cherished and beautiful symbols. Our calling then is to hold on to Jesus himself, to continue to trust him, to believe that the one who was vindicated by God in the first century will one day be vindicated before the whole world. We too are called to live with the birth pangs of God's new age, and to trust that in his good time the new world will be born.[8]

Matthew 24:1–35

Eschatological Discourse
Being Prepared for Jesus' Return

Big Idea *Jesus predicts his return (parousia), which will usher in the end of the age and the final judgment, and warns that, because the time of his return is unexpected, his followers should be always ready for his return.*

Understanding the Text

The Text in Context

In the latter part of chapter 24 and the first parable in chapter 25, Jesus' teachings turn from the signs portending the temple's imminent destruction (24:4–35) to his reappearing (his *parousia* at the end of the age [see 24:3]), which will occur without warning (24:36–51). The overriding discipleship theme of this section is the importance of being prepared or "watchful" (since there will be no warning signs for Jesus' return). This theme is heard particularly in the two brief parables in 24:42–51 and the parable of the ten virgins in chapter 25. The final two parables of chapter 25 (which cap all of Jesus' teaching in Matthew) will highlight the way to be prepared: faithful and merciful living.

Interpretive Insights

24:36 *nor the Son.* This phrase is not included in some Greek manuscripts. Yet it is very likely original to Matthew, since it

is easy to understand how early Christian scribes copying Matthew might have found these words troubling (showing Jesus to lack knowledge of the timing of his own return) and omitted them.

24:37 *so it will be at the coming of the Son of Man.* The word for "coming" here is *parousia* and refers to Jesus' return or reappearing at the "end of the age" (see 24:3), the topic of 24:36–40. This language is distinct from the word used for the "coming" of the Son of Man earlier in the chapter, which refers to God's vindication of Jesus' predictions about the fall of the temple. There the term *erchomai* is used to evoke the picture of vindication and enthronement from Daniel 7 (see comments on 24:30).

24:39 *they knew nothing about what would happen.* The comparison between the time of Noah and the return of the Son of Man centers on the suddenness of both events. Just as the arrival of the flood provided no warning, so Jesus' reappearing will have no precursor signs that would help people prepare for it. This suddenness contrasts with the many warning signs preceding the temple's destruction in 24:4–35.

24:40 *one will be taken and the other left.* The picture painted is of normal, everyday activity interrupted by the *parousia.* Again, the emphasis is on the sudden, unexpected timing of the return of the Son of Man.

24:42 *Therefore keep watch.* Keeping watch is a key exhortation of this section of the Eschatological Discourse, based on the unpredictability of the timing of Jesus' return.

24:43–44 *the thief.* These verses provide a brief analogy (or parable) about the unexpected timing of Jesus' return (like a thief at night [cf. 1 Thess. 5:2]) and the consequent importance of constant readiness (24:44).

24:45 *faithful and wise servant.* With this parable about servants being entrusted with a task, Matthew begins a series of parables that speak to being prepared for the Son's return (24:45–51; 25:1–13, 14–30). Here the task is the care of the master's other servants, and two scenarios are provided. In the first, a "faithful and wise servant" is found doing what he was tasked to do when the master arrives (24:45–47) and so receives greater responsibilities (cf. 25:29). In the second, the servant mistreats his fellow servants and lives a dissipated life. He will be punished

by the master, who returns "when he does not expect him and at an hour he is not aware of" (24:50). The unexpectedness of the return is again emphasized.

24:51 *cut him to pieces and assign him a place with the hypocrites.* The verb *dichotomeō* means "to cut in two" (BDAG 253). It is hard to see how someone who has been cut into pieces could subsequently be assigned a place with the hypocrites (presumably, in judgment), and so some scholars have suggested that this verb be understood

"Two women will be grinding with a hand mill; one will be taken and the other left" (24:42). In first-century life, if bread or flour was not purchased commercially, grinding grain for the bread needs of a family was done daily by hand. Shown here are two women operating the tools used for hand milling. The woman at the top is using a grindstone, and the woman at the bottom is using a rotary hand quern.

metaphorically, as in "cut off" from the community. This would fit well with the language of being "assigned a place" (*meros*; i.e., his "lot" will be among them). An example of the pairing of these concepts is found in the Dead Sea Scrolls: "May God set him apart for evil that he may be cut off from all the Sons of Light. . . . May he put his lot among those who are cursed forever" (1QS 2:16–17).[1] Nevertheless, there is no additional evidence for this metaphorical use outside of Matthew 24:51 and its parallel, Luke 12:46 (see NRSV). In either case, this verse bridges the story of the parable and its outside referent.

with the hypocrites, where there will be weeping and gnashing of teeth. The parable's conclusion signals judgment for lack of preparedness. The master of the unfaithful servant will assign that servant his place with the "hypocrites," a group that has borne the brunt of Jesus' critique in Matthew (see 6:1–18; 23:13–32). The Matthean phrase "weeping and gnashing of teeth" occurs here (as at 8:12; 13:42, 50; 22:13; 25:30), signaling despair and remorse at the final judgment.

25:1 *the kingdom of heaven will be like ten virgins.* This parable, with the preceding one (24:45–51), communicates the importance of being prepared for the *parousia*, the coming of the Son of Man. In this

kingdom parable the story revolves around ten unmarried women ("virgins" [see 1 Cor. 7:25], likely in their early teens) who wait for a bridegroom who is delayed (25:5).

bridegroom. Jesus uses a very familiar social setting for this kingdom parable. Weddings were joyous and important occasions in the Jewish world of the first century, and the festivities went on for a number of days (seven, according to Judg. 14:12; Tob. 11:18). The parable envisions a wedding procession. These began at the bride's home and concluded at the groom's.[2] The ten young women presumably are waiting for the groom (and his bride) to arrive at his home, where the wedding feast would be held.

25:2 *Five of them were foolish and five were wise.* Matthew has introduced the motif of wisdom or prudence at 24:45, where a "faithful and wise servant" is characterized by constant readiness. This same pairing of "wise" (*phronimos*) and "foolish" (*mōros*) is used in Jesus' first parable in Matthew, that of the wise and foolish builders (7:24–27).

25:4 *The wise ones . . . took oil in jars along with their lamps.* Lamps for outdoor use typically were made of cloth rags wrapped around the top of a stick and soaked in oil.[3] Since the lamp would burn through the oil before long, it was sensible (wise) to

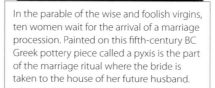

In the parable of the wise and foolish virgins, ten women wait for the arrival of a marriage procession. Painted on this fifth-century BC Greek pottery piece called a pyxis is the part of the marriage ritual where the bride is taken to the house of her future husband.

bring along a jar of oil to resoak the cloth and keep the lamp lit.

25:5 *The bridegroom was a long time in coming.* This detail of the parable, along with similar references at 24:48 and 25:19, suggests that Matthew offers these parables about the return of the Son of Man to address, in part, a delay in the expected timing of his return. See comments on 25:19.

25:9 *"No," they replied, "there may not be enough for both us and you."* This statement provides a point of color to the story but should not be extrapolated to mean something outside the parable's metaphor (see the sidebar "Interpreting Parables" in the unit on 19:27–20:16).

25:11 *Lord, Lord.* The protestations of the five young women who were unprepared for the unexpected timing of the groom are reminiscent of 7:21, where Jesus warns, "Not everyone who says to me, 'Lord, Lord,' will enter the kingdom of heaven." It is doing God's will (7:21)—here, being ready by being faithful—that will bring about kingdom life.

25:12 *I don't know you.* With these words of pronouncement, the parable shifts from metaphor to meaning, since a bridegroom would know the identity of the bride's attendants. The import of the declaration seems to be a severing of relationship (or a statement of a lack of relationship), as in the parallel at 7:23: "I never knew you."

25:13 *Therefore keep watch, because you do not know the day or the hour.* Jesus' concluding application of the parable forms an inclusio with 24:36, which began this passage. Jesus' words there—"about that day or hour no one knows"—provide the reason for watchfulness throughout this passage (24:42, 43),

culminating in the exhortation to "keep watch" (*grēgoreō*).

Theological Insights: Being Watchful

Themes of being watchful and alert cross the New Testament, often in relationship to discussion of Jesus' return, as in Matthew (parallels in Mark 13:34–37). For example, Paul exhorts the Thessalonians in relation to "the day of the Lord" to "be awake and sober" (1 Thess. 5:6, 8; see also Rev. 3:2–3; 16:15). The Epistle of 1 Peter, written to believers being slandered for their allegiance to Jesus, has multiple admonitions to be alert and sober. The first occurs within an exhortation to hope in the grace that will be given at Jesus' coming (1 Pet. 1:13). Here, as in Matthew, preparation is tied to keen anticipation of what is to come—grace (1 Peter) and joy (Matt. 25:1–13). A second reference comes in 1 Peter 4:7, where the purpose is to encourage prayer (similar connection at Col. 4:2). The final admonition to watchfulness comes at the end of the letter, tied to a concluding promise of God's restoration (1 Pet. 5:8, 10).

Teaching the Text

1. *Jesus' return at the end of the age will not be preceded by signs indicating its arrival.* The refrain of this passage is the unanticipated timing of the return of the Son of Man (24:36–41, 42–44, 50; 25:5). In contrast to the temple's destruction, which will have warning signs (23:4–35), Jesus' return will come unexpectedly. Given this clear theme, it is ironic that many preachers and teachers offer so much theological rumination on Jesus' return and spend

considerable time and energy delineating the signs that will precede his coming. Some of the confusion comes from applying Matthew's precursor signs for the fall of the temple (AD 70) to Jesus' final return. Yet Jesus' teachings about his *parousia* emphasize its unexpected timing and delay (24:48; 25:5, 19).

And why do we see in certain circles an obsession with end-time events? There seems to be a sense of comfort that many derive from eschatological timelines and charts. Perhaps they give the illusion of having control over what we perceive as disturbing, unpredictable events. If we could just map out how and when Jesus will return, we will be ready. In Matthew 24–25, however, Jesus calls his followers to be ready at all times, since no one knows the day or hour of his return (24:36; 25:13). Timing and knowledge about his return are not something that we can obtain; knowledge of the timing was even outside of Jesus' purview (24:36). Thus, looking forward, anticipating Jesus' return, is a matter of trust—Matthew's answer to so many issues of the Christian life. And it is a matter of staying alert. These are themes that will preach.

2. *Jesus' parables stress being watchful and faithful at all times so that his followers will be ready for his return.* The theme of readiness pervades this passage. The way to be ready is to faithfully live out one's calling (e.g., servant's assigned tasks in 24:46; keeping lamps lit in 25:4). For Matthew, the person who is living faithfully need not worry about the unexpected timing of Jesus' return. Thus, Matthew's teaching, with its analogy to a thief in the night or a bridegroom arriving later than expected, is not meant to cause fear or obsession about the timing of Jesus' return in the future (which cannot be predicted). Instead, Matthew's teaching about the end actually focuses on faithful living in the present. Matthew might be a good standard for our own teaching about Jesus' second coming. Do our preaching and teaching cause people to reflect on their own present way of living out faithfulness to Jesus' teachings? Or do we distract their attention toward speculation and generate fearfulness of "the end"? These words from

Jesus illustrates the importance of watchfulness with his parable of the wise and foolish virgins. The virgins who had brought extra oil were ready to light their lamps when the bridegroom made his appearance. These lamps were more like torches and may have looked like those held by Artemis in this sculpture from the second century AD.

1 Peter focus on proper attentiveness and positive hope (not fear), as we look ahead to Jesus' return: "With minds that are alert and fully sober, set your hope on the grace to be brought to you when Jesus Christ is revealed at his coming" (1 Pet. 1:13).

Illustrating the Text

Jesus' return at the end of the age will not be preceded by signs indicating its arrival.

News: Jesus made it clear that we will not know the day or the hour of his return, yet Christian history is filled with examples of people who miss this point. In the last two centuries alone entire movements have coalesced around teachers who confidently asserted they knew the day and time. William Miller was sure that Jesus would return before 1843. Alternately, some are convinced that the formation of Israel in 1948 lit the fuse for a coming tribulation. In 2011 Harold Camping predicted that the world would end on May 21. When that date came and went, he revised the date to October 21, 2011. Perhaps it is safest to remember Jesus' words that people will not be able to anticipate the arrival of the final day by its alignment with other events. Readiness, as a result, is the best course of action.

Quote: Calvin Miller, in his fictional and humorous book *The Philippian Fragment*, purports to have discovered a letter from Eusebius of Philippi, a young pastor, filled with his reflections on church issues that mirror contemporary church life. At one point, Eusebius introduces a debate raging

in "scroll study" about the timing of Jesus' return. Phoebe, one of the women in the study, is put in the position of casting the deciding vote on the issue. She agonizes over it as other study members "bring their parchment charts on the final signs of the times."[4] Yet Eusebius finds her one afternoon visiting lepers rather than attending scroll study.

> "Phoebe," I blurted out. "Don't you care? Is our Lord coming back before or after the tribulation? When he comes back, where do you want to be found—in this state of indecision or at the Second Coming study?"
>
> "This is where I want to be found," she said, pointing to a circle of low, thatched huts. A little boy came running up to us from the compound. His face was badly blighted and part of his hand was gone.
>
> "When do you think the Lord is coming back, my child?" asked Phoebe. A single tear ran down across his cheek. I handed her a bandage and couldn't remember why I thought the question was so important.[5]

Jesus' parables stress being watchful and faithful at all times so that his followers will be ready for his return.

Song: "Getting Ready for Christmas Day." This song from Paul Simon's album *So Beautiful or So What* (2011) nicely illustrates the need for preparation, with an old recording of a preacher in the background that provides rhythm, cadence, and theme for the song. If your context allows, it would be effective to play a part of this song.

Eschatological Discourse
Being Faithful and Merciful

Big Idea *Jesus tells two more parables that demonstrate how his followers should be ready for his return: they should pursue covenant faithfulness and show mercy to the most vulnerable, who are hungry, poor, sick, and imprisoned.*

Understanding the Text

The Text in Context

Chapter 24 concludes and chapter 25 begins with a call to be prepared, since there will be no precursor signs for Jesus' reappearing (24:36–51). Matthew 25:14–46 continues with this theme of readiness by narrating two more parables of Jesus, one focusing on faithfulness as the way to continually stay prepared (25:14–30), and one on actions of mercy and justice as the way to live out covenant faithfulness (25:31–46). Themes of faithfulness, mercy, and justice

have already been introduced as hallmarks of Torah adherence (23:23), which are to typify Jesus' followers. Chapter 25 concludes the fifth and final Matthean discourse of Jesus' teachings (chaps. 24–25). The final words of Matthew's Gospel will make clear that Jesus expects his followers to obey all his teachings (28:20; see 26:1).

Interpretive Insights

25:14 *Again, it will be like a man going on a journey.* The parable of the bags of gold (traditionally, talents) is another kingdom parable (see 25:1). In this parable a wealthy householder takes a journey and leaves three servants or slaves (*doulos*) with varying amounts of his money to invest.

25:15 *five bags of gold . . . two bags . . . one bag.* The money allocated is expressed

The faithful servants in the parable invest their master's money and double the amount they are initially given. One source of investment during this time period was to lend funds to money changers and receive a share of their profits. This relief from the third century AD depicts a money changer with a customer.

in terms of *talanton* ("talent"). One *talanton* equals approximately twenty years' worth of wages. So five talents would exceed what a day laborer would earn in a lifetime.

25:16–18 *put his money to work . . . dug a hole in the ground and hid his master's money.* The key distinction of the parable is that the faithful servants invest the householder's money and the last servant hides it, ignoring the possible investment gains.

25:19 *After a long time.* As with the previous two eschatological parables, where a delay is mentioned (24:48; 25:5), this wealthy man returns home after a long absence. With this detail, Matthew appears to highlight the delay of Jesus' *parousia*. If the people in Matthew's audience (ca. AD 75–85) were expecting Jesus' return in conjunction with the fall of the temple (see 24:3), they would need to hear that his return might be longer in coming than expected (25:5).

25:21, 23 *Well done, good and faithful servant!* The man returns and commends his two faithful servants. Their faithfulness adheres in "putting to work" what they had been given. This will prove to be the thrust of the parable in its metaphor—a call to faithfulness to use what has been given for the work of the kingdom while awaiting the final day.

You have been faithful with a few things; I will put you in charge of many things. This saying of the householder also has implications outside the parable's story, given its reiteration at the climax of the story (25:29–30; also 25:23). Faithfulness begets opportunities for greater faithfulness.

25:24–25 *you are a hard man . . . So I was afraid.* The servant who hid the money

Key Themes of Matthew 25:14–46

- Disciples must remain faithful.
- Disciples must be merciful in action to the "least of these."
- Jesus is the judge and the criterion for judgment.

without investing it did so from fear of his harsh master. It is not necessary to apply this detail of the story to reality. Unlike the reiterated theme of faithfulness begetting greater opportunity for faithfulness (25:21, 23, 29–30), this element (mentioned just once) gives color to the story and does not provide a picture of what God is like. Certainly, Matthew has not portrayed God in this way in his Gospel (e.g., 5:45; 7:11; see the sidebar "Interpreting Parables" in the unit on 19:27–20:16).

25:31 *When the Son of Man comes in his glory.* The final parable (or judgment scene) of the Eschatological Discourse is set at the time of final judgment. By referring to the Son of Man (the King) coming in glory as judge over all the nations, Matthew evokes Daniel 7:13–14 in the Septuagint and highlights the universal authority that Jesus as Son of Man will exercise (see 28:18).

25:32 *All the nations.* There is debate over whether "the nations" (*ethnē*) refers exclusively to Gentiles or to all nations, including Jews and Gentiles. It is most likely that *ethnē* refers to all peoples, Jews and Gentiles, given the modifier "all" and Matthew's use of *ethnē* inclusively to refer to Jews and Gentiles earlier in the Eschatological Discourse (24:9, 14; in 21:43 *ethnē* must refer to a people comprised of both Jews and Gentiles).

25:34 *take your inheritance, the kingdom prepared for you.* The inheritance that Jesus speaks of is identified as "the kingdom prepared for you." This coheres with Matthew's picture of reward more generally; reward is conceived of not as something additional to receiving the kingdom and eternal life but rather as the kingdom itself (e.g., 6:1–18; 19:28).

25:35–36 *I was hungry . . . thirsty . . . a stranger . . . needed clothes . . . sick . . . in prison.* Jesus expresses his solidarity with those who are dispossessed and in great need. The level of identification between Jesus and those in need as portrayed here should discourage viewing altruism as simply a means to the end of caring for Jesus. As Gustavo Gutiérrez argues, "The neighbor is not an occasion, an instrument for becoming closer to God. We are dealing with a real love of [humanity] for [its] own sake."[1]

25:37 *the righteous.* Matthew has emphasized "righteousness" or "justice" (often using *dikaiosynē, dikaios*) across his Gospel, defining it, in part, as covenant loyalty expressed through merciful action (e.g., 1:19; 5:7; 12:7; 23:23). This final teaching of Jesus reiterates the connection between mercy and covenant loyalty.

Lord, when did we see you hungry . . . ? An important feature of this judgment scene is the surprise expressed by both groups that they have encountered Jesus in their interactions with the poor, the hungry, the thirsty, the stranger, the sick, and the prisoner (cf. 25:44). Given the trajectory of Matthew's Gospel, it is not unexpected to hear that all peoples will be judged by their responses to Jesus. What is surprising is that they encounter Jesus in their care for the needy. The element of surprise makes most sense if those who received aid were not transparently believers in Jesus (see

25:40). As R. T. France suggests, "They have helped . . . not a Jesus recognized in his representatives, but a Jesus *incognito.* . . . [The needy] seem closer to what some modern theologians call 'anonymous Christians' than to openly declared supporters of Jesus himself."[2]

25:40 *whatever you did for one of the least of these brothers and sisters of mine, you did for me.* As the superlative of *mikros* ("little ones" [10:42; 18:6, 10, 14]), the word *elachistos* ("least of these") highlights the theme of care for the most vulnerable with little status.[3] The term is qualified here (though not in 25:45) by "brothers and sisters" (*adelphos*), which has been used by Matthew primarily to refer to believers (possible exceptions are 5:21–24, 47; 7:3–5). Scholars and theologians debate whether *adelphos* limits the scope of "the least of these" to Christians. A significant number argue that it does, so that the criterion of judgment for the nations is the way they have treated Jesus' followers who were dispossessed and needy.[4] Alternately, many scholars argue that the referent is to the dispossessed of the world. For example, Arland Hultgren argues that because the descriptors for "the least of these" (e.g., hungry, in prison) are broad in scope, *elachistos* should be understood universally.[5] Given the point made by R. T. France regarding "Jesus *incognito*" (see discussion on 25:37) and the wide scope of the description of the "least," it is likely that "the least of these" does refer beyond the church. Or at least the text implies this trajectory of application.[6]

25:44 *Lord, when did we see you hungry . . . and did not help you?* In spite of their reference to Jesus as "Lord," the group on his left proves unfaithful and unmerciful and so not among his true followers (cf. 7:21).

25:45 *whatever you did not do for one of the least of these, you did not do for me.* This use of *elachistos* is not modified by "brothers and sisters" and so may suggest that "the least of these" is to be understood broadly (see 25:40).

25:46 *they will go away to eternal punishment, but the righteous to eternal life.* Matthew has emphasized God's work as judge in the final day ("the end of the age" [13:39–40, 49]). Here it is Jesus who is judge, adjudicating on the basis of people's responses to himself as he acts in solidarity with the dispossessed (see the sidebar "Relation of 'Faith' and 'Works' in Matthew").

Teaching the Text

1. *Believers in Jesus are exhorted to exercise faithfulness in all things, so that they are always ready for the Lord's return.* It is a rather common mistake in preaching the parable of the talents (bags of gold) to simply transfer the meaning of "talent" (i.e., a skill or aptitude) in English to the traditional rendering of *talanton* as "talent." In that scenario, the parable becomes about being faithful in using one's talents for God. The story of the parable, however, is about a master's servants being faithful (or unfaithful) with money invested. In the metaphor, money stands in for all that a person has and what has been entrusted to the church corporately. Faithfulness is judged based on the church's attention to using all resources for the kingdom—the gospel, God's gracious provision, money, talents, strengths, health, and more. As

Relation of "Faith" and "Works" in Matthew

The parable of the sheep and the goats, with its apparent judgment based on works, raises the issue of the relationship between faith and works in Matthew. However, this framing (faith versus works) is drawn from Reformation categories rather than Matthean ones. Matthew has consistently highlighted the importance of action as well as words and intention (e.g., 6:1–18; 7:21; 12:33–37). It is integrity between one's inner life and one's actions that is important for Matthean ethics (e.g., 15:11–20; 23:25–28). Thus, final judgment will reveal the true character of a person, which only God can know at present (13:29–30). One's actions reflect one's identity and basic allegiances.[a] And allegiance to Jesus as God's Messiah and so obedience to his teachings (28:20) will be the basis of judgment (16:27; 25:31–46).

[a] Wesley G. Olmstead, "Judgment," *DJG* 460.

When Christ comes to judge, "he will separate the people one from another as a shepherd separates the sheep from the goats" (25:32). This Israeli herd contains both sheep and goats.

William Davies and Dale Allison suggest, "The parable implies that the gifts are various, so it makes little sense to be specific. We must rather think of God's gifts in general."[7]

2. *Believers in Jesus are exhorted to practice mercy toward the needy as an expression of their covenant loyalty to Jesus himself.* Given the importance of this final

teaching of Jesus in Matthew (25:31–46), it is crucial that we preach this passage and preach it well. Yet given potential concern, at least within Protestant circles, over its emphasis on judgment based on actions done, it is easy to go off point and preach this text by defending justification by grace through faith.[8] Against this tendency, we might preach a holistic message that attends to the covenantal balance of trust and loyalty across the Gospel. Matthew makes clear that grace comes in Jesus, "God with us" (1:23 [cf. 28:20]), and that trusting in Jesus the Messiah is crucial (e.g., 9:22; 15:28). And Matthew also communicates that doing the will of God as expressed in his own teachings is essential (7:21, 28–29; 28:20), and that all people will someday be judged by their actions (16:27; 25:31–46).

In preaching this text, it is also helpful to communicate that the actions done as for Jesus are significant actions of mercy and justice to alleviate the suffering of those in need. The surprise of those on the king's right and left side is not based on the seeming insignificance (littleness) of their actions;[9] rather, it is based on the surprising solidarity shown by Jesus with those usually treated as least significant—the "least of these." So teaching this passage could highlight this surprising solidarity and its importance for the way we treat those deemed least valuable in our own contexts. Such acts of justice and mercy are not insignificant. As Gutiérrez suggests, "To offer food or drink in our day . . . means the transformation of a society structured to benefit a few who appropriate to themselves the value of the work of others."[10]

Illustrating the Text

Believers in Jesus are exhorted to exercise faithfulness in all things, so that they are always ready for the Lord's return.

Popular Culture: We live in a culture that prizes ownership. We work our whole lives to own our own house, our own car(s), and all that goes with and in them. Even when it would make sense to share material possessions communally, our tendencies toward buying and owning are strong (e.g., would it not be better for several households in a neighborhood to share a lawnmower rather than each one owning its own?). The parable of the bags of gold encourages believers to think of all resources, material and otherwise, as entrusted to us rather than belonging to us. Stewardship rather than ownership is the theme of this parable.

Cultural Institution: Every year, a publicly traded company must give an account of how it has performed. Those who own company stock gather to hear the report and hold the board of directors accountable. For this illustration, you might provide a contemporary example of a contentious shareholder meeting. You might ask those gathered this question: If a stockholder meeting based on the investments of your life or the life of your congregation was held, how would this meeting go?

Believers in Jesus are exhorted to practice mercy toward the needy as an expression of their covenant loyalty to Jesus himself.

Church Missions: Give examples from your own church context or beyond of service organizations that are actively participating in solidarity with those in prison or in need of food, clothing, or shelter (you might consider non-Christian organizations as well). This passage provides a strong impetus to help your church think through ways to live in solidarity with the poor and downtrodden.

Quote: Author and activist Shane Claiborne comments,

> When we get to heaven, though, I'm not convinced Jesus is going to say, "When I was hungry, you gave a check to the United Way and they gave me something to eat," or, "When I was naked, you donated clothes to the Salvation Army and they clothed me." Jesus is not seeking distant acts of charity. He seeks concrete acts of love: "*you* gave me something to eat . . . *you* gave me something to drink . . . *you* clothed me . . . *you* invited me in . . . *you* looked after me . . . *you* came to visit me [in prison]" (Matthew 25:35–36).[11]

"The King will reply, 'Truly I tell you, whatever you did for one of the least of these brothers and sisters of mine, you did for me'" (25:40). In Catholicism these deeds became known as the "Corporal Works of Mercy" and include providing food, drink, clothing, and shelter; visiting the sick and imprisoned; and burying the dead. These activities have been the subject of many paintings, including *Seven Works of Mercy* by Pieter Brueghel the Younger (1564–1638), shown here.

Jesus Is Anointed and Celebrates the Passover with His Disciples

Big Idea *Matthew contrasts the Jewish leaders and Judas, who conspire against Jesus, and even the disciples, who continue to lack understanding about Jesus' impending death, with an unnamed woman who anoints Jesus for his burial, pointing toward his missional death to bring covenant renewal through the forgiveness of sins.*

Understanding the Text

The Text in Context

Chapters 26–28 narrate the passion and resurrection of Jesus. After Jesus predicts his coming death again (26:2; also 16:21; 17:22–23; 20:17–19), Matthew narrates the plot against Jesus by the Jewish leaders (26:3–5; also 12:14; 21:45–46). The woman who anoints Jesus (26:6–13) is the first of a number of women highlighted in the Passion Narrative who display discipleship qualities or remain with Jesus when the Twelve desert him (27:19, 55–56, 61; 28:1–10). The scene in which Jesus shares the Passover with his disciples (26:17–30) highlights Judas's betrayal (26:23–25; see 26:14–16, 47–50) and Jesus' sacrifice and death "for the forgiveness of sins" (see 1:21).

The chief priests and elders plot how to secretly arrest and kill Jesus so as not to incite a riot that would come to the attention of the Romans (26:3). Roman troops were stationed in Jerusalem to keep order, especially during festivals like the Passover, when the city was crowded with visitors. The Antonia Fortress, on the left side in this photo, provided barracks for the soldiers as well as a commanding view of the activities occurring in the temple courts.

Interpretive Insights

26:1 *When Jesus had finished saying all these things.* This formula has concluded each of the major Matthean discourses containing Jesus' teaching (7:28; 11:1; 13:53; 19:1). In this final repetition

of the formula Matthew includes "all" to provide a summative reference to the teachings of Jesus. At this point in the story Jesus has concluded his teachings as he turns to his final days in Jerusalem.

26:2 *the Passover is two days away.* Matthew sets the context for Jesus' coming death during the Passover festival (as do all the Gospels) and will portray Jesus making specific connections between the Passover meal and his death (26:20–29).

the Son of Man will be handed over to be crucified. Jesus has predicted his crucifixion during his travels to Jerusalem (16:21; 17:22–23; 20:17–19). Here he reaffirms that his journey will end on a cross.

26:3 *Caiaphas.* Caiaphas was high priest in the years AD 18–36, a religious and political role. According to Josephus, (Joseph) Caiaphas was appointed by Pilate's predecessor, Valerius Gratus (*Ant.* 18.35).

26:5 *there may be a riot among the people.* During Passover, one of the three major Jewish festivals, Jerusalem and its environs swelled with pilgrims coming to celebrate. Given its ties to Israel's deliverance from Egypt (Exod. 12–14), Passover held the potential for revolutionary activity. Josephus, for instance, speaks of the Roman procurator Cumanus (mid-first century), who feared that the large number of people attending the Passover "might afford occasion for an uprising [and] ordered one company of soldiers to take up arms and stand guard on the porticoes of the temple so as to quell any uprising that might occur" (*Ant.* 20.106 [see also Matt. 27:24]).

26:6 *alabaster jar of very expensive perfume.* Perfumes were used in preparing a body for burial. If the woman intended her

actions to prepare for Jesus' burial (26:12), then it is ironic that she, although not privy to Jesus' passion predictions, understands his mission, while his disciples, who have heard of his coming death four times now, do not (16:21; 17:22–23; 20:17–19; 26:1–2).

26:11 *The poor you will always have with you.* Jesus justifies the unnamed woman's act of anointing him for burial by alluding to Deuteronomy 15:11. In Deuteronomy the context focuses on care for the poor, with its refrain about being "openhanded toward your fellow Israelites who are poor and needy" (15:11 [cf. 15:8, 10]). And this context is certainly something that Jesus and Matthew would have been aware of. So it is inappropriate to take this statement from Matthew (or Deuteronomy) and universalize what was quite specific to the unique event of Jesus' coming death; that is, this statement should not be interpreted proverbially as an excuse to avoid merciful care for the poor. In fact, by allusion to Deuteronomy, the context of care for the poor is likely relevant to the Matthean context. In other words, care for the poor should be a Christian duty because ongoing poverty will require such action (cf. 25:31–46).

26:13 *what she has done will also be told, in memory of her.* The woman who has anointed Jesus as preparation for his burial, although unnamed, is promised that her action will be recounted wherever the gospel itself is proclaimed. This statement highlights the centrality of Jesus' death within the good news.

26:14 *Judas Iscariot.* Matthew has referred to Jesus' disciple Judas Iscariot previously with the descriptor "who betrayed him [Jesus]" (10:4). So the reader is prepared for the act of betrayal here, although there is no specific reason provided for his betrayal other than his request for payment.

26:16 *Judas watched for an opportunity to hand him over.* Matthew has already indicated that the Jewish leaders desire to arrest Jesus in secret and, if at all possible, not during the Passover festival, so as to avoid rioting (26:3–5). This sets the context for Judas watching for an opportune time to betray Jesus to the authorities, presumably at night and outside the city in order to avoid a public arrest in front of a sympathetic crowd (see 26:47). In fact, hints of secrecy occur across the rest of this chapter (e.g., 26:18, 20 [see commentary], 48; and in Jesus' rather cryptic responses at 26:25 and 64).

26:17 *On the first day of the Festival of Unleavened Bread.* Although the Passover and the Festival of Unleavened Bread originally seem to have been two distinct feasts (Exod. 12:1–30), at some point they began to be celebrated as a single festival (Deut. 16:1–8; Philo, *Spec. Laws* 2.150). The combined festival lasted from Nisan (the Jewish month corresponding to March/April) 14 to 21, with the first day (Nisan 14) being the day on which the lambs were sacrificed; presumably this is the day Matthew refers to here.[1]

26:18 *Go into the city to a certain man.* The Greek word for "a certain man" (*deina*) occurs only here in the New Testament and is used when a speaker wants the person's identity to remain unknown (or simply does not know it [BDAG 215]). With *deina*, Matthew indicates that Jesus has prearranged a location for the Passover meal that he will share with his disciples. The reference may also indicate the secretive nature of their plans, especially if Jesus is planning to celebrate the meal on Nisan 14 rather than Nisan 15 (see comments on 26:20).

26:20 *When evening came.* This clause (*opsias genomenēs*) is usually taken to indicate that Jesus and his disciples celebrate the Passover meal on Nisan 15 (as all Jews would), since in Jewish reckoning each new day begins at nightfall. In this scenario, the disciples have prepared for the Passover meal sometime during the daytime hours on Nisan 14 and eat the meal with Jesus after sundown (per Jewish custom) on Nisan 15.

R. T. France persuasively suggests that this temporal clause refers to later the same evening ("later on"), as in 14:23 (*opsias genomenēs*), where it does not make sense to have an inauguration of evening when evening has already arrived at 14:15 (*opsias genomenēs*). If this is correct, then Jesus has prearranged a clandestine Passover meal with his disciples (see 26:18). He then has his disciples prepare the meal at the beginning of Nisan 14 just after sundown, when they would attract less attention than in daylight. Even later into the evening (Nisan 14), they celebrate the Passover in secrecy, the day before the large crowds in Jerusalem would be celebrating it. By that time, Jesus will already be dead. This scenario fits the hints of secrecy that run through chapter 26 (see 26:16), explains

the omission of a lamb at the meal, and coheres with John's chronology of Jesus' death.[2]

26:24 *just as it is written about him.* Throughout Matthew's Gospel the theme of Scripture's fulfillment in Jesus has been emphasized. Jesus' passion is also deliberately set in the context of Scripture's fulfillment. Here and at 26:54 and 26:56 Scripture and the prophets provide the context and reason for Jesus' arrest and missional death.

26:26 *Take and eat; this is my body.* Jesus draws on the Passover meal to infuse meaning into his coming death. Matthew has already highlighted the theme of Jesus as enacting return from exile and new exodus (as these themes converge in Isaiah [e.g., Matt. 1–4; 14:19]). The same connection is made here by identifying Jesus with the Passover sacrifice that brings forgiveness and freedom.

26:28 *This is my blood of the covenant, which is poured out for many for the forgiveness of sins.* The phrase "blood of the covenant" is an allusion to Exodus 24:8, where Moses sprinkles sacrificial blood on the people to ratify Yahweh's covenant with them (with identical wording in the Septuagint). This allusion points to Jesus as the climax of the covenant. Some commentators also see an allusion to Isaiah 53:11–12 in the language of "poured out for many," a text already evoked at 20:28 ("a ransom for many").[3] Finally, this climactic narrative moment brings full circle the promise of the

angel that Jesus will "save his people from their sins" (1:21).

Some manuscripts include the adjective "new" before "covenant," but it is more likely that copyists added the word to conform to Luke 22:20 than that scribes omitted it. Also, Matthew seems to be cautious in using this adjective (see the sidebar "What's 'New' in Matthew?" in the unit on 9:9–34).

Teaching the Text

Jesus as the Messiah will bring covenant renewal and forgiveness of sins by his missional death. By connecting Jesus' coming death with the Passover celebration in very specific ways, Matthew indicates that Jesus ushers in a new exodus or deliverance. The hope for such a new exodus comes from Isaiah's vision of God returning to Israel in restoration; this Isaianic vision is drawn with allusions to the exodus from Egypt, with its parting of the waters and God's victory over Pharaoh (e.g., Isa. 43:16–19; 48:20–21; 51:9–11). Isaiah's message is implicit but clear: just as God redeemed Israel from their Egyptian oppressors, so God would bring restoration from Babylon. Matthew picks up this theme as fitting to the redemption God brings through Jesus at the fullness of time. With his statement that the Passover bread is his body (26:26),

> Jesus was drawing into one event a millennium and more of Jewish celebrations. The Jews had believed for some while that the original Exodus pointed on to a new one, in which God would do at last what he had long promised: he would forgive the sins of Israel and the world, once and for all. Sin, a far greater slave-master than Egypt had ever been, would be defeated in the way God defeated not only Egypt but also the Red Sea. And now Jesus, sitting there at a secret meal in Jerusalem, was saying, by what he was doing as much as by the words he was speaking: this is the moment. This is the time. And it's all because of what's going to happen to me.[4]

So how can this theme of Jesus inaugurating the new exodus impact our preaching? This theme seems particularly fruitful as we prepare people to celebrate the Lord's Supper or Eucharist. As we commemorate Jesus' death in the Lord's Supper, we can provide rich resources to people by highlighting the connections between Jesus' offering of himself for our salvation and the Jewish celebration of and hope for God's continued saving work. We can preach with confidence that it is God's pattern to save and redeem; salvation does not begin with Jesus, though it most certainly culminates in him. And by emphasizing the connection between the Lord's Supper and the Jewish hopes for God's new exodus, we tap a deep vein within the Scriptures about God's commitment to restoration and the newness of salvation available then and now for God's people; as we read in Isaiah 43:16–19,

> This is what the LORD says—
>   he who made a way through the sea,
>   a path through the mighty waters,
> who drew out the chariots and horses,

Matthew connects the approaching death of Jesus with the Passover celebration. Just as God rescued the Israelites from their Egyptian oppressors, God will redeem Israel (and the nations) through Jesus' death. The carving on this fourth-century AD sarcophagus shows Pharaoh and his army being engulfed by the waters while Moses and the Israelites are safe on dry land.

the army and reinforcements
together,
and they lay there, never to rise again,
extinguished, snuffed out like a
wick:
"Forget the former things;
do not dwell on the past.
See, I am doing a new thing!
Now it springs up; do you not perceive it?
I am making a way in the wilderness
and streams in the wasteland."

Illustrating the Text

*Jesus as the Messiah will bring covenant
renewal and forgiveness of sins by his
missional death.*

Christian Liturgy: Alexander Schmemann
describes the Lord's Supper (Eucharist) as
a kind of entry into a fourth dimension.
By doing so, he intimates the way this celebration of the church points ahead to the
newness of salvation and the final consummation of the kingdom.

The liturgy of the Eucharist is best understood as a journey or procession. It is the
journey of the Church into the dimension
of the Kingdom. . . . Our entrance into
the presence of Christ is an entrance into
a fourth dimension which allows us to
see the ultimate reality of life. It is not
an escape from the world, rather it is the
arrival at a vantage point from which we
can see more deeply into the reality of
the world.[5]

Quote: N. T. Wright explores the connection between sin and death, helping us to
understand more deeply Jesus' reflection

on his coming death "for the forgiveness
of sins" (26:28).

To be released from sin is to be released
from death, and since Jesus died in a representative capacity for Israel, and hence
for the whole human race, and hence for
the whole cosmos (that is how the chain
of representation works), his death under
the weight of sin results immediately in
release for all those held captive by its
guilt and power. . . . Forgiveness of sins in
turn (just as in Isaiah 54–55) means new
creation, since the anti-creation force of
sin has been dealt with. And new creation
begins with the word of forgiveness heard
by the individual sinner.[6]

Christian Music: African American spiritu-
als often draw on exodus imagery, with its
vision of God's action to free Israel from
Egyptian slavery. Because African Ameri-
cans experienced brutal slavery themselves,
many songs of the slave community spoke
to their longing for freedom from slavery
and for freedom in Christ. One such song,
"Oh, Mary," celebrates God's victory in
the exodus as an expression of the singer's
hopes for freedom.

Oh, Mary, don't you weep, don't you
mourn.
Oh, Mary, don't you weep, don't you
mourn.
Pharaoh's army got drowned.
Oh, Mary, don't you weep.
Some of these mornings bright and
fair,
Take my wings and cleave the air.
Pharaoh's army got drowned.
Oh, Mary, don't you weep.

Jesus Is God's Faithful Son in Gethsemane and at His Arrest and Trial

Big Idea *Although Jesus predicts and witnesses the disciples' desertion and prays for God to change his fate, he as the Messiah, the Son of God, proves himself faithful to God's will even to the point of suffering and death.*

Understanding the Text

The Text in Context

Matthew's passion story continues with Jesus' prediction of the disciples' desertion and Peter's denial (26:31–35), Jesus' time of prayer in Gethsemane and arrest there (26:36–56), and Jesus' trial before the Sanhedrin (26:57–68) followed by Peter's denial (26:69–75). Matthew's thematic emphases include the stumbling of the disciples ("fall away" [26:31, 33]), prophetic fulfillment (26:31, 54–56), and Jesus' commitment to doing God's will even to the point of death (26:39). The antagonism of the Jerusalem leaders toward Jesus, which has been palpable since his arrival in the city (21:23–27, 45–46; 22:15–40; 26:3–4), culminates in Jesus' trial before the Sanhedrin. Jesus' citation of Daniel 7:13–14 (see 26:64; see also 24:30–31) and the implicit claim that he is the Son of Man result in the charge of blasphemy and propel the story to the next political level, a trial before Pilate (27:1–2, 11–26).

Interpretive Insights

26:31 *This very night you will fall away on account of me.* Matthew draws on the thematic *skandalizō* to describe the disciples' falling away or stumbling over Jesus. The Pharisees (15:12) and Jesus' hometown (13:57) have stumbled over Jesus and his teachings. Yet Jesus has tried to avoid causing stumbling (17:27) and has pronounced a blessing over those who do not stumble over his messianic identity (11:6). It is ironic that Jesus' closest followers will stumble over him in his darkest hour.

I will strike the shepherd. Jesus cites Zechariah 13:7 to describe the disciples' desertion, a text that draws on the common image of shepherd for Israel's leaders and offers a final vision of Israel restored after Yahweh purifies them (13:1, 9).

26:32 *after I have risen, I will go ahead of you into Galilee.* Jesus' prediction of the disciples' desertion is followed by a hint of future restoration. His saying about meeting his disciples in Galilee (see also 28:7, 10) points ahead to Matthew's final commissioning scene in Galilee (28:16–20).

26:36 *to a place called Gethsemane.* Gethsemane was an olive orchard located on the Mount of Olives. This will be the scene of both Jesus' fervent prayer and his arrest.

26:38 *keep watch with me.* The admonition for Jesus' followers to be watchful (*grēgoreō*) has been thematic in the Eschatological Discourse (24:42–43; 25:13) and now is at the center of Jesus' exhortation to Peter, James, and John, his closest friends, as he goes off alone to pray (also 26:40–41).

26:39 *may this cup be taken from me. Yet not as I will, but as you will.* The image of a "cup" in the Old Testament often refers to God's judgment (e.g., Jer. 25:15; 49:12; see also Matt. 20:22). Jesus desires that he not experience his coming trial, crucifixion, and death, but as he prays, he puts his future in God's hands.

26:45 *the Son of Man is delivered into the hands of sinners.* This prediction of what will happen at Jesus' arrest echoes his earlier words about his coming passion at 17:22: "The Son of Man is going to be delivered into the hands of men."

26:47 *a large crowd . . . sent from the chief priests and the elders.* As

the arrest scene begins, Judas arrives in Gethsemane along with a large crowd sent by the Jewish leaders. Once they deliver Jesus to the high priest and the Sanhedrin, the crowd reappears during Jesus' trial before Pilate (27:17).

26:48 *The one I kiss is the man; arrest him.* The signal that Judas has arranged is a kiss. This detail indicates either that Jesus is not readily recognizable to those coming to arrest him, or, more likely, that the darkness of night made it difficult to distinguish him from the many other visitors to Jerusalem who might be spending the night in the olive grove. For the motif of secrecy across chapter 26, see 26:16.

26:53 *twelve legions of angels.* Matthew ties the scene in Gethsemane to the temptation narrative (4:1–12) by means of

In Gethsemane Jesus prays before his arrest. This grove of ancient olive trees adjacent to the Church of All Nations is one site traditionally considered to be the location for this scene.

an echo of Psalm 91: angels are at Jesus' disposal to rescue him. Ironically, the devil used Psalm 91:11–12 (4:6) in order to tempt Jesus. Jesus did not succumb to that temptation, nor does he turn his focus away from his God-given mission at his arrest.

26:54 *how then would the Scriptures be fulfilled . . . ?* Jesus indicates that the Scriptures will be fulfilled by his faithful completion of his mission. Here Matthew, rather than characteristically citing particular Old Testament texts, emphasizes in the Passion Narrative how Jesus fulfills the Scriptures broadly (also 26:56).

26:56 *Then all the disciples deserted him and fled.* For the Twelve, who have been called to follow Jesus and have been with him for most of the story (note 26:71: "with Jesus"), their desertion signals a fundamental act of disloyalty and abdication of their mission.

26:57 *Caiaphas the high priest.* See comments on 26:3.

26:59 *the whole Sanhedrin.* The ruling Jewish council in Jerusalem, the Sanhedrin, was led by the high priest and consisted of prominent priests, scribes, and influential citizens who heard cases, made decisions and judgments, and were the central Jewish liaison with Rome.[1]

looking for false evidence against Jesus. Given that the search for false evidence surfaces nothing, the charges eventually lodged will be based on something that Jesus has said, though misconstrued (see comments on 26:61).

26:61 *I am able to destroy the temple of God and rebuild it in three days.* Matthew includes no such statement by Jesus in his Gospel, but John's Gospel records Jesus' enigmatic riddle: "Destroy this temple, and I will raise it again in three days" (2:19). This Jesus tradition likely provides the basis of the accusation from these two witnesses. And although they get the details wrong (e.g., in John's text Jesus is not the agent of the temple's destruction, and he speaks figuratively), the high priest accepts their testimony, probably because it comes from the mouths of "two or three witnesses" (see Deut. 19:15).

26:63 *But Jesus remained silent.* Jesus chooses to remain silent rather than defend himself (again at 27:14). Those prone to hear allusions to Isaiah 53 elsewhere in Matthew (20:28; 26:28) also suggest an echo of Isaiah 53:7 here: "He [the servant] was oppressed and afflicted, yet he did not open his mouth."

I charge you under oath. When Caiaphas binds him by an oath, Jesus answers the question about his identity. In doing so, Jesus does not contravene his teaching about avoiding oaths (5:34), since that teaching addressed voluntary oaths and not oaths placed on one person by another.

Tell us if you are the Messiah, the Son of God. The titles "Messiah" and "Son of God" refer to Jesus' kingly identity. While modern readers are prone to hear "Son of God" as a divine title, in first-century Judaism it is a messianic one. Drawing from 2 Samuel 7:14 and Psalm 2, Jewish use of "son of God" could refer to Israel's king and so certainly the Messiah (see 2 Esd. 7:28–29). This seems to underlie Matthew's use of the title here and elsewhere (see 14:33; 16:16). For Matthew's Israel Christology, which may be relevant here, see comments on 4:3, 6.

26:64 *You have said so.* Jesus answers the high priest, but in somewhat cryptic fashion (see also 26:25; cf. 27:11). As John Nolland notes, "Though formally noncommittal, it is to be taken as an obliquely expressed affirmative [answer]."[2]

From now on you will see the Son of Man . . . coming on the clouds of heaven. Jesus clearly alludes to Daniel 7:13–14 in his response to Caiaphas, a text also evoked at 10:23; 16:28; 24:30. Psalm 110:1 is also echoed in the reference to being seated at God's right hand. Daniel 7:13–14 pictures a "son of man" figure entering the heavenly court and being vindicated and glorified. So Jesus is implicitly claiming and asserting his coming vindication by God in spite of his present trial and impending death. His vindication occurs most clearly at his resurrection but also upon the vindication of his predictions about the temple's destruction (see 24:30).

26:65 *He has spoken blasphemy!* Blasphemy is a broad enough charge, at least in the first century, to characterize Jesus' response.[3] Through reference to Daniel 7, Jesus has claimed implicitly a unique relationship with God and his (future) universal authority. He has also spoken against God's temple and God's leaders (see Exod. 22:28).[4]

26:66 *He is worthy of death.* According to the Torah, the punishment for blasphemy is death (Lev. 24:13–15).

26:69 *Now Peter was sitting out in the courtyard.* The scene of Peter's denial (introduced at 26:58) involves three intensifying claims by Peter that he does not know Jesus.

26:72 *He denied it again, with an oath.* Peter not only denies Jesus again; he does so by rashly taking an oath, something that Jesus has prohibited his followers from doing (5:34).

26:73 *your accent gives you away.* This statement highlights the distinction, linguistic and social, that existed between Jews from Judea and Jerusalem and Jews from Galilee. Earlier (21:10–11), Matthew has distinguished between the Jerusalem crowds and those from Galilee (see comments on 4:12).

Theological Insights: Jesus as Faithful Son

Jesus' faithfulness to God's plan is emphasized across the arc of Matthew's story, especially here in Gethsemane. In spite of temptation to go another (easier) path, Jesus remains God's faithful son in contrast to Israel's historical failings as God's son (Hosea 11:1; Matt. 2:15). Each of the Gospels tells this story of Jesus' faithfulness to God's plan (e.g., Mark 14:36; Luke 9:51; John 12:27–28). And particularly if Paul speaks of God's righteousness being displayed through Jesus' faithfulness in Romans 3:22 (also Gal. 2:16; Phil. 3:9), then Paul calls people to trust in the faithful work of Christ demonstrated and enacted in his suffering and death.[5] The author of the Epistle to the Hebrews gives significant space to the theme of Jesus' faithfulness: "Christ is faithful as the Son over God's house" (3:6 [cf. 3:2]). Although he was "tempted in every way, just as we are . . . he did not sin" (4:15). Instead, "he learned obedience from what he suffered" (5:8 [cf. 2:10]). Because of his faithfulness, he has brought salvation (5:9) and provides help for believers when tempted (2:18).

Teaching the Text

1. *Jesus as obedient son, facing the greatest of all temptations, remains faithful to his mission.* Matthew has portrayed Jesus as faithful and obedient to his Father and his mission from the start. He is baptized by John in solidarity with the people of Israel (3:15–17 ["to fulfill all righteousness"]) and, as faithful representative of Israel, resists all temptations to turn aside from God's will for him (4:1–12). Although tempted to take a different path (16:22–23), he stays the course to the cross. Here in Gethsemane we see the most heart-wrenching of moments in Jesus' journey to the culmination of his mission to "give his life as a ransom for many" (20:28). Yet even with his death looming before him, Jesus remains faithful and obedient.

In preaching and teaching this passage, we can follow our inclination to interpret Jesus' faithfulness as a model for our own, since Matthew has authorized this analogy in his focus on Jesus as representative Israel: he is the faithful Israelite par excellence (see "Matthew's Narrative Christology" in the introduction). It can help those we minister to and with to know of Jesus' struggle to follow an easier path and of his own desire to avoid the cross (to do what he wills [26:39]). To overcome temptation as Jesus did is not about some superhuman ability to avoid feeling deep ambivalence toward the sacrifice involved in following God's path for our lives; rather, it is about placing ourselves in the hands of the covenant God, who cares deeply for us as we say yes to our God-given mission.

2. *Matthew portrays the commitment to "being with" Jesus as fundamental to discipleship.* In the scene of Jesus' desertion by his disciples we get a glimpse of how important it is for followers of Jesus to remain loyal to him. For the Twelve, who have been present with Jesus for much of Matthew's narrative and whose call to follow has been about presence (4:18–22), to desert Jesus now at his most vulnerable and difficult hour is an abdication of their most important role. In church contexts where we often highlight the importance of activity ("doing ministry" and "serving the church"), it may be helpful in preaching and teaching to encourage Christians to think of their fundamental identity as disciples having to do with "being with Jesus." Presence precedes activism, and relationship precedes service. Jesus' words provide the

This panel of the altarpiece from the Siena Cathedral, Italy, painted by Duccio di Buoninsegna in the early fourteenth century AD depicts Jesus praying in Gethsemane (bottom register) and his disciples fleeing after his arrest (top panel).

proper order when he calls four fishermen to a new vocation: "Come, follow me, and I will send you out to fish for people" (4:19).

Illustrating the Text

Jesus as obedient son, facing the greatest of all temptations, remains faithful to his mission.

Science: In spite of great temptation to do so, Jesus does not choose the "path of least resistance." In physics, this phrase describes the way in which an object is most likely to move. For example, water in a river will flow downhill, pulled by gravity, moving around rocks and obstacles in its path. This phrase is also an idiom describing the way people often take the easier path in life, avoiding conflict and obstacles. Unique levels of commitment are needed to choose a path that is more difficult. In the Gethsemane narrative we get a glimpse of the difficulty of the path that Jesus takes.

Scripture: In Joshua 4 Israel has just passed over the Jordan River and into the promised land. Their time of desert journeying is over, but many challenges lie ahead. In this moment of transition God has Israel stop and set up twelve memorial stones. These stones provided Israel with a tangible and long-lasting reminder of God's covenant faithfulness. These stones were meant to keep Israel from the temptation of idolatry. As we seek to endure moments of temptation, we might mark moments of God's salvation and loyalty for us with "memorial stones" of our own.

This illustration might lead to application. You might encourage people to try one of the following ways of setting up their own memorial stones:

- Create a memorial box: Either individually or as a family, record memories of God's faithfulness on slips of paper and keep them in a box. Each family member might add a memory each year, possibly as part of a Thanksgiving Day tradition.
- Set aside a memory shelf: Dedicate a shelf in your home to objects chosen as symbols of God's faithfulness. Perhaps you can snap a photograph of a place or thing that will help you remember a moment when God was quite evidently at work.

Matthew portrays the commitment to "being with" Jesus as fundamental to discipleship.

Quote: To live in relationship with the living God in a way that focuses on being prior to doing, it can be helpful to return to the truth that being with Jesus begins and ends with his initiating presence with us. We depend on his presence (not vice versa).

Dependence assumes that God is already at work, so a centering question that emerges is: Where is God in this? In whatever situations, questions, or experiences we encounter, we can ask how God is already present, involved, and directing us precisely in the middle of these life experiences. This question—a foundational one in the practice of spiritual direction—is quite different from . . . the commonplace refrain: If you're not feeling close to God, guess who moved?[6]

Jesus Is Tried before Pilate and Sentenced to Death

Big Idea *Although Jesus is innocent of all charges and is truly the king of the Jews, he is delivered to be crucified by Pilate, the Roman governor, at the instigation of the Jewish leadership in Jerusalem, aided by Judas.*

Understanding the Text

The Text in Context

Following Jesus' trial before the Sanhedrin, the chief priests and elders bring him to Pilate, the governor (27:1–2). Matthew narrates the self-inflicted death of Judas, emphasizing Judas's belief in the innocence of Jesus, a theme that continues through this chapter (27:4, 19; see 27:24; cf. 12:7). In the account about Judas, Matthew also highlights the way in which Jesus' story fulfills Scripture (27:9–10, one of Matthew's ten fulfillment quotations). Continuing with the trial before Pilate (27:11–26), Matthew emphasizes Jesus' kingly

Pontius Pilate was the Roman prefect over Judea and Samaria from AD 26 to 36. This building inscription with Pilate's name and title was found at Caesarea.

identity (27:11, 17, 22), a theme that will pervade the crucifixion scene that follows (27:27–44). Matthew alone of the evangelists narrates the role of Pilate's wife in advocating for Jesus' innocence; this plot element fits the theme of Gentile inclusion in Matthew (e.g., 2:1; 8:5–13; 15:21–28; 28:19).

Interpretive Insights

27:1 *made their plans how to have Jesus executed.* Matthew intimates that although the Jewish leaders plan to use their influence to get Jesus executed, it is not in their power to enact the death penalty, since they are an occupied people. As the Jewish leaders are portrayed responding to Pilate in John, "We have no right to execute anyone" (John 18:31 [see also

Josephus, *J.W.* 6.126]). Only Rome could legally enact the death penalty, and crucifixion is a distinctly Roman brand of execution.

27:2 *Pilate the governor.* Pontius Pilate was the Roman governor (prefect) of Judea in the years AD 26–36. He was not particularly attuned to Jewish sensibilities, as illustrated by his frequent ignorance and transgression of Jewish customs. For example, he brought his army with their military standards, displaying images (forbidden by the Torah), into Jerusalem (see Josephus, *Ant.* 18.55–62).

27:3 *thirty pieces of silver.* This monetary amount echoes Zechariah 11:12–13, where Yahweh (or the shepherd-leader who rules for him) scorns the pitifully small amount of money (the value of a slave [see Exod. 21:32]) that the people think his shepherding is worth (with great irony, "the handsome price at which they valued me!" [11:13]). How little Jesus' life is worth to the Jewish leaders and Judas is meant to stagger Matthew's readers (26:15).

27:4 *innocent blood.* Matthew thematizes and connects innocence and blood in the Passion Narrative. Here Judas laments that he has betrayed Jesus' innocent (*athōos*) blood; Pilate's wife suffers in a dream over the innocent (*dikaios*) Jesus (27:19); Pilate attempts to claim that he is innocent (*athōos*) of Jesus' blood (27:24); and the people at Jesus' trial try to take responsibility for Jesus' blood (27:25; see also 23:35). Through this theme Matthew emphasizes Jesus' innocence while spreading culpability for his death rather broadly (see comments on 27:25).

27:9 *what was spoken by Jeremiah the prophet was fulfilled.* The reference to

Key Themes of Matthew 27:1–26

- Jesus is innocent of all charges.
- Judas, the Jewish leaders, and Pilate are culpable.
- Jesus is the true king of the Jews.

Jeremiah picks up allusions and themes from both Zechariah 11:12–13 and Jeremiah, particularly 19:1–13; 32:6–9. While the thirty pieces of silver and devaluing of God's shepherd(ing) come from Zechariah, the references to a purchase of a potter's field and the involvement of priests and elders derive from Jeremiah.

27:11 *Are you the king of the Jews?* Pilate's question is essentially a contextualization of the high priest's question (whether Jesus is the Messiah) in a Roman context, demonstrating that "messiah" is a kingly category and claim in the first-century world.

You have said so. Jesus' response here (*sy legeis*) is very similar to his answer to Caiaphas at 26:64 (*sy eipas*). It has a cryptic quality to it that does not allow Pilate to level a clear charge of treason, although Matthew's audience can hear the messianic affirmation in it, given the broader context of the Gospel.

27:12 *he gave no answer.* As in his trial with Caiaphas, Jesus does not answer Pilate regarding the charges and accusations made against him. For a possible echo of Isaiah 53:7, see comments on 26:63.

27:15 *governor's custom at the festival to release a prisoner.* While there is no external corroboration for this custom attributed to Pilate, we also hear about it in Mark 15:6 and John 18:39, which add the detail that Pilate was deferring to local custom in offering to release a prisoner at Passover. Craig Keener provides evidence of Roman officials deferring to local customs in regard to leniency.[1]

27:17 *Jesus Barabbas, or Jesus who is called the Messiah?* Some manuscripts include the name "Jesus" before the surname "Barabbas"; others do not. Given a clear disposition by Christian scribes copying the New Testament to hold Jesus' name in reverence, it is easy to understand how they might omit that name when used to refer to a criminal. It is less discernible why some scribes might add the name if it was not originally in Matthew. For this reason, it is likely that both prisoners to whom Pilate refers have the name "Jesus," a quite common Jewish name in the first century.[2] The choice between the two men named "Jesus" is set before the people: Jesus Barabbas or Jesus the Messiah.

27:18 *self-interest*. Most translations attribute the action of the Jewish leaders against Jesus as arising from jealousy or envy (*phthonos* [see BDAG 1054]), but R. T. France argues that these are rather weak descriptors, since the motivations of the leaders were political: "The Jewish leaders saw Jesus as a threat to their position and authority; it was a matter of competing claims of self-interest."[3]

27:19 *his wife sent him this message*. Matthew's Gospel is the only one that includes this scene with Pilate's wife. It accents Gentile inclusion (cf. 1:3, 5, 6) and also heightens the culpability of Pilate for Jesus' death.

Don't have anything to do with that innocent man. Matthew uses *dikaios* here to describe Jesus' innocence. This use connects back to 23:35, where Jesus speaks of the righteous blood spilled across Jewish history, pointing ahead to his own death

and the spilling of his blood. Jesus' innocence is asserted also in 12:7; 27:4.

in a dream. The early part of Matthew's Gospel narrates a number of dreams through which God's protection and direction are communicated (1:20; 2:12, 13, 19). Here the warning of the dream goes unheeded by Pilate.

27:20 *But the chief priests and the elders persuaded the crowd*. Throughout Matthew the Jewish crowds are portrayed as susceptible to the influence of the Jewish leaders (e.g., 12:22–24; 15:14; 16:12; 21:33–46; 23:13–15). Here the leaders persuade the crowd to call for Jesus' death.

27:24 *an uproar was starting*. Pilate fears a riot, given the large crowds present and the latent revolutionary fervor that could accompany the Passover festival (see comments on 26:5). This leads him to quickly conclude his deliberations and send Jesus to be crucified.

I am innocent of this man's blood. Pilate attempts to wash his hands of responsibility for Jesus' death, but his words do not exonerate him. Narratively, it is helpful to attend to issues of point of view, asking whether Matthew authorizes Pilate's perspective (see the sidebar "Characterization and Narrative Authorization" in the unit on 4:1–11). Given that Pilate represents the full power of Rome in this decision, and that he is the one who sends Jesus to be crucified (27:26), we can legitimately question Pilate's perspective. In fact, Matthew emphasizes only Jesus' innocence in the Passion Narrative, not that of other characters or groups (see 27:4, 19; cf. 23:35).

27:25 *His blood is on us and on our children!* These words, if extracted from context, indict the Jewish people for Jesus'

Pilate washes his hands, claiming he is innocent of Jesus' blood. A sarcophagus from AD 350–75 pictures this event carved in relief.

in no way represents all of Judaism.[4] Third, in addition to Pilate, Matthew highlights the culpability of the Jewish leaders, who persuade the crowd to call for Jesus' death (27:20; see also 16:21; 20:17–19). Fourth, this is not the final word on the "people" (*laos*). In 27:64 the chief priests and Pharisees express concern that the people might be deceived by reports of Jesus being raised from the dead, showing that the people are still potentially receptive to him. In the end, Matthew spreads culpability for Jesus' death quite broadly; it is all humanity that is responsible (*cheiras anthrōpōn* as "human hands" [17:22]).

27:26 *he had Jesus flogged, and handed him over to be crucified.* Despite Pilate's attempt to absolve himself of responsibility (27:24), Matthew indicates here that it is Pilate who delivers Jesus to be crucified, as was his and no one else's prerogative (see 27:1).

death. However, attention to immediate context and the narrative contours of the Gospel suggest a more nuanced response to who is responsible for Jesus' death in Matthew. First, Pilate, as Roman authority over Judea, cannot absolve himself of responsibility (see 27:24). Second, the "people" (*laos*) speaking here are the crowd that has gathered at Pilate's residence (27:17) and possibly the crowd "sent from the chief priests and elders" during Jesus' arrest (26:47). As such, it is likely primarily a Jerusalemite crowd rather than the Galilean crowds that have followed Jesus into Jerusalem (note Matthew's distinction in 21:10–11). Thus, for Matthew, this group

Teaching the Text

1. *Jesus is innocent of the charges lodged against him, because he is the true king of Israel, the Messiah.* This theological truth likely seems obvious to us, as readers of Matthew, and we will not be surprised by it. But it may be helpful to remind ourselves and our hearers that the crowds that have followed Jesus from Galilee (e.g., 21:8–11), welcoming him into Jerusalem as Messiah-King, would have expected this king to do precisely what Rome and the Jewish leaders were afraid of: confront Roman rule and take his rightful place as Israel's king. In this expected scenario Jesus' kingship would be defined by sedition against Rome, not exoneration from such charges. Jesus,

in a surprising turn based on Daniel 7, claims that his vindication and enthronement most certainly will happen. However, it will happen not by an overthrow of Rome, but somehow precisely through his representative death. God's ways are not ours: Jesus comes as a king who gives up rather than asserts power to bring about God's restoration and people's salvation.

2. *Matthew shows that, in the end, all humanity is responsible for Jesus' death.* It has been a stain on the history of Jewish-Christian relations that the words of 27:25, "His blood is on us and on our children," have been used not only to focus blame (exclusively) on Jews but also to inflict harm on them. As Amy-Jill Levine suggests, "The failure to understand the Jewish Jesus within his Jewish context has resulted in the creation and perpetuation of millennia of distrust, and worse, between church and synagogue."[5]

Yet a careful reading of Matthew, in both its historical and literary contexts, does not support this interpretation and use of the text. Matthew is a Jew who writes to other Jews who believe in Jesus; any argument that he has with other first-century Jews is by definition an intramural one. And as we have noted (see comments on 27:25), Matthew highlights the culpability of the Jewish leaders who influence the Passover crowds (27:20) and of Pilate, who cannot remove his guilt in sentencing Jesus to death (27:19, 24, 26). And the Roman and Jewish leaders have already been referenced as the actors in Jesus' death in 20:17–19 (also 16:21). Thus, assigning blame to all the Jewish people across history moves far beyond Matthew's message to his first-century audience. Additionally, Matthew intimates

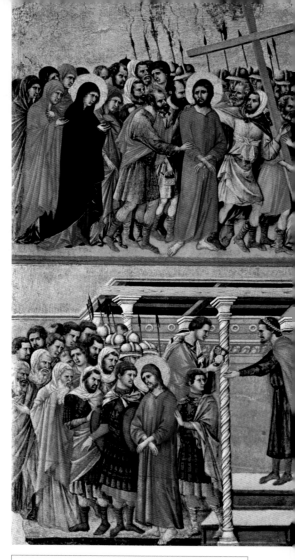

Duccio di Buoninsegna paints the crucifixion scene showing Pilate washing his hands (lower register) and Jesus being led to Golgotha (upper register) in this panel of the altarpiece from the Siena Cathedral, Italy (fourteenth century AD).

a theological widening of responsibility for Jesus' death at 17:22, where Jesus is delivered into "human hands." We could say, with justification, that all humanity is responsibile for Jesus' death. And yet assigning blame for something that Matthew has portrayed Jesus willingly accepting as his God-given mission seems, in some ways, to miss the mark. Especially given that Jesus' death brings salvation (1:21; 26:28) and life (27:52), assigning blame loses sight of the divine activity that is at the center of Jesus' death and resurrection. Teaching and preaching Jesus' death can focus where Matthew does: God's work in Jesus the Messiah's life, death, and resurrection to usher in the kingdom and bring restoration.

Illustrating the Text

Jesus is innocent of the charges lodged against him, because he is the true king of Israel, the Messiah.

Film: *Catch Me If You Can*. In this 2002 movie, Leonardo DiCaprio portrays the life of Frank Abagnale Jr., a real-life con artist who was a master of impersonation. Eventually, law enforcement catches up with Abagnale. After years on the run, forging multiple false identities, the true Frank is exposed to judgment. In contrast, Jesus is true to his identity and calling, demonstrated not by overthrowing Roman rule but by laying down his life.

Matthew shows that, in the end, all humanity is responsible for Jesus' death.

History: Matthew's account of Jesus' trial and condemnation has been used throughout subsequent history to justify anti-Semitism (27:25). For a survey of how the charge of "Christ killer" has been used for centuries to enflame passions and accuse Jews as a people of killing Jesus, you might refer to Jeremy Cohen's book *Christ Killers: The Jews and the Passion from the Bible to the Big Screen*,[6] which provides examples of this accusation and its devastating results.

Quote: *Church Dogmatics*, by Karl Barth. Blaming the Jewish people for Jesus' death can be done only by distancing Jesus from his Jewish identity. Barth provides an important corrective in this regard.

> The Word did not simply become any "flesh," any man humbled and suffering. It became Jewish flesh. The Church's whole doctrine of the incarnation and the atonement becomes abstract and valueless and meaningless to the extent that this comes to be regarded as something accidental and incidental. The New Testament witness to Jesus the Christ, the Son of God, stands on the soil of the Old Testament and cannot be separated from it. . . . The Christian kerygma as it is addressed to the world has this statement about an Israelite at its very heart.[7]

Book: *Plenty of Blame to Go Around*, by Eric Wittenberg and David Petruzzi. In their book, the authors analyze the commonplace view that Jeb Stuart was responsible for the Confederate Army's loss at Gettysburg. Stuart, a cavalry commander, led his troops on a roundabout ride to Gettysburg and finally arrived on the afternoon of the second day of the battle.[8] Wittenberg and Petruzzi's historical analysis suggests that the picture is more complicated: there is good reason to assign blame more broadly than has been done.

Through His Faithful Death, Jesus as Messiah Redefined Brings Life

Big Idea *In his narration of the crucifixion Matthew intertwines his affirmation of Jesus as the true king of the Jews with his use of Psalm 22 to indicate Jesus as the one who trusts God when suffering unjustly, thereby demonstrating Jesus' death as the completion of his faithful mission, a redefinition of kingship, and a cosmic life-giving event.*

Understanding the Text

The Text in Context

The crucifixion narrative (27:27–50) brings together various christological threads of Matthew's Gospel. The kingly (messianic) identity of Jesus is emphasized (27:29, 37, 40, 42, 43) and interpreted through the lens of Psalm 22 (27:31, 35, 39, 41, 46). The resulting portrait is a Messiah who willingly suffers for the sake of doing the will of God. Jesus' death also proves to be of cosmic significance, bringing life to humanity (27:52). There is great irony in this passage. Although those who crucify and taunt Jesus assume that God will not rescue him (27:42–43, 49), and though that assumption seems to be confirmed by Jesus' death (27:50), they are quite wrong. Not only will Jesus be vindicated in his resurrection (28:1–10), but also it is his death that will enact life and salvation for others (1:21; 20:28).

Interpretive Insights

27:27 *the governor's soldiers took Jesus into the Praetorium.* Pilate's soldiers carry out the death sentence that Pilate has imposed on Jesus; Pilate is unable to deflect responsibility for Jesus' death from himself (see 27:24). The Praetorium was the governor's official residence.

27:28–29 *scarlet robe . . . crown of thorns . . . staff in his right hand.* The soldiers mock Jesus by dressing him in royal attire: a scarlet robe, a crown (though of thorns), and a staff (standing in for a royal scepter). Then they kneel as they would before a king and jeer, "Hail, king of the Jews!" The irony of this scene is that readers know the identity of Jesus as king, and so they understand that what the soldiers say as mockery is actually true.

27:34 *he refused to drink it.* Jesus refuses the wine mixed with gall (*cholē*) offered to him. Gall is bitter and can refer to poison (BDAG 1056). If Matthew's reference to wine mixed with gall alludes to Psalm 69:21, then it heightens the sense of the mockery of Jesus' enemies during his crucifixion. "You know how I am scorned, disgraced and shamed; . . . my enemies . . . put gall in my food and gave me vinegar for my thirst" (Ps. 69:19, 21 [see Matt. 27:48]).

27:37 *THIS IS JESUS, THE KING OF THE JEWS.* The accusation placed over the cross is Jesus' claim to be king of the Jews. Matthew's readers know that although the Romans consider this a false charge (for them, only Caesar is king of the Jews), Jesus is the true and rightful Jewish king, the Messiah.

27:38 *Two rebels were crucified with him.* These rebels have most likely participated in some act of rebellion against Rome. The term *lēstēs* was often used for those causing insurrection. For example, according to Josephus, "bands of brigands" were responsible for "deceiving the mob" during the time of Felix's governorship of Judea (*Ant.* 20.160 [Gk. *lēstērion*, a band of rebels]). Rome crucifies Jesus, whom it considers a royal pretender and a political threat, along with other rebels.

27:40 *You who are going to destroy the temple and build it in three days.* This accusation is the same charge lodged against Jesus at his trial before the Sanhedrin (26:61).

if you are the Son of God! Matthew's ready interchange of the titles "King of Israel" (i.e., Messiah) and "Son of God" (cf. 27:40, 42, 43) indicates that he understands these to be essentially synonymous (see comments on 26:63). Jesus' claim to be the Messiah-King is thematic in the crucifixion scene.

27:46 Eli, Eli, lema sabachthani? The opening words of Psalm 22 spill from Jesus'

Key Themes of Matthew 27:27–66

- Jesus is the true king of the Jews, who trusts God when suffering unjustly.
- The death of Jesus is a cosmic event that completes his faithful mission and redefines his kingship.
- Many women and Joseph of Arimathea demonstrate faithful service.
- The possibility of Jewish mission and responsiveness continues.

mouth in his final moments of life, and Matthew provides them in Aramaic (as in Mark 15:34), along with their translation, "My God, my God, why have you forsaken me?"[1] Although Matthew has omitted or translated into Greek other Aramaic phrases from Mark (e.g., Mark 5:41 // Matt. 9:25; Mark 14:36 // Matt. 26:39), here he retains Mark's Aramaic rendering of Psalm 22:1 (with slight differences in spelling). The Aramaic is necessary to explain why some bystanders think that Jesus calls for Elijah (27:47, 49). Matthew also may retain it because these are Jesus' final words before his death, and hearing them in Jesus' mother tongue heightens the solemnity of this climactic moment.[2]

Matthew's use of Psalm 22 throughout the crucifixion scene is clearly intentional (see the sidebar "Psalm 22 in Matthew's Crucifixion Scene"). This psalm portrays the suffering of an afflicted Israelite who nonetheless trusts in God for deliverance. Drawing from this pattern, Matthew portrays Jesus as the faithful representative of Israel who trusts God despite all indications that God has left him to his enemies. In this framing of 27:46, Jesus truly laments God's apparent desertion of him while still trusting God to the end, as the psalmist does.

Psalm 22 in Matthew's Crucifixion Scene

Matthew 27	Psalm 22
"[The soldiers] mocked him" (v. 31). "[The Jewish leaders] mocked him" (v. 41).	"All who see me mock me" (v. 7).
"They . . . crucified him" (v. 35).	"They pierce my hands and my feet" (v. 16).
"They divided up his clothes by casting lots" (v. 35).	"They divide my clothes among them and cast lots for my garment (v. 18).
"Those who passed by hurled insults at him, shaking their heads" (v. 39).	"They hurl insults, shaking their heads" (v. 7).
"He trusts in God. Let God rescue him now if he wants him" (v. 43).	"He trusts in the LORD, . . . let the LORD rescue him" (v. 8).
"My God, my God, why have you forsaken me?" (v. 46).	"My God, my God, why have you forsaken me?" (v. 1).

27:49 *Let's see if Elijah comes to save him.* The name "Elijah" (*Ēlias*) sounds similar to the Aramaic word for "God" (*Ēli*), so some bystanders provide a taunt, calling for Elijah to save Jesus (also 27:47).

27:50 *he gave up his spirit.* Matthew has expanded Mark 15:37 ("breathed his last") to "gave up his spirit." Matthew's rendering might suggest a deliberate action on Jesus' part, more like the voluntary act in John's Passion Narrative (John 19:30; cf. Luke 23:46).

27:51 *the curtain of the temple was torn in two from top to bottom.* The curtain referred to here could be either the outer curtain separating the temple from its courts (making the event publicly accessible) or the inner curtain separating the most holy place from the rest of the temple (Exod. 26:31–36). Daniel Gurtner

argues that the inner curtain was torn, an apocalyptic sign granting a new kind of access to God's presence (see 1:23; 28:20) no longer tied to the temple.[3]

27:52 *The bodies of many holy people who had died were raised to life.* Apocalyptic signs accompany Jesus' death and confirm its cosmic import (see, e.g., Ps. 18:6–8, which uses earthquakes as cosmic imagery to signify historical events). Unique to Matthew is the reporting of the raising of many "holy people." It is significant that this apocalyptic sign is caused by Jesus' death, not his resurrection. One person's death brings resurrection for many (see 1 Cor. 15:21–22; Matt. 20:28). This narration of resurrection may allude to Ezekiel's vision of the dry bones. If so, Matthew understands Jesus' death as bringing about Israel's return from exile (Ezek. 37:11–14), anticipating the destruction of God's final enemy, death (see 1 Cor. 15:26).

27:54 *Surely he was the Son of God.* A Roman centurion and other guards at the crucifixion are unlikely sources of this confession. Yet Matthew has accented Gentile perceptiveness about Jesus' identity (see 2:1–12; 8:5–13; 15:21–28; 27:19), so this scene contributes to his theme of Gentile inclusion.

27:55 *Many women . . . had followed Jesus from Galilee to care for his needs.* Matthew uses the term *diakoneō* ("care for, serve") and in doing so connects the service of these women to Jesus' exhortation for his followers to serve rather than be served (20:25–28; also 8:15). They, like Jesus himself (20:28), provide a positive discipleship example for Matthew's readers.

27:56 *Mary Magdalene, Mary the mother of James and Joseph.* The name "Mary" was common in first-century

Palestine. According to Richard Bauckham's analysis, Mary was the most popular female name among Palestinian Jews.[4] As such, those with this name were often distinguished by place (e.g., Magdalene) or family relationship (e.g., the mother of James and Joseph).

27:62 *The next day, the one after Preparation Day.* Given the likelihood that Joseph completed Jesus' burial before sundown, when the Sabbath began, the next day was the Sabbath (through Saturday at sundown). Matthew may have specified "the [day] after Preparation Day" to emphasize that in this particular year the Friday on which Jesus died functioned as preparation to both the Sabbath and the Passover (with both landing on Nisan 15 [see comments on 26:17, 18, and 20]).

27:64 *This last deception will be worse than the first.* Matthew's final word about the "people" (*laos*) is not their statement at 27:25 ("his blood is on us") but rather the Jewish leaders' concern that the people might be deceived by the "rumor" that Jesus has risen (27:62–64). This demonstrates that, for Matthew, the Jewish people remain receptive to the truth about Jesus and so are included in Jesus' ongoing mission (28:19).

throughout his ministry; they are described in the same terms as the Twelve—they are "with" Jesus (8:1–3)—and are likely part of the mission of the seventy-two (10:1–20). Each Gospel testifies to women as first witnesses of the resurrection (Matt. 28:1; Mark 16:1; Luke 24:1, 10; John 20:1). Acts narrates key points where women provide leadership in the early Christian movement (e.g., Lydia in 16:11–15; Priscilla in 18:24–26). And Paul's greetings in Romans 16 illuminate female involvement in the ministry of the Roman church. About a third of the people mentioned are women (nine of twenty-six names), and a few of them are described by terms implying leadership roles: Phoebe, a "deacon of the church in Cenchreae" and "benefactor" (16:1–2 [possibly the letter's courier]); Junia, "outstanding among the apostles" (16:7); and a number of women described as Paul's "co-workers" or those who "worked very hard in the Lord."

Teaching the Text

1. *By intersecting Jesus' identity as the Messiah with the portrait of the*

Theological Insights: Women in the Early Church

At Jesus' death and burial, of those who have followed Jesus from Galilee, only the women remain with him. Luke narrates more about the women who followed Jesus

The Church of the Holy Sepulchre was built to mark the presumed site of the crucifixion and burial of Jesus.

righteous sufferer of Psalm 22, Matthew redefines the kind of kingship that Jesus embodies. A succinct title for the crucifixion scene might be "Kingship Redefined." Kings in the ancient world had absolute power over their realm; this scope of authority did not lend itself to attitudes and behaviors of divesting power in service to others. Yet

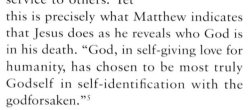

These ivory figurines from the fourteenth century AD show Christ on the cross flanked by two women who remained with him.

this is precisely what Matthew indicates that Jesus does as he reveals who God is in his death. "God, in self-giving love for humanity, has chosen to be most truly Godself in self-identification with the godforsaken."[5]

So preaching Jesus' kingship in light of the cross will have countercultural implications, even in a contemporary context that values democratic process and principles. For the kind of self-giving that characterizes Jesus' actions as he reveals who God is has no parallel. As Susan Eastman expresses it, Jesus' incarnation and way of life "culminating in self-humbling and crucifixion render visible and accessible God's character and relationship to humanity." She calls this "Christ's downward mobility."[6] Matthew has most clearly expressed this downward mobility in Jesus' words in 20:28: "The Son of Man did not come to be served, but to serve, and to give his life as a ransom for many."

2. Jesus' death has cosmic implications for humanity, as death is overcome by life.

It is quite appropriate to preach and teach that Jesus' death brings forgiveness of sins (26:28; see 1:21), and this is often the focus of preaching Jesus' death. Beyond this, Matthew demonstrates that resurrected life springs from Jesus' death (27:52). So we can preach with confidence about the life that comes to humanity from Jesus' death—not only life after death but also the hope of the bodily resurrection of all believers at that final day (what N. T. Wright refers to as "life after life after death"). And that resurrection life has somehow burst into the present through Jesus' death. As Jesus claims in John 10:10, "I have come that they may have life, and have it to the full." Jesus' death brings this fullness of life, and his resurrection confirms that we too will be raised (1 Cor. 15:20–22).

3. Matthew highlights discipleship as "being with" Jesus and serving him. Joseph of Arimathea and the women at the cross and tomb model true discipleship by serving Jesus and remaining "with Jesus" when the Twelve desert him (27:55). Matthew holds up these and other followers of Jesus as exemplars for his readers (e.g., those with [great] faith who trust Jesus for healing [8:8–10; 9:2, 22, 29; 15:28]). Preaching Matthean discipleship can include drawing on these positive portraits of discipleship to encourage those whom we teach to practice loyalty and service to Jesus.

Illustrating the Text

By intersecting Jesus' identity as the Messiah with the portrait of the righteous sufferer of Psalm 22, Matthew redefines the kind of kingship that Jesus embodies.

Popular Culture: Our culture is one that emphasizes accumulation and consolidation—of wealth, of power, of authority. Jesus, however, shows us that true life is about divesting. And we are called to join him. As we do this for Jesus' sake, we, like Jesus, trust in a God whose resources are limitless. In seeing how Jesus triumphs over death even as he gives up his life, we can have confidence to walk in the footsteps of our king.

This illustration could easily lead to application. Consider including one of the two action steps below, or create your own. It would be helpful to research your local context for specific examples of people or groups divesting their resources.

- Divest time: One of the most valuable commodities is our time. Almost everyone seems to have a to-do list that expands beyond twenty-four hours a day. In this kind of world, divesting time to serving others who cannot return the favor is a countercultural act. Volunteering in your community is one such action.

- Divest dignity: Our culture places a high premium on appearances and accolades. How might you divest yourself of the desire or opportunities for honor or status? Are there places you might serve that will help you take a humble position (see 18:2–3)?

Jesus' death has cosmic implications for humanity, as death is overcome by life.

Film: *The Princess Bride*. In this 1987 movie, two hapless friends of the hero, Westley, have carried his dead body to Miracle Max, hoping to purchase resuscitation. They are surprised to learn that Westley is only "mostly dead." Further, they are told, "mostly dead" is still "slightly alive." According to Max, when someone is "all dead," there is only one thing to do: check the deceased's pockets for loose change. Jesus, who was fully dead but has been resurrected by the living God, changes that whole equation.

Poetry: "Death Be Not Proud," by John Donne. In this triumphant poem, Donne glories in the paradox of death dying. Building toward that joyful declaration, he recognizes that death seems immutable and irresistible. But the great hope from Christ's resurrection is that in the final day death itself will be swallowed up by life. The final two lines of the poem read,

> One short sleep past, we wake
>   eternally,
> And death shall be no more; death,
>   thou shalt die.

Scripture: In the face of death and losses of all kinds, Jesus' followers can have hope of resurrection to come. As Paul reminds the church in 1 Thessalonians 4:13–14 (CEB),

> Brothers and sisters, we want you to know about people who have died so that you won't mourn like others who don't have any hope. Since we believe that Jesus died and rose, so we also believe that God will bring with him those who have died in Jesus.

The Resurrected Jesus Is Vindicated by God and Given All Authority

Big Idea *Matthew narrates Jesus' resurrection, demonstrating God's vindication and authorization of Jesus' mission, and Jesus' commission of his followers to disciple the nations through baptizing and teaching obedience to all that he has taught.*

Understanding the Text

The Text in Context

Chapter 28 narrates Jesus' resurrection (28:1–15) and his commissioning of the disciples (28:16–20). The resurrection story picks up plot elements introduced at the end of chapter 27, including the presence of certain women at the cross and the tomb (27:56, 61; 28:1), the placing of guards at the tomb (27:62–66; 28:4), and an earthquake (27:51–52; 28:2). The women and the eleven disciples encounter the risen Jesus and worship him (28:9, 17), concluding the Gospel as it began, with worship of Jesus (2:2, 11). In the final scene Matthew asserts that Jesus, who has demonstrated messianic authority in his healings and miracles (e.g., chaps. 8–9), now is given "all authority" (28:18). The mission that Jesus gives to his disciples now includes "all nations" (28:19; cf. 10:5–6), culminating the theme of Gentile inclusion (e.g., 1:3, 5–6; 2:1; 4:15). And the promise of Jesus' presence with his followers to the "very end of the age" links to the description of Jesus as "God with us" (1:23).

"I know that you are looking for Jesus, who was crucified. He is not here; he has risen" (28:5–6). Corpses were typically placed on a bench or slab like the U-shaped one shown here in this first-century AD family tomb on the Mount of Olives.

Interpretive Insights

28:2 *There was a violent earthquake.* As Jesus' death was accompanied by the earth shaking (*seiō* [27:51]), so an earthquake (*seismos*) attends his resurrection. Matthew thereby indicates the cosmic implications of Jesus' death and resurrection.

28:6 *He is not here; he has risen, just as he said.* This affirmation of Jesus' prediction of his resurrection picks up the three passion predictions in 16:21; 17:22–23; 20:17–19, each of which mentions Jesus' resurrection.

28:7 *go quickly and tell his disciples.* It would have been noteworthy to Matthew's original audience that women were the first witnesses to Jesus' resurrection, given that male testimony was considered preferable to female witness, since women were considered weaker in character and less rational than men and so less reliable (e.g., Josephus, *Ant.* 4.219; cf. Origen, *Cels.* 2.55).

28:9 *They . . . clasped his feet and worshiped him.* Matthew highlights worship of Jesus by the women and the eleven disciples after his resurrection (28:9, 17). In and of itself, resurrection of a person does not compel worship (i.e., it does not prove divinity), but Jesus' resurrection in light of the link with his future vindication by God (see 16:28; 26:64; Dan. 7:13–14) means for Matthew that Jesus participates in the divine identity and is worthy of worship (see comments on 28:18).

28:10 *Go and tell my brothers to go to Galilee; there they will see me.* Jesus has offered future hope of reconciliation with his disciples when he predicts that they will desert him (26:32). Here that restoration is intimated by his reference to the eleven as his "brothers."

28:12 *the chief priests had met with the elders.* Even at the end of the Gospel the chief priests and elders continue to attempt to derail Jesus' ministry and mission (cf. 21:23; 26:3, 47; 27:1, 12). They bribe the soldiers to falsely attribute Jesus' missing body to a plot hatched by his disciples.

28:15 *And this story has been widely circulated among the Jews to this very day.* With this comment, Matthew steps outside the story world of the narrative and speaks more directly to his audience. The evangelist's use of "Jews" distinct from his own community finds precedent in Josephus's use of the same term for part of the Jewish people.[1]

28:17 *When they saw him, they worshiped him; but some doubted.* The eleven disciples respond ambivalently to Jesus: they worship, but some also doubt.[2] The nature of their doubt is not indicated (e.g., some have suggested that they wonder if it is really Jesus because his resurrected body is not fully recognizable to them). So it might be most consistent exegetically to interpret this doubt (*distazō*) as a further expression of the disciples' characterization as those of "little faith," since the only other occurrence of the word occurs at 14:31, where it is defined by "little faith" (*oligopistos*). Even in this climactic scene of Matthew's Gospel, the disciples are not those of exemplary faith, but they do rightly worship Jesus (cf. 14:33). By portraying the disciples in worship here, Matthew begins and ends his narrative with people worshiping Jesus (2:2, 11).

28:18 *All authority in heaven and on earth has been given to me.* Matthew has identified Jesus with the "son of man" figure from Daniel at key narrative points (e.g., 10:23; 16:28; 24:30; 26:64). Daniel 7:13–14 is also evoked here with Jesus' reference to "all authority" being "given" to him (*edothē . . . exousia* [Dan. 7:14 LXX; Matt. 28:18]) and also in the reference to "all the nations" (Dan. 7:14; Matt. 28:19). The universal authority given to Jesus upon his resurrection/vindication implies his inclusion in the divine identity, given that universal authority is something attributed to God alone in the Jewish Scriptures.[3]

28:19–20 *go and make disciples of all nations.* The key exhortation Jesus gives to his disciples is to "disciple" the nations, with the verbal form used here (*mathēteuō* [also 13:52; 27:57; cf. Acts 14:21]). All the accompanying verbs ("go," "baptize," "teach") are participles in the Greek text and so attend or augment Jesus' primary command to disciple the nations. The inclusive reference to "all nations" (*panta ta ethnē* [see 25:32]) indicates that the scope of the church's mission is universal (mirroring the scope of Jesus' authority in 28:18). The apostolic mission during Jesus' ministry

After rising from the dead, Jesus meets with his disciples on a mountain in Galilee. The resurrected Christ stands with a group of his disciples in this scene from an ivory box (Rome, AD 420–30).

was limited to Israel (10:5–6, 23; 15:24), but the church's mission after his resurrection includes both Jew and Gentile (see comments on 25:32).

baptizing . . . and teaching. Jesus' commission to disciple all the nations involves two activities of ministry: baptizing and teaching. Baptism is a sign of covenantal inclusion and so initiates a person into identification with the Messiah and into the messianic community. Teaching constitutes a central aspect of discipling, as understood in a Jewish context in which disciples would study and learn under a teacher or leader.[4] Teaching has also been an important aspect of Matthew's Christology; Jesus is portrayed as the consummate teacher (e.g., 7:28–29).

in the name of the Father and of the Son and of the Holy Spirit. This trinitarian baptism formula is clearly rooted in a monotheistic sensibility. The reference to "the name" (*to onoma*) is singular followed by the tripartite distinction "Father, Son, and Holy Spirit," indicating the Christian affirmation of the name of the one God.

teaching them to obey everything I have commanded you. Jesus' reference to everything that he has commanded certainly refers to all teachings that Matthew has included in his Gospel. Yet given Matthew's careful arrangement of Jesus' teaching primarily into five major discourses (chaps. 5–7, 10, 13, 18, 24–25), these discourses are likely brought to mind for the reader here. Jesus' kingdom teachings are to be obeyed by his followers as they live out their covenant loyalty to and with Jesus. Although Jesus has commended faithful obedience to the Law and the Prophets throughout his ministry, after his resurrection a development occurs so that it is Jesus' teachings—themselves a true expression of the Torah—that are to guide the lives of his disciples.

And surely I am with you always, to the very end of the age. Matthew's concluding line promises Jesus' presence to his followers, providing a frame to the whole Gospel that began by introducing Jesus as "God with us" (1:23; see also 18:20). Jesus' presence ensures the success of the disciples' ministry of baptizing and teaching, since it is Jesus himself who will be with them in mission. "Jesus' effective presence . . . is the final assurance that his teaching will be both preserved and spread to all the nations."[5] Jesus has spoken of the authority that the Twelve and the church will receive (16:19; 18:18). In this commissioning scene it becomes clear that their authority is a derivative one. Jesus, who has been given all authority, goes with them, so that they participate in his authority only as they remain with him and follow his lead.

Theological Insights: Jesus and Divine Prerogatives

Matthew asserts that Jesus is granted universal lordship upon his resurrection (28:18; cf. 11:27). According to Richard Bauckham, this is one of two central divine prerogatives (only God holds them) that, according to the New Testament writers, belong to Jesus. In this way, Jesus the Messiah is portrayed as sharing in the divine identity.[6] Other New Testament texts that affirm Jesus' universal authority include John 3:35; 13:3; 16:15; 1 Corinthians 15:27–28; Philippians 3:21. Worship of Jesus is often a counterpart to his universal authority, as seen at Philippians 2:9–11. Matthew emphasizes worship of Jesus by beginning and concluding his Gospel with Jesus being worshiped (2:2, 11; 28:9, 17), tying worship to his universal authority at 28:17–18. The second divine prerogative, according to Bauckham, is participation in creation. This prerogative, exercised by the Son, is highlighted in John 1:1–4; 1 Corinthians 8:6; Colossians 1:15–17; Hebrews 1:3.

Teaching the Text

1. *Jesus' resurrection is the sign of God's vindication of Jesus' identity and mission as the Messiah.* Matthew has highlighted Daniel 7:13–14 at a number of key points in his Gospel to indicate that Jesus understood himself as the "son of man" from Daniel's vision who would be vindicated by God and given universal authority. Jesus has connected his time of vindication with his resurrection (16:28; 26:64), and Matthew affirms this connection in chapter 28, where Jesus is resurrected and given "all authority in heaven and on earth" (28:18). We can know that Jesus is God's true Messiah because of his resurrection to universal reign.

So how does this help us preach Jesus' resurrection? Modernist suspicions about the miraculous, including and especially resurrection, have often set the agenda for preaching Jesus' resurrection primarily in apologetic terms, with the goal being proofs for it. This is not inappropriate, but an apologetic for the resurrection is not at the heart of what Matthew provides. He is much more interested in the meaning of the resurrection for his Christology. And understanding Jesus' resurrection as his vindication by God gets at this meaning. Jesus' resurrection shows us that he is the Messiah, and that his particular way of living out that messianic mission—in service and death for others—is God's way of making all things right and ushering in the kingdom. And that is a message that we can preach all year long, not simply at Easter time.

2. *Jesus, as universal king and Lord, promises his presence to his followers and is worthy of their worship.* The promise of Jesus' presence with his followers to "the very end of the age" is eminently teachable. Given a certain tension in the New Testament between Jesus' absence after his ascension (e.g., John 16:5–7) and his involvement in the life of the church (e.g., Acts 16:7), Matthew's thematic offering of Jesus as God with us (1:23; 18:20; 28:20) is a rich resource for helping the church conceive of living in light of Jesus' presence in the present.

3. *Matthew calls people to respond to Jesus as Messiah and Lord by following him in discipleship.* As Michael Wilkins expresses it, "To 'be discipled' means that one who is a disciple continues to learn from Jesus about the kingdom of heaven (13:52; 27:57)."[7] The metaphor of following lends itself to

understand Christian faith as a journey. Learning from Jesus, or what Luke Johnson calls "learning Jesus," is a lifelong endeavor and commitment based on God's initiative in our lives. As Johnson expresses it,

> We are pursuing the implications of a strong belief in the resurrection for knowledge of Jesus. If we are dealing not with a dead person of the past but with a person whose life continues, however mysteriously, in the present, then it is better to speak of "learning Jesus" than of "knowing Jesus." We are concerned with a *process* rather than a *product*.[8]

Illustrating the Text

Jesus' resurrection is the sign of God's vindication of Jesus' identity and mission as the Messiah.

Quote: N. T. Wright, in *Matthew for Everyone*, sums up nicely the way that Jesus' resurrection helps to interpret the whole of Matthew and vindicates Jesus' identity and mission.

> Take away the resurrection of Jesus . . . and you leave Matthew without a gospel. The cross is the climax of his story, but it only makes the sense it does as the cross of the one who was then raised from the dead. The great discourses of the gospel—the

According to Matthew 28:1–6, the stone is rolled away and the tomb is empty, confirming Jesus' identity as Messiah and God's vindication of him. Shown here is a first-century AD rolling-stone tomb in lower Galilee.

Sermon on the Mount, and all the rest—are his way of saying that Jesus is . . . Israel's Messiah. He is the one who is giving Israel and the world the new Law through which God's new way of being human has been unveiled before the world. But all this is true only because the one who proclaimed God's blessings on his followers, the one who announced God's woes on those who went their own ways, and the one who spoke God's kingdom-message in parables, is now the risen Lord.[9]

Jesus, as universal king and Lord, promises his presence to his followers and is worthy of their worship.

Quote: Richard Fox provides an interesting, alternate perspective on the commonplace question "What would Jesus do?"

Evangelical Protestants like to ask, "What would Jesus do?" but many Catholics and non-evangelical Protestants prefer to ask, "What does Jesus do?" In their eyes Christ makes his body and his Holy Spirit available to believers in the sacraments, and he models selfless surrender to his Father's will. Since the nineteenth century, Word-centered Protestant evangelicals have focused on Jesus as speaker and doer, not mystical presence or submissive servant.[10]

Holding both visions—Jesus as speaker and doer and Jesus as presence with us—would resonate with Matthew's christological portrayal.

Summary: 16:21–28:20. Matthew portrays Jesus setting out toward Jerusalem and predicting his impending suffering, death, and resurrection. While they travel to Jerusalem, Jesus teaches his disciples about a way of living that adequately reflects the reality of the kingdom in his ministry and mission. It is a way of life that renounces status and position in order to serve others in the believing community, especially the little ones and the least of these. Jesus rides into Jerusalem as a peaceable and humble king and demonstrates his messianic authority over the temple and the Jewish leaders. These leaders plot his demise, as he answers all their challenges and tests with wisdom and God-given authority. Jesus predicts the destruction of the temple and links that event to his coming vindication by God. As the Passover arrives, Jesus celebrates and redefines that festival by reference to his coming death and resurrection. Throughout his arrest, trials, and crucifixion, Jesus remains the faithful son who gives his life as "a ransom for many." His resurrection demonstrates God's vindication of his mission and message.

Notes

Introduction to Matthew

1. The story line or plot is one aspect of a narrative analysis. Another important part of narrative study of a Gospel is how the story is told—that is, attention to characterization, point of view, and use of stylistic devices. See J. K. Brown, *Scripture as Communication*, 157–63.

2. Green, *Luke*, 19.

3. J. K. Brown, *Scripture as Communication*, 246–50. Generally speaking, it is important to evaluate whether an application of a biblical text has enough consistency with that particular text (coherence) and whether the application fulfills the original goals of the text (purpose).

4. Donald Hagner (*Matthew*, 1:xlv–xlvi), however, considers the *logia* to refer to sayings of Jesus unique to Matthew's Gospel.

5. So Gundry, *Matthew*, 619.

6. Hagner, *Matthew*, 1:lxxvii.

7. Throughout the commentary Matthew will be referred to as the author, with the focus being on the implied author. "The implied author is the author that can be known through the reading of the narrative alone . . . the one who tells the story using various narrative devices to communicate with and persuade the implied reader" (J. K. Brown, *Disciples in Narrative Perspective*, 36).

8. Luz, *Matthew*, 1:58–59.

9. Garland, *Reading Matthew*, 3.

10. Carter, *Matthew*, 15–16.

11. Saldarini, *Christian-Jewish Community*, 7–8.

12. Luz, *Matthew*, 1:50; Stanton, *Gospel for a New People*, 139–40.

13. Bauckham, *Gospels for All Christians*.

14. See M. M. Thompson, "Holy Internet."

15. Matthew's unique expression "kingdom of heaven" (*basileia tōn ouranon*) is used essentially synonymously with "kingdom of God" while possibly heightening the heavenly origin of the kingdom (on the latter point, see Pennington, *Heaven and Earth*). The latter is used a few times in Matthew and extensively in Mark and Luke, often in parallel contexts to Matthew's "kingdom of heaven" (e.g., Matt. 3:2 // Mark 1:15; Matt. 19:23 // Mark 10:23).

16. The title "Son of God" likely points to Jesus as the Messiah (and as representative Israel); see discussion at 4:3, 6.

17. Bauckham, *God Crucified*, viii. See also Jesus' identification with Yahweh in citations from Isaiah 40:3 at Matthew 3:3 and from Malachi 3:1 in Matthew 11:10.

18. Hurtado, *Lord Jesus Christ*, 338.

Matthew 1:1–17

1. Wright, *New Testament*, 268–72.

2. Against this notion, see Cohick, *Women*, 155–56.

3. William Davies and Dale Allison point out that the author of the First Gospel appears to have a penchant for "scattering items in his Greek text whose deeper meaning could only be appreciated by those with a knowledge of Hebrew" (*Matthew*, 1:279). They cite 1:21; 2:23 as additional examples.

4. Bauer, "Function of the Genealogy," 156.

Matthew 1:18–25

1. Jeremias, *Jerusalem*, 364–68. For the importance of and help with discerning the dating and relevance of rabbinic materials for the New Testament, see Instone-Brewer, *Traditions*, 1:28–40.

2. Keener, *Matthew*, 91.

3. On the latter emphasis and the translation issues between the Hebrew text of Isaiah 7:14 (*'almā*, "young woman") and the Septuagint's rendering that Matthew draws upon (*parthenos*, "virgin"), see France, *Matthew*, 55–58.

4. What Raymond Brown refers to as "legal paternity" (*Birth of the Messiah*, 138–39). See *m. B. Bat.* 8:6.

Matthew 2:1–23

1. The Hasmoneans were the dynasty of Jewish priest-kings who ruled in Israel following the successful revolt of the Maccabees against the Syrian king Antiochus IV (166–64 BC).

2. "Herod" is a family name, so it is not surprising that more than one of Herod the Great's offspring bore that name.

3. See also examples from Greco-Roman and midrashic Jewish literature in Powell, *Chasing the Eastern Star*, 138–43.

4. Ibid., 147.

5. Nolland, *Matthew*, 128.

6. Davies and Allison, *Matthew*, 1:278–79.

7. J. K. Brown, "Matthew," 959.

Matthew 3:1–17

1. Everett Ferguson, "Baptism," *DJG* 66.

2. Keener, *Spirit in the Gospels*, 93.

3. Ferguson, "Baptism."

4. Bauckham, *God Crucified*, 219.

5. For a helpful discussion of this topic, see Lynn Cohick, "Pharisees," *DJG* 673–79.

6. Keener, "'Brood of Vipers,'" 11.

7. Saldarini, *Christian-Jewish Community*, 7.

8. See the chapter "The Holy Spirit," in Brown and Roberts, *Matthew*.

9. Note that *dikaiosynē* occurs in synonymous parallelism with "salvation" (*sōtēria/sōtērion*) in a number of Old Testament texts (e.g., Isa. 46:13; 51:6; 63:1). See Hagner, *Matthew*, 1:56.

10. J. K. Brown, "Justice, Righteousness," *DJG* 463–67.

11. In addition, Matthew has changed the "you" in Mark 1:11 to third person, as in Isaiah 42.

12. See Brown, Dahl, and Reuschling, *Whole and Holy*, 72–76.

13. Quoted in Becknell and Ashcroft, *Beginning of Wisdom*, 141.

14. For an example, see http://www.textweek.com/art/baptism_of_Jesus.htm.

15. Jerry Sittser, *The Adventure: Putting Energy into Your Walk with God* (Downers Grove, IL: InterVarsity, 1985), 44.

Matthew 4:1–11

1. C. S. Lewis, *The Screwtape Letters* (New York: Macmillan, 1958), chap. 21.

Matthew 4:12–16

1. France, *Matthew*, 6.

2. Mark Twain, *The Adventures of Tom Sawyer*, in *Mississippi Writings*, The Library of America (New York: Library of America, 1982), 194.

Matthew 4:17–25

1. Pennington, *Heaven and Earth*. The use of the plural "heavens" in this phrase in the Greek likely reflects the linguistic reality that "heaven" occurs in the plural in the Hebrew Scriptures.

2. See Anders Runesson, "Synagogue," *DJG* 903–10; Keener, *Matthew*, 156–57.

3. For example, Carter, *Matthew*, 3.

4. Wright, *Challenge of Jesus*, 178.

Matthew 5:1–16

1. Hagner, *Matthew*, 1:91. As Hagner notes, "In Israel . . . poverty and piety often went together, the poor . . . having no other recourse than their hope in God."

2. Carter, *Matthew*, 133.

3. Powell, "Matthew's Beatitudes," 467. Hagner (*Matthew*, 1:93) concurs that justice is the correct sense of *dikaiosynē* in this context.

4. Garlington, "Salt of the Earth."

5. Simonetti, *Matthew 1–13*, 79.

6. The stuffed animals that formed the basis of A. A. Milne's stories about the Hundred Acre Wood are kept at the New York Public Library (http://www.nypl.org/locations/tid/36/node/5557).

Matthew 5:17–48

1. Snodgrass, "Matthew and the Law."

2. J. K. Brown, "Matthew," 965.

3. France, *Matthew*, 192n48.

4. BDAG 903.

5. Wink, "Beyond Just War," 200; Carter, *Matthew*, 150–54.

6. Keener, *Matthew*, 203.

7. Brown, Dahl, and Reuschling, *Whole and Holy*, 93–97.

8. Victor Hugo, *Les Misérables*, trans. Julie Rose, Modern Library Classics (New York: Modern Library, 2009), 90.

9. C. Timothy Floyd, "Giving Aid and Comfort to the Enemy: A Surgeon's View of the War in Iraq," *AAOS Now* 5, no. 2 (2011): http://www.aaos.org/news/aaosnow/feb11/youraaos5.asp.

Matthew 6:1–18

1. This is clearly a Matthean theme, with the word "hypocrite" (*hypokritēs*) occurring thirteen times in Matthew (Mark: 1; Luke: 3; John: 0).

2. David M. Crump, "Prayer," *DJG* 688.

3. Keener, *Matthew*, 227.

4. Johnson, *Prophetic Jesus*, 124.

5. Christopher Webber, ed., *Give Us Grace: An Anthology of Anglican Prayers* (Harrisburg, PA: Morehouse, 2004), 359 (italics added).

Matthew 6:19–34

1. France, *Matthew*, 260.

2. Green, *Luke*, 465.

3. For the model derived from Steven Friesen and Bruce Longenecker's adjustments to it, see Longenecker, "Economic Middle." This model is a heuristic device for understanding urban life in the first-century world. Adjustments would inevitably be needed for its application to rural or village settings and/or to specific regions such as Galilee, as Longenecker notes.

4. Ibid., 269.

5. For the coupling of "cubit" with time/age, see BDAG 812.

6. Dennis Linn, Sheila Fabricant Linn, and Mathew Linn, *Sleeping with Bread: Holding What Gives You Life* (Mahwah, NJ: Paulist Press, 1995), 1.

Matthew 7:1–12

1. Keener, *Matthew*, 243.
2. Carter, *Matthew*, 182.
3. See Wilkins, *Matthew*, 313–14. Wilkins (315) also provides a number of other parallels outside Judaism.
4. See Brown, Dahl, and Reuschling, *Whole and Holy*, 80–82.
5. J. D. Salinger, *The Catcher in the Rye* (New York: Little, Brown, 1951), 19.

Matthew 7:13–29

1. Hagner, *Matthew*, 1:305.
2. France, *Matthew*, 294.
3. See Wright, *Surprised by Hope*.
4. Lambrecht, *Out of the Treasure*, 29.
5. Wilkins, *Matthew*, 328.

Matthew 8:1–17

1. The contrast derives from the fact that the pronoun is not needed in Greek because it is indicated in the form of the verb, *therapeusō* ("[I] will heal"). Note the use of Greek pronouns to indicate contrast at 3:11: "I [*egō*] . . . he [*autos*] . . .").
2. Episcopal Church, *The Book of Common Prayer* (New York: Church Publishing, 1979), 461.

Matthew 8:18–9:8

1. There are a number of text-critical options regarding the location that Matthew designates. Some manuscripts read "Gerasenes," located thirty-three miles from the Sea of Galilee; others read "Gergesenes," located on the seashore.
2. G. K. Chesterton, *Orthodoxy* (1908; repr., San Francisco: Ignatius, 1995), 65–66.

Matthew 9:9–34

1. Levine, "Discharging Responsibility," 387.
2. David Kinnaman and Gabe Lyons, *unchristian: What a New Generation Really Thinks about Christianity—and Why It Matters* (Grand Rapids: Baker Books, 2007), 146.

Matthew 9:35–10:23

1. J. K. Brown, "Apostle," 471.
2. Keener, *Matthew*, 320.
3. Henri J. M. Nouwen, *In the Name of Jesus: Reflections on Christian Leadership* (New York: Crossroad, 1989), 67.
4. Corrie ten Boom, *The Hiding Place* (Peabody, MA: Hendrickson, 2009), 240.

Matthew 10:24–11:1

1. Jeffers, *Greco-Roman World*, 221.

2. J. K. Brown, "Direct Engagement."
3. J. K. Brown, "Matthew," 973.
4. J. K. Brown, "Matthew's 'Least of These' Theology," 293–94.
5. Davies and Allison, *Matthew*, 2:239.
6. So Weaver, *Matthew's Missionary Discourse*, 152–53.
7. As recorded in Kenneth W. Osbeck, *25 Most Treasured Gospel Hymn Stories* (Grand Rapids: Kregel, 1999), 41–42; Jane Stuart Smith and Betty Carlson, *Great Christian Hymn Writers* (Wheaton: Crossway, 1997), 193.
8. See http://www.ecclesia.org/truth/martyrdom.html.

Matthew 11:2–19

1. Nolland's translation (*Matthew*, 453) and interpretation (457–58).
2. J. K. Brown, "Rhetoric of Hearing," 268.

Matthew 11:20–30

1. Cornelis Bennema, "Wisdom," *DJG* 998.
2. M. M. Thompson, *Colossians and Philemon*, 30.
3. Charles Dickens, preface to *A Christmas Carol*, in *Dickens' Christmas Spirits: "A Christmas Carol" and Other Tales* (1843; reprint, Mineola, NY: Dover, 2010), 3.

Matthew 12:1–14

1. Also Davies and Allison, *Matthew*, 2:314.
2. Levine, *Misunderstood Jew*, 125.

Matthew 12:15–21

1. For a study on this theme, see J. K. Brown, "Rhetoric of Hearing."
2. Neyrey, "Thematic Use of Isaiah," 461.
3. Beaton, *Isaiah's Christ*, 165.
4. http://usnews.nbcnews.com/_news/2012/10/18/1453 6848-hikers-rescued-from-montana-wilderness-describe -six-day-ordeal (accessed March 18, 2014).

Matthew 12:22–50

1. Davies and Allison, *Matthew*, 2:195–96.
2. Timmer, *Four-Dimensional Jesus*, 41.
3. For a definition and description of repentance derived from the biblical story, see Brown, Dahl, and Reuschling, *Whole and Holy*, 72, 77.

Matthew 13:1–23

1. J. K. Brown, "Rhetoric of Hearing."
2. Ibid.
3. Thiselton, *Thiselton on Hermeneutics*, 517.
4. NIV footnote rendering.

Matthew 13:24–53

1. J. K. Brown, *Disciples in Narrative Perspective*, 110–11.
2. The video available through PBS: http://video.pbs .org/video/2179152804/.
3. Johnson, *Living Jesus*, 195.
4. Ibid., 197.

5. Barbara Brown Taylor, *Leaving Church: A Memoir of Faith* (New York: HarperCollins, 2006), 111.

Matthew 13:54–14:12

1. Hagner, *Matthew*, 2:411.
2. France, *Matthew*, 553.
3. For the motif of fear in Matthew, see J. K. Brown, *Disciples in Narrative Perspective*, 142–45.
4. Schweitzer, *Quest*, 397 (italics added).
5. Scot McKnight, "The Jesus We'll Never Know," *Christianity Today* (April 9, 2010): http://www.christianitytoday.com/ct/2010/april/15.22.html (accessed March 20, 2014).

Matthew 14:13–36

1. Verseput, "Faith of the Reader," 15.
2. Timothy Keller, *The Reason for God: Belief in an Age of Skepticism* (New York: Dutton, 2008), 234.

Matthew 15:1–20

1. France, *Matthew*, 580–81.
2. See J. K. Brown, "Rhetoric of Hearing."
3. And Matthew does intimate this movement when the resurrected Jesus calls his followers to obey "everything I have commanded," not the Torah itself (28:20 [see comments there]).
4. deSilva, *Honor*, 244.
5. Parker J. Palmer, *A Hidden Wholeness: The Journey toward an Undivided Life; Welcoming the Soul and Weaving Community in a Wounded World* (San Francisco: Jossey-Bass, 2004), 8.

Matthew 15:21–39

1. Davies and Allison, *Matthew*, 2:546.
2. J. K. Brown, "Genesis in Matthew's Gospel," 57.
3. Matthew adds to his Markan source (Mark 7:26–27) Jesus' initial silence, his disciples' plea to dismiss the woman, and his statement about being sent only to the lost sheep of Israel.
4. For more examples, see Davies and Allison, *Matthew*, 2:569.
5. Verseput, "Faith of the Reader," 19.
6. C. S. Lewis, *The Lion, the Witch and the Wardrobe* (1950; repr., New York: HarperCollins, 2005), 80.

Matthew 16:1–20

1. J. K. Brown, *Disciples in Narrative Perspective*, 105–6.
2. For an expansion of this idea, see Knowles, *Jeremiah in Matthew's Gospel*, 81–95.
3. Powell, "Binding and Loosing," 438.
4. J. K. Brown, *Disciples in Narrative Perspective*, 138–42.

Matthew 16:21–28

1. "Cruciformity" refers to the way of the cross, characterized by serving others rather than self. The word is related to the verb "crucify" and so refers to a "cross-shaped" way of life. See Gorman, *Cruciformity*.

2. Wright, *Challenge of Jesus*, 94.
3. Miroslav Volf, *Exclusion and Embrace: A Theological Exploration of Identity, Otherness, and Reconciliation* (Nashville: Abingdon, 1996), 92.

Matthew 17:1–13

1. Allison, *New Moses*.
2. J. K. Brown, *Disciples in Narrative Perspective*, 63–64.
3. Roland Barthes, *The Responsibility of Forms: Critical Essays on Music, Art, and Representation*, trans. Richard Howard (New York: Hill & Wang, 1985), 245.
4. Wright, *Matthew for Everyone*, 2:15.

Matthew 17:14–27

1. J. K. Brown, *Disciples in Narrative Perspective*, 47–48.
2. Verseput, "Jesus' Pilgrimage," 111.
3. J. K. Brown, "Matthew," 985.

Matthew 18:1–20

1. J. K. Brown, "Direct Engagement."
2. Wiedemann, *Adults and Children*, chap. 1.
3. Davies and Allison, *Matthew*, 2:757.
4. J. K. Brown, "Matthew's 'Least of These' Theology," 294.
5. Stein, *Interpreting the Bible*, 185.
6. J. K. Brown, *Disciples in Narrative Perspective*, 72n49.
7. J. K. Brown, "Matthew," 988.

Matthew 18:21–35

1. J. K. Brown, "Genesis in Matthew's Gospel," 50–51.
2. See the helpful distinctions and definitions provided by Shults and Sandage, *Faces of Forgiveness*, 204–5.

Matthew 19:1–26

1. J. K. Brown, "Genesis in Matthew's Gospel," 45.
2. For another possibility related to marriages of kinship forbidden in Judaism but allowed in non-Jewish contexts, see Garland, *Reading Matthew*, 69–70.
3. As Craig Keener notes, "in most of Palestinian Judaism only the husband could initiate divorce" ("Adultery, Divorce," *DNTB* 6).
4. J. K. Brown, *Disciples in Narrative Perspective*, 78.
5. Manning, *Ragamuffin Gospel*, 17–18.

Matthew 19:27–20:16

1. France, *Matthew*, 745.
2. Brown, Dahl, and Reuschling, *Whole and Holy*, 82.
3. Manning, *Ragamuffin Gospel*, 23–24.

Matthew 20:17–28

1. For a review of the interpretive options, see Carter, *Matthew*, 392–93.
2. J. K. Brown, *Disciples in Narrative Perspective*, 90.
3. Luz, *Matthew*, 2:545.
4. http://www.nobelprize.org/nobel_prizes/peace/laureates/1979/teresa-bio.html (accessed March 26, 2014).

5. "Vatican Suspends German Bishop Accused of Lavish Spending on Himself," http://www.nytimes.com/2013/10/24/world/europe/vatican-suspends-german-bishop-known-for-spending.html?_r=1& (accessed March 26, 2014).

Matthew 20:29–21:11

1. France, *Matthew*, 776.
2. Davies and Allison, *Matthew*, 3:126.

Matthew 21:12–22

1. Davies and Allison, *Matthew*, 3:136.
2. Keener, *Matthew*, 497.
3. France, *Matthew*, 784.
4. Ibid., 788.
5. Wright, *Jesus and the Victory of God*, 334–35.
6. Perrin, *Jesus the Temple*, 47.
7. Hauerwas, *Matthew*, 182–83.

Matthew 21:23–22:14

1. Setha Low, *Behind the Gates: Life, Security, and the Pursuit of Happiness in Fortress America* (New York: Routledge, 2003), 149.
2. John Stott, *Authentic Christianity*, ed. Timothy Dudley-Smith (Downers Grove, IL: InterVarsity, 1995), 327.

Matthew 22:15–46

1. Davies and Allison, *Matthew*, 3:216.
2. J. K. Brown, "Genesis in Matthew's Gospel," 46–47.
3. Wright, *Resurrection*, 415–23.
4. Snodgrass, "Matthew and the Law," 108.
5. Gary Burge, "Commandment," *DJG* 151.
6. Snodgrass, "Matthew and the Law," 111.

Matthew 23:1–12

1. Powell, "What Moses Says."
2. Ibid., 431–32.
3. Davies and Allison, *Matthew*, 3:273.
4. Pliny, *Epistolae* 2.6, trans. Betty Radice, Loeb Classical Library 55 (Cambridge: Harvard University Press, 1969), 95–97, quoted in Gordon D. Fee, *1 Corinthians*, New International Commentary on the New Testament (Grand Rapids: Eerdmans, 1987), 542.

Matthew 23:13–39

1. Stein, *Method and Message*, 13.
2. Keener, "'Brood of Vipers,'" 9.
3. J. K. Brown, "Genesis in Matthew," 52. On the possible conflation of the two Zechariahs (2 Chron. 24:20; Zech. 1:1), see Nolland, *Matthew*, 946–47.
4. Hamilton, "'His Blood Be upon Us,'" 86.
5. Garland, *Reading Matthew*, 236.
6. Ibid., 232.
7. Marshall, "Who Is a Hypocrite?"
8. Bruce Watson, "Science Makes a Better Lighthouse Lens," *Smithsonian* 30 (August 1999), http://www.smithsonianmag.com/science-nature/object_aug99.html?c=y&page=2 (accessed on 03/28/13).

Matthew 24:1–35

1. France, *Matthew*, 902.
2. Ibid., 903.
3. Garland, *Reading Matthew*, 242.
4. France, *Matthew*, 917.
5. Wright, *New Testament*, 333.
6. Hays, *Moral Vision*, 188.
7. J. K. Brown, *Scripture as Communication*, 243.
8. Wright, *Matthew for Everyone*, 2:115.

Matthew 24:36–25:13

1. See Davies and Allison, *Matthew*, 3:390.
2. Keener, *Matthew*, 596.
3. France, *Matthew*, 948.
4. Calvin Miller, *The Philippian Fragment* (Downers Grove, IL: InterVarsity, 1982), 65.
5. Ibid., 66.

Matthew 25:14–46

1. Gutiérrez, *Theology of Liberation*, 202.
2. France, *Matthew*, 959.
3. See J. K. Brown, "Matthew's 'Least of These' Theology," 293–94.
4. For example, Ulrich Luz ("Final Judgment," 308) argues that this is the text's original sense.
5. Hultgren, *Parables of Jesus*, 321.
6. Luz, "Final Judgment," 310.
7. Davies and Allison, *Matthew*, 3:405.
8. For an analysis of sermons on Matthew 25:31–46 that do just that, see J. K. Brown, "Matthew's 'Least of These' Theology."
9. Ibid., 296–98.
10. Gutiérrez, *Theology of Liberation*, 202.
11. Shane Claiborne, "The Great Divide," *Relevant* 45 (May 5, 2010): 84–85.

Matthew 26:1–30

1. France, *Matthew*, 981.
2. See France, *Matthew*, 981–85; J. K. Brown, "New Testament Chronology," *DTIB* 113–14.
3. For the thematic and linguistic connections to Isaiah 53, see France, *Matthew*, 994.
4. Wright, *Matthew for Everyone*, 2:156–57.
5. Schmemann, *Life of the World*, 26–27.
6. Wright, *Evil and the Justice of God*, 90.

Matthew 26:31–75

1. Keener, *Matthew*, 614–16.
2. Nolland, *Matthew*, 1131.
3. Bock, *Blasphemy and Exaltation*, 111.
4. Ibid., 111–12.
5. An issue of translation is whether the Greek *pistis Christou* is best translated as "faith in Christ" or "the faithfulness of Christ" (e.g., see NIV footnote on Rom. 3:22).
6. Brown, Dahl, and Reuschling, *Whole and Holy*, 79.

Matthew 27:1–26

1. Keener, *Matthew*, 668–70.

2. According to Richard Bauckham (*Jesus and the Eyewitnesses*, 85), "Jesus" was the sixth most popular male name among Palestinian Jews in the period 330 BC–AD 200.

3. France, *Matthew*, 1046n4.

4. Saldarini, *Christian-Jewish Community*, 33.

5. Levine, *Misunderstood Jew*, 21.

6. Jeremy Cohen, *Christ Killers: The Jews and the Passion from the Bible to the Big Screen* (New York: Oxford University Press, 2007).

7. Karl Barth, *Church Dogmatics* IV/1 (Edinburgh: T&T Clark, 1956), 166–67.

8. Eric J. Wittenberg and J. David Petruzzi. *Plenty of Blame to Go Around: Jeb Stuart's Controversial Ride to Gettysburg* (New York: Savas Beatie, 2006).

Matthew 27:27–66

1. There is some debate over whether "Eli, Eli" is Aramaic or Hebrew.

2. Davies and Allison, *Matthew*, 3:624.

3. Gurtner, *Torn Veil*, 199–201.

4. Data gathered from sources between 330 BC and AD 200 (Bauckham, *Jesus and the Eyewitnesses*, 89).

5. Bauckham, *God Crucified*, 268.

6. Eastman, "Philippians 2:6–11," 17.

Matthew 28:1–20

1. As demonstrated by Saldarini, *Christian-Jewish Community*, 36–37.

2. On the exegetical question of whether some or all the disciples doubt, see J. K. Brown, *Disciples in Narrative Perspective*, 117–18.

3. Bauckham, *God Crucified*, 23, 56–57.

4. Wilkins, *Discipleship in the Ancient World*, 124–25.

5. J. K. Brown, *Disciples in Narrative Perspective*, 123.

6. Bauckham, *God Crucified*.

7. Wilkins, *Discipleship in the Ancient World*, 163.

8. Johnson, *Living Jesus*, 57.

9. Wright, *Matthew for Everyone*, 2:200.

10. Richard Wightman Fox, *Jesus in America: Personal Savior, Cultural Hero, National Obsession* (San Francisco: HarperSanFrancisco, 2004), 396.

Bibliography

Recommended Resources

Brown, Jeannine K. "Matthew." In *The Baker Illustrated Bible Commentary*, edited by Gary M. Burge and Andrew E. Hill, rev. ed., 950–1006. Grand Rapids: Baker Books, 2012.

Brown, Jeannine K., and Kyle Roberts. *Matthew*. Two Horizons New Testament Commentary. Grand Rapids: Eerdmans, forthcoming.

Davies, William D., and Dale C. Allison. *A Critical and Exegetical Commentary on the Gospel according to Saint Matthew*. 3 vols. International Critical Commentary. Edinburgh: T&T Clark, 1988–1997.

France, R. T. *The Gospel of Matthew*. New International Commentary on the New Testament. Grand Rapids: Eerdmans, 2007.

Garland, David E. *Reading Matthew: A Literary and Theological Commentary*. Reading the New Testament. Macon, GA: Smyth & Helwys, 2001.

Green, Joel B., Nicholas Perrin, and Jeannine K. Brown. *Dictionary of Jesus and the Gospels*. Rev. ed. Downers Grove, IL: IVP Academic, 2013.

Hagner, Donald A. *Matthew*. 2 vols. World Biblical Commentary 33A, 33B. Dallas: Word, 1993–1995.

Keener, Craig S. *A Commentary on the Gospel of Matthew*. Grand Rapids: Eerdmans, 1999.

Luz, Ulrich. *Matthew: A Commentary*. Translated by James E. Crouch. Edited by Helmut Koester. 3 vols. Hermeneia. Minneapolis: Fortress, 2001–2007.

Nolland, John. *The Gospel of Matthew: A Commentary on the Greek Text*. New International Greek Testament Commentary. Grand Rapids: Eerdmans, 2005.

Wright, N. T. *Matthew for Everyone*. 2nd ed. 2 vols. Louisville: Westminster John Knox, 2004.

Select Bibliography

Allison, Dale C. *The New Moses: A Matthean Typology*. Minneapolis: Fortress, 1993.

Bauckham, Richard. *God Crucified: Monotheism and Christology in the New Testament*. Grand Rapids: Eerdmans, 1998.

———, ed. *The Gospels for All Christians: Rethinking the Gospel Audiences*. Grand Rapids: Eerdmans, 1998.

———. *Jesus and the Eyewitnesses: The Gospels as Eyewitness Testimony*. Grand Rapids: Eerdmans, 2006.

Bauer, David R. "The Literary and Theological Function of the Genealogy in Matthew's Gospel." In *Treasures New and Old: Recent Contributions to Matthean Studies*, edited by Mark A. Powell and David R. Bauer, Society of Biblical Literature Symposium Series 1, 129–59. Atlanta: Scholars Press, 1996.

Beaton, Richard. *Isaiah's Christ in Matthew's Gospel*. Society for New Testament Studies Monograph Series 123. Cambridge: Cambridge University Press, 2002.

Becknell, Thomas, and Mary Ellen Ashcroft, eds. *The Beginning of Wisdom: Prayers for Growth and Understanding*. Nashville: Moorings, 1995.

Bock, Darrell L. *Blasphemy and Exaltation in Judaism: The Charge against Jesus in Mark 14:53–65*. Grand Rapids: Baker Books, 2000.

Brown, Jeannine K. "Apostle, New Testament." In vol. 2 of *Encyclopedia of the Bible and Its Reception*, edited by Hans-Josef Klauck et al., 471–76. Berlin: de Gruyter, 2008.

———. "Direct Engagement of the Reader in Matthew's Discourses: Rhetorical Techniques and Scholarly Consensus." *New Testament Studies* 51 (2005): 19–35.

————. *The Disciples in Narrative Perspective: The Portrayal and Function of the Matthean Disciples*. Society of Biblical Literature Academia Biblica 9. Atlanta: Society of Biblical Literature, 2002.

————. "Genesis in Matthew's Gospel." In *Genesis in the New Testament*, edited by Maarten J. J. Menken and Steve Moyise, Library of New Testament Studies 466, 42–59. New York: T&T Clark, 2012.

————. "Matthew's 'Least of These' Theology and Subversion of 'Us/Other' Categories." In *Matthew*, edited by Nicole Wilkinson Duran and James P. Grimshaw, Texts @ Contexts, 287–301. Minneapolis: Fortress, 2013.

————. "The Rhetoric of Hearing: The Use of the Isaianic Hearing Motif in Matthew 11:2–16:20." In *Built upon the Rock: Studies in the Gospel of Matthew*, edited by Daniel M. Gurtner and John Nolland, 248–69. Grand Rapids: Eerdmans, 2008.

————. *Scripture as Communication: Introducing Biblical Hermeneutics*. Grand Rapids: Baker Academic, 2007.

Brown, Jeannine K., Carla M. Dahl, and Wyndy Corbin Reuschling. *Becoming Whole and Holy: An Integrative Conversation about Christian Formation*. Grand Rapids: Baker Academic, 2011.

Brown, Raymond E. *The Birth of the Messiah: A Commentary on the Infancy Narratives in the Gospels of Matthew and Luke*. Anchor Bible Reference Library. New York: Doubleday, 1993.

Carter, Warren. *Matthew and the Margins: A Sociopolitical and Religious Reading*. Journal for the Study of the New Testament, Supplement Series 204. Sheffield: Sheffield Academic Press, 2000.

Cohick, Lynn H. *Women in the World of the Earliest Christians: Illuminating Ancient Ways of Life*. Grand Rapids: Baker Academic, 2009.

deSilva, David A. *Honor, Patronage, Kinship and Purity: Unlocking New Testament Culture*. Downers Grove, IL: InterVarsity, 2000.

Eastman, Susan Grove. "Philippians 2:6–11: Incarnation as Mimetic Participation." *Journal for the Study of Paul and His Letters*, sample issue (fall 2010): 1–22.

Garlington, Don B. "'The Salt of the Earth' in Covenantal Perspective." *Journal of the Evangelical Theological Society* 54 (2011): 715–48.

Gorman, Michael J. *Cruciformity: Paul's Narrative Spirituality of the Cross*. Grand Rapids: Eerdmans, 2001.

Green, Joel B. *The Gospel of Luke*. New International Commentary on the New Testament 3. Grand Rapids: Eerdmans, 1997.

Gundry, Robert H. *Matthew: A Commentary on His Literary and Theological Art*. Grand Rapids: Eerdmans, 1982.

Gurtner, Daniel M. *The Torn Veil: Matthew's Exposition of the Death of Jesus*. Society for New Testament Studies Monograph Series 139. Cambridge: Cambridge University Press, 2007.

Gutiérrez, Gustavo. *A Theology of Liberation: History, Politics and Salvation*. Translated and edited by Sister Caridad Inda and John Eagleson. Maryknoll, NY: Orbis Books, 1973.

Hamilton, Catherine Sider. "'His Blood Be upon Us': Innocent Blood and the Death of Jesus in Matthew." *Catholic Biblical Quarterly* 70 (2008): 82–100.

Hauerwas, Stanley. *Matthew*. Brazos Theological Commentary on the Bible. Grand Rapids: Brazos Press, 2006.

Hays, Richard B. *The Moral Vision of the New Testament: Community, Cross, New Creation—A Contemporary Introduction to New Testament Ethics*. San Francisco: HarperSanFrancisco, 1996.

Hultgren, Arland J. *The Parables of Jesus: A Commentary*. The Bible in Its World. Grand Rapids: Eerdmans, 2000.

Hurtado, Larry W. *Lord Jesus Christ: Devotion to Jesus in Earliest Christianity*. Grand Rapids: Eerdmans, 2003.

Instone-Brewer, David. *Traditions of the Rabbis from the Era of the New Testament*. 6 vols. Grand Rapids: Eerdmans, 2004–11.

Jeffers, James S. *The Greco-Roman World of the New Testament Era: Exploring the Background of Early Christianity*. Downers Grove, IL: InterVarsity, 1999.

Jeremias, Joachim. *Jerusalem in the Time of Jesus: An Investigation into Economic and Social Conditions during the New Testament Period*. London: SCM Press, 1969.

Johnson, Luke Timothy. *Living Jesus: Learning the Heart of the Gospel*. San Francisco: HarperSanFrancisco, 1999.

————. *Prophetic Jesus, Prophetic Church: The Challenge of Luke-Acts to Contemporary Christians*. Grand Rapids: Eerdmans, 2011.

Keener, Craig S. "'Brood of Vipers' (Matthew 3.7; 12.34; 23.33)." *Journal for the Study of the New Testament* 28 (2005): 3–11.

————. *The Spirit in the Gospels and Acts: Divine Purity and Power*. Peabody, MA: Hendrickson, 1997.

Knowles, Michael P. *Jeremiah in Matthew's Gospel: The Rejected Prophet Motif in Matthaean Redaction*. Journal for the Study of the New Testament, Supplement Series 68. Sheffield: JSOT Press, 1993.

Lambrecht, Jan. *Out of the Treasure: The Parables in the Gospel of Matthew*. Louvain Theological and Pastoral Monographs 10. Louvain: Peeters; Grand Rapids: Eerdmans, 1991.

Lawrence, Louise Joy. "'For Truly I Tell You, They Have Received Their Reward' (Matt. 6:2): Investigating Honor Precedence and Honor Virtue." *Catholic Biblical Quarterly* 64 (2002): 687–702.

Levine, Amy-Jill. "Discharging Responsibility: Matthean Jesus, Biblical Law, and Hemorrhaging Woman." In *Treasures New and Old: Recent Contributions to Matthean Studies*, edited by David R. Bauer and Mark A. Powell, Society of Biblical Literature Symposium Series 1, 379–97. Atlanta: Scholars Press, 1996.

———. *The Misunderstood Jew: The Church and the Scandal of the Jewish Jesus*. San Francisco: HarperSanFrancisco, 2006.

Longenecker, Bruce W. "Exposing the Economic Middle: A Revised Scale for the Study of Early Urban Christianity." *Journal for the Study of the New Testament* 31 (2009): 243–78.

Luz, Ulrich. "The Final Judgment (Matt 25:31–46): An Exercise in 'History of Influence' Exegesis." In *Treasures New and Old: Recent Contributions to Matthean Studies*, edited by David R. Bauer and Mark Allan Powell, Society of Biblical Literature Symposium Series 1, 271–310. Atlanta: Scholars Press, 1996.

Manning, Brennan. *The Ragamuffin Gospel*. Sisters, OR: Multnomah, 2000.

Marshall, I. Howard. "Who Is a Hypocrite?" *Bibliotheca sacra* 159 (2002): 131–50.

Milgrom, Jacob. *Leviticus 1–16: A New Translation with Introduction and Commentary*. Anchor Bible 3. New York: Doubleday, 1991.

Neyrey, Jerome H. *Honor and Shame in the Gospel of Matthew*. Louisville: Westminster John Knox, 1998.

———. "The Thematic Use of Isaiah 42:1–4 in Matthew 12." *Biblica* 63 (1982): 457–73.

Pennington, Jonathan T. *Heaven and Earth in the Gospel of Matthew*. Grand Rapids: Baker Academic, 2009.

Perrin, Nicholas. *Jesus the Temple*. Grand Rapids: Baker Academic, 2010.

Powell, Mark Allan. "Binding and Loosing: A Paradigm of Ethical Discernment from the Gospel of Matthew." *Currents in Theology and Mission* 30 (2003): 438–45.

———. *Chasing the Eastern Star: Adventures in Biblical Reader-Response Criticism*. Louisville: Westminster John Knox, 2001.

———. "Do and Keep What Moses Says (Matthew 23:2–7)." *Journal of Biblical Literature* 114 (1995): 419–35.

———. "Matthew's Beatitudes: Reversals and Rewards of the Kingdom." *Catholic Biblical Quarterly* 58 (1996): 460–79.

Saldarini, Anthony J. *Matthew's Christian-Jewish Community*. Chicago Studies in the History of Judaism. Chicago: University of Chicago Press, 1994.

Schmemann, Alexander. *For the Life of the World: Sacraments and Orthodoxy*. 2nd ed. Crestwood, NY: St. Vladimir's Seminary Press, 1973.

Schweitzer, Albert. *The Quest of the Historical Jesus: A Critical Study of Its Progress from Reimarus to Wrede*. London: Adam & Charles Black, 1910.

Shults, F. LeRon, and Steven J. Sandage. *The Faces of Forgiveness: Searching for Wholeness and Salvation*. Grand Rapids: Baker Academic, 2003.

Simonetti, Manlio, ed. *Matthew 1–13*. Ancient Christian Commentary on Scripture 1A. Downers Grove, IL: InterVarsity, 2001.

Snodgrass, Klyne N. "Matthew and the Law." In *Treasures New and Old: Recent Contributions to Matthean Studies*, edited by David R. Bauer and Mark Allan Powell, Society of Biblical Literature Symposium Series 1, 33–127. Atlanta: Scholars Press, 1996.

Stanton, Graham N. *A Gospel for a New People: Studies in Matthew*. Louisville: Westminster John Knox, 1992.

Stein, Robert H. *A Basic Guide to Interpreting the Bible: Playing by the Rules*. 2nd ed. Grand Rapids: Baker Academic, 2011.

———. *The Method and Message of Jesus' Teaching*. Rev. ed. Louisville: Westminster John Knox, 1994.

Thiselton, Anthony C. *Thiselton on Hermeneutics: Collected Works with New Essays*. Grand Rapids: Eerdmans, 2006.

Thompson, Marianne Meye. *Colossians and Philemon*. Two Horizons New Testament Commentary. Grand Rapids: Eerdmans, 2005.

Thompson, Michael B. "The Holy Internet: Communication between Churches in the First Christian Generation." In *The Gospels for All Christians: Rethinking the Gospel Audiences*, edited by Richard Bauckham, 49–70. Grand Rapids: Eerdmans, 1998.

Timmer, John. *Four-Dimensional Jesus: Seeing Jesus through the Eyes of Matthew, Mark, Luke, and John*. Grand Rapids: CRC Publications, 2001.

Verseput, Donald J. "The Faith of the Reader and the Narrative of Matthew 13:53–16:20." *Journal for the Study of the New Testament* 46 (1992): 3–24.

———. "Jesus' Pilgrimage to Jerusalem and Encounter in the Temple: A Geographical Motif in Matthew's Gospel." *Novum Testamentum* 36 (1994): 105–21.

Weaver, Dorothy J. *Matthew's Missionary Discourse: A Literary Critical Analysis*. Journal for the Study of the New Testament, Supplement Series 38. Sheffield: JSOT Press, 1990.

Wiedemann, Thomas E. J. *Adults and Children in the Roman Empire*. New Haven: Yale University Press, 1989.

Wilkins, Michael J. *Discipleship in the Ancient World and Matthew's Gospel*. 2nd ed. Grand Rapids: Baker Books, 1995.

———. *Matthew*. NIV Application Commentary. Grand Rapids: Zondervan, 2004.

Wink, Walter. "Beyond Just War and Pacifism: Jesus' Nonviolent Way." *Review & Expositor* 89 (1992): 197–214.

Wright, N. T. *The Challenge of Jesus: Rediscovering Who Jesus Was and Is*. Downers Grove, IL: InterVarsity, 1999.

———. *Evil and the Justice of God*. Downers Grove, IL: InterVarsity, 2006.

———. *Jesus and the Victory of God*. Christian Origins and the Question of God 2. Minneapolis: Fortress, 1996.

———. *The New Testament and the People of God*. Christian Origins and the Question of God 1. Minneapolis: Fortress, 1992.

———. *The Resurrection of the Son of God*. Christian Origins and the Question of God 3. Minneapolis: Fortress, 2003.

———. *Surprised by Hope: Rethinking Heaven, the Resurrection, and the Mission of the Church*. New York: HarperOne, 2008.

Image Credits

Unless otherwise indicated, photos, illustrations, and maps are copyright © Baker Photo Archive.

The Baker Photo Archive acknowledges the permission of the following institutions and individuals.

Photo on page 116 © Baker Photo Archive. Courtesy of the Archaeology Museum of Nazareth.

Photos on pages 4, 78, 142, 216, 255, 277 © Baker Photo Archive. Courtesy of the British Museum, London, England.

Photos on page 199 © Baker Photo Archive. Courtesy of the Bode Museum, Berlin, Germany.

Photos on pages 164, 230, 249 © Baker Photo Archive. Courtesy of the Eretz Museum, Tel Aviv, Israel.

Photo on page 112 © Baker Photo Archive. Courtesy of the Greek Ministry of Antiquities and the Archeological Museum of Thessaloniki, Greece.

Photos on pages 191, 292 © Baker Photo Archive. Courtesy of the Holyland Hotel. Reproduction of the City of Jerusalem at the time of the Second Temple, located on the grounds of the Holyland Hotel, Jerusalem, 2001. Present location: The Israel Museum, Jerusalem.

Photo on page 205 © Baker Photo Archive. Courtesy of the Jordanian Ministry of Antiquities and the Amman Archaeological Museum.

Photo on page 54 © Baker Photo Archive. Dr. James C. Martin, courtesy of The Greek Ministry of Antiquities and Thessaloniki Archaeological Museum, Thessaloniki, Greece.

Photo on page 172 © Baker Photo Archive. Courtesy of the Masada Museum.

Photo on page 224 © Baker Photo Archive. Courtesy of the museum at Sepphoris.

Photos on pages 29, 107, 181, 187, 206, 212, 233, 314 © Baker Photo Archive. Courtesy of the Musée du Louvre; Autorisation de photographer et de filmer. Louvre, Paris, France.

Photo on page 258 © Baker Photo Archive. Courtesy of the Skirball Museum, Hebrew Union College–Jewish Institute of Religion, 13 King David Street, Jerusalem 94101.

Photo on page 295 © Baker Photo Archive. Courtesy of the Skulpturensammlung, Germany.

Illustration on page 281 © Baker Photo Archive / Timothy Ladwig.

Photo on page 2, 32, 192 © Baker Photo Archive. Courtesy of the Turkish Ministry of Antiquities and the Antalya Museum, Turkey.

Photos on pages 110, 144, 182 © Baker Photo Archive. Courtesy of the Turkish Ministry of Antiquities and the Istanbul Archaeological Museum.

Photos on pages 20, 62, 65, 97, 114, 170, 203, 234, 242, 273, 286, 296, 307 © Baker Photo Archive. Courtesy of the Vatican Museum.

Photo on page 168 © Baker Photo Archive. Courtesy of the Yigal Allon Centre, Kibbutz Ginosar, on the western shore of the Sea of Galilee, Israel.

Additional image credits

Photo on page 99 © Archives of the Billy Graham Center, Wheaton, Illinois.

Illustration on page 248 © Balage Balogh / Archaeology Illustrated (www.archeologyillustrated.com).

Photo on page 15 © Bibliothèque nationale de France.

Contributors

General Editors Mark. L. Strauss John H. Walton	*Project Editor* James Korsmo
Associate Editors, Illustrating the Text Kevin and Sherry Harney	*Interior Design* Brian Brunsting William Overbeeke
Contributing Author, Illustrating the Text Adam Barr	*Visual Content* Kim Walton
Series Development Jack Kuhatschek Brian Vos	*Cover Direction* Paula Gibson Michael Cook

Index

denarius, 227, 257
"den of robbers," 246
deservedness, 230
deSilva, David, 176
devil, 35
Dickens, Charles, 129, 243
discernment, 78, 79, 261
disciples, 46, 47
    as audience of Sermon on
        the Mount, 53
    confession of, 186
    desertion of, 298, 299, 300
    empowerment to heal,
        106–7
    inability to heal, 202
    mission to Israel, 115
    misunderstanding of,
        175, 234
    as unwelcoming to chil-
        dren, 222
discipleship, 7–8, 33, 47–48,
    50, 51, 98, 188, 190,
    192, 204, 207, 237, 255,
    302, 314, 320
    as cruciform, 194, 199,
        207
    humility required of, 265
    modeled by Jesus, 235–36
discipline, 87
divesting resources, 315
divorce, 16–17, 221–22
dogs, 78, 180, 182
donkey, 239–40
doubt, 72, 169, 247, 249,
    317
dreams, 17, 22, 24, 306

earthly life, 192–93
earthquake, 312, 317
Eastman, Susan, 314
Egypt, 11, 23, 32
elders, 250–51
Elijah, 29, 120–21, 186, 197,
    198–99, 311, 312
"end of the age," 156, 275,
    280
engagements, 16
Eschatological Discourse,
    85, 274–78, 280–85,
    286–90
eschatological restora-
    tion, 96
eschatological timelines, 284
Essenes, 174
eternal life, 289
eternal punishment, 289
Eusebius, 3
evil, resistance to, 61
evil one, 66
evil thoughts and actions,
    175–76
exalting, of humble, 265

exile and restoration, 11–12,
    14, 15, 24, 25–26, 45,
    91, 182
exodus, 32, 167–68, 169–70,
    295–96
exorcism, 179, 202
extravagant forgiveness,
    217–19
eye, 71
eye for eye, tooth for tooth,
    60
eye of the needle, 223

faith, 3, 96, 247, 249
    examples of, 249
    lack of, 161
    and works, 289
faithful and wise servant,
    parable of, 281, 282
faithfulness, 31, 268, 269,
    272, 284, 286, 287, 289
false messiahs, 276
false prophets, 83, 276
family loyalty, 98, 114,
    116, 145
farmer sowing seed, parable
    of, 149–50
fasting, 64–65, 67, 266
favoritism, toward the rich,
    73, 212
fear, 72, 113, 116, 251
fear of God, 113
feeding miracles, 181, 185
feeding the five thousand,
    166–67
feeding the four thousand,
    167, 178, 181
Festival of Unleavened
    Bread, 294
fig tree, cursing of, 244,
    247, 277
final judgment, 126, 154,
    193, 282, 287
fire, 30
"first" and "last," in the
    kingdom, 227–29, 231,
    234–35, 265
"fishing" for others, 50
flogging, of Jesus, 307
following Jesus, 95, 98,
    303, 320
food laws, 174–75
forgiveness, 67, 96, 212–13,
    217–18
forgiving others, 67, 214–15
form criticism, 2
fourteen generations, 12–13
France, R. T., 41, 239, 246,
    275, 276, 288, 294
Francis, Pope, 213, 237
fruit bearing, 82, 83, 86,
    148, 150, 157, 252, 254

fulfillment quotations, 4, 18,
    24, 239

Gadarenes, 95
Galilee, 24–25, 40–41, 42,
    44, 49, 241
gall, 310–11
Garland, David, 276
gematria, 13
genealogies, 10, 12
generation, 121
generosity, 230
Gennesaret, 169
genre, 278
Gentile inclusion, 4, 5, 12,
    14, 26, 40, 42–43, 45,
    88, 90–93, 137, 139–40,
    175, 181, 304, 306, 316
Gentiles, 78, 95, 232, 235
Gerasenes, 325
Gergesenes, 325
Gethsemane, 299, 301
giving, 64–65, 266
gnat, 269
gnosticism, 150, 152
God
    answers prayer, 79–80,
        81, 247
    faithfulness of, 93, 303
    as Father, 72, 79, 113
    generosity of, 230
"God with us," 7, 10, 16,
    19, 20, 208
Golden Rule, 76, 79
Gomorrah, 108
good fruit, 30, 83, 144
good news, 48–50
good Samaritan, 259
good soil, 149–51
good trees, 83
Gospels
    as biography, 4
    harmonization of, 1
grace, 63, 79, 193, 230–31
grammateus, 157
great faith, 90, 96, 102,
    180, 182
greatness, 209, 211, 233–34,
    265
Greco-Roman society, 53,
    71, 73, 211, 212, 224,
    229, 234, 264, 266
greed, 270
guardian angels, 210
Gurtner, Daniel, 312
Gutiérrez, Gustavo, 288, 290

Hades, 125, 186
Hagner, Donald, 84
hands of men, 205
Hauerwas, Stanley, 249
Hays, Richard, 278
healing, 48–49, 88–89, 96–
    97, 106, 119, 125, 202

on the Sabbath, 133
hearing, 121, 138, 148,
    150–51, 174, 200
heart, 70–71, 141
heavenly temple, 248
heavens, 324
"heavy loads," 263
Herod Agrippa I, 233
Herod Antipas, 22, 120,
    161–63, 185, 199
Herodians, 256
Herodias, 162–63
Herod the Great, 22, 23,
    26, 217
Hillel, 79, 221
Holy Spirit, 17, 30, 32,
    34, 109, 137–38, 142,
    143, 146
honor, 264–67
honor of father and mother,
    173
hope, 139
Hosanna, 240
Hultgren, Arland, 288
humbling, of exalted, 265
humiliation, 54
hungering and thirsting for
    righteousness, 55
Hurtado, Larry, 7
hyperbole, 77, 91, 210, 223
hypocrisy, 55, 64–66, 76, 77,
    173–74, 256–57, 262,
    272–73, 282
    of Jewish leaders, 264
    of Pharisees, 265–66, 268

imagery, in Jesus' teach-
    ing, 77
Immanuel, 17, 18, 20, 45
imperial tax, 256–57
impurity, 104
incarnation, 19
inheritance, 287
innocent blood, 305
insiders and outsiders, 154
instructor, 264–65
integrity, 177, 270
irony, 310
Isaianic servant, 31–32, 88,
    91, 92, 119, 136–39,
    197, 199, 235–36
Israel
    covenant disloyalty, 34,
        35–36
    as God's son, 32
    restoration of, 11, 120–23
    in the wilderness, 28, 35,
        144, 167, 169–70, 202–3

James (brother of John),
    117, 197, 232, 233
James the Lesser, 117
Jeremiah, 186
Jericho, 238–39

woes pronounced on, 268–72

temple
  cleansing of, 241, 244–49
  destroyed and rebuilt in three days, 300
  destruction of, 109, 271, 274–79, 283
  as place of prayer, 246
  tearing of the curtain, 312

temple tax, 202, 205

ten virgins, parable of, 282–83

theophany, 168, 197, 198

third day, 191–92

thirty pieces of silver, 305

Thiselton, Anthony, 152–53

"this generation," 118, 121, 122, 203, 277

Thomas, 117

Timmer, John, 146, 147

tithing spices, 269

Torah, 31, 58–59, 62, 262
  fulfillment of, 1, 4, 5, 6, 263
  interpretation of, 221, 258–59, 268, 272
  not burdensome, 127
  obedience to, 17, 31, 92–93, 134, 172–73, 256

Pharisees on, 130

torture, 217

tradition criticism, 2

tradition of the elders, 172–73

transcendent life, 192–93

transfiguration, 196–201

treasure, as hidden, 156, 158, 159

treasures in heaven, 70, 223

treasures on earth, 70

Trinity, 318

trust, 74, 98, 104, 113, 290

Twelve, 226, 232
  mission of, 108–9
  preaching of, 110

twelve (number), 168

two or three witnesses, 210–11, 300

two sons, parable of, 251–52, 254

"two ways," 83

typological reading, 18

Tyre, 125, 178–79

unbelief, 202–3

uncleanness, 174

understanding, 156–57

unforgiving servant, parable of, 67, 215–18

Uriah's wife, 12

Verseput, Donald, 167, 205

vineyard and tenants, parable of, 252

violence, 218

vipers, 30

virtue list, beatitudes as, 55–56

wandering sheep, parable of, 210

watchfulness, 281, 283–84, 299

wealth, 73–74, 151, 152, 223, 224, 225

wedding banquet, parable of, 253, 254

weeds and wheat, parable of, 154–55, 158, 174

wholeness, 61

wicked generation, 144–45

widows, 269

wilderness generation, 35, 144, 202–3

Wilkins, Michael, 320

will of God, 66, 84–85, 86

Wink, Walter, 61

wisdom, 5, 6–7, 119, 123, 126, 128

Wisdom literature, 126, 260

witness, 255

woes, 52, 120, 268–72

women
  at crucifixion, 292, 312
  in early church, 313
  in genealogy of Matthew, 12, 14, 26
  low status of, 223, 234
  as witnesses to resurrection, 317

word and deed, 50

words, 144, 147

workers in vineyard, parable of, 227–31

worry, 71–72, 74, 151, 152, 169

worship, of Jesus, 26–27, 317–18, 320

Wright, N. T., 51, 201, 258, 276, 279, 297, 314, 320–21

yeast, 154, 155, 158, 167, 185

yoke, 127, 128, 130

zealot movements, 107

Zebulun, 41

Zechariah, 271

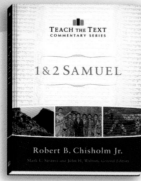

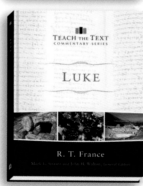

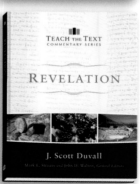